Romanticism

The Romantic period coincided with revolutionary transformations of traditional political and human rights discourses, as well as witnessing rapid advances in technology and a primitivist return to nature. As a broad global movement, Romanticism strongly impacted on the literature and arts of the late eighteenth and early nineteenth centuries in ways that are still being debated and negotiated today.

Examining the poetry, fiction, non-fiction, drama and the arts of the period, this book considers:

- important propositions and landmark ideas in the Romantic period;
- key debates and critical approaches to Romantic studies;
- new and revisionary approaches to Romantic literature and art;
- the ways in which Romantic writing interacts with broader trends in history, politics and aesthetics;
- European and global Romanticism;
- the legacies of Romanticism in the twentieth and twenty-first centuries.

Containing useful, reader-friendly features such as explanatory case studies, chapter summaries and suggestions for further reading, this clear and engaging book is an invaluable resource for anyone who intends to study and research the complexity and diversity of the Romantic period, as well as the historical conditions which produced it.

Carmen Casaliggi is a Senior Lecturer in Nineteenth-Century Literature at Cardiff Metropolitan University, UK.

Porscha Fermanis is an Associate Professor in Romantic Literature at University College Dublin, Ireland.

Romanticism

A Literary and Cultural History

**Carmen Casaliggi and
Porscha Fermanis**

Routledge
Taylor & Francis Group

LONDON AND NEW YORK

First published 2016
by Routledge
2 Park Square, Milton Park, Abingdon, Oxon OX14 4RN

and by Routledge
711 Third Avenue, New York, NY 10017

Routledge is an imprint of the Taylor & Francis Group, an informa business

British Library Cataloguing-in-Publication Data
A catalogue record for this book is available from the British Library

Library of Congress Cataloging-in-Publication Data
Names: Casaliggi, Carmen, author. | Fermanis, Porscha, 1975- author.
Title: Romanticism: a literary and cultural history/Carmen Casaliggi and Porscha Fermanis.
Description: Milton Park, Abingdon, Oxon; New York: Routledge, 2016. | Includes bibliographical references and index.
Identifiers: LCCN 2015037829 | ISBN 9780415679077
(hardback: alk. paper) | ISBN 9780415679084 (pbk.: alk. paper) |
ISBN 9781315749501 (ebook)
Subjects: LCSH: Romanticism.
Classification: LCC PN603.C37 2016 | DDC 809/.9145–dc23LC record available at http://lccn.loc.gov/2015037829

ISBN: 978-0-415-67907-7 (hbk)
ISBN: 978-0-415-67908-4 (pbk)
ISBN: 978-1-315-74950-1 (ebk)

Typeset in Times New Roman
by Sunrise Setting Ltd, Paignton, UK

Contents

Figures

Preface

Over the past thirty years, literary scholars have increasingly questioned the reiteration of familiar stories about our literary past, making the writing of literary history a more tentative – but perhaps more necessary – project than ever before. As David Perkins has pointed out in the opening pages of *Is Literary History Possible?* (1992), two of the three principal assumptions of traditional literary history – that works are formed by their historical contexts, that changes in literary forms and styles take place developmentally and that these changes are the products of an overarching idea – have gradually been eroded by less teleological ways of thinking about periodicity and by the inclusion of previously neglected and less easily accommodated writers in literary canons. In the context of Romantic studies this destabilisation of periods and canons has led to concerns about how to characterise the relationship between eighteenth-century, Romantic and Victorian writing, and ultimately to fears that the term 'Romanticism' itself may have become obscured and even meaningless.

Until recently these anxieties have been felt primarily at the level of academic scholarship, but they are now permeating classrooms and pedagogical discussions. Students of British Romanticism will no longer encounter just the 'Big Six' Romantic poets in their seminars and lectures, but will most likely be exposed to the work of female, working-class, transatlantic, Scottish, Irish and Welsh writers. This book is intended as a useful guide for undergraduate and postgraduate students navigating these difficult new waters, but it will also be of interest to scholars and teachers of Romanticism more generally. The Introduction to the book ('Romanticism and its discontents') offers an overview of debates surrounding the definition of Romanticism, as well as providing a survey of different critical approaches. Seven substantive chapters follow: 1) 'Contexts of Romanticism', 2) 'Romantic forms, genres and language', 3) 'Romantic groups and associations', 4) 'National, regional and local Romanticism', 5) 'Romanticism in the arts', 6) 'European Romanticism' and 7) 'Global Romanticism'. The Conclusion ('Legacies of Romanticism') considers the ways in which Romanticism has influenced nineteenth-, twentieth- and twenty-first-century literary cultures. Each of these chapters can be read individually in its own right, but the book is designed to promote adaptive reading strategies by pointing out links and connections between a variety of ideas, events, themes, genres and concepts across chapters and sections. At the same time, case studies, or close readings, of selected individual texts provide specific examples of the broader ideas and contexts raised in the book.

Some of the book's narratives will already be familiar to students and scholars of British Romanticism, others less so. It is traditional, for example, to find chapters on Romantic groups and on genres/forms in literary histories of Romanticism, but we are less used to seeing chapters on European Romanticism, Romanticism and the arts and global Romanticism. While these chapters contribute to the book's distinctive flavour, their primary purpose is to provide readers with a sense of the ways in which key Romantic paradigms have been tested and revised in recent years, in particular by new studies on the transnational, European-wide origins of the novel, inter-disciplinary studies on the Romantic arts and studies of native and non-Anglophone literary cultures within the British Empire and beyond. In other words, while the book's aim is to introduce readers to the principal ideas, concepts, texts, art works and events of the Romantic period – and to be as comprehensive and accessible as possible – it also aspires to provide its readers with the tools with which to question traditional understandings of Romanticism and even the arguments made in the book, which are themselves the product of particular critical positions and institutional biases.

Without indulging repeatedly in metaphysical musings on its own ontological construction, the book hopes to raise the kinds of questions that literary scholars have themselves been grappling with in the last thirty years. Is Romanticism best understood as a remedy, reaction to or extension of the Enlightenment? Does Romanticism involve a wholesale rejection of empiricism and mechanism? Did Romantic and neoclassical literary models coexist? Did the French Revolution really coincide with radical aesthetic changes? How does our understanding of the period alter when female, regional and working-class Romantic writers are allowed into the canon? Is there such a thing as a pan-European Romanticism? Is there still a Romanticism to be found when we extend the temporal, diachronic and spatial co-ordinates of Romanticism to include writers outside traditional periodisations (1789–1832) and geographical spaces (England and especially metropolitan London)?

The answers to these questions have changed and will continue to change over time. Nor are there always answers to the questions raised: in some cases – for example, in relation to whether Romanticism is best defined as a literary movement or historical phenomenon/period – there is no overwhelming critical consensus. The plurality of critical opinions raised in the book, and the intensity of debates surrounding changing understandings of Romanticism, is suggestive not only of the diversity of the period itself, but also of the exceptionally innovative work being done by colleagues in the field. That chapters with a European-wide coverage and with a focus on comparative, transnational and global methodologies should now make their way into a literary history of Romanticism is a testament to the strength of the revisionary body of scholarly work produced in recent years, work that has countered the long-standing dominance of nation-centric explanations of the rise and development of Romanticism without subscribing to older notions of a coherent, holistic, pan-European and/ or world literary movement. Such innovation shows no sign of abating and, as such, there will always need to be 'yet another' book on Romantic literary history.

Carmen Casaliggi and Porscha Fermanis
Cardiff and Dublin, 2015

Acknowledgements

We are grateful to Polly Dodson at Routledge for suggesting that we write this book and for her commitment to the project, as well as to Liz Levine and Ruth Hilsdon for their advice and assistance on editorial matters. We are also indebted to the readers consulted by Routledge for their astute comments and suggestions: Duncan Wu, John Strachan, Daniel S. Roberts, Deirdre Coleman and Marc Canuel. To colleagues and friends we would like to express our sincere thanks, in particular to Michael Cooke, Nick Daly, Dimitra Fimi, Anna Fochi, Robert Gerwarth, Santi Pérez Isasi, Jon Kear, Gina Morgan, Kate North, Michelle O'Connell, Diego Saglia, Angelo Silvestri and Jeff Wallace. As the book took its final shape we benefited from the helpfulness of the staff at the Library of Trinity College Dublin. Our greatest debt of gratitude goes to our families.

***

The authors would like to acknowledge the following for permission to reproduce material: Nottingham City Museum and Galleries, Newstead Abbey; the Museum of Fine Arts, Boston; the National Gallery, London; Musée du Louvre, Paris; the Fitzwilliam Museum, Cambridge; the Ashmolean Museum, Oxford; and the Walker Art Gallery, Liverpool. Every effort has been made to trace or contact all copyright holders of illustrations reproduced in *Romanticism: A Literary and Cultural History*. The authors would be pleased to rectify any omissions brought to their notice at the earliest convenience.

Note on texts

Unless otherwise stated, all references to primary texts are taken from the following editions and are cited parenthetically by line, volume or page number in the main text.

Austen, Jane (2013) *The Cambridge Edition of the Works of Jane Austen*, gen. ed. Janet Todd, 9 vols, Cambridge: Cambridge University Press.

Blake, William (2008) *The Complete Poetry and Prose of William Blake*, ed. David V. Erdman, Berkeley, CA and London: University of California Press.

Clare, John (1978) *Selected Poems and Prose of John Clare*, eds. Eric Robinson and Geoffrey Summerfield, Oxford: Oxford University Press.

Coleridge, Samuel Taylor (1971–2001) *The Collected Works of Samuel Taylor Coleridge*, 16 vols, gen. ed. Kathleen Coburn, Princeton, NJ: Princeton University Press.

Coleridge, Samuel Taylor (1983) *Biographia Literaria*, 2 vols, eds. James Engell and W. Jackson Bate, Bollingen Series 75, Princeton, NJ: Princeton University Press.

Byron, George Gordon, Lord (1973–94) *Byron's Letters and Journals*, ed. Leslie A. Marchand, 13 vols, London: John Murray.

Byron, George Gordon, Lord (1980–93) *The Complete Poetical Works*, 7 vols, ed. Jerome J. McGann, Oxford: Clarendon Press.

Hazlitt, William (1930–4) *The Complete Works of William Hazlitt*, ed. P. P. Howe, 21 vols, London and Toronto: J. M. Dent.

Hemans, Felicia (2001) *Felicia Hemans: Selected Poems, Letters, Reception Material*, ed. Susan J. Wolfson, Princeton, NJ and Oxford: Princeton University Press.

Keats, John (1978) *The Poems of John Keats*, ed. Jack Stillinger, London: Heinemann.

Keats, John (1958) *The Letters of John Keats, 1814–1821: Volumes I–II*, ed. Hyder Edward Rollins, Cambridge, MA: Harvard University Press.

Shelley, Percy Bysshe (1964) *The Letters of Percy Bysshe Shelley*, ed. Frederick L. Jones, 2 vols, Oxford: Clarendon Press.

Shelley, Percy Bysshe (1977) *Shelley's Poetry and Prose: Authoritative Texts, Criticism*, eds. Donald H. Reiman and Sharon B. Powers, New York and London, W. W. Norton.

Southey, Robert (2004) *Robert Southey Poetical Works 1793–1810*, eds. Tim Fulford and Lynda Pratt, 5 vols, London: Pickering and Chatto.

Southey, Robert (2012) *Robert Southey: Later Poetical Works 1811–1838*, gen. eds. Tim Fulford and Lynda Pratt, 4 vols, London: Pickering and Chatto.

Wordsworth, William (2008) *The Prelude*, in *The Major Works*, ed. Stephen Gill, Oxford: Oxford University Press.

Wordsworth, William and Samuel Taylor Coleridge (2013) *Lyrical Ballads*, 2nd ed., ed. Michael Mason, London and New York: Routledge.

Note on translations

Chapter 6 of this book makes extensive use of citations from prose and poetry in German, French, Italian and Spanish. Except for relatively short passages, all such citations are given in the main text in English. Translation is based on texts indicated in the Bibliography. Where such translations do not already exist, they are our own.

Romanticism timeline (1789–1837)

(The following is a timeline of traditional Romantic periodisation: from the outbreak of the French Revolution to the accession of Queen Victoria to the British throne.)

Year	Historical background	Literature	Arts
1789	Outbreak of the French Revolution; storming of the Bastille		
1790		Publication of Edmund Burke's *Reflections on the Revolution in France*	
1791	Slave rebellions in St. Domingue (1791–1804)		
1792	Proclamation of the French Republic	Publication of Mary Wollstonecraft's *A Vindication of the Rights of Woman*; Birth of Percy Bysshe Shelley	Death of Sir Joshua Reynolds
1793			
1794		Publication of William Blake's *Songs of Innocence and of Experience*; William Godwin's *Caleb Williams*; Ann Radcliffe's *The Mysteries of Udolpho*	
1795		Birth of John Keats	
1796			
1797			
1798	United Irishmen rebellion in Ireland; Nelson's great victory in Aboukir Bay near the mouth of the Nile, securing the Mediterranean for the British and the East from conquest by Napoleon	Publication of William Wordsworth and Samuel Taylor Coleridge's *Lyrical Ballads with a few other Poems*; First edition of Joanna Baillie's *Plays on the Passions*	

Year	Historical background	Literature	Arts
1800	Ireland enters into political union with Great Britain	Publication of the second edition of *Lyrical Ballads*, with Wordsworth's radical 'Preface'	Antoine-Jean Gros returns to Paris from Italy and is employed by Napoleon to record his military successes
1801			Jacques-Louis David paints *Napoleon Crossing the Alps*; Jean-Auguste-Dominique Ingres wins the Prix de Rome
1802	Peace of Amiens between Great Britain and France	Publication of Wordsworth and Coleridge's *Lyrical Ballads* with expanded version of the 1800 'Preface'; Second edition of Joanna Baillie's *Plays on the Passions*; Birth of Letitia Elizabeth Landon and Victor Hugo; William Hazlitt visits Paris	John Constable first exhibits at the Royal Academy; J. M. W. Turner makes first trip to the continent; Birth of Richard Parkes Bonington; Death of Thomas Girtin
1803	War between Britain and France resumes; Robert Emmet's uprising in Dublin; Emmet executed		
1804	Napoleon crowned Emperor of France; Pitt re-elected as British Prime Minister	Blake begins *Jerusalem*; Death of William Gilpin, Joseph Priestley and Immanuel Kant	
1805	Nelson killed in the Battle of Trafalgar, where the French and Spanish fleets are destroyed	Publication of Walter Scott's *The Lay of the Last Minstrel*; Robert Southey's *Madoc*; Hazlitt's *An Essay on the Principles of Human Action*; Godwin's *Fleetwood: Or, The New Man of Feeling*	David Wilkie moves to London; Foundation in London of the British Institution and Society of Painters in Water Colours
1806	Napoleon invades Prussia; British army defeats French army in Italy; Death of Pitt and Charles James Fox; Lord Grenville becomes Britain's Prime Minister	Publication of Sydney Owenson's *The Wild Irish Girl*; Thomas Moore's *Epistles, Odes, and Other Poems*; Lord Byron's *Fugitive Pieces*; Scott's *Ballads* and *Lyrical Pieces*; Death of Charlotte Smith	David Wilkie's work celebrated at the Royal Academy; Ingres travels to Rome

Year	Historical background	Literature	Arts
1807	France invades Spain and Portugal; Napoleon defeats Russia; Abolition of slave trade	Publication of Byron's *Hours of Idleness*; Southey's *Letters from England*; Wordsworth's *Poems in Two Volumes*; Madame de Staël's *Corinne, or Italy*	David completes *The Coronation of Napoleon*
1808	Peninsular War begins; Joseph Bonaparte becomes King of Spain; Spanish American Wars of Independence (1808–33)	Publication of Scott's *Marmion*; Moore's *Irish Melodies*; Johann Wolfgang von Goethe's *Faust*; *Examiner* founded	Ludwig van Beethoven completes *Fifth Symphony*
1809	Wellington commands British army in Portugal	Publication of Byron's *English Bards, and Scotch Reviewers*; Tory *Quarterly Review* is founded; Death of Thomas Paine	Blake organises his own private exhibition in London
1810		Publication of Scott's *The Lady of the Lake*; Baillie's *The Family Legend*	Francisco Goya begins *Disasters of War*; Birth of Frédéric Chopin
1811	George, Prince of Wales, made Prince Regent; Luddite uprisings in Britain	Publication of Scott's *The Vision of Don Roderick*; Jane Austen's *Sense and Sensibility*; Percy Shelley expelled from Oxford	
1812	Wellington enters Madrid; Napoleon invades Russia; Lord Liverpool becomes Britain's Tory Prime Minister; Luddite reform bill in Britain; Spanish Constitution of Cádiz	Publication of Byron's *Childe Harold's Pilgrimage* (Cantos I and II)	William Bullock's Egyptian Hall opened in London; First exhibition of Théodore Géricault at the Paris Salon
1813	Wellington defeats French army and invades France; Napoleon defeated at Leipzig; Belfast riots	Publication of Austen's *Pride and Prejudice*; Coleridge's *Remorse*; Byron's *The Giaour, A Fragment of a Turkish Tale* and *The Bride of Abydos*; Scott's *Rokeby*; Shelley's *Queen Mab*; Southey becomes Poet Laureate after Scott declines the honour; Leigh Hunt imprisoned	Opening of the Dulwich Picture Gallery, England's first public art gallery; Birth of Giuseppe Verdi and Richard Wagner

Year	Historical background	Literature	Arts
1814	Napoleon abdicates and is exiled to the island of Elba	Publication of Byron's *The Corsair, Lara* and *The Ode to Napoleon*; Scott's *Waverley*; Wordsworth's *The Excursion*; Austen's *Mansfield Park*	Wilkie, Robert Haydon and John Crome visit Paris
1815	'Hundred Days' of Napoleon; Britain defeats France at Battle of Waterloo; Napoleon exiled to St Helena; Corn Laws in Britain	Publication of Byron's *Hebrew Melodies*; Scott's *Guy Mannering* and *The Field of Waterloo: A Poem*; Wordsworth's *Poems*; Byron marries Annabella Milbanke	Turner exhibits *Crossing the Brook* at the Royal Academy
1816	Spa Fields riots in London; Shipwreck of the Medusa	Publication of Austen's *Emma*; Byron's *The Prisoner of Chillon*, *Childe Harold* (Canto III), *The Siege of Corinth*; Coleridge's *Christabel and Other Poems*; Scott's *The Antiquary*; Hunt's *The Story of Rimini*; Shelley's *Alastor; or, The Spirit of Solitude and Other Poems*; Byron's final departure from England	Elgin Marbles exhibited at the British Museum; First British Institution competition for 'Grand Historical Painting'; David exiled to Brussels; Géricault travels to Italy; Rossini's *Otello*
1817		Publication of Byron's *Manfred* and *The Lament of Tasso*; Scott's *Rob Roy* and *Harold the Dauntless*; Keats's *Poems*; Percy Shelley's *The Revolt of Islam*; Mary and Percy Shelley's *History of a Six Weeks' Tour through a part of France, Switzerland, Germany, and Holland*; *Blackwood's Edinburgh Magazine* is founded; Stendhal visits London; Death of Jane Austen	Narrative accounts of the *Medusa* shipwreck by Alexander Corréard and Henri Savigny published in Paris
1818		Publication of Mary Shelley's *Frankenstein, or, the Modern Prometheus*; Austen's *Northanger Abbey* and *Persuasion*; Byron's *Childe Harold* (Canto IV) and	Turner exhibits *Field of Waterloo* at the Royal Academy; English translation of Corréard and Savigny's accounts of the *Medusa*

Year	Historical background	Literature	Arts
		Beppo; Hazlitt's *Lectures on the English Poets*; Keats's *Endymion: A Poetic Romance*; Scott's *The Heart of Midlothian*; Percy Shelley's final departure from England; Keats attacked in *Blackwood's Edinburgh Magazine*	shipwreck published in London
1819	Peterloo Massacre in Manchester; Birth of Victoria, later Queen of England	Publication of Byron's *Don Juan* (Cantos I and II) and *Mazeppa*; Scott's *Ivanhoe* and *The Bride of Lammermoor*; Percy Shelley's *The Cenci: A Tragedy* and *Peter Bell the Third*; Wordsworth's *Peter Bell: A Tale in Verse*; John William Polidori's *The Vampyre*; Birth of John Ruskin	Géricault exhibits *The Raft of the Medusa* at the Paris Salon; John Constable exhibits *The White Horse*; Turner visits Italy
1820	Death of George III and accession of George IV	Publication of John Clare's *Poems Descriptive of Rural Life and Scenery*; Keats's *Lamia, Isabella, The Eve of St. Agnes, and Other Poems*; Maturin's *Melmoth the Wanderer*; Percy Shelley's *Prometheus Unbound and Other Poems*; Scott's *The Abbott* and *The Monastery*; Scott is knighted	Death of Benjamin West, President of the Royal Academy (Thomas Lawrence succeeds); Géricault exhibits *The Raft of the Medusa* at Bullock's Egyptian Hall in London; Bonington meets Delacroix in the Louvre; Marshall's panoramas tour Scotland (and conclude in Dublin in 1821)
1821	Greek War of Independence begins; Death of Napoleon at St Helena; Famine in Ireland	Publication of Byron's *The Two Foscari; Cain; Sardanapalus* and *Don Juan* (Cantos III–V); Percy Shelley's *Adonais: An Elegy on the Death of John Keats*; Southey's *A Vision of Judgement*; Scott's *Kenilworth*; Hazlitt's *Table-Talk*; Death of John Keats in Rome; Death of John Polidori; Birth of Charles Baudelaire, Gustave Flaubert and Fyodor Dostoevsky	Géricault spends the year in London; Wilkie visits Paris

Year	Historical background	Literature	Arts
1822	Greece declares independence; Massacre of Chios by the Turks; Congress of Verona decides the partition of Europe; Robert Steward – Viscount Castlereagh commits suicide	Publication of Scott's *The Fortunes of Nigel* and *Peveril of the Peak*; Byron's *The Vision of Judgement*; Shelley's *Hellas*; Thomas De Quincey's *Confessions of an English Opium-Eater*; Wordsworth's *Ecclesiastical Sketches* and *A Description of the Scenery of the Lakes in the North of England*; Death of Shelley in Italy	Wilkie's *The Chelsea Pensioners Reading the Waterloo Dispatch* exhibited at the Royal Academy; Opening of the Paris diorama by Charles Bouton and Louis Daguerre; David visits London
1823	Byron sails to Greece to take part in the Revolution	Publication of Byron's *Don Juan* (Cantos VI–XIV); Scott's *Quentin Durward*; Mary Shelley's *Valperga, or, the Life and Adventures of Castruccio, Prince of Lucca*; Hazlitt's *Liber Amoris, or, The New Pygmalion*; Charles Lamb's *Essays of Elia*; Lamartine's *Nouvelles Méditations Poétiques*; Death of Robert Bloomfield and Ann Radcliffe	Opening of the first British diorama in Regent's Park
1824	Charles X becomes King of France	Publication of Byron's *Don Juan* (Cantos XV–XVI); James Hogg's *The Private Memoirs and Confessions of a Justified Sinner*; Scott's *Redgauntlet* and *St. Ronan's Well*; Letitia Elizabeth Landon's *The Improvisatrice, and Other Poems*; Athenaeum Club founded in London; Death of Lord Byron at Missolonghi and Charles Maturin	Society of British Artists formed; Foundation of the National Gallery in London; Delacroix's *Massacre at Chios* creates a sensation; Constable, Bonington and Anthony Vandyke Copley Fielding awarded a gold medal at the British Salon in Paris; Death of Géricault and Girodet; Beethoven finishes *Ninth Symphony*
1825	The first steam-locomotive railway opens, from Stockton to Darlington	Publication of Hazlitt's *The Spirit of the Age*; Coleridge's *Aids to Reflection*; Scott's *The Betrothed*; Felicia Hemans's *The Forest Sanctuary, and Other Poems*; Death of Anna Letitia Barbauld and Henry Fuseli	Daguerre's diorama *Ruins of Holyrood Chapel* displayed in London; Bonington and Delacroix travel to London in the summer; Wilkie visits Paris; Death of David in Brussels

Year	Historical background	Literature	Arts
1826	Missolonghi falls to the Turks	Publication of Scott's *Woodstock*; Mary Shelley's *The Last Man*; Disraeli's *Vivian Grey*; Alfred de Vigny's *Cinq-Mars*	Bonington exhibits for the first time in London at the British Institution; he shares a studio in London with Delacroix; Bonington and Delacroix visit Venice; Scott visits Paris and attends Rossini's adaptation of *Ivanhoe*
1827	George Canning becomes Prime Minister of Britain after resignation of Lord Liverpool; Independence of Greece declared by the Treaty of London	Publication of Scott's *The Life of Napoleon Buonaparte* and *Chronicles of the Canongate*; Clare's *The Shepherd's Calendar*; Landon's *The Golden Violet, With Its Tales of Romance and Chivalry, and Other Poems*; Victor Hugo's 'Preface' to *Cromwell*; Scott acknowledges authorship of the Waverley novels; Death of Blake	Constable exhibits *The Cornfield* at the Paris Salon; Delacroix shocks critics with his *Death of Sardanapalus*; Paul Delaroche visits London; Death of Beethoven and George Canning (after less than four months in office)
1828	Wellington becomes Prime Minister of Britain	Publication of Hazlitt's first two volumes of *Life of Napoleon Buonaparte*; Hemans's *Records of Woman with Other Poems*; Death of Lady Caroline Lamb	Delacroix's first exhibition at the British Institution in London; Bonington's last exhibition in London and Paris; Hector Berlioz composes the *Waverley Overture*; Death of Bonington, Goya and Franz Schubert
1829	Catholic Emancipation Act passed in Britain	Publication of Hugo's *Les Orientales*	Constable elected Royal Academician; Premieres of Rossini's *William Tell* and Donizetti's *Kenilworth*
1830	Death of George IV and accession of William IV; Earl Charles Grey becomes Prime Minister of Britain; July Revolution in France	Publication of Hemans's *Songs of the Affections, with other Poems*; Volumes three and four of Hazlitt's *Life of Napoleon Buonaparte*; Stendhal's *The Red and the Black*; Death of Hazlitt	Hugo stages *Hernani*; First performance of Berlioz's *Symphonie fantastique*

Year	Historical background	Literature	Arts
1831	Whigs introduce Reform Bill into Parliament, but it is defeated in House of Lords; National Union of the Working Classes founded in London with assistance of Robert Owen	Publication of Mary Shelley's revised edition of *Frankenstein*	Delacroix's exhibition of *Liberty Leading the People*; Berlioz conducts *Rob Roy*; Death of Hegel in Berlin
1832	Passing of the Great Reform Act; Britain proclaims sovereignty over the Falkland Islands	Publication of Shelley's *The Mask of Anarchy*; Death of Scott and Goethe	Turner exhibits *Childe Harold's Pilgrimage* at the Royal Academy
1833	Abolition of slavery in the British Empire; Factory Act limits child labour in Britain	Death of Hannah More	
1834	The Tories, under Robert Peel, take office in Britain	Death of Coleridge	Delaroche exhibits *The Execution of Lady Jane Grey* at the Paris Salon
1835	Whigs in power in Britain under Melbourne; Press Law passed	Publication of De Musset's *Confession d'un enfant du siècle*; Vigny's *Chatterton*	Gold medal awarded to John Martin for his exhibition of *The Deluge* at the Paris Salon; Premiere in Naples of Donizetti's *Lucia di Lammermoor*; Gros commits suicide
1836	Founding of London Working Men's Association by William Lovett		
1837	Death of William IV and accession of Victoria		Death of Constable

Introduction

Romanticism and its discontents

> Romanticism: an ambiguous question, like everything modern.
>
> Friedrich Nietzsche, *The Will to Power* (1885–6)

Overview

This introductory chapter is concerned with the ways in which Romanticism has been defined and understood from the nineteenth century to the present day. The first part of the chapter explores the difficulties of defining Romanticism, examining the history of the term; the ways in which the period is marked by various (and competing) dates of political, social and cultural significance; the efficacy (or otherwise) of period markers such as 'early' or 'pre-' Romanticism; questions of canonicity and representativeness; and the usefulness of rubrics such as the 'Age of Feeling', the 'Age of the Individual', the 'Age of the Lyric' and the 'Age of Nationalism'. This part of the chapter therefore primarily examines issues surrounding periodisation, including the various theories or hypotheses that have been used to explain the relationship between eighteenth-century and Romantic literature, such as 'rupture', 'continuity', 'developmental' and 'emergence' theses. The second part considers critical approaches to Romanticism such as deconstruction, New Historicism, cultural materialism, gender criticism and ecocriticism. As Jon Klancher has pointed out, disputes about what constitutes Romanticism are deeply entangled with its institutional and critical history (Klancher 1989: 77–88). This second part therefore also explores the ways in which our inherited notions of Romanticism (as discussed in the first part) have increasingly been undermined by revisionist approaches and methodologies.

Defining Romanticism

The history and meaning of the term

It is by now a commonplace to acknowledge that the designation 'Romantic' is anachronistic or, in other words, a term applied retrospectively to the literature of the late eighteenth and early nineteenth centuries. Although the word 'Romantic' did appear in writing of the period – William Wordsworth (1770–1850) uses it ten times in his poetry, Samuel Taylor Coleridge (1772–1834) five times, John Keats (1795–1821) four times, Percy Bysshe Shelley (1792–1822) three times and Lord Byron (1788–1824) fifteen times (Whalley 1972: 164, 178, 194–5) – it was never applied to a school of British writing or a group of British writers, and 'none of the English poets of the time . . . recognized himself as a romanticist' (Wellek 1955: 110–11). Some critics have even maintained that early nineteenth-century writers either disavowed or deliberately avoided the word 'Romantic' (Isbell 2004: 37–57; Whalley 1972: 159), which has, in turn, lead to claims that its continued use has obfuscated, rather than clarified, the nature of literary writing in the period. Marilyn Butler, for example, has argued that '[g]oing out to look for "romanti-cism" means selecting in advance one kind of answer' and that the term itself is 'historically unsound' (Butler 1988: 37; 1981: 186–7). At the same time, few critics go so far as to suggest that Romanticism is solely an arbitrary 'convention/necessary fiction' or that we should abandon it altogether (Pittock 2008: 3). As John Reider has rightly pointed out, the status of the term continues to 'hover[s] uneasily between its critical usefulness and its obfuscation of historical complexity' even as we persist in using it (Reider 1997: 145).

Raymond Williams's definition of 'Romantic' in *Keywords* (1976) is a useful place to start when considering the term's history. Williams points out that the origins of the word 'romantic' lie in the verse and prose quest romances of the medieval and early modern periods (Williams 1976: 230), a link seized on by critics such as Harold Bloom, who describes Romanticism as an 'internalization' of these older forms of 'quest-romance' (Bloom 1970: 3–24). As early as 1650 in Britain, the word 'romantick' was applied to the adventurous, fantastic, absurd or unrealistic (Eichner 1972: 5), but by the early to mid eighteenth century it was used in a more positive sense to refer to striking, dark, remote or mysterious land-scapes (Immerwahr 1972: 24). By the 1760s, 'romantic' had an established usage in art criticism on painters such as Salvator Rosa (1615–73) and Claude Lorrain (1600–82) (see Chapter 5), and in writing on the picturesque by William Gilpin (1724–1804), Uvedale Price (1747–1829) and others (see Chapter 2). Towards the end of the eighteenth century, the word was increasingly used to refer to emerging sentimental and Gothic genres (Whalley 1972: 242) or what Wordsworth described, in more negative terms, in the 1802 'Preface' to *Lyrical Ballads* (1798) as 'frantic novels, sickly and stupid German tragedies, and deluges of idle and extravagant stories in verse' (65).

In seventeenth- and eighteenth-century France, on the other hand, a distinction was made between *Romanesque* (a derogatory term) and *Romantique* (tender, sentimental or gentle) (Eichner 1972: 5). In Germany the term *Romanisch* or *Romantische* was used in a negative sense in the seventeenth century, but by the mid eighteenth century it too had come to mean tender, gentle or melancholy. Drawing on Thomas Warton's (1728–90) juxtaposition of 'classical' and 'roman-tic' in his *Observations on the Faerie Queene* (1754), Friedrich Schlegel (1772–1829) defined *Romantische* literature very widely in his 1798 *Athenaeum* fragment as 'literature depicting emotional matter in an imaginative form' (cited in Grange 2011: 32). Other German philosophers and aestheticians such as

Friedrich Schiller (1759–1805) and Wilhelm Schlegel (1767–1845) used *Romantische* in a slightly more technical sense to refer to 'modern' rather than 'classical' literature (see Chapter 6), but, arguably, the impact of these debates in Britain was limited (Isbell 2004: 44).

Throughout the eighteenth and early nineteenth centuries the terms 'Romantic', 'Romantique' and 'Romantische' were therefore vague and diffuse labels. Even in the mid to late nineteenth century, writers and critics did not often or habitually use the term 'Romantic' to refer to the literary productions of their predecessors. Mrs Oliphant's (1828–97) 1882 *Literary History of England*, for instance, avoids the term altogether. Victorian critics were nonetheless highly influential on the way in which the field of Romantic studies developed; and an interest in Romantic forms and styles did not simply fade away as the nineteenth century progressed (Cronin 2002). Although he never used the words 'Romantic' or 'Romanticism', Matthew Arnold (1822–88), for example, tended to de-politicise the work of Wordsworth, Byron, Keats and Shelley, representing it as an escape from the history and politics of its time. Establishing what subsequently became known as a Romantic 'cult of sensitivity', he famously referred to Shelley as 'a beautiful and ineffectual angel beating in the void his luminous wings in vain' (cited in Culler 1961: 380), an idea of the Romantic poets that was later invoked by the New Critical academy of T. E. Hulme, F. R. Leavis and T. S. Eliot, who dismissed Romanticism as escapist and even fantasist when arguing for the deep division between Romantic and classical styles. The German philosopher Friedrich Nietzsche also saw Romanticism as an escape from conflict through dreams, visions and other forms of self-deception. As the epigraph to this chapter suggests, Nietzsche's attitude towards Romanticism was deeply ambivalent, attributing to the new movement a hunger or desire for change combined with a decadent philosophical pessimism that devalued the present in favour of the past and future (Nietzsche 1968: 445–6).

The application of the word 'Romantic' to a literary movement began in the late nineteenth century when the French literary historian Hyppolite Taine (1828–93) applied the term *Romantique* first to a group of late-eighteenth- and early-nineteenth-century French writers, and then later to a 'school' of English writers of the same period in his *History of English Literature* (1862–7, trans. 1871–2). But while the idea of a 'Romantic school' was established by the end of the nineteenth century, the concept of literary Romanticism as a distinct academic field is primarily a twentieth-century phenomenon. Early studies by Irving Babbit (1919) and Carl Schmitt (1919) tended to consider Romantic writing in a wider European setting (see Chapter 6). This kind of comparativism was largely a product of European politics following World War I (Klancher 1989: 78), but it also meant that the differences between various nations, countries and regions could be elided. It was partly for this reason that, as early as 1924, Arthur O. Lovejoy argued for the 'discrimination' of Romanticisms on the basis that the term Romanticism had 'come to mean so many things that, by itself, it means nothing' (Lovejoy 1924: 232). Lovejoy's key points were that diversity was the leading characteristic or principle of Romanticism and occurred even within national contexts; and that the term itself was a problem rather than a solution to the questions of national particularity and specificity that were only just being identified and debated by literary critics.

The period following Lovejoy's essay was both a period of discrimination, as national Romanticisms were given separate critical histories and institutional identities, *and* a period of consolidation, as a number of critics attempted to demonstrate that the designation 'Romantic' was not just a convenient fiction. In a direct response to Lovejoy, René Wellek, for example, described a holistic pan-European Romanticism as:

> part of a great endeavor to overcome the split between subject and object, the self and the world, the conscious and the unconscious. This is the central creed of the great Romantic poets in England, Germany and France. It is a closely coherent body of thought and feeling
>
> (Wellek 1963: 220)

Between 1945 and 1970 similarly recuperative attempts to define Romanticism as a cohesive aesthetic or cultural movement by critics such as Walter Jackson Bate, M. H. Abrams, Earl Wasserman, Northrop Frye, Carl Woodring, Geoffrey Hartman and Harold Bloom were less pan-European in their orientation but also tended to portray Romantic writers as 'triumphantly internalizing their traumatic encounter with history and politics' (Klancher 1989: 79).

Many of the orthodoxies or the most enduring ideas and popular perceptions of Romanticism emerged from the work of these critics in the post-war period: for example, the idea of Romantic poetry as an expression of emotion or feeling; the idea of the lyric poem as the movement's representative form of expression; the idea of the creative and solitary Romantic genius; and the idea that the imaginative faculty allowed the poet to transcend the material world. In formulating this 'interiority' model of Romanticism very little attention was paid to Romantic-era dramas, novels and narrative poems, or to female, working-class, Irish, Scottish and Welsh writers. Nor were the historical, material and intellectual contexts in which Romantic writers lived and worked a primary site of investigation. As Ian Duncan has put it, Romanticism was for many years solidified in the university system as 'an ideologically potent account of lyric poetry . . . which escaped or resisted the collected pressures of society and history' (Duncan 2004: 5).

The most serious challenge to this understanding of Romanticism came in the 1980s in the form of works such as Marilyn Butler's *Romantics, Rebels and Reactionaries* (1981) and Jerome McGann's *The Romantic Ideology* (1983). McGann pointed out that both Romantic writing and its scholarship were 'dominated . . . by an uncritical absorption in Romanticism's own self-representations' (McGann 1983: 137), accusing Abrams, Wellek and others of perpetuating the myths about genius, originality and isolationism that Romantic writers told about themselves (see also Siskin 1988). McGann also pointed to the tension between two central approaches to Romanticism, the first of which sees it as an aesthetic movement, and the second as a historical phenomenon or distinct historical period. As he later noted, the distinction between 'Romanticism' and the 'Romantic period' is 'important not merely because so much of the work of [the] period is not "romantic", but even more, perhaps, because the period is noted for its many ideological struggles ... [and] sharp cultural conflict; some of the fiercest engagements were internecine – the civil wars of the romantic movement itself' (McGann 2002: 236–7).

In similarly rejecting 'Romanti-centric' criticism, Butler went further than McGann in her attempt to define the historical specificity of the Romantic period, arguing that Romanticism was deeply entangled with the emergence of a culture of modernity: 'Romanticism is inchoate because it is not a single intellectual movement but a complex of responses to certain conditions which Western society has experienced and continues to experience since the middle of the eighteenth century' (Butler 1981: 184; see also 178–87). Like McGann, Butler sees the period as one characterised by ideological struggles, but she grounds the varied and conflicted responses to those struggles more fully in the historical conditions in which Romantic writers lived and wrote. If some critics see this 'common historical ground' definition of Romanticism as problematically 'neutral', 'colourless' and 'odourless', in that it attempts to encompass virtually all literary activity produced in Britain (and beyond) from the American Revolution to the First Reform Bill of 1832 (Reider 1997: 146, 147), it is nonetheless one to which numerous other critics have subscribed in various guises. Anne Janowitz, for example, has argued that Romanticism is a response (progressive or otherwise) to the emergence of capitalist modernity in that it is 'the literary form of a struggle taking place on many levels of society between the claims of *individualism* and the claims of *communitarianism*' (Janowitz 1998: 13; see also Chandler 1998; Makdisi 1998; Siskin 1988).

The continued unease about whether or not Romanticism exists as a cohesive movement may point, as Mark Parker has noted, to a desire among Romantic scholars for less prescribed period boundaries and definitions: 'Perhaps we have come to a place where an ironic counterhistory of Romanticism, one less intent on closure, one more alive to the accidents and contingencies of descent, is at once possible and necessary' (Parker 1991: 247). But while literary criticism has moved away from the essentialism of Wellek's position, it has arguably not 'fully addressed the difficulties of defining periodicity when the literary movement it is supposed to capture has lost the definition which made it worth capturing' in the first place (Pittock 2008: 3). Murray Pittock, for one, is unsettled not only by the pervasiveness of old, ahistorical ideas about Romantic transcendence, but also by durability of the term Romanticism, which he sees as 'the doughtiest survivor, the "last of the race" if you like, of the use of historical eras as a stalking-horse for aesthetic assumptions in literary history' (Pittock 2008: 2). Pittock is right in suggesting that the traditional view of the Romantic period is still very powerful in institutional settings, but an increasing number of scholars are removing the capital from the term 'romantic' or avoiding the 'R-word' altogether (Galperin and Wolfson 1997: n.p.). Others have even suggested that Romanticism might be better understood as an isolated or 'relative phenomenon' within a broader picture of the period's literary productions (Wolfson cited in Cox 1996: 8).

Periodising hypotheses

Despite continued debates about the definition and meanings of Romanticism, literary historians have consistently agreed that 'something' changed between 1700 and 1800. Even those scholars who argue against 'rupture' narratives (or the idea that 1789 marks a turning point in British literary culture) accept that what began as neoclassical or Augustan somehow ended as 'Romantic'. Yet neither eighteenth-century nor Romantic scholars are in agreement about the nature of this change. The idea that 1789 and the French Revolution marks a rupture in literary and aesthetic styles was first introduced by Romantic writers themselves, and has been reinforced by the work of influential critics such as Abrams and Bloom. Continuity and emergence theses, on the other hand, see the birth of Romanticism as emerging either from a crisis within eighteenth-century thinking or from the gradual evolution of shared ideas and aesthetic styles. These kinds of theses not only argue against Romantic exceptionalism in favour of continuous changes over the 'long eighteenth century', but also highlight the ways in which Romantic and neoclassical styles could coexist.

Despite Marilyn Butler's contention that a revival of neoclassical writing began with Byron's *Childe Harold* (1812–18) and marked the writing of the second generation of Romantic poets (Butler 1981: 180–1), modern critics have often argued that around the 1790s writers rejected neoclassical (and, in particular, French) models of literature in favour of a new and uniquely English or British model that carried with it an appreciation of older, Gothic tastes. In 'Sleep and Poetry' (1816), for example, Keats refers to the schism caused by John Dryden (1631–1700) and Alexander Pope (1688–1744) – 'with a puling infant's force/ They sway'd about upon a rocking horse,/ And thought it Pegasus. Ah dismal soul'd!' (ll. 185–8) – before considering the partial recovery of poetry in his own age: 'yet in truth we've had/ Strange thunders from the potency of song;/ Mingled indeed with what is sweet and strong,/ From majesty' (ll. 230–3). April London has rightly described these kinds of narratives, championed by Francis Jeffrey (1773–1850), Leigh Hunt (1784–1859) and William Hazlitt (1778–1830), among others, as part of a gradual standardisation of literary history after 1800s, in which 'the defense of a uniquely British "national mind"' was 'vested in a canonic "national literature"' (London 2006: 111), but such narratives (and their modern counterparts) arguably underestimate the continued appreciation and adoption of neoclassical models after the 1790s.

A second rupture argument emerged from Abram's view that the 1790s in Britain saw a shift from neoclassical 'mimesis' to Romantic 'expressionism'. Wordsworth's 'Preface' to *Lyrical Ballads* is seen as a key text in explaining this change from the 'mirror' to the 'lamp' as a model for literary creation and production (Abrams 1971a) (see Chapter 2). In the 'Preface' Wordsworth famously describes poetry as 'the spontaneous overflow of powerful feelings' and argues that the primary aim of his poetry is to 'follow the fluxes and refluxes of the mind when agitated by the great and simple affections of our nature' (62, 63). Butler has not only argued against the representative status accorded to *Lyrical Ballads* (Butler 1981: 57, 58; see also Moore 2011: 253) – its publication is sometimes seen as a 'manifesto' or period marker for the beginnings of British Romanticism – but has also suggested that the radical spontaneity of Wordsworth's view of poetry in the 'Preface' is tempered by subsequent comments, which put 'rational thought, moral intention and social utility above the subjective, emotional side of the mind, and above the claims of self-expression' (Butler 1981: 60). Butler – and an increasing number of other critics – therefore reject the idea of Romantic writing as a product of pure expressionism.

Such a view of *Lyrical Ballads* and the kind of poetry it represents has largely deflated a third rupture argument concerning the relationship between Enlightenment and Romanticism. Although Irving Babbitt's *Rousseau and Romanticism* (1919) had long repudiated the thesis of a divide between Romantic and Enlightenment ideology, arguing that Romanticism was in fact deeply immersed in Enlightenment systemisation, disciplinarity and the will to power, the traditional view of Romanticism is that it is a late form of 'counter-Enlightenment', in which writers rejected Enlightenment mechanism, rationality and progress, and instead promoted anti-rationalist, vitalist, spiritual and organic values. This view has come under much interrogation of late, partly because of its misrepresentation of Romantic attitudes towards the Enlightenment and partly because it misleadingly presupposes that there was a relatively unified Enlightenment followed or superseded by a relatively unified Romanticism (Schmidt 2006: 651–5). Marshall Brown, for example, has argued that the Romantics' distaste towards systematic and speculative thought – or what Keats in his *Letters* calls 'consecutive reasoning' (I. 171) – should be thought of as only the surface or theatrical manifestation of a deeper process of reflection 'that was the Romantic working-through of its roots' (Brown 1993: 38). Romanticism is therefore increasingly being characterised not as a form of rupture from the philosophies and values of the eighteenth century but rather as a series of literary and philosophical responses that emerged from the sentimental critiques of Enlightenment progress, rationalism and mechanism undertaken by late Enlightenment figures (such as Adam Smith (1723–90) and David Hume (1711–76)) themselves (Phillips 2000; Chandler 1998; O'Brien 1997).

But while the idea of a sharp conceptual break between Romanticism and the Enlightenment has quite rightly been interrogated, the Romantic period is still often represented as the locus of a corrective shift towards subjectivity, transcendence and feeling, whereby Romantic writing culminates all the literature that has gone before it. 'Pre-Romanticism' – now an unfashionable term – has sometimes been used to valorise certain kinds of eighteenth-century literature (such as primitivism, Graveyard poetry and the literature of sensibility) over other kinds, while simultaneously subordinating it to the literature of the Romantic period. Although the term has been somewhat reinvigorated by Brown, who uses the 'pre' to point to the productive affinities and differences between Romantic writers and their immediate predecessors (Brown 1991), it no longer seems adequately to capture the nature and scope of eighteenth-century writing.

More recently, Clifford Siskin has maintained that we need to think of literary history in dialectic rather than linear terms, arguing against 'developmental', 'continuity' and 'revelation' theses in favour of theories of 'emergence'. In a 2011 article Siskin and William Warner argue that Romanticism was not the radical break with the past that has been supposed but an outcome of long-term changes in various forms of mediation: new ways of transporting and communicating texts; new genres such as the newspaper; new spaces and associational practices in which these texts were read; and finally new rules or 'enabling constraints'. Enlightenment, they claim, was 'an event' of which Romanticism was an outcome or 'eventuality' and the Victorian period 'a variation' rather than an absolute departure (Siskin and Warner 2011: 289). Siskin has elsewhere argued for the idea of a 'second Enlightenment' emerging in the 1780s, an idea which not only stresses 'the continuity underlying that change', but also points to the Enlightenment's overlap with Romanticism. For Siskin, 'Enlightenment 2', by extending knowledge in new directions, meant that Romanticism, 'far from being a nightmare turn from the dream of Enlightenment knowledge, is the moment in which the reorganization of that knowledge leads to unprecedented productivity' (Siskin 2009: 119).

Dates, the canon and representativeness

The Romantic era has been described as a 'hot chronology', or a period in which certain kinds of ideological, technological and political changes appear to have precipitated and even accelerated social and cultural transformations (Chandler 1998: 3). Events such as the American Revolution (1776), the French Revolution (1789), the Union with Ireland (1800), Waterloo (1815), the Peterloo Massacre (1819), the Great Reform Act (1832) and the Indian Rebellion (1848) all suggest that the Romantic era is one of those periods to which the anthropologist Claude Lévi-Strauss ascribes an intensified 'pressure of history', which is differentially 'coded' from other periods by a larger number of important dates and historical events (cited in Chandler 1998: 67). Wordsworth captures this sense of the dizzying speed of change in the period in the 'Preface' to *Lyrical Ballads*, when he notes that 'the great national events which are daily taking place, and the increasing accumulation of men in cities' produces 'a craving for extraordinary incident, which the rapid communication of intelligence hourly gratifies' (64). While the Romantic period may have been granted 'representation out of all proportion to its duration' (Chandler 2009: 9), Lévi-Strauss's idea that some cultures are 'compressed' or develop more quickly than others at certain periods of time chimes with the Romantics' own sense that they were living through a difficult and revolutionary time (see the case study of Hazlitt later in this Introduction), although it also reveals the extent to which the Romantics' own view of themselves has coloured and even defined the way in which modern criticism has understood the period.

We have certainly been conditioned by the Romantic notion that political causes and events mark shifts in literary practices. For example, British Romantic writers tended to portray the period after the French Revolution as a new beginning, and modern scholarly analyses of the Romantic period have also associated the 'politicised metaphors' of Wordsworth's personal 'dawn' in *The Prelude* (published 1850) with the French Revolution (Robertson 2014: 246). More recently, several critics have raised the case for competing dates or events. Fiona Robertson, among others, has demonstrated that the American War of Independence was in some ways more crucial for the generation of thinkers that preceded it than the French Revolutionary wars or even the French Revolution itself (Robertson 2014: 246–7), proposing that we begin the Romantic period in 1776 rather than 1789. Regional and national studies have also raised all kinds of questions about Romantic periodicity. For example, is Romanticism in Scotland initiated by the so-called 'vernacular revival' signalled by Allan Ramsay's (1686–1758) Scots-language collections of the 1720s or by the publication of James Macpherson's (1736–96) enormously influential Ossianic texts in the 1760s? Alternatively, does the publication of Robert Burns's (1759–96) first poetic collections in the late 1780s better mark the beginnings of Scottish Romanticism? Either way, it is necessary to begin accounts of Romanticism in Scotland well before 1789, just as Wales and Ireland raise very different dates and agendas from those that commonly mark English literary history (Pittock 2008: 2; see also Chapter 4).

Pre-empting both transatlantic and national/regional scholars, Butler has argued that 1760 is a more appropriate start date for Romanticism both because the conditions that galvanised the American and French Revolutions date back to the 1760s and because it is naïve to suggest that Romanticism can be dated within precise or prescriptive boundaries. Butler avoids categorising the period 1760–89 as 'pre-romantic' (Butler 1981: 11), instead vindicating Pittock's view that an extended set of period dates usefully points to 'the range of possibilities, the choice of cultural options, which their own and succeeding generations could neglect, but which had been simply unavailable earlier' (Pittock 2008: 4). Within the period 1760–1830, Butler isolates four inter-related and overlapping phases: the first from about 1760 to the mid or late 1790s (which she calls neoclassical), the second from 1790–1820 (in which national loyalties replaced universality), the third from 1815 to the early 1820s (centred on a 'cult of the South') and the fourth up until the early 1830s (characterised by a new interest in the 'modern artist'). Whether or not the Romantic period can or should be divided in this way, Butler's study presents a vision of the period that is primarily latitudinal rather than longitudinal in perspective, and allows for the existence of contradiction in literary history. Her argument for a wider set of periodising dates has more recently been taken up in William Galperin and Susan Wolfson's suggestion that we might embrace a 'long Romanticism' or 'long Romantic century' from 1750–1850 instead of a 'long eighteenth century' (Galperin and Wolfson 1997: n.p.).

Romanticism is usually said to end in 1832 (the Great Reform Act) or in 1837 (the ascension of Queen Victoria (1819–1901)), but as Butler has astutely pointed out, 'the political and constitutional reforms arrived at in 1832 were hardly of an order to account for the sense . . . of a change that amounted to a social revolution' (Butler 1981: 178). Moreover, if we look outside Britain and even Europe, the traditional beginning and end dates of Romanticism become far less compelling, and are threatened by alternative dates such as the American Revolution of 1775, the Haitian Revolution of 1791–1804, the liberation of Spanish America from 1808–33, the Rebellion in India of 1857, the dissolution of the East India company in 1858 and the American Civil War of 1861–5. While this broadening of geographic space and deepening of historical time has proved crucial to recent transnational and global reconceptions of Romanticism (see Chapters 6 and 7), in some ways using a historical definition of Romanticism is just as problematic as an aesthetic definition because, as Gillian Russell points out, it 'tend[s] to elide the magnitude and scope of cultural change after 1760' (Russell 2013: 72).

Interrogations of period dates have been accompanied by, and work in tandem with, a rethinking of the Romantic canon and canonicity more generally. Traditional conceptions of Romanticism were based on a very small (and highly unrepresentative) canon of Romantic writers, in the main limited to the 'Big Six' Romantic poets: Blake (1757–1827), Wordsworth, Coleridge, Byron, Shelley and Keats. Primarily consolidated between 1950 and 1970, this canon tended to privilege the so-called 'High' Romanticism of Wordsworth and Coleridge. In his seminal book *Natural Supernaturalism*, for example, Abrams states that the aim of his project is to show that 'Wordsworth (as his English contemporaries acknowledged, with whatever qualifications) was the great and exemplary poet of the age' (Abrams 1971b: 14). Wordsworth's ability to stand as the representative figure of his age has long since been interrogated. McGann, for example, has proposed that Byron and Shelley's 'key experience', which involves 'the complexities of mortally ordered worlds', is just as representative of the period as the Wordsworthian key experience, which 'is intensely personal and quasi-mystical. . . . a psychic experience' (McGann 2002: 289). More recently, critics have begun to question the whole notion of representativeness itself. While the Romantics were deeply concerned with questions of representativeness – Chandler has rightly dubbed the Romantic period 'the age of the spirit of the age' (Chandler 1998: 78) – they were nonetheless careful not to provide glib or simple answers to those questions, as suggested by the following case study of William Hazlitt's *The Spirit of the Age* (1825).

Case study: William Hazlitt, *The Spirit of the Age* (1825)

In support of his contention that Wordsworth is *the* representative writer of the Romantic age, M. H. Abrams cites William Hazlitt's essay on Wordsworth in his collection *The Spirit of the Age*. 'Mr. Wordsworth's genius', Hazlitt writes, 'is a pure emanation of the Spirit of the Age' because it 'partakes of, and is carried along with, the revolutionary movement of our age: the political changes of the day were the model on which he formed and conducted his poetical experiment' (11: 86). Yet, as James Chandler has pointed out, if we consider Hazlitt's collection of essays in its entirety we can see that it is not only Wordsworth for whom Hazlitt advances the claim of representativeness. Hazlitt in fact constructs a 'scheme of contradictions' that is emphasised throughout the arrangement of his text (Chandler 1998: 177–85): writers are contrasted with other writers both within essays (e.g. Mr. Thomas Campbell (1777–1844) and Mr. George Crabbe (1754–1832)) and between essays (Lord Byron and Sir Walter Scott (1771–1832)), but, ironically, the paired figures are almost complete opposites. Byron and Scott, for example, are said to be 'the greatest geniuses of the age', but they 'afford a complete contrast to one another. In their poetry, in their prose, in their politics, and in their tempers, no two men can be more unalike' (11: 69). The larger point here, as Chandler so admirably demonstrates, is that Hazlitt refuses either to capture the spirit of the age in a 'single portrait that could stand as its total representation' or to select from among the figures he discusses 'one proxy to be its representative', and instead makes every effort to 'block the identification of any single contradiction' to which the representation of his age could be said to be reduced (Chandler 1998: 185, 183). Indeed, Hazlitt's text, written in 1824 when he felt himself to be dealing with the end of an era, reveals 'how fragile and how fractured the era . . . looked to those who lived it' (Kelley 2011: para. 16).

The idea of representativeness, so cleverly and self-consciously distressed by Hazlitt, allowed mid-twentieth-century critics to focus on one or two figures as the pivotal centers of the Romantic period, and hence to attribute value to a very small number of writers, who were often judged hierarchically according to their similarities with, or differences from, more ostensibly central figures. Writing in response to this institutionalised history of inclusion and exclusion, Butler noted in 1989 that Romantic critics were now facing 'the unfortunate intellectual consequences of letting a small set of survivors, largely accidentally arrived at, dictate the model many of us seem to work with, of a timeless, desocialized, ahistorical literary community' (Butler 1989: 72). Butler's complaint about the narrowness of the Romantic canon initiated the recovery of a number of 'lost' Romantic voices, including those of working-class, female, Irish, Scottish and Welsh writers (see Chapter 4), as well as instigating a new interest in neglected genres, styles and forms such as drama, sentimental and popular literature and various types of prose writing (see Chapter 2).

Rubrics and markers

Along with the expansion of the canon has come an interrogation of the ostensibly key markers of the Romantic world-view. For example, the myth of the Romantic poet as a solitary genius and the Romantic age as one of isolationism or the 'Age of the Individual' has been replaced by a new understanding of Romantic literary production as a 'collective activity' in which Romantic writers were not solitaries but 'citizens' (Butler 1981: 9–10) (see Chapter 3). At the same time, studies of Romantic drama and prose writing have questioned the idea that the representative Romantic voice is a primarily lyric voice (Langbaum 1957), arguing against the idea of the Romantic period as the 'Age of the Lyric' or 'Lyric Age' (see Chapter 2). The idea of the Romantic period as the 'Age of Feeling' has also been undermined by studies demonstrating that sentimental themes were present in British culture long before the 1790s (Phillips 2000), while understandings of the Romantic period as the 'Age of Nationhood' or 'Age of Nationalism' have recently come under threat from new transnational and global methodologies (see Chapters 6 and 7), which argue for 'a *widened* eighteenth century' as well as a '*long* eighteenth century' (Nussbaum 2003: 1).

Other rubrics have similarly come under sustained interrogation: the classification of the Romantic period as the 'Age of Revolution' has increasingly been revised by studies that acknowledge the conservatism of English society in the period (Gilmartin 2007; Eastwood 1989; Butler 1981: 5); and new work on religion in the Romantic era has forced us to rethink the notion of Romanticism as an essentially 'secularized form of devotional experience' (Abrams 1971b: 65) by examining the institutional and political, rather than purely personal implications, of secularisation (Canuel 2002: 4), as well as acknowledging the enormous impact of Evangelical religions in the period. The next part of the chapter considers some of these revisionary approaches and methodologies in more detail. Further critical approaches are considered in other chapters: for example, queer theory (Chapter 1); new regionalism, 'four nation' studies and archipelagic studies (Chapter 4); postcolonial criticism (Chapter 7); and transnational and global approaches (Chapters 6 and 7).

Critical approaches to Romanticism

Deconstruction, New Historicism and cultural materialism

The prestige of Romantic literature was somewhat dented in the early to mid twentieth century by New Critical representations of it as escapist and self-indulgent. Deconstructive critics such as Jacques Derrida and Paul de Man (both part of the Yale School in the 1970s and early 1980s) helped to restore the institutional status of Romantic literary texts, even if they primarily focused on the work of canonical writers such as Wordsworth, Coleridge and Shelley. Other scholars of the Yale School such as Harold Bloom, Geoffrey Hartman and J. Hillis Miller collaborated with De Man and Derrida on *Deconstruction and Criticism* (Bloom 1979), which set out their revisionary approach to literary texts. In simple terms, deconstructive critics reject the idea of any stable, autonomous meaning to which a text can be reduced in favour of the existence of an unlimited number of interpretive contexts and a multiplicity of meanings. Typically, a deconstructive reading will draw on the conflicting forces within a text in order to challenge dominant readings or to question the authority of the text's structure. Hillis Miller's controversial reading of Wordsworth's 'A Slumber Did My Spirit Seal' (1798), for example, finds in it a whole host of meanings surrounding Wordsworth's desire to efface his mother's death, some of which relate to sexuality and hidden incestuous desires (Miller 1979). Similarly, De Man sees in some of the characters in Wordsworth's *Prelude* (such as the Boy of Winander and the Drowned Soldier) uncanny doubles of Wordsworth himself, even if these Wordsworthian selves are unconsciously submerged within the text (De Man 1984).

By the mid 1980s, two criticisms of deconstruction had emerged: the first concerned its predictability, the second its erasure of political and historical contexts. Ironically, New Historicism, which challenged the primacy of deconstructive interpretation in the late 1980s, borrowed many of its interpretive strategies from deconstruction, in particular its focus on the 'unsaid' of a literary text (see the case study on *Tintern Abbey* later in this Introduction). The so-called 'turn to history' in the 1980s marks the beginnings of what Damian Walford Davies has called a 'critical orthodoxy' that continues to define Romanticism as a discipline several decades later (Walford Davies 2009: 4). New Historicist criticism tends to see texts as having no fixed or universal literary value above and beyond the ways in which specific societies read them in specific contexts. Other key assumptions of New Historicist criticism include a belief in the historical and material embeddedness of texts; the idea that literary and non-literary texts circulate inseparably; and the idea that no critical discourse provides access to unchanging truths or inalterable human nature (Veeser 1989: xi). Drawing on the work of Michel Foucault and Fredric Jameson, New Historicism therefore 'distinguishes itself by its heightened consciousness of criticism's institutional past, and of how its methodological changes might have served particular cultural interests' (Hamilton 2003: 131).

Materialist criticism shares many of the interests and practices of the New Historicist agenda but is more fully focused on the ideological implications of cultural forces. With its roots in Marxist theory (particularly ideas surrounding the economic base of cultural phenomena), English cultural materialism 'ranges between social history and semiotic and deconstructive reading strategies to ask how literature is produced, read, and reproduced among institutions, cultural formations, and social structures' (Klancher 1989: 77–8). In other words, cultural materialism, as developed in England, is primarily concerned with the material conditions surrounding literary production and consumption. Examples of materialist criticism include E. P. Thompson's cultural history of the English working classes (1966) and Raymond Williams's brilliant ideological examinations of cultural formations and the uses of language in *Culture and Society* (1987) and elsewhere. More recent materialist criticism in Romantic studies can be found in the work of Daniel P. Watkins (1993, 1996), John Barrell (2000) and David Worrall (2006), as well as in the more explicitly Marxist work of Christopher Caudwell (1937), John Lucas (1982) and Roger Sales (1983).

Despite its apparent openness and relativism, New Historicism (and to a lesser extent cultural materialism) has come under increasing criticism in recent years. In Romantic studies the New Historicist effort to read texts in relation to the historical contexts in which they were produced and consumed has tended to lead to what Chandler has called 'critical renunciations' of a Romanticism that is deemed 'dehistoricizing' (Chandler 1998: 4). History as 'displacement' has been central to David Simpson (1987) and Alan Liu's (1989) work on Wordsworth's historical consciousness, while scholars such as Marjorie Levinson (1986) have focused heavily on the 'unsaid', negations or historical absences of Romantic writing. In *Wordsworth's Great Period Poems*, for example, Levinson's primary argument is 'that the extreme disinterest [in political, social, and interpersonal conflicts] evinced by these works indicates their resumption of those problematic themes at the level of image and metaphysics, precisely because they were deadlocked at the practical level' (Levinson 1986: 5). For many cultural materialists, too, the Romantics, while reacting to the alienating and dehumanising forces of encroaching modernity, tended to reify or idealise poverty from the privileged position of bourgeois sentimentalism, and thus unconsciously elided the reality of class and other antag-onisms. The argument proffered by Levinson, Liu and some other New Historicist critics that the supposed Romantic denial, displacement or idealisation of history is, in fact, 'also the strongest kind of engagement of history' (Liu 1989: 35) has been rejected by critics such as Abrams as subscribing to 'a "necessitarianism" of historical determination based on purely negative evidence' (cited in Liu 1988: 176), a 'fetishization of allegories of absence' (McFarland 1992: 29), and as a 'pardon' for the perceived (and politically incorrect) occlusion of social realities (O'Neill 1995: 28). For all of these critics, the New Historicist demystification of Romantic literature is a form of reductionism that implicitly denies the value of the aesthetic (Walford Davies 2009: 6). An example of a New Historicist reading, which also draws on deconstructive techniques, is provided by the following *Tintern Abbey* case study.

Case study: William Wordsworth, *Lines Composed a Few Miles Above Tintern Abbey, On Visiting the Banks of the Wye During a Tour. July 13, 1798* (1798)

The starting point of Marjorie Levinson's influential essay 'Insight and Over-sight: Reading "Tintern Abbey"' from *Wordsworth's Great Period Poems* (1986) is the 'strange fact' that Wordsworth does not anywhere in the poem refer to the Abbey itself, even though he had visited the ruin and read William Gilpin's *Observations on the River Wye* (1782), which describes the monastery as the abode of beggars and the poor. Nor does Wordsworth men-tion that the river Wye was then overloaded and polluted with ships carrying coal and timber, and that Tintern was a manufacturing town. Why, Levinson asks, is Wordsworth so specific in his title about the circumstances of his visit – 'Composed a Few Miles Above Tintern Abbey, on Revisiting the Banks of the Wye During a Tour' – and so vague about them in the poem? Why call attention to a famous ruin and then ignore it? Levinson's conclu-sion is that the absences of *Tintern Abbey* look uncomfortably like suppres-sions. Selectively blind to the beggars and ironworkers around the abbey's ruins, Wordsworth elides or negates these material realities in favour of the sublime transcendence of selfhood. Levinson's essay goes on to look in detail at the text–title incongruity, providing descriptions of how the Abbey would have looked to Wordsworth in 1798 and showing how fragile the pastoral prospect of the poem really is, assembled, as it were, by 'acts of exclusion' (Levinson 1986: 32). She maintains that *Tintern Abbey*'s doctrinal affirmations about the self exist mainly in textual rather than in material space: ' "Tintern Abbey's" subject is . . . profound and universal, its mode of address lofty and abstract, and its questions and answers seem to originate in textual space' (Levinson 1986: 14). In other words, Levinson restores history in the poem as 'willfully repressed content' (Klancher 1989: 81).

Gender criticism

In 1981 Gayatri Spivak traced a 'sexual-political program' of gender exclusion in 'the texts of the Great Tradition' through an analysis of one of Romanticism's central works (Spivak 1981: 57, 76): Wordsworth's 1805 *Prelude*. In 1989 Mary Jacobus also focused on *The Prelude* to showcase the ways in which Wordsworth's High Romanticism or 'master-plot' resulted in the elision of sexual difference and the occlusion of women (Jacobus 1989: 106). While neither Spivak nor Jacobus concentrated on the construction of the Romantic canon, their arguments about the 'Great Tradition' and the Romantic 'master-plot' illuminated the neglect of women writers in literary histories of Romanticism – an idea more explicitly taken up by Isobel Armstrong's 1995 essay 'The Gush of the Feminine', in which she explores the fallacies of contemporaneous male readings of female Romantic poetry. Similarly drawing on Romantic-era criticism and literary histories, Sonia Hofkosh has noted Hazlitt's total exclusion of female writers in *The Spirit of the Age* and his earlier displacement of all but three women – Anna Letitia Barbauld (1743–1825), Hannah More (1745–1833) and Joanna Baillie (1762–1851) – in his *Lectures on the Living Poets* (1818), arguing that '[w]hat Hazlitt did and what we have done with Hazlitt is to make a tradition of that displacement' (Hofkosh, cited in Chandler 1998: 113). Hazlitt's gendered literary history was extended in Victorian and twentieth-century literary criticism, which largely ignored the once popular (and influential) Charlotte Smith (1749–1806) and nearly all of her contemporary female poets, as well as neglecting genres traditionally favoured by women, such as the Gothic novel, the sentimental novel, the national tale and the novel of manners.

Over the last thirty years, this remarkable gap in British Romantic scholarship has been filled by a number of important studies. Stuart Curran's brilliant counter-factual in his 1988 essay 'The I Altered', in which all of the 'Big Six' Romantic poets die young and only female writers remain, is suggestive not only of the amount of writing done by and for women in the period, but also puts into perspective the relatively limited readership of at least five of the 'Big Six' Romantic poets (Curran 1988: 185). Identifying both a 'masculine' and a 'feminine' Romanticism, Anne K. Mellor has examined the relationship between genres and gender, arguing that genres such as epistles and diaries are culturally feminine genres, allowing for a fluid, relational subjectivity and an 'ethic of care' that contributed to the formation of 'an alternative counter-public sphere' (Mellor 1993: 83–4). Susan Wolfson too has identified the relationship between gender and genre in her insightful formalist studies on the politics of literary style, while her more recent work, *Borderlines: The Shifting of Gender in British Romanticism*, rejects 'schematic binaries' (Wolfson 2006: xvi) in order to consider the fluid nature of gender shapes and definitions, looking at examples of strategic cross-dressing, effeminate males and masculine women.

Mellor has rightly argued that the inclusion of women writers in the canon has radically changed our understanding of Romanticism, in that many of the most popular female writers of the period actively rejected male Romantic tenets. Mary Shelley (1797–1851), for example, 'was profoundly disturbed by what she saw to be a powerful egotism at the core of the Romantic ideology' (Mellor 1990: 284). But as Marlon Ross has shown us, and as Mellor too points out, it was not just female writers who objected to the egotistical sublime: Keats's 'chameleon poet' (*Letters*, I. 386–88), for example, has been read as a feminised version of the Romantic sublime (Mellor 1993: 183; Ross 1989). A number of other important studies by Gary Kelly (1993), Mary Favret (1993) and Adriana Craciun (2005), to name but a few, have focused on the ways in which the Revolution debates of the 1790s redefined notions of gender in the nineteenth century, while a cluster of critics has recently discussed the importance of history as a genre for women writers. Devoney Looser (2000), Mary Spongberg (2002), Miriam Burstein (2004), Fiona Price (2009), Lisa Kasmer (2012) and Greg Kucich (2014), among others, have shown us how women writers of the period from Smith to Jane Porter (1776–1850) developed an impressive variety of historiographical innovations to formulate what Kucich has called an 'alternative or feminist historiography' in the service of women's rights as well as other types of political reform (Kucich 2014: 36).

Ecocriticism

Also known as 'Green Romanticism', Romantic ecocriticism is concerned with the ways in which Romantic writers responded to the political, scientific and ethical issues surrounding nature, ecology, animal rights, urbanisation and environmental activism. Pioneered by Jonathan Bate in the early 1990s, Romantic ecocriticism is now a relatively well-established field, encompassing such varied proponents as ecopoeticists, ecolinguists, archipelagic theorists and ecofeminists. As Kevin Hutchings has pointed out, Romantic ecocriticism has approached the literature of the period from two markedly different perspectives: the first privileges 'ecopoesis', which is primarily concerned with an imaginative engagement with the non-human (see, for example, Bate 1991), while the second is more concerned with ecological activism and the 'politics of nature's social construction in literature' (Hutchings 2007: 188). James McKusick has attempted to link these two modes of inquiry by considering the ideological implications of language in ecological studies, arguing for the existence of 'linguistic ecotones' (McKusick 2000: 50), or contact zones between writers and natural objects. Onno Oerlemans, on the other hand, has considered the 'material sublime' as a mode of perception where it is recognised that the mind cannot always subjugate the material world (Oerlemans 2004: 5). Greg Garrard has influentially critiqued the notion of 'pastoral ecology', or the idea that nature exists in a harmonious state, in favour of the existence a darker, more 'radical' Romantic pastoral (Garrard 2004; 1996), while Kate Rigby has argued for a sense of nature's agency in Romantic writing (Rigby 2004).

Other studies have considered the Romantic contribution to the history and development of ecology. Bate, McKusick and Karl Kroeber (1995) emphasise the Romantic contribution to a progressive form of environmentalism. For example, the Romantic craze for picturesque travel was influential on understandings of ecology, leading to the development of attitudes favourable to wildlife protection, national parks, sanctuaries and other preservationist practices (Hutchings 2007: 179–80).

Moreover, as Maureen McLane has shown, it was in the Romantic period that species extinction became a pressing concern, merging with older discourses surrounding natural history, catastrophism and the trope of the 'last man' (McLane 2000) and culminating in Robert Malthus's (1766–1834) demographic treatise on population crisis in his *Essay on the Principle of Population* (1798) (see the case study in Chapter 1). Malthus's interest in resource deficit is taken up in numerous Romantic works such as Mary Shelley's novel *The Last Man* (1826) and Byron's famous poem, 'Darkness' (1816), which is the subject of the following case study.

Case study: Lord Byron, 'Darkness' (written 1816)

'Darkness' was composed in July 1816, during the so-called 'Year without a Summer' caused by the eruption of Mount Tambora in the Dutch East Indies in the previous year, which led to abnormal weather patterns across much of northeast America and northern Europe. Crop failures, famines and cholera and typhus epidemics swept through Europe. In Switzerland, where Byron was living, the Swiss government declared a state of emergency, and this state of general panic inspired Byron to write his poem narrating a dark history of resource deficit and ecocrisis:

> I had a dream, which was not all a dream.
> The bright sun was extinguish'd, and the stars
> Did wander darkling in the eternal space,
> Rayless, and pathless, and the icy earth
> Swung blind and blackening in the moonless air (ll. 1–5)

As this passage suggests, the suffix 'less' is repeated again and again in the poem, enclosing the reader in a world of suffocating, repetitive gloom: 'rayless', 'pathless', 'moonless', 'useless', 'seasonless', 'herbless', 'treeless', 'manless', 'lifeless'. To some extent, the poem represents the underside of Romanticism or the triumph of irrationality. Byron takes great delight in heaping up details of horror: humanity and freedom are defeated; religious faith is parodied in the image of a dog's pointless loyalty to his dead master; and two men die when they see their own face reflected in the other's visage. Even more interesting is the way in which the poem simultaneously describes a meteorological and a socio-political condition (Bate 1996), suggesting that there is no guarantee of human health and happiness or even species security. Human life is contingent on natural forces and an unforeseeable natural or ecological disaster in some distant part of the world can spread death and destruction around the globe. Byron thereby suggests that much of what we take for granted (sunlight, food, harvest, social order) can disappear and that there is nothing in human nature that guarantees that our response will be civilised or noble.

Conclusion

- This Introduction explored competing understandings and definitions of Romanticism, providing an overview of debates concerning periodicity, canonicity and representativeness. It argued that definitions of Romanticism are still contested, particularly in relation to whether the term is best understood as a cohesive literary movement (either national or European) or as a historical phenomenon/time period.

- It considered the varies hypotheses or theses used to explain relationships between Romantic and eighteenth-century writing, arguing that Romantic critics have increasingly rejected rupture arguments in favour of continuity and emergence arguments, which see Romanticism as developing from changes within the late Enlightenment itself or from the gradual evolution of shared ideas, forms and styles.

- It argued that our understanding of the Romantic period as a 'hot chronology' and our tendency to use historical/political events in order to frame its period boundaries is an inheritance from the Romantics themselves, while acknowledging that new transnational and global studies are widening Romantic period dates and frames of reference.

- It pointed out that, relatively recently, traditional rubrics and markers such as the 'Age of the Individual' and the 'Age of Feeling' have been contested by critics, just as a traditionally very small canon limited to the 'Big Six' Romantic poets has been expanded by a new interest in a variety of literary genres and forms, as well as by the recognition of the achievements of female, working-class, Scottish, Irish and Welsh writers.

- The second part of this Introduction considered a number of critical approaches to Romantic literature, including deconstruction, New Historicism, cultural materialism, gender criticism and ecocriticism.

1   Contexts of Romanticism

> Poets, not otherwise than philosophers, painters, sculptors and musicians, are in one sense the creators and in another the creations of their age.
>
> Percy Bysshe Shelley, 'Preface' to *Prometheus Unbound* (1820)

Overview

This chapter outlines some of the most important events, ideas and contexts for understanding the conditions in which British Romantic writing was produced, published and read. It does so not only in order to situate the writers discussed in this book within a particular cultural milieu, or even because of the inherent historical embeddedness or locatedness of literary texts, but also because the Romantic period was one in which both writers and readers repeatedly engaged with 'questions about the conditions within which their own literary efforts were inscribed' (Keen 2009: 101). If, as James Chandler has argued, the Romantic period was 'the age of the spirit of the age' or, in other words, an age self-consciously obsessed with defining itself (Chandler 1998: 78), the events and ideas set out below become much more than just background, contextual or anecdotal material for the study of British Romanticism, and instead form a cultural matrix that Romantic writers both informed and passionately critiqued. Poets, as Percy Shelley puts it in the epigraph to this chapter, are simultaneously 'the creators' and the 'creations of their age' (*Poetry and Prose* 206). The first section of the chapter considers historical and political contexts such as the American and French Revolutions; the political landscape of Britain pre and post-Waterloo; and industrialisation and urbanisation. The second part of the chapter looks at circulating intellectual currents, including scientific developments from Isaac Newton (1643–1727) to Joseph Priestley (1733–1804); philosophical ideas from John Locke (1632–1704) to Adam Smith; religious discourses; and political economy. The final part of the chapter examines social and cultural contexts such as gender and sexuality; classes and conflicts; the literary market place, focusing on publishing and print cultures; and leisure and lifestyle, including tourism, the theatre, art galleries and sport.

Historical and political contexts

Wars, revolutions and revolution debates

In 1783 the Treaty of Paris ended the American Revolutionary War of 1775–83 and secured the independence of the United States of America from the British Empire. In 1789 the Constitution of the United States set out principles such as the separation-of-powers doctrine and federalism; and in 1791 the United States Bill of Rights enshrined many of the liberties and natural rights that had been used to justify the Revolution in the first place such as freedom of religion, speech and assembly. The events leading up to American independence primarily concerned issues of parliamentary sovereignty or whether the British Parliament had the right to extend its legislative authority over the colonies (Ammerman 1976: 473). At the First Continental Congress assembly of 1774, the Americans rejected the authority of the British Parliament to tax the Thirteen American Colonies, thereby validating more local protests such as the infamous Boston Tea Party of 16 December 1773.

British opinion on the American 'crisis' was sharply divided (see Chapter 7). Some British commentators such as the Irish MP Edmund Burke (1729–97) agreed with the Americans, arguing in his 'Speech on Conciliation with the Colonies' (1775) that the American devotion to liberty was founded on English principles and that any attempt to curb American disobedience was an affront to the principle of liberty itself. Like Burke, several of the most popular British newspapers expressed sympathy for the American cause and admiration for George Washington (1732–99). For those on the margins of British society – such as radicals, religious dissenters and the working classes – the American Revolution was an event to be encouraged and even celebrated. More conservative commentators, on the other hand, felt that the American colonists owed Britain a great deal for their protection and for the ongoing provision of goods and services (Weintraub 2005). Still others were concerned that Britain's rivals (especially France and Spain) would use the Revolutionary War to expand their empires at Britain's expense.

When the French Revolution erupted in 1789 many commentators in Britain felt that the French monarchy was receiving its just deserts for the part it had played against Britain in the American Revolutionary Wars. Materially, France had gained little by its involvement in the wars, and Louis XVI (1754–93) ascended the throne during a financial crisis largely caused by France's participation in the American Revolution. Indeed, it was partly in response to a new and unpopular tax code, initiated to raise revenue, that the Third Estate of the French Estates-General (*Etats-Généraux*) on 17 June 1789 declared itself the National Assembly, or the assembly of the people. The first year of the French Revolution in 1789 saw a series of popular revolts such as the storming of the Bastille in July, the Declaration of the Rights of Man and of the Citizen in August and the march on Versailles by working-class women in October. A Republic was proclaimed in September 1792 and Louis XVI was executed in January 1793.

British reactions to the French Revolution ranged from despairing to jubilatory. For Burke, the French Revolution – even before the onset of the Terror – was a 'monstrous tragi-comic scene' in which 'everything seem[ed] out of nature' in a 'strange chaos of levity and ferocity' (Burke 1986: 92). For the poet Helen Maria Williams (1761–1827), '[i]t was a triumph of human kind . . . and it required but the common feelings of humanity to become in that moment a citizen of the world' (Williams 1790: 14). Anna Seward (1742–1809) wrote her admiring 'Sonnet to France on Her Present Exertions' in 1789. Although not published until 1834, Samuel Taylor Coleridge's *Destruction of the Bastille* (written 1789) was similarly celebratory, and annual festivals commemorating the fourteenth of July were held in Britain by Whigs and radicals during the early years of the French Republic. Yet admiration for the new Republic quickly soured when it invaded Belgium and the Netherlands in 1792. Fearing the impact of such expansionary ambitions on the European balance of power, Britain declared war on France soon after.

During the French Revolutionary Wars, popular agitation and the threat of civil war radicalised the Revolution significantly, resulting in the rise of Maximilien Robespierre (1758–94) and the Jacobins at the expense of the more moderate Girondists. The so-called 'Reign of Terror', from 1793–4, resulted in the deaths of an estimated 40,000 people in France. By 1794 Coleridge and Robert Southey's (1774–1843) three-act play, *The Fall of Robespierre*, was less admiring of the Revolution, portraying the French politician as a bloodthirsty tyrant. A similar trajectory can be traced in William Wordsworth's views on the Revolution in the 1805 version of *The Prelude*. For the young Wordsworth, 'Bliss was it in that dawn to be alive' (10. 692), but he later compares the Revolution to a 'volume, whose contents he knows/ Are memorable, but from him locked up,/ Written in a tongue he cannot read' (10. 59–61). Wordsworth's visceral reaction in *The Prelude* to the remains of the blood and bodies piled on the Carousel during the French Terror stands in stark contrast to his original support for revolutionary violence in his unpublished *Letter to the Bishop of Llandaff* (written 1793), where he argues that liberty must often borrow the methods of tyranny in order to triumph.

Commentators on all sides of the political spectrum – Whigs, Tories, Liberals and Radicals – quickly realised the implications of the French Revolution, and the debate that ensued in Britain was about nothing less than the relationship between monarchy and people (or the principle of 'contractual government') and the desirability (or otherwise) of a more democratic and participatory political process (Verhoeven 2013: 1). These debates about the contractual nature of government have led some historians and philosophers to argue that the French Revolution 'marks the birth of political modernity' (Claeys 1995: I. xvii). The Revolution certainly initiated one of the most important ideological debates to have ever taken place in Britain, but the American Revolution also played a central role in debates concerning political reform. Not only did some of the most radical British writers flee to America to escape persecution, but many radical commentators such as Thomas Paine (1737–1809) and William Cobbett (1763–1835) believed that revolutionary forces and discourses about human rights in Europe had originally been generated in America rather than in France (Verhoeven 2013).

Case study: Richard Price, Edmund Burke, Mary Wollstonecraft and Thomas Paine, 'The Revolution Debate' (1789–92)

The dissenting minister Richard Price (1723–91) opened the debate on the French Revolution in Britain with his 1789 sermon to the London Corresponding Society celebrating the 'Glorious Revolution' of 1688, arguing in his *Discourse on the Love of our Country* (1789) that 'a King is no more than the first servant of the public, created by it, maintained by it, and responsible to it' (cited in Butler 1984: 28). Price's *Discourse* received an infamous response from Edmund Burke in the form of his *Reflections on the Revolution in France* (1790). Although Burke had supported the American Revolution, he denounced the French Revolution for its violence and excesses. Burke's strategy was instead to celebrate the stability of the British nation, appealing to Britain's history of bloodless, organic and gradual improvement. For Burke, the nation was 'entailed' or left in trust for the next generation, and many of his metaphors invoke private property and domestic ties, arguing for the 'binding up the constitution of our country with our dearest domestic ties; adopting our fundamental laws into the bosom of our family affections' (Burke 1986: 120).

Mary Wollstonecraft's (1759–97) *A Vindication of the Rights of Men* (1790) was one of nearly 200 responses to Burke's *Reflections*. Using the same form, metaphors and style as Burke, Wollstonecraft reverses his arguments in order 'to shew you to yourself, stripped of the gorgeous drapery in which you have enwrapped your tyrannic principles' (Wollstonecraft 1993: 37). Despite her focus on Burke's sophistry, Wollstonecraft's larger goal is to censure British political elites for their opulence, corruption and inhumane treatment of the poor. Unlike Burke, Wollstonecraft saw the hereditary class structure of English society as 'unnatural, unjust and artificial': 'why was it a duty to repair an ancient castle, built in barbarous ages, of Gothic materials?' (Wollstonecraft 1993: 41). Thomas Paine's *Rights of Man* (1791–2) also rejects Burke's notions of inheritance and entailment, arguing that '[M]an has no authority over posterity in matters of personal right, and therefore, no man, or body of men, had, or can have, a right to set up hereditary government. . . . To inherit a government, is to inherit the people as if they were flocks and herds' (cited in Butler 1984: 110).

Like the Revolution itself, the Revolutionary and Napoleonic Wars with France initiated a number of social and political debates in Britain. Rejecting traditional views that British Romantic writers were largely unconcerned by the wars of the period, works by Simon Bainbridge (2003), Mary Favret (2010), Catriona Kennedy (2013) and Gillian Russell and Neil Ramsey (2015), as well as a digital edition of Betty Bennett's 1976 collection of the period's war poems, demonstrate the extent to which British writers responded to war activities, with Bennett even suggesting that '[w]ar was the single most important fact of British life from 1793–1815' (Bennett 1976: 448). If, for Marilyn Butler, the Napoleonic Wars led to a more repressive cultural nationalism that increasingly politicised and stratified literature according to class allegiances (Butler 1981: 114), they nonetheless also sharpened responses to issues such as industrialisation, poverty and the balance of power in Europe. British war policy was therefore seen to have a unique moral status, which only increased after Napoleon Bonaparte (1769–1821) overthrew the Directory during the coup of 18 Brumaire in 1799 and established the Consulate, later proclaiming himself emperor. Like Wordsworth and Coleridge, the latter of whom led a vigorous campaign in *The Courier* against what he saw as Whiggish defeatism about the Napoleonic Wars, Robert Southey (1774–1843) saw the Peninsular War, during which Britain supported Portugal and Spain against Napoleon, as a 'just' or 'holy' war, claiming in the opening chapter of his *History of the Peninsular War* (1823) that 'this was no common war . . . it was as direct a contest between the principles of good and evil as the elder Persians, or the Manicheans imagined in their fables' (Southey 1823: I. 1–2).

Napoleon's eventual defeat at Waterloo in 1815 by an allied army under the the Duke of Wellington (1769–1852) was largely represented as the victory of good over evil in the British press, becoming in later years the ultimate symbol of national cohesion (Shaw 2002; Bainbridge 1995). But liberals, such as the essayist William Hazlitt and his friend Leigh Hunt (1784–1859), felt that the Congress of Vienna, held from September 1814 to June 1815 in order to restore long-term peace and the balance of power in Europe, was a decisive step backwards rather than forwards, as reactionary regimes were reasserted in France, Spain and elsewhere, and the liberties and natural rights associated with the American and French Revolutions disappeared on the continent. As Hunt put it in his journal *The Examiner* in 1815: 'Monks with their mummeries begin to parade the streets again; the age seems fairly sliding back into old times' (Hunt 1815: 786). For Hunt, the political landscape of post-Waterloo Europe was not a period of international peace, but rather of ideological betrayal: '[T]he Allies, with their violated promises, would not have it otherwise; and they will inevitably see the blessed fruit of that Divine Right which they would have re-planted' (Hunt 1816: 534).

Politics: conservatives, radicals and reformists

Like his friend Hunt, John Keats, writing to his brothers in 1819, felt that the 'unlucky termination' of the French Revolution had produced the temporary effect of returning Europe to the age of autocracy and 'horrid superstition' (*Letters*, II, 193). After the Revolution, 'social deviance' in Britain came to include radical political views, and a series of societies were formed to prevent 'vice', beginning with the Proclamation Society (1787) and the Society for the Suppression of Vice (1802). These societies attempted to expose those who published and distributed obscenity, including seditious and blasphemous publications, as in the case of the 1817–19 trials of publishers and booksellers such as Thomas Wooler (1786–1853), William Hone (1780–1842) and Richard Carlile (1790–1843), and the earlier 1794 treason trials. Many liberals and radicals saw the period immediately following the French Revolution, which included the prosecution of Thomas Paine in 1792 and the 1794 treason trials of John Thelwall (1764–1834), John Horne Tooke (1736–1812) and other members of the London Corresponding Society (a group formed in 1792 by artisans who sought parliamentary reform), as 'the institution of a system of TERROR, almost as hideous in its features, almost as gigantic in its stature, and infinitely more pernicious in its tendency, than France ever knew' (Anon 1795: I. iv). This idea lies at the heart of William Godwin's (1756–1836) novel *Things as they are; or, the Adventures of Caleb Williams* (1794), where the pattern of Caleb's persecution and flight mirrors the vicissitudes of radicals like Paine and Thelwall.

When in October 1795 crowds threw refuse at George III (1738–1820), demanding a cessation of the war with France and lower bread prices, the Government passed the so-called 'Two Acts': the Seditious Meetings Act and the Treasonable Practices Act. Under these new laws, it was almost impossible to hold public meetings, and radicalism was effectively muted during the later 1790s and 1800s. During and after the Napoleonic Wars periods of famine and chronic unemployment were intensified by imported-grain tariffs known as the Corn Laws, which kept grain prices artificially high in Britain even when food supplies were short. As a result, mass meetings were held at Spa Fields, Islington on 15 November and 2 December 1816. In response, the government passed the so-called 'Gagging Acts' of 1817: the Treason Act and the Seditious Meetings Act. By 1819 poor economic conditions had further enhanced the appeal of political radicalism. The Manchester Patriotic Union, for example, organised a demonstration by the radical orator Henry Hunt (1773–1835) on 16 August 1819. Around 60,000 people attended the peaceful demonstration. When local magistrates asked military authorities to arrest Hunt fifteen people were killed and over 400 injured. The event was dubbed the 'Peterloo Massacre' in an ironic comparison to the apparently glorious and nationally cohesive Battle of Waterloo. Many Romantic writers reflected, either directly or indirectly, on the Peterloo Massacre. Percy Shelley, for example, wrote *The Masque of Anarchy*, subtitled *Written on the Occasion of the Massacre at Manchester*, in response to this event, although it was not published until 1832. Shelley's sonnet 'England in 1819', discussed below, also makes reference to the Peterloo Massacre.

Case study: Percy Bysshe Shelley, 'England in 1819' (1819)

The first twelve lines of Shelley's sonnet are a list or catalogue of social ills: the people – 'starved and stabbed in the untilled field' (l. 7) – are clearly the victims of Peterloo; the comparison between rulers and leeches in line 5 represents the monarchy and government as corrupt; the army is a 'two-edged sword' (l. 9), using its power to 'prey' (l. 8) on the weak and to attack liberty itself ('liberticide' (l. 8)); and religion is 'Christless' and 'Godless' (l. 11), a matter of form rather than substance ('a book sealed' (l. 12)). Yet, as James Chandler has pointed out, the poem ends with the thematic pivot of the closing couplet, suggesting that these ills may somehow be transcended in an illuminating resurrection (Chandler 1998: 27): all of the miseries in the first twelve lines '[a]re graves from which a glorious Phantom may/ Burst, to illumine our tempestuous day' (ll. 13–14). For England, then, the dark moment of 1819 holds out the possibility of an illumination that will mark its rebirth. Moreover, as Chandler points out, the catalogue of social ills in the first twelve lines is more complex than it first appears. While George III's loathsome qualities are partly a function or symbol of his age, this fact is also a redeeming feature of the situation, as he will soon be dead (and in fact died only a few weeks after Shelley wrote his poem). Similarly the fact that the Princes are 'the dregs of their dull race' (l. 2) – a view no doubt amplified by Shelley's interest in the ongoing Princess Caroline (1768–1821) scandal, which would peak during her trial for adultery in 1820 – seems an evil, until one stops to think that, being dregs, their flow through 'public scorn' (l. 3) cannot go on indefinitely. 'Leechlike' (l. 5) they eventually drop 'without a blow' (l. 6); that is, of their own accord. In Chandler's masterful reading the 'glorious phantom' of the closing couplet is not unrealistic but instead arises from the very evils described in the poem (Chandler 1998: 29).

By the end of 1819 the government had introduced the so-called 'Six Acts' to suppress political meetings and publications, and by 1820 every significant working-class radical reformer was either in jail or in exile. The Six Acts were the Training Prevention Act (making it unlawful to receive training or drill in weapons), the Seizure of Arms Act (giving local magistrates the power to search private property for weapons), the Misdemeanors Act (reducing the opportunities for bail); the Seditious Meetings Prevention Act (requiring permission for a public meeting of more than 50 people), the Blasphemous and Seditious Libels Act (toughening existing laws and sentences for blasphemy and libel) and the Newspaper and Stamp Duties Act (increasing taxes to include those papers publishing opinion rather than news). George Cruickshank's (1792–1878) famous cartoon of a 'A Free Born Englishman!' (1819) encapsulates the resentment felt by many liberals and radicals during this period, when a number of high-profile prosecutions took place. In the cartoon a figure in rags (possibly Leigh Hunt) is bound in chains with his jaws in a padlock inscribed 'No Grumbling'. One foot rests on the Bill of Rights and the other on the Magna Carta, across which lies an axe whose blade is inscribed 'Law of Libel'. Behind him a banner reads: 'Free discussion – a farce. Right of Petitioning reserved to Families only'. In his hand he holds a note, reading: 'Freedom of the Press – Transportation'.

Despite the persecution of liberals and radicals, the early nineteenth century is also marked by reform in some areas, such as religious toleration (especially

Catholic emancipation) and an increased franchise. In Ireland the campaign for Catholic emancipation was led by Daniel O'Connell (1775–1847), who had himself been denied the opportunity to take a seat in Parliament because he was a Catholic. O'Connell was supported by the Prime Minister, Arthur Wellesley, the Duke of Wellington, as well as by Robert Peel (1788–1850), and many other Whigs and liberal Tories. The Catholic Emancipation Act of 1828 permitted members of the Catholic Church to sit in Parliament at Westminster and no longer required them to take an oath of loyalty to the reigning government (as per the earlier Papists Act of 1778). As Eric Evans has pointed out, one important effect of the Catholic Emancipation Act is that it split the anti-reformers and diminished their ability to block future reform, such as the Great Reform Act of 1832 (Evans 1996). This act, proposed by the Whigs and led by the then prime minister, Charles Grey (1764–1845), introduced wide-ranging changes to the electoral system of England and Wales, reducing the number of boroughs and extending the franchise or the right to vote to owners of land in copyhold and holders of long-term leases. Yet the Reform Act did little to appease the working classes, since voters were required to possess property worth at least 10 pounds. Some historians have therefore questioned the assumption that the Reform Act marked the beginning of a recognisably modern political system of representative democracy in Britain, which was arguably more fully realised by the Second Reform Act of 1867 (Evans 1983).

Industrialisation, urbanisation and social conditions

Industrialisation occurred relatively early in Britain in comparison to the rest of Europe. Certainly, by the end of the eighteenth century significant changes had taken place to the ways in which both agriculture and manufacturing were undertaken. In the first half of the eighteenth century new agricultural techniques, such as more advanced tools, fertilisers and harvesting procedures, led to widespread changes in both country and town: not only were increasing amounts of food more efficiently produced, but such productivity led to a surplus of cheap agricultural labour. As a result, many people left the countryside in favour of towns and cities, providing a new urban workforce for larger-scale, labour-intensive factories. Changes in steam technology also radically altered the face of British industry, with James Watt's (1736–1819) improvements to the steam engine rapidly increasing the efficiency of coalmines, textile mills and dozens of other industries by 1800. Other new technologies, such as Richard Arkwright's (1732–92) water frame for the cotton-spinning wheel and power looms, similarly led to the development of large industrial buildings and factories.

The metal industry – particularly iron, copper and steel – was one of the most profitable industries in Britain from the late eighteenth century onwards: for example, part of the West Midlands was known as the 'Black Country' because of its number of furnaces, while Birmingham was well known for its metalwork. These industries were significant in themselves but they also played an important role in changes to Britain's infrastructure and transportation networks, as the demand for both raw materials and manufactured goods grew. By 1815 networks of canals and roads – and subsequently ship-building and carriage-building – flourished. Docks and warehouses were also constructed in significant numbers to support maritime trade. A new scholarly interest in infrastructural studies, in the work of Claire Connolly (2015) and Nicola Lloyd (2013), among others, is suggestive of the transformative force of new technologies, as schemes of infrastructural improvement not only facilitated industrialisation but also transnational political, social and literary networks.

But not everyone was convinced by Britain's new industrial power. In his *Songs of Innocence and of Experience* (1789, 1794) the poet William Blake explores radical subjects such as poverty, child labour and working conditions. The bleakness of early nineteenth-century London is conveyed in 'London' (1794), where 'the Chimney-sweepers cry/ Every blackning Church appalls/ And the hapless Soldiers sigh/ Runs in blood down Palace walls' (ll. 9–12). Living conditions were certainly grim in most cities and towns, as the demographic shift from country to town resulted in huge pressure on cheap housing. Slum areas quickly grew, and many families lived in unspeakable conditions in tenement housing or in damp cellars with no sanitation, windows or air. Despite the Romantic idealisation of childhood (Plotz 2001), child mortality rates were very high. Workers, including children, worked up to twelve-hour days, and accidents were frequent in unregulated factories, leading to increasing demands for improved social welfare, education and political equality by reformers such as the Welsh social reformer Robert Owen (1771–1858) in his *Observations on the Effect of the Manufacturing System* (1815).

Owen's call for free education for the poor fed into a concerted effort to improve social conditions and the British Poor Laws in the late eighteenth and early nineteenth centuries. Acts of 1782 and 1795 had established poorhouses for the aged and infirm but preserved the right of non-settled people to stay in the community unless they applied for relief. Social attitudes to poverty began to change after 1815, when the Poor Law system was increasingly criticised for distorting the free market. Following the Sturges-Bourne Acts of 1816 and the 1817 Poor Employment Act, workhouses were built to reduce the cost of poor relief. The Poor Law Amendment Act of 1834 further encouraged the development of workhouses and significantly modified the existing system of local poor relief from a parish level to a highly centralised system. It also increasingly distinguished between the 'deserving' and the 'undeserving' poor, and denied relief to unwed mothers and illegitimate children, leading to increased rates of infanticide. William Wordsworth attacks this emerging system of poor relief in poems such as 'The Last of the Flock' (1798) and 'The Old Cumberland Beggar' (1800) in *Lyrical Ballads*, as discussed in the following case study.

Case study: William Wordsworth, 'The Old Cumberland Beggar' (written 1798, published 1800)

In a note to 'The Old Cumberland Beggar', Wordsworth maintains that '[t]he class of Beggars to which the old man here described belongs, will probably soon be extinct' (*Lyrical Ballads*, 309). He is, of course, referring to forthcoming changes to the Poor Laws, which will soon be introduced by the kinds of statesmen 'Who are so restless in your wisdom, ye/ Who have a broom still ready in your hands/ To rid the world of nuisances' (ll. 68–70). Attacking but also appropriating utilitarian justifications for the new Poor Laws, Wordsworth goes on to suggest that the beggar is, in fact, socially useful: he is both a 'silent monitor' (l. 123) and registry of charitable deeds – 'a record which together binds/ Past deeds and offices of charity/ Else unremembered' (ll. 89–91) – as well as an object of habit and association: 'Where'er the aged Beggar takes his rounds,/ The mild necessity of use compels/ To acts of love; and habit does the work/ Of reason' (ll. 98–101). The poem's multiple metaphors of vision – 'I saw an aged Beggar in my walk'; 'Watches the aged Beggar with a look'; 'she sees/ the aged beggar coming' (ll. 1, 31, 34–5) – suggest the importance of the visibility of suffering for the moral sanctity of a community. Yet many commentators have noted the poem's uncomfortably glib response to the Beggar's suffering – 'As in the eye of Nature he has lived,/ So in the eye of Nature let him die!' (ll. 196–7) – as well as commenting on the Beggar's mimicry of charitable acts and his own disturbing lack of vision (Langan 1995: 71–2): 'On the ground/ His eyes are turned. . . . Instead of common and habitual sight/ Of fields with rural works, of hill and dale/ And the blue sky, one little span of earth/ Is all his prospect' (ll. 45–6, 48–51). If, as some of these commentators have argued, Wordsworth's confrontation with poverty and injustice seems muted in that it does not address the root cause of social inequality, the poem nonetheless contains a strong humanitarian sub-argument that transcends its arguments about utility value: 'man is dear to man . . . for this single cause,/ That we have all of us one human heart' (ll. 147, 152–3).

Industrialisation also led to significant changes to Britain's physical and social, as well as moral, landscape. In particular, the years between 1760 and 1820 saw an accelerated process of 'enclosure' in which scattered land holdings, open fields and other common-law land rights were consolidated into private farms. This largely ended traditional rights such as mowing meadows for hay or grazing livestock on common land in an open-field system, and created a landless working class that provided the labour for the new industries described above. As early as 1770, in his poem *The Deserted Village,* Oliver Goldsmith (1728–74) deplored the rural depopulation taking place in Britain, but the process was accelerated in the early nineteenth century (see Chapter 3). Enclosure was enacted in an even more brutal way in Scotland. In a process that became known as the 'Clearances', thousands of Highlanders were evicted from their land and deported to Canada or other parts of Scotland in order to allow for more land for grazing sheep. Like the enclosure movement, the Clearances were driven by a discourse of improvement, but they were also arguably justified by newer colonial and imperialist discourses

(Makdisi 1998: 78). For Saree Makdisi, the Highlands thus became 'a site for the rehearsal of Britain's larger colonial project [in Africa and Asia]' (Makdisi 1998: 79–80) (see Chapter 7). Indeed, as Walter Scott noted in his 'Culloden Papers' (1816), the Clearances were so brutal that few Highlanders were left to remember the event.

Intellectual contexts

Science

The late eighteenth and early nineteenth centuries are often given an important role in the history of science, sometimes being described as a 'second scientific revolution', which 'marked the shift from natural philosophy to "science"' as we know it (Wood 2004: 6). If in the 1770s the naturalist Thomas Ramsay, writing in praise of the geologist and naturalist Thomas Pennant (1726–98), could claim that '[n]atural history is, at present, the favourite science over all Europe, and the progress which has been made in it will distinguish and characterize the eighteenth century in the annals of literature' (Ramsay 1774: 174), the old scientific disciplines bound up with natural history, such as astronomy and botany, were nonetheless increasingly being transformed, and new disciplines such as biology and physiology were rivalling the techniques and methodologies of natural philosophers. Older disciplines such as chemistry, physics and mathematics were also increasingly transformed or reconfigured. Jan Golinski has shown us that the Romantic period saw the beginning of a new era of scientific specialisation, disciplinisation and professionalisation that systemised and extended the inductive, experimental and mathematical methodologies of Francis Bacon (1561–1626), Isaac Newton and other seventeenth-century scientists and natural philosophers, who are credited with initiating the 'first scientific revolution' (Golinski 1992).

The period also saw a new emphasis on the empirical and practical uses of science: the establishment of the British Association for the Advancement of Science in 1831, for example, was set up not only to separate the 'true' sciences from the 'false' or 'pseudo' sciences (such as astrology), but also to counteract the amateur, gentlemanly culture of the Royal Society and the Royal Institution of London. The Society for the Encouragement of Arts, Commerce, and Manufacture, set up by William Shipley (1715–1803) in 1754, similarly encouraged useful scientific innovation in the practical and decorative arts, as did Henry Brougham's (1778–1868) Society for the Diffusion of Useful Knowledge of 1828. Much of this emphasis on the practical application of scientific discoveries stemmed from the popularisation of Newton's work on mechanics in his 1687 *Mathematical Principles of Natural Philosophy*, which provided, among other things, a foundation for ideas as varied as the natural religion of Richard Bentley (1662–1742), theories of sensibility in which body and mind were intertwined, and the philosophic empiricism of John Locke, David Hume and David Hartley (1705–57) (see later in this chapter), as well as being central to the development of modern physics and mathematics. It also incited a heated public debate, as some thinkers found scientific mechanism to be incapable of explaining the complexities of the natural world. The surgeon John Hunter (1728–1793) and the botanist and poet Erasmus Darwin (1731–1802), for example, used vitalist, rather than mechanical, principles to explain special features of animal and plant life such as sexual or generative principles (Ruston 2005).

As Golinski points out, it was Newton's audience, practitioners and popularisers that made the new science the cornerstone of so many emerging disciplines. In the 1770s and 80s Joseph Priestley, for example, described his discovery of new types of air or gases in *Disquisitions Relating to Matter and Spirit* (1777) in accessible and 'carefully crafted' narratives, while also encouraging his associates to stage demonstrations of scientific principles for the public (Golinski 1992: 8). The increasing specialisation of science, and its movement into restricted spaces in the nineteenth century, was therefore tempered by an enormous popular interest in scientific discoveries, as scientific ideas circulated in 'general literate culture' (Golinski 2009: 527) via popular periodicals and books addressed to middle-class readers such as Oliver Goldsmith's eight-volume *History of the Earth and Animated Nature* (1774), and even working-class readers via the popular press (Porter 2000: 144).

New work on Romanticism and science by Sharon Ruston, Noah Heringman and others has clearly demonstrated that the Romantics were not 'anti-science' and that very few Romantic writers believed that there was an inherent conflict between poetry and science, or that scientific progress entailed poetic decline (Ruston 2005; Heringman 2003 and 2004). Mary Shelley's *Frankenstein* (1818) is, perhaps, the best-known example of the moral dangers of a Promethean attempt to mimic and control the sublime forces of nature through the use of science – in particular, electricity – but many other Romantic writers referred to new scientific discoveries and principles in their work. One cannot but notice, for example, the medical and scientific flavour of one of Keats's remarks on sensations in his *Letters*: 'Axioms in philosophy are not axioms until they are proved upon our pulses' (I. 279). John Aikin's *Essay on the Application of Natural History to Poetry* (1777) was echoed in Anna Letitia Barbauld's poem 'The Invitation', where she argued that 'Where science smiles, the Muses join the train' (I. 109). Wordsworth draws a distinction between the poet and the man of science in the 'Preface' to *Lyrical Ballads*, but he (along with Coleridge and Southey) was part of the physician Thomas Beddoes's (1769–1808) circle in Bristol in the late eighteenth century. While William Blake detested Newton, Wordsworth's view of Newton in *The Prelude* is ambivalent but certainly not dismissive: 'Newton with his prism and silent face/ the marble index of a mind forever,/ Voyaging through strange seas of Thought, alone' (3. 61–3).

Philosophy and social theory

Along with their apparent dismissal of scientific mechanism, Romantic writers have traditionally been seen as rejecting empirical philosophy, or the 'philosophy of mechanism', originated in Britain by John Locke (Abrams 1971: 51, 308).

Locke argued in his *Essay Concerning Human Understanding* (1690), for example, that we are born without innate ideas – that is, at birth the mind is a blank slate or *tabula rasa* – and that knowledge (and even identity) is instead derived from sense perceptions. Locke, Hume, Hartley and other British empiricists agreed that the mind could build complex ideas out of these simple sense perceptions through the principle of association, but that new thoughts were really only new combinations of simple ideas or parts of more complex ones. These theories saw the human mind as a mechanism and tended, albeit to varying degrees, to deny the active ability of the imagination to create, invent or frame entirely new ideas divorced from initial sensory experiences.

'Associationalism', as it became known, appealed to some Romantic writers because it suggested that the poet could be inspired by uncontrollable powers separate from the exertion of the will, but other writers tended either to modify or oppose these ideas in favour of promoting a vital or active imagination. In *A Defence of Poetry* (written 1820, published 1821), for example, Percy Shelley argues that 'Man is an instrument over which a series of external and internal impressions are driven, like the alternations of an ever-changing wind over an Aeolian lyre', but he nonetheless concludes that 'there is a principle within the human being, and perhaps within all sentient beings, which acts otherwise than in the lyre, and produces not melody alone, but harmony' (480). Hazlitt's *Essay on the Principles of Human Action* (1805) concedes that knowledge is produced by the impressions created on our minds by sensations, but argues that these sensations are nonetheless framed into ideas by the imagination or the active powers of the mind (I. 38–9). Wordsworth's idea of 'a wise passiveness' (l. 24) in the poem 'Expostulation and Reply' (1798) and Keats's representation of the passivity of the human mind in his *Letters*, on the other hand, seem closer to the associationalism of the British empiricists. For Keats, the 'negative' state of 'receiving' is preferable to the more restless and aggressive state of 'giving' or 'seeking' (*Letters*, I. 232), an idea which helps to clarify his concept of 'negative capability' or the ability of the mind to exist in 'uncertainties, Mysteries, doubts, without any irritable reaching after fact & reason' (*Letters*, I. 193).

Alongside empirical philosophies, various forms of idealism also circulated in the eighteenth and early nineteenth centuries. The British or 'subjective idealism' of George Berkeley (1685–1753) and others argued that external objects have an existence or being only when they are perceived by an observer. Transcendental idealism as propounded by Immanuel Kant (1774–1804), on the other hand, argued that there are things in themselves (noumena) that exist other than being merely sensations or ideas drawn from the perceiving mind, although the mind has a central role in influencing how the world is experienced (phenomena). German idealism, on the whole, tended to reject Kant's idea of the existence of noumena. Johann Gottlieb Fichte's (1762–1814) influential *Wissenschaftslehre*, or *Theory of Scientific Knowledge* (1794–5), for example, argued that our representations, ideals and mental images are merely the productions of the 'knowing subject', transforming Kant's transcendental idealism into an absolute idealism.

Some Romantic writers such as Coleridge, Wordsworth, Hazlitt, Shelley, Thomas De Quincey (1785–1859) and later Thomas Carlyle (1795–1881) were familiar with aspects of German idealism, as is suggested by poems such as Shelley's *Hymn to Intellectual Beauty* and *Mont Blanc* (both written 1816), where Shelley pre-empts his argument in *A Defence of Poetry* (1821) that 'all things exist as they are perceived' (505); but it is far harder to trace the particular sources of idealist thinking in British Romantic poetry. A number of recent studies have questioned the extent to which German idealism was a major influence on British Romanticism, arguing that even Coleridge's readings of Kant, Fichte and Friedrich Schelling (1775–1854) in *Biographia Literaria* were 'informal' (Hamilton 2007: 6), 'idio-syncratic' (Budge 2007: 23) and reshaped by British philosophical contexts, such as the Common Sense philosophy of Thomas Reid (1710–96) and others (Milnes 2010; Budge 2007).

More influential on Romantic writers were the so-called Scottish 'social theorists' such as Lord Kames (1696–1782), Adam Smith, William Robertson (1721–93) and Adam Ferguson (1723–1816), who argued that man progressed towards modern or civilised society through a series of predictable stages, such as hunting, pasturage, agriculture and commerce. Although they recognised the cost of modernity, the Scottish social theorists tended to reject both the 'state of nature' and 'social con-tract' explanations of society proposed by Locke, Thomas Hobbes (1588–1679) and Jean-Jacques Rousseau (1712–78), among others, who had all argued that in the 'natural' state of mankind there is no personal property or injustice because there are no laws other than the laws of nature, which are governed by reason. In *Of the Social Contract* (1762) Rousseau outlines his theory of the 'noble savage', or an idealised concept of uncivilised man, arguing that men in a state of nature do not understand good or evil but that their ignorance of vice nonetheless prevents them from doing harm. Injustice and inequality arise only because of the enlarged wants or desires that accompany civilisation, as enshrined in the laws of private property.

Rousseau's arguments encouraged a vogue for cultural primitivism, or 'the preference of "nature" and "the natural" over "art" and the "artificial" in any field of human culture and values' (Abrams and Harpham 2012: 315), but in *The Theory of Moral Sentiments* (1759) Adam Smith refutes Rousseau by maintaining that society is held together by positive virtues rather than by selfish interests or even by reason (Smith 1759: 308–14). His primary argument is that motive rather than consequence is at the heart of why men approve or disapprove of an action. Men are able to understand each other's motives through sympathy, which allows them to enter vicariously into the situation of another person 'by changing places in fancy with the sufferer' (Smith 1759: 9–10). It is by and through the imagination that we are able to 'place ourselves in his situation': 'we enter as it were into his body, and become in some measure the same person with him, and thence form some idea of his sensations' (Smith 1759: 9). As James Chandler has pointed out, Smith's spectatorial ideas of the 'like situation' and 'psychic projection' were cen-tral to theories of the imagination in the early nineteenth century and permeate the work of Byron, Hazlitt, Shelley and Keats, among other writers (Chandler 1998: 229), as the following case study of Shelley suggests.

Case study: Percy Bysshe Shelley, *A Defence of Poetry* (1821)

Shelley's definition of the poet in *A Defence of Poetry* amounts to an attempt to define poetry and the poet in moral and ethical rather than aesthetic terms (see also the epigraph to this chapter): that is, as one who seeks or 'acts to produce the moral improvement of man' rather than one who is concerned only with the arrangement of language or dramatic effect (487). Like Adam Smith, Shelley defines moral judgment as a process of sympathetic identification or 'a going out of our own nature': 'The great secret of morals is love; or a going out of our own nature, and an identification of ourselves with the beautiful which exists in thought, action, or person, not our own' (487). Here Shelley adapts the Smithean idea of the 'like situation', whereby a man must project himself into circumstances not his own or put himself in the place of another. Even more importantly, Shelley emphasises the role of the imagination in achieving this function, arguing that one can only project oneself into the feelings of others by and through the imagination:

> A man, to be greatly good, must imagine intensely and comprehensively; he must put himself in the place of another and of many others; the pains and pleasure of his species must become his own. The great instrument of moral good is the imagination; and poetry administers to the effect by acting upon the cause.
>
> (487–8)

Poetry therefore has a crucial role to play in moral improvement and acts to bind society together in ways that more narrowly utilitarian discourses cannot: 'Poetry strengthens the faculty which is the organ of the moral nature of man [the imagination] in the same manners as exercise strengthens a limb' (488).

Religion

Despite the fact that most Irish people were Catholics and most Welsh people were non-Conformists, the Anglican Church of England was the establishment church in Romantic-era Britain. Following the French Revolution, various types of religious difference, such as atheism, deism and 'rational dissent', while legal under the Act of Toleration of 1689, were increasingly considered political as well as religious deviations. Deism, or 'natural religion', largely emerged from the work of eighteenth-century French philosophers such as Voltaire (1694–1778), who argued in his *Dictionnaire philosophique* (1764) that the moral law inscribed upon the heart was the only thing that proclaimed the existence of a great Original: 'Almost everything that goes beyond the worship of a supreme Being, and the submission of one's heart to his eternal commands, is superstition' (cited in Gay 1977: 396).

Deism was influential on writers and thinkers of the so-called 'Cockney School' (see Chapter 3). Leigh Hunt proclaimed in his *The Religion of the Heart* (1853), for example, a model of religious thinking that found in man's instincts and emotions the basis for piety and morality; and Voltaire's natural religion was also a major influence on Keats's thought (Ryan 1997; 1976: 41–2), as suggested by the following case study.

Case study: John Keats, 'Vale of the Soul Making' (1819)

In his 'Vale of the Soul Making' letter, written at the end of April 1819, Keats argues that we enter the world as pure 'Intelligence' but that we only gain a 'Soul' or 'sense of Identity' through the lessons provided by 'Circumstances': in other words, we only acquire an identity or soul through the process of experience. In his letter Keats demonstrates an increasing awareness of the role of suffering for the development of the soul: 'Do you not see how necessary a World of Pains and troubles is to school an intelligence and make it a soul?' (*Letters*, II. 102). As Robert Ryan has pointed out, the problem of suffering was a major intellectual concern for Keats (Ryan 1976: 117), who was increasingly unable to accept the Christian 'doctrine of atonement' and rejected a Calvinist interpretation of redemption in which man is powerless to influence his salvation: 'The common cognomen of this world among the misguided and superstitious is "a vale of tears" from which we are to be redeemed by a certain arbitrary interposition of God and taken to Heaven – What a little circumscribe[d] straightened notion!' (II. 102) Like Voltaire and other Enlightenment sceptical thinkers, Keats uses Greek and Roman myths to question Christianity's claims to an exclusive spiritual truth: 'It is pretty generally suspected that the chr[i]stian scheme has been copied from the ancient persian and greek Philosophers' (II. 103). Keats's own, alternative system of redemption recognises the importance of the 'medium of the Heart' for the development of the soul and places sorrow and suffering at the centre of salvation: 'Not merely is the Heart a Hornbook, It is the Minds Bible, it is the Minds experience, it is the teat from which the Mind or intelligence sucks its identity' (II. 103). Ryan suggests that Keats's system involves salvation through adversity rather than from it, and that it is therefore based on the view that man works towards his own salvation by coming to terms with his natural condition (Ryan 1976: 208).

Unlike atheists and deists, Unitarians and other 'rational dissenters' believed in the value of organised or institutionalised religion, but they rejected several conventional Christian notions. Joseph Priestley's *History of the Corruptions of Christianity* (1782), for example, rejects the idea of the trinity, questions Jesus's divinity and argues against doctrines such as original sin and predestination. Unitarian networks of writers and readers included circles surrounding the publisher

Joseph Johnson, the Aikin family and authors such as Anna Letitia Barbauld, Mary Hayes (1759–1843), Harriet Martineau (1802–76) and Elizabeth Gaskell (1810–65). Many of these individuals and groups were involved with the establishment of dissenting academies, such as the Hoxton and Warrington Academies, which played a key role in fuelling the expansion of religious dissent in the nineteenth century (see also Chapter 3). Unitarianism was increasingly accepted following the Doctrine of the Trinity Act of 1813, the repeal of the Test and Corporations Acts in 1828 and the Dissenting Chapels Act of 1844, all of which contributed to a new discourse of toleration in the period that was bound up with political models of social inclusion and state protection (Canuel 2002).

Although Christianity was increasingly under threat from deism and scientific discourses, the eighteenth century nonetheless saw a Protestant revival with Evangelicals and Methodists privileging enthusiasm and personal faith over institutionalised religion. John Wesley's (1703–91) 'religion of the people', as Methodism was known, proposed a simple, direct and accessible mode of worship that appealed to believers in a wide array of social circles, particularly the middle and labouring classes. Evangelicalism was similar to Methodism in its focus on the emotional experience of conversion and its belief in the power of prayer, but moral reform was even more central to the Evangelical message than that of Methodism. The poet Hannah More's religious tracts such as *Radical Piety* (1811), *Christian Morals* (1813) and *Moral Sketches* (1819), for example, are entangled with her philanthropic work on abolitionism, Poor Law amendments, universal education and rights for women.

Despite drawing on the hymnody and inspirational flavour of this Evangelical revival, many Romantic writers seriously challenged institutionalised or organised religion. In *The Necessity of Atheism* (1811), for example, Shelley argues that God acts as a substitute for reason and that there is no empirical evidence for his existence. In *Tintern Abbey* (1798) William Wordsworth describes nature as 'the anchor of my purest thoughts, the nurse,/ the guide, the guardian of my heart, and soul/ of all my moral being' (ll. 110–12), leading M. H. Abrams to conclude that Wordsworth's pantheism or belief in a spiritual life-force flowing through nature involves a secularisation of spiritual-crisis narratives (Abrams 1971). Coleridge's attitude towards religion is more complicated, ranging from deism to the Greek Eleusinian mysteries to pantheism and the so-called 'one life' to Unitarianism and finally orthodoxy. Byron's dissent from orthodox Christian belief mainly takes the form of Manicheanism, such as in *Manfred* (1816–17), where the dualistic or opposite forces of 'dust' and 'divinity' are equally necessary.

William Blake was greatly influenced by the theologian Emanuel Swedenborg (1688–1772), who promoted a non-literal biblical exegesis and also influenced the development of so-called 'Higher Criticism', which transformed the study of the Bible through the use of literary-critical methods (Roston 1965). Some of Blake's prophetic poems, such as *The First Book of Urizen* (1794), are characterised by antinomianism, or the belief that a new age of direct inspiration is imminent. Blake's claims to visionary experience emerge from Morton Paley's famous 1978 study not so much as exceptional but as associated with the millenarian discourses of religious sects led by Joanna Southcott (1750–1814) and Richard Brothers (1757–1824), as well as being typical of a wider artisan culture (Paley 1978). More recent studies on millenarianism, or a belief in a gradually approaching millennium without a preceding apocalypse, by Tim Fulford (2002), Jon Mee (2002) and others have shown us that writers as diverse as William Cowper (1731–1800), Priestley, Coleridge and Byron were also influenced by millenarianism.

Political economy

Apart from growing preoccupations with working conditions and the poor, a primary concern for many observers of the newly industrialised Britain was whether the privatisation of interests that accompanied an advanced commercial society would undermine civic virtue and corrupt the state. Drawing on older republican narratives, Adam Smith argued as early as 1776 in his *Wealth of Nations* that while commerce encouraged liberty because each man was governed by self-interest, the division of labour could prove harmful to community and citizenship. If, as Smith also argued, an individual's attempt to pursue their own interest frequently results in unplanned and unintended benefits to society as if by an 'invisible hand', it could also lead to unwanted results, such as gluttony and luxury, which could prove incompatible with both individual happiness and socio-political stability. Leigh Hunt, for example, frequently laments in *The Examiner* that England has become a society dominated by the commercial spirit and a new desire-based mode of consumption: '*la nation bouquetiere,* not *boutiquiere*; – the bloom-keeping, not the shop-keeping nation' (Hunt 1817: 817).

Other attacks on commercialism in the period related to finance and, in particular, to the national debt and the so-called 'paper system'. Percy Shelley followed the radical editor William Cobbett in arguing that the national debt favours the wants of the 'indolent' over the hard-working, as well as decrying the Bank of England's suspension of payment on banknotes in his *A Philosophical View of Reform* (written 1819–20) (cited in Gallagher 2006: 83). Thomas Paine's 1796 pamphlet *The Decline and Fall of the English System of Finance*, like similar tracts written by David Ricardo (1772–1823) and Cobbett, argues that any wealth divorced from its referent (i.e. the labour of the people) is illusory. Alex Dick (2013), Mary Poovey (2008) and Catherine Gallagher (2006), among others, have shown us the extent to which arguments about monetary policy, such as those surrounding the introduction of the gold standard, were central to the story of literary Romanticism, as suggested not only by collections such as Thomas Moore's (1779–1852) *Odes on Cash, Corn and Catholics* (1828) and Thomas Love Peacock's (1785–1866) *Paper Money Lyrics* (1825–6), but also by the inter-relationship between political economy and Romantic aesthetics. Gallagher, for example, has noted the complex relationship between Wordsworth's own poetic labour and that of the labourers he is depicting in *The Prelude* (Gallagher 2006: 93–4).

The question of 'use' or 'utility-value' was also an important issue for debate in the period. Thomas De Quincey's *Dialogues of Three Templars on Political Economy* (1824) and *The Logic of Political Economy* (1844), for example, are not so much concerned with questions of labour as with issues surrounding personal or individual utility value. Hunt too often considers the issue of utility value and, more specifically, the idea that a utilitarian approach to monetary policy can cure the nation of its ills (Hunt 1818: 129). The Utilitarians argued that the proper course of action is the one that maximises utility, or provides 'the greatest happiness of the greatest number' (Bentham 1776: ii). In *An Introduction to the Principles of Morals and Legislation* (written 1780, published 1789) Jeremy Bentham (1748–1832) argued that this principle concerned the calculation of the relative value of pleasures and pains, and should be applied not just to private individuals but also to governments. Unlike Bentham, John Stuart Mill's (1806–73) later *Utilitarianism* (1863) rejected a purely quantitative measure of utility, but he too argues that government policy should maximise utility value. Robert Malthus's *Essay on the Principle of Population* (1798) infamously applies utilitarian principles to pressing demographic problems, as discussed in the following case study.

Case study: Robert Malthus, *An Essay on the Principle of Population* (1798)

Linked to utilitarian principles and initially written as a response to the ideals of perfectibility and enlightened progress in William Godwin's proto-anarchical tract *An Enquiry Concerning Political Justice* (1792), Robert Malthus's *Essay on the Principle of Population* argues that continued population growth will inevitably lead to resource deficit and poverty, preventing 'any great permanent amelioration' of the lower classes of society and therefore limiting any future improvement of society (Malthus 1798: 14). Malthus claimed that two types of checks could control population: positive checks that raise the death rate (such as hunger, disease and war) and preventative ones that lower the birth rate (such as celibacy, birth control and abortion). He supported the establishment of state-wide education because lessons concerning moral virtue and sexual restraint were fundamental to the principles of growth restraint recommended by his *Essay*. Some Romantic writers wrote direct refutations of Malthus. William Hazlitt, for example, argued in his *Letters in Answer to Malthus, &c.* (1807) that Malthus's grim inevitability and passiveness had turned 'selfishness into a regular code': 'The poor, Sir, labour under a natural stigma; they are *naturally* despised. Their interests are at best but coldly and remotely felt by the other classes of society. Mr. Malthus's book has done all that was wanting to increase this indifference and apathy' (IX. 182). Godwin's *Of Population* (1820) argues against Malthus's notion that, unless checked, population increases exponentially. The impact of Malthus's *Essay* was nonetheless substantial and led to the introduction of the Poor Law Amendment Act of 1834, as well as being a key influence on the development of Charles Darwin's (1809–82) theory of natural selection.

Social and cultural contexts

Gender and sexuality

Women in the Romantic period were substantially constrained by the legal framework under which they existed, especially their lack of political representation or suffrage and their subjection to the law of coverture, which put them under the authority and protection of their husbands after marriage. While the fundamental rights of personal security, liberty and private property theoretically applied to women, in reality a woman's 'uninterrupted enjoyment . . . of life . . . depended on her father or husband respectively' (Swan 1997: 19). In 1753 Parliament enacted the Marriage Act to prevent clandestine marriages because of the fear that 'patrimonies were threatened by the clandestine marriages of minors' (Outhwaite 1995: 13). This Act (until it was overturned in 1823) not only required parental consent for marriage, but could also potentially render a marriage without consent invalid (Probert 2009).

Another severe limitation on women was the lack of a legal right to education. In her *Vindication of the Rights of Woman* (1792) Mary Wollstonecraft argues that all women should receive an education equal to that of men, in order to rid them of 'artificial grace' and 'female weakness', and allow them to develop an active or 'conscious virtue' rather than a passive or unthinking one (Wollstonecraft 1993: 167, 107, 92). For Wollstonecraft, true virtue cannot exist without a well-developed mind. Even motherhood should be a rational undertaking: 'If children are to be educated to understand the true principle of patriotism, their mother must be a patriot; and the love of mankind. . . . can only be produced by considering the moral and civil interest of mankind' (Wollstonecraft 1993: 66). Anything less, she famously argues, subjects women to a 'state of perpetual childhood' (Wollstonecraft 1993: 73).

Several other female writers in the period made compelling arguments for female education. In *Letters on Education* (1790) the historian Catherine Macaulay (1731–91) argued for the natural equality of the sexes. In her *Letters for Literary Ladies* (1790) the Irish novelist and educationalist Maria Edgeworth (1768–1849) maintained that a focus on conduct prevented women from developing serious intellects. In her *Appeal to the Men of Great Britain* (1798) Mary Hayes asserted that female education is essential to the prosperity of the nation, and Mary Darby Robinson (1757–1800) compared the position of women to that of slavery in *A Letter to the Women of England, on the Injustice of Mental Subordination* (1799). More provocatively, Wollstonecraft finds one of the sources of inequality in women's own behavior and their habit of making a 'gilt cage' of their bodies (Wollstonecraft 1993: 112): 'The thoughts of women ever hover round their persons, and is it surprising that their persons are reckoned most valuable?' (Wollstonecraft 1993: 148).

As Wollstonecraft suggests, female education often centred around fashion, conduct manuals and domestic duties. Many educational theories, such as those presented in Rousseau's *Emile, Or On Education* (1762), were inherently gendered when they argued, for example, that a dislike of the physical was natural to women. Wollstonecraft countered that a young girl 'whose spirits have not yet been damped by inactivity, or innocence tainted by false shame, will always be a romp' (Wollstonecraft 1993: 110). Caroline Bingley's mocking dismissal of Lizzie Bennett's sunburnt face and flushed cheeks when she walks for miles to visit her sister Jane in *Pride and Prejudice* (1813) is suggestive of Lizzie's rejection of 'feminine' inactivity. Edgeworth's novel *Leonora* (1806) is another example of a novel that critiques false femininity and sensibility. Olivia claims to be a woman of sensibility or heightened feeling but her behaviour is unsupported by strong moral beliefs.

Drawing on texts such as these, Richard Sha has rejected the mischaracterisation of the Romantic period as a 'seemingly asexual zone between eighteenth-century Edenic "liberated" sexuality and guiltless pleasures, and the repressive sexuality of the Victorians that enabled real sexuality to emerge' (Sha 2001: para. 6). Although several scholars have demonstrated that women, sexuality and the body are occluded in canonical Romantic writing (see Introduction), Daniel P. Watkins (1996) and Claudia Johnson (1995) have considered scenes of sadism and violence against women in a wide range of both male and female Romantic writing, while questions relating to masculinity have been examined by Tim Fulford (1999) and Mike Goode (2009). Yet as Michael O'Rourke and David Collings have recently pointed out, many of the existing studies on gender present Romantic-era sexuality as solely or primarily hetero-normative (O'Rourke and Collings 2004: para. 2). Sha's own *Perverse Romanticism* (2008) brilliantly unites studies of sexuality and aesthetics in considering the ways in which sexual pleasure, liberation and perversity inform the work of writers as diverse as Wollstonecraft, Byron, Blake and Shelley, but it tends to shy away from some of the more radical aspects of Romantic writing about sexuality such as pornography, paedophilia, obscenity and sodomitical desire, particularly evident in work by writers such as William Beckford (1760–1844) and Matthew Lewis (1775–1818) (Mudge 2001). While most studies of homosexual and pornographic literature focus on the Victorian period, Romantic critics have found numerous representations of homosexuality or proto-homosexuality in literary texts before 1860 (Elfenbein 1999), as well as noting the existence of voyeuristic, deviant and transgressive sexualities in Romantic works.

Case study: Matthew Lewis, *The Monk* (1796)

The Gothic novel tends to raise the spectre of sexualised bodies in ways that do not arise in the realist novel of manners (see Chapter 2), but Matthew Lewis's *The Monk* uses much more explicitly sexual content than most Gothic novels both to critique religion and to titillate the reader. The novel begins with an obviously sexualised account of the monk's public oration in the Capuchin Church. Recalling the impassioned political speeches of the orators of the French Revolution (Paulson 1983), Ambrosio's discourse produces in the listening crowd and, in particular, in the heroine Antonia 'a pleasure fluttering in her bosom which till then had been unknown to her' (Lewis 1973: 18). From this representation of public mass arousal we move to Ambrosio's private but equally sexualised reaction to a portrait of the Virgin Mary, who he sees not as an object of religious devotion but as a fetishised and masturbatory object of sexual temptation and desire: 'Were I permitted to twin round my fingers those golden ringlets and press with my lips the treasures of that snowy bosom' (Lewis 1973: 40). Even the series of (forced) confessions in the novel, through which the plot essentially progresses, are related to illicit sexual desires (Matilda/Rosario for Ambrosio, Agnes for Raymond, Ambrosia for Antonia), suggesting not only the important role of the confessional in the workings of civil and religious power, but also its profound connection to self-hood and the liberation or unburdening of the 'essential' self (Foucault 1978: 59). If, as Michel Foucault has argued, the confession has now become widely dispersed in modern society ('Western man has become a confessing animal' (59)), Ambrosio's voyeurism, secret desires and perversions ultimately implicate the reader as much as the monk himself: 'The scene was a small closet belonging to her apartment. She was undressing to bathe herself . . . The amorous monk had full opportunity to observe the voluptuous contours and admirable symmetry of her person. She threw off her last garment' (Lewis 1973: 271).

Classes and conflicts

There is considerable disagreement about how to classify the social and class structures of the Romantic period. On the one hand, there are those historians who emphasise the continuity of a hierarchical, landed society; on the other hand, there are those who have identified a more open, mobile and commercial one. John Cannon (1984), J. C. D. Clark (1985) and J. V. Beckett (1986), for example, have pointed to an aristocratic dominance and even resurgence in the period, while also acknowledging the forces that led to the Reform Acts (see above). McKendrick *et al.* (1982) and Paul Langford (1989), on the other hand, point to the birth of Britain's consumer society and the importance of metropolitan Whig aristocrats in promoting economic change and modernising influences. Clarke's provocative view of eighteenth-century England as 'Christian, monarchical, aristocratic, rural, traditional and poor' (Clark 1985: 9) is not one that is currently in favour, since it does not capture either the making of a global empire or the processes of long-term industrialisation.

While both imperial expansion and industrialisation were to greatly increase the possibility of self-advancement from the nineteenth century onwards, E. P. Thompson's influential *The Making of the English Working Classes* (1966) sees the period as one dominated more by a struggle between plebeians and patricians than one in which either class triumphed, although arguably Thompson's study downplays the role of the middle classes in early nineteenth-century society. The agrarian revolution, the industrial revolution and enclosure (see earlier in this chapter and Chapter 3) saw a demographic shift from country to town, and the rise in the eighteenth century not only of a new urban middle class, but also of what Jürgen Habermas has called the 'bourgeois public sphere', which 'may be conceived above all as the sphere of private people coming together as a public . . . whose institutions were the coffee-houses, the salons, and the table societies' (Habermas 1989: 27). For Habermas, this public sphere was driven by the newly emerging middle classes, comprised of merchants, manufacturers, bankers, capitalists, entrepreneurs and managers (the economic middle class), as well as teachers, civil servants, professors, clergy and other intellectuals (the educated middle class).

The increasingly diminished role of the aristocracy in eighteenth-century English society resulted in a shift in values, most notably encapsulated in popular eighteenth-century magazines like the *Tatler* (1709–11) and *The Spectator* (1711–12), which not only promoted a new model of gentlemanly behavior based on conduct rather than birth, but also envisaged a new kind of openness grounded in the free circulation of people and print. Yet despite the increasing mobility of late eighteenth-century society and the existence of some very influential figures who made their money in India or the West Indies, such as William Beckford, Robert Clive (1735–74) and other 'nabobs', stately homes and their grounds remained a testimony to the wealth, power, confidence and income of the upper classes. The power of the landed elite rested not only in their houses and grounds, but also in their control over the whole local environment in which their grounds were situated, as well as in their dominance in both major parties in Parliament (Whig and Tory) and the House of Lords. While this dominance was challenged by the Reform Act of 1832, significant changes to suffrage and political representation arguably did not occur until later in the nineteenth century.

In the arts, landowners or the landed elite were still 'the most influential individual patrons' of the eighteenth and early nineteenth centuries (Black 2005: 42). The control of the aristocracy over the arts was certainly in decline following the success of middle-class journals such as *The Edinburgh Review*, but many of the most powerful patrons in the Romantic period were nonetheless aristocrats; for example, the Irish poet Thomas Moore's patron was Francis Rawdon-Hastings (1754–1826), the Earl of Moira, and Moore's journals contain some wry reflections about his dependent status among the Holland House set. Patrons such as Josiah Wedgwood (1730–95) countered the aristocratic hold on intellectual and creative patronage with some high-profile protégés of their own, and newer institutions funded by middle-class subscriptions challenged the hold of the Royal Academies over the arts and sciences; but these emerging middle-class patrons did not altogether shake the class structures of the period (on patronage in the arts, see also Chapter 5).

A substantial body of scholarly work has focused on the working classes in Romantic-era Britain and, in particular, on working-class experiences and the development of a working-class consciousness. According to Thompson, in the years between 1780 and 1832, English working people 'came to feel and articulate the identity of interests as between themselves, and as against other men whose interests are different from (and usually opposed to) theirs' (Thompson 1966: 11). Thompson sees the core English working-class values emerging in the period as solidarity, collectivism, political radicalism and Methodism, but his book contains an enormous range of ethnographic detail from popular religious traditions to millenarian preaching to conspiracy theories to weavers' houses. Drawing on Thompson's idea of a distinct working-class consciousness, Kevin Gilmartin has rightly pointed out that a great number of working-class publishers, writers and activists were active and conscious participants in their own class formation, seeking to 'appropriate and mock the authority of a system that was not easily transcended or superseded' (Gilmartin 1996: 57). Terry Eagleton has even argued that what emerged in the England of the early nineteenth century was nothing less than a 'counter public sphere', invading the 'dominant consensus threatening to fragment it from within' (Eagleton 1984: 36). Thompson's interest in working-class artisans has certainly permeated literary scholarship: an impressive range of studies on Romantic-era radical culture in a field of inquiry often now called 'plebeian studies' (Janowitz 1998: 4) includes work by Jon Klancher (1987), Iain McCalman (1988), Michael Scrivener (1992), Jon Mee (1992, 2003), David Worrall (1992), Paul Thomas Murphy (1994) and Leonora Nattrass (1995).

The literary marketplace

The eighteenth century has been described as enjoying both a consumer and a reading revolution (Klancher 1987). Instead of a luxury afforded only to the privileged and educated few, books, magazines and newspapers changed the nature of daily life for a large part of Britain's population. Certainly, printed materials rose at a rapid rate in the eighteenth and early nineteenth centuries. Roy Porter has estimated that while 6,000 titles appeared in England in the 1620s, the number climbed to almost 21,000 in the 1710s and had reached over 56,000 by the 1790s (Porter 2000: 73). Prominent in this print explosion were newspapers, magazines, pamphlets and other printed ephemera. As Porter notes, the annual total sale of newspapers in 1713 was around 2.5 million. By the 1770s there were nine London daily newspapers and fifty provincial weekly papers, and the figure rose to over 12 million. By 1801, when London alone had thirteen daily papers and ten tri-weekly papers, the figure was around 16 million (Porter 2000: 78). Despite the increase of press regulation in 1790s, with the introduction of libel, sedition and blasphemy laws and stamp duties on pamphlets and the cheap press, William Cobbett and other radical journalists managed to circumvent the laws for a time by producing their own local, unstamped weeklies.

The sharp increase in the printed word between 1700 and 1800 hinged on high literacy rates in Britain. By 1750 at least 60 per cent of adult men and 40 per cent of adult women in England could read and write, creating new types of reading audiences that included women, children and the middle and working classes. By the mid century, too, a series of subscription and circulating libraries had sprung up in London and most major towns; and the new commercial classes created an audience with the means, education and leisure time to read them. The provision of libraries expanded quickly in the early nineteenth century. In 1800 there were 1,000 libraries in the provinces and around 100 in London; by the 1820s there were around 1,500 libraries (Johns 2009: 396). With the increased circulation or distribution of books, the period also saw a shift from 'intensive' to 'extensive' readers, who had access to a far greater range of materials than they could afford to buy.

The proliferation of print had a profound influence on the print business itself. Not only did the demands of newspapers and magazines for copy turn authorship into a trade or profession, but the demand for cheap copy and periodical literature led to a drop in the prices of printers and the establishment of a larger body of working-class printers. Technological changes such as steam printing, the mechanisation of papermaking and manufacture, and stereotyping also led to what has been called 'a second printing revolution' (Johns 2009: 390, 392–3). With the explosion of print culture came cheap editions printed on Grub Street by the likes of Minerva Press rather than on the reputable Paternoster Row or St Paul's Churchyard. Certainly, as Adrian Johns had pointed out, the Romantic period saw the 'English book trade change from a craft to something that might plausibly be called an industry' (Johns 2009: 377).

In 1774 the House of Lords effectively demolished the principle of common-law copyright. William St Clair has called this event 'the most decisive event in the history of reading in England since the arrival of printing 300 years before' (St Clair 2004: 109). The changes that ensued from the freeing up of copyright laws were a rapid expansion of publishers and the rise of specialists devoted to particular genres, such as textbooks, children's books and Gothic fiction. The Minerva Press, for example, specialised in popular fiction of the kind satirised by Jane Austen (1775–1817) in *Northanger Abbey* (1818) and sold its novels through its own library. Firms such as Longman and John Murray in London, and Archibald Constable and Cadell in Scotland, on the other hand, were the leading conventional publishers of the period, divorcing themselves entirely from retail and bookselling. Publishing was concentrated in London, Edinburgh and Dublin (until the 1800 Act of Union made Ireland subject to British copyright laws), but from the late eighteenth century industrial towns such as Bristol increasingly challenged the domination of London publishers.

Leisure and lifestyle

In a three-part article in *The Examiner* entitled 'Christmas and Other Old National Merry-Makings Considered' (1817–18), Leigh Hunt compares the 'inauthentic' festivities of modern times with 'the Christmas greens and gambols . . . the pleasures, the leisures, the real treasures' of 'Merry Old England' (Hunt 1817: 801). Hunt's attack is not only on the utilitarian principles underlying the new political economy, but also on the changing role of leisure in a commercialised society: 'Virtue is too much made to consist of compromises with really vicious and foolish and overworked states of society, which of necessity *cannot* attain to pleasure'

(Hunt 1818: 2). A number of other writers and poets in the Hunt circle decried the gloominess and selfishness that characterised modern society, and argued for a return to the sociability of an older England of good living and fellowship. In his 'Robin Hood' poems, for example, John Keats notes the increasing commodification of literary culture: 'strange! that honey/ Can't be got without hard money' ('Robin Hood: To A Friend' (1818), ll. 47–8). As these works suggest, the role and value of leisure activities were much debated topics in the Romantic period, as long working hours and a new culture of consumerism vied for precedence.

Tourism became the model for a new democratised view of leisure, as the shift in focus from the expensive and elite Grand Tour of the aristocracy and wealthy upper-middle classes to a more local or domestic touring (as a result of the French Revolution, the Napoleonic Wars and other tensions on the continent) saw the birth of a more inclusive attitude towards travel and leisure. To be sure, the new domestic tourism – and, in particular, pedestrian travel (Jarvis 1997) – was partly fuelled by the elitism of picturesque aesthetics (see Chapter 5), literary tourism and a culture of antiquarianism (see Chapter 4), but it nonetheless emphasised the mass appeal of local sites, as the improvement of main roads gradually made travel easier, cheaper and more accessible. Middle-class writers like Keats, for example, made trips both within Britain and abroad. If Keats's final trip to Italy in 1821 was fuelled by illness and desperation, his *Letters* describe the joys and tribulations of Romantic-era pedestrian and coach travel during his 1818 trip to the Lake District and Scottish Highlands (see, for example, *Letters*, I. 298, 322, 331).

One of the primary means of affordable entertainment for all social classes in the Romantic period was the theatre (see also Chapter 2). Melodrama, burlesque, burletta and pantomime were particularly popular because of their songs and visual appeal, and even the patent theatres were forced to attract larger audience through these genres, effectively leading to the abolition of distinctions between legitimate and illegitimate theatre via the Theatre Regulation Act of 1843. Julie Carlson has described the 'cavernous' and 'noisy' experience of going to Drury Lane or Covent Garden, which seated over 3,000 people in mixed audiences that simultaneously included the higher orders, critics and the middle classes, working people, sellers of food and merchandise, and prostitutes (Carlson 2009: 494). The enormous popular appeal of Romantic-era theatre is evident in the so-called 'Old Price Riots' of 1809, in which spectators disrupted shows at Covent Garden for sixty-seven nights by staging their own dramas in order to protest a rise in ticket prices and the number of private boxes.

Apart from the theatre, the men and women of the eighteenth and early nineteenth centuries amused themselves in pleasure gardens (such as Vauxhall Gardens), the great 'melting pots' of the period, where both aristocrats and tradesmen enjoyed entertainments side by side. Ranelagh Pleasure Gardens in Chelsea were first opened in 1746 and had acres of formal gardens with pavilions and fountains where pedestrians could stroll on summer evenings. Francis Burney (1752–1840) refers to just such an outing in her novel *Evelina* (1778), and the pleasure gardens remain popular settings for twentieth and twenty-first-century historical novels and romances set in the Georgian period. Most towns celebrated traditional holidays or saints and feast days through fairs known as 'wakes', such as St Bartholomew's Fair, which was held for four days in September and attracted thousands of people (see discussions of this fair in Chapters 5 and 7). Other fairs were linked to civic celebrations and, increasingly, to the sale and marketing of consumer products. Wordsworth represents the consumer-based economy of London as a series of theatrical spectacles that verge on simulation in Book VII of *The Prelude* – 'Shop after shop, with symbols, blazoned names,/ And all the tradesman's honours over-head–/ Here, fronts of houses, like a title-page,/ With letters huge inscribed from top to toe' (7. 176–9) – leading Andrea Henderson to link a Romantic anxiety about the temporary or impermanent status of ideal concepts and objects to this new culture of commercialism and consumerism (Henderson 2008).

The display and viewing of visual culture as a commodified leisure activity is discussed in Chapter 5 of this book, which considers the marketing of panoramas, dioramas and phantasmagorias to the general public, as well as commercial exhibitions such as John Boydell's (1720–1804) Shakespeare Gallery and Henry Fuseli's (1741–1825) Milton Gallery. Like strategically marketed exhibitions of art, exhibitions of curiosities drew large audiences. The Strand in London often displayed exotic animals such as lions and tigers in taverns or assembly rooms. Human curiosities such as native slave women, giants or mad people were also exciting to the public. Scientific lectures and experiments such as balloon flights and that of a bird in the air pump (as in Joseph Wright of Derby's painting (1734–1797)) attracted widespread public interest and promoted a public culture of science.

Sport was another popular leisure activity in the Romantic period. Along with reputable and elite sports such as whist, fencing and horse racing (which was centred around Newmarket), animal baiting and blood sports were common forms of entertainment. Bull baiting, bull running and cock fighting were popular with all social classes, until animal baiting was made illegal in 1800. Boxing was also an enormously popular sport, and straddled the divide between respectable and disreputable sports. By 1719 the sport was established enough to have a leading pugilist of the day, James Figg (1684–1734). From 1734 to 1750 Jack Broughton (1704–89) brought a sense of respectability and order to the sport by devising an accepted set of rules centred on safety and fairness. Broughton also opened an academy in the Haymarket to which he attracted young gentlemen. Daniel Mendoza (1764–1836), the champion of the 1790s, even wrote a book on the subject: *The Art of Boxing* (1789). Prize-fighting took another step towards respectability when several aristocrats launched the Pugilistic Club in 1821. In 1839 a new set of rules (the London Prize King rules) were established, preventing kicking, gouging and head-butting, which lasted until the Queensbury rules of 1867.

Conclusion

* This chapter traced a variety of political, social and intellectual contexts of relevance for the study of British Romantic writing, arguing that these contexts are of more than just anecdotal or background interest because of the

Romantics' own self-conscious engagement with the conditions in which their works were produced, read and circulated.

- The chapter explored the prominence of debates concerning the meaning and legacies of the French Revolution in Britain, while also arguing for the importance of the American Revolution in setting the agenda for discussions about human rights and other revolutionary discourses in the period. The examinations of Romantic-era politics more generally considered both conservative and radical positions, as well as presenting various perspectives on industrialisation and social conditions.
- The discussion of intellectual contexts in part two dismissed traditional views of Romanticism as anti-science and anti-empiricism, suggesting that Romantic writers adapted ideas relating to scientific and philosophic mechanism, as well as exploring other philosophic ideas such as vitalism and idealism. Similarly, religious discourses informed Romantic writing in ways that did not always involve secularising impulses.
- The chapter's examination of social contexts considered gender and sexuality, including homosexuality; classes and conflict, noting conflicting views of the roles of aristocratic, middle-class and working-class groups; the literary marketplace; and leisure and lifestyle, noting the democratisation and commodification of entertainment in the period.

2 Romantic forms, genres and language

> The language of Prose may yet be well adapted to Poetry; [. . .]. Poetry [. . .] can boast of no celestial choir that distinguishes her vital juices from those of prose; the same human blood circulates through the veins of them both.
>
> William Wordsworth, 'Preface' to *Lyrical Ballads* (1800)

Overview

This chapter reappraises the role of genre and genre theory in studies of British Romanticism, as well as considering the development of literary forms, styles and language during the period. On the one hand, the chapter argues that Romanticism was fundamentally hostile to traditional genres, forms and dictions: Romantic ideas of originality, spontaneity and self-expression, and the associated preference for 'organic form', were incompatible with traditionally constrained literary genres grounded in neoclassical notions of decorum, convention and imitation. On the other hand, the chapter acknowledges the period's fascination with, and revival of, archaic forms such as the ballad and romance, as well as its adoption of a less ornate style of language that emulated the simpler forms of a uniquely British or national school of literature. Although particular attention is given to poetry, the novel, the long-neglected Romantic drama and women's writing, minor genres such as essays, reviews, memoirs, confessions, letters, periodicals and biographies are also examined. The chapter concludes by discussing the importance of the sublime, symbolism and other aspects of Romantic language.

***

In his overview of the uses of genres in the Romantic period, David Duff outlines the generic innovations and experiments which propelled the Romantic revolution in literature, arguing that 'the coexistence of . . . contradictory tendencies – towards the dissolution and transcendence of genres, and towards their consolidation and exploitation' were akin to the political revolutions in France (Duff 2009: ix). Duff also, however, examines the age's fascination with archaic forms such as the ballad, sonnet, epic and romance, whose revival and transformation make Romanticism a 'retro' movement as well as a new and original one. Yet despite its antiquarian interest in conserving and reviving archaic forms, Romanticism, with its focus on imagination and creativity, was nonetheless hostile to traditional forms, and its fascination with genres was therefore often for the purpose of dissolving, distressing or transcending them (Duff 2009: 1).

As outlined in the Introduction to this book, Romanticism has traditionally been associated with lyric poetry, often at the expense of other genres or forms of expression, including Romantic fiction, drama and narrative poetry. Although there is ample evidence to show that Romantic poets were among the most prolific and proficient writers of the period, this chapter – drawing on studies by Duff, Stuart Curran (2010a), Nicholas Roe (2005) and Duncan Wu (1998) – is concerned to celebrate the great diversity of literary forms in the Romantic period, including the rise of the novel in all its forms (Gothic, historical, manners), the distinctiveness of the national tale, the re-emergence of satire, the significance of non-fictional prose writing, the value of the fragment and the importance of Romantic drama. Beginning with a discussion of Graveyard poetry, the chapter goes on to discuss the 'hybrid genre' of Wordsworth's and Coleridge's *Lyrical Ballads*, the lyric and the sonnet, songs, conversation and narrative poems, the ode, the epic and satire; and it shows how Romantic poetry was affected by new ideas relating to simplicity and democratisation whereby the artificial 'poetic diction' of the eighteenth century was replaced by 'a selection of the language really spoken by men' ('Preface' to *Lyrical Ballads*, 59).

The second half of the chapter begins by discussing the Gothic novel and considers how it discovered the charm of horror and the power of sensation, recovering all that had been repressed by eighteenth-century rationalism, such as the grotesque, the body and the supernatural. Foreshadowed by a discussion of the national tales of Maria Edgeworth and Sydney Owenson (Lady Morgan) (1776–1859), the chapter considers Walter Scott's historical novels and the ways in which they combine a contemporary interest in the distant and Romantic past with 'true', 'probable' and historically 'accurate' contexts in an emerging realist tradition before concluding with an analysis of Jane Austen's 'novel of manners', traditionally read as the kind of fiction that is faithful to reality, conventional in its plots and characters and focused on everyday routine life and events, but here considered in light of Austen's interest in the events and ideas of her own time. The chapter also looks at the flourishing of prose essays during the second half of the eighteenth century, when the genre became more philosophical and speculative. It suggests that the period's literary criticism was guided and accompanied by a profound sense of speculation on human understanding, following the work of philosophers and social theorists such as Robert Malthus, James Mill (1773–1836), William Godwin and Jeremy Bentham, while works by Charles Lamb (1775–1834), William Hazlitt, Leigh Hunt, Thomas de Quincey and James Hogg (1770–1835) all attest to the importance not only of literary criticism, but also of memoirs, letters, confessions and biographies. The last part of the chapter evaluates the significance of Romantic drama, before concluding with an examination of the importance of the sublime as a distinct form of Romantic expression, arguing that the Romantic attempt to 'express the inexpressible' with pauses, breaks and silences (the mute Dorothy in Wordsworth's *Tintern Abbey*, for example) is not only characteristic of Romantic language but of modern literature more generally.

Poetry

In their impressive *Cambridge Companion to British Romantic Poetry* (2008), James Chandler and Maureen McLane discuss the central role played by poetry in the Romantic period and rightly argue that it 'emerges as a project of cultural inquiry; national fantasy; and socio-political critique as much as a poetry of self and nature' (Chandler and McLane 2008: 5). In other words, the idea that poetry 'came to mean . . . many different things' (Chandler and McLane 2008: 6) is reflected in the diversity of poetic forms and styles found in the Romantic period: poets were experimenting with blank verse (Wordsworth and Shelley), the Spenserian stanza (Keats), the Italian *terza rima* (Shelley), the Italian *ottava rima* (Byron), the folk ballad stanza (Coleridge and Keats) or inventing their own forms (Blake, Wordsworth and Coleridge) (Steward 2008: 53). Somewhat ironically, it is in the major prose works of the period that the cardinal functions of poetry are explained. For example, Percy Bysshe Shelley's focus on the ideal nature and essential value of poetic compositions in his *Defence of Poetry* (1821) can be read as a clear challenge to poets to fulfil their prophetic task to 'lift the veil from the hidden beauty of the world' (487) and 'make immortal all that is best and most beautiful in the world' (505). Even as it defends poetry from those who think poetic works unlikely to produce social improvement, Shelley's essay highlights the relationship of poetic fervour and political activism by declaring poets 'the unacknowledged legislators' of their age (508).

Despite recent challenges to its significance, meaning and radical agenda (see Introduction), Wordsworth's 'Preface' to *Lyrical Ballads* has traditionally been considered the manifesto of British Romanticism. Written as a response to the objections raised by some critics to the new and experimental poems of the 1798 edition, Wordsworth outlines in the 'Preface' the characteristics of this 'experiment', or new type of poetry, such as 1) the subject matter of the poetic works (Wordsworth's 'ordinary' and Coleridge's 'extraordinary' situations (366)); 2) the language (that commonly 'used by men', although purified from disgusting defects (59)); 3) the role of imagination ('a certain colouring of imagination' (59)); 4) poetry as memory or remembered incident ('emotions recollected in tranquillity' (82)); and 5) the task of the poet, who, despite Wordsworth's famous claim that the poet is 'a man speaking to men' (71), is also addressed in the 'Preface' as a 'prophet' and moral teacher. In other words, the poet stands apart from the rest of society because he is 'possessed of more than usual organic sensibility' (62) and is therefore best suited to get at the very essence of things and communicate them in a simple and unelaborated language. As the epigraph to this chapter suggests, Wordsworth does not only exert his readers to find beauty in the ordinariness of everyday life, but also the prose in poetry; in other words, to make audible the 'simple produce of the common day' ('Prospectus' to *The Recluse*, l. 55).

Graveyard poetry, romances, ballads and lyrics

The 'extraordinary' situations of Coleridge's poetry in *Lyrical Ballads* – as, for example, in *The Rime of the Ancient Mariner* (1798) (see the case study in Chapter 7) – draw their inspiration from the Gothic resonances of the so-called Graveyard School of poetry, whose favourite subjects were graves, death, the darkness of night and general themes of sorrow and despair. The changes in taste that were taking place around the middle of the eighteenth century are particularly evident in the productions of Thomas Gray (1716–71), Edward Young (1683–1765), Robert Blair (1699–1746), James Macpherson (1736–96), and Thomas Percy (1729–1811), whose works were characterised by an interest in death and the transitoriness of life, as well as macabre and solitary descriptions of churchyard settings. Gray's *Elegy Written in a Country Churchyard* (1751) is suggestive of the period's gradual shift from neoclassical to Romantic poetry in its reconciliation of the formal conventions of a still classical poetic diction with Romantic reflections on ruin, loss and loneliness. Edward Young's *Night Thoughts on Life, Death and Immortality* (1742–6), inspired by the premature death of his wife, is a long religious meditation set against the unchanging and gloomy background of nocturnal darkness. A morbid attraction to death and physical dissolution is taken to the extreme in Robert Blair's poem *The Grave* (1743) (see also William Blake's illustrations of the poem), whose duty was 'To paint the gloomy horrors of the tomb' (l. 5) where only 'silence reigns, and night, dark night' (l. 13). Death is also the theme of a number of ballads in Thomas Percy's *Reliques of Ancient English Poetry* (1765), which, by following the vogue of Ossianism (James Macpherson's *Works of Ossian* was published in the same year), significantly attracted the attention of the reading public to the popular poetry of a remote past.

The increasing public interest in old ballads extended to the romance genre, which typically recorded the exploits of heroic characters in foreign and distant settings. As Clara Reeve (1729–1807) pointed out in *The Progress of Romance* (1785), the form encompassed any type of narrative in prose or verse that ventured into exotic terrain and included medieval sceneries and landscapes, the chivalric exploits of young knights and love relations. After the disillusionments of the French Revolution and the Napoleonic Wars, Romantic writers tended to look idealistically towards the distant, chivalric past. Examples of the widespread Romantic engagement with this literary genre include Wordsworth's *Prelude*, in which he describes Revolutionary France as a country in a chivalric romance; Coleridge's *Christabel* (1816); Byron's earliest poem 'To Romance' (1807), *Childe Harold's Pilgrimage: A Romaunt* (1812–18) and his Turkish tales; Walter Scott's *The Lay of the Last Minstrel* (1805) and *The Minstrelsy of the Scottish Border* (1802); Southey's *Thalaba* (1802); Keats's *The Eve of St Agnes, Isabella* (1818), *Lamia* (1819) and *La Belle Dame Sans Merci* (1819); and Thomas Moore's *Lallah Rookh* (1817).

Romances and ballads are characterised by archaisms and a genuine and simple style of expression, both of which made powerful contributions to the renovation of eighteenth-century poetic diction. As a primitive, popular and plebeian form of poetry, ballads were seen by Thomas Percy as examples of 'pleasing simplicity, and many artless graces, which . . . have been thought to compensate for the want of higher beauties, and, if they do not dazzle the imagination, are frequently found to interest the heart' (Percy 1866: xiv). The old ballads contained much that Wordsworth and Coleridge's *Lyrical Ballads* tried to emulate, albeit with some significant changes: they dealt with the elementary passions of human nature; they conformed to the idea of a simple language without extreme finery or elegance; and they tried to moralise and philosophise: 'each of these poems has a purpose' ('Preface' to *Lyrical Ballads*, 63). Yet Wordsworth and Coleridge also attempted to refine their archaic models. In *Romantic Verse Narrative* Hermann Fischer perceptively suggests that *Lyrical Ballads* 'departed from its external medievalism by raising it to a higher level philosophically and poetically and by using it for highly intellectual and up-to-date subjects' (Fischer 1991: 62). Fischer's argument is borne out by Alan Bewell's reading of the rustic figures encountered in the poems as modern-day noble savages (Bewell 1989: 58) as well as by debates about the political meanings of *Lyrical Ballads* (Fulford 1996; Levinson 1986; Chandler 1984). For example, as a revolutionary collection of poems in terms of style and content, *Lyrical Ballads* suggests an analogy with the political ideas of the French Revolution (see *Tintern Abbey*'s subtitle of *13 July 1789*), which both Wordsworth and Coleridge embraced as young men. Some poems also criticise the effects of enclosure, rural poverty, changes to the Poor Laws and the repressive policies of the then government (see 'The Female Vagrant', 'The Old Cumberland Beggar' (note the case study in Chapter 1) and 'The Last of the Flock'). Moreover, the simple tales of 'Simon Lee', the once famous huntsman who is now old, weak and poor, and 'Michael', the old shepherd lamenting the loss of a way of life; the Ancient Mariner's supernatural tale of a crime, its punishment, expiation and final redemption; the depths of human feelings in 'The Idiot Boy'; the compelling attitude of 'The Mad Mother'; and the innocent yet profound view of the cycle of life and death in 'We are Seven' not only present characters, subjects and themes not generally written about in poetry, but they also challenge the reader's expectations about what poetry is in their enigmatic conclusions and didactic scope.

Case study: William Wordsworth, 'Michael: A Pastoral Poem' (written 1798; published 1800)

In 'Michael', Wordsworth presents a nostalgic image of the peace and simplicity of the life 'Of shepherds, dwellers in the vallies, men/ Whom I already loved – not verily/ For their own sakes, but for the fields and hills/ Where was their occupation and abode' (ll. 23–6). Set in a small, rural community in the English Lake District, Michael, the Good Shepherd, constructs an alternative lifestyle of old-fashioned pastoral values in the face of modern industrialisation, in which his symbiotic relationship with the land is a living memorial to a life of labour (ll. 62–79). When Michael is forced 'to sell/ a portion of his patrimonial fields' (ll. 233–4), his son Luke, the Prodigal Son, is sent to work in 'the dissolute city' (l. 453), which is represented as the centre of artificial civilisation and degeneration, and is the setting of Luke's subsequent fall from his Edenic (Rousseauian) innocence. Luke's failure either to adapt to life in the city or to return home represents a disruption of relations between land and family, and foreshadows the tragedy associated with the loss of the family farm. In other words, 'Michael' suggests the deadening effects of modernity: it is a poem that discusses the depopulation of the countryside and the dizzying effects of urbanisation, reflecting the loosened hold of rural society in Britain brought about by new forms of capital and the enclosure of communal land (see Wordsworth's association of 'nature' with 'permanence' in the 'Preface' to *Lyrical Ballads*). The poem is also particularly preoccupied with the plight of small landowners – families who passed the same plot of land from one generation to the next over many centuries (ll. 235 ff.).

The hybrid form of Wordsworth's and Coleridge's lyrical ballads matures in the Romantic period into a lyric voice which is reinvented in the work of other fellow poets. Lyrics in the Romantic period offered an opportunity to recover what eighteenth-century poetry had lost, or as Paul D. Sheats has so perceptively put it, they released 'language's organic power to awaken responses rooted deep within the living, unthinkable body' (Sheats 2005: 313). In 1911 Edmund Gosse contended that, while the lyric was originally a poem suitable for musical accompaniment, it had become 'really, nothing more than another name for poetry itself' (cited in Sheats 2005: 310). Such a view certainly dominated modern criticism of the poetry of the period until the 1980s, when critics began to acknowledge a much wider variety of Romantic poetic forms and styles.

Songs, sonnets and fragments

Although 'the lyric assumed its modern cultural role as the poetic voice of the individual self' (Sheats 2005: 318) in the Romantic period, it did so through and within a variety of traditional and emergent forms, in particular songs. It was Wordsworth himself in the 'Preface' to *Lyrical Ballads* who suggested that a 'split between music and lyric took place in the nineteenth century' (Sheats 2005: 310). Yet musical effects were key features of Thomas Moore's *Irish Melodies* (1808–34), a collection of national ballads whose mixture of graceful lyrics and Irish folk songs invite comparisons with the *Lyrical Ballads* themselves. Byron's *Hebrew Melodies* (1815) and Felicia Hemans's *Welsh Melodies* (1822) are similarly lyrical songs, which attest not only to a popular interest in music in the period, but also to an emerging national taste within the public domain (see Chapter 4). The lyricism of Blake's *Songs of Innocence and of Experience* (1789–94), which highlights the social and political issues that characterised the England of his own time (Hilton 1998: 103–12); Coleridge's 'The Eolian Harp' (1795), an emblem for poetic inspiration that beautifully symbolises the union of nature (the wind) and man (the musical instrument), and the natural perfection that could be enhanced by that union – 'A light in sound, a sound-like power in light/ Rhythm in all thought, and joyance everywhere' (ll. 28–9); the harmonious paradise of the lyre and dulcimer in *Kubla Khan* (1797); and the '"Most musical, most melancholy bird!"' (l. 13) in 'The Nightingale, A Conversation Poem' (1798), whose song conveys 'A pleasure in the dimness of the stars' (l. 11), all evoke the musical resonances of Romantic lyricism. Wordsworth's 'Solitary Reaper' (1807) more explicitly focuses on the relationship between words, sounds and meanings ('Reaping and singing by herself; . . ./ And sings a melancholy strain, . . ./ Will no one tell me what she sings?' (ll. 3, 6, 17)), while the skylark's music in Shelley's homonymous poem and the 'fled . . . music' (l. 80) of Keats's *Ode to a Nightingale* (1819) can all be understood as examples of lyrical songs, where poetry and music work hand in hand as symbiotic forms.

Songs and sonnets are formally related as the *sonetto*, or little song, was originally intended to be set to music. There is little doubt that experimentations with the sonnet in the Romantic era mark a movement away from the origin of the form in the thirteenth century towards a focus on more personal, internalised and/or transcendental themes relating to nature, the supernatural, imagination and individualisation. Yet David Fairer has rightly noted a paradox in the revival of the sonnet in the Romantic period, observing that 'in an age that breathed the spirit of liberty, explored the visionary sublime, and cultivated the incompleteness of the fragment', Romantic poets rediscovered the 'discipline, tightness and wholeness' of this genre (Fairer 2005: 292). With the exception of Blake and Byron, most Romantic poets experimented with the sonnet form. Significant examples are Charlotte Smith's description of grief and indignation in her *Elegiac Sonnets* (1784); Coleridge's domestic experiences in 'To the River Otter' (1793); Mary Robinson's (1757–1800) re-visitation of the myth of 'Sappho and Phaon' (1796); Anna Seward's collection of *Original Sonnets* (1799); Wordsworth's beautiful and peaceful view of London at dawn in 'Composed upon Westminster Bridge' (1802); Keats's rediscovery of the Greek past in 'On Seeing the Elgin Marbles for the First Time' (1817) and 'On First Looking into Chapman's Homer' (1816); and Shelley's commemoration of the 'kings of kings' (l. 10), 'Ozymandias' (1818), as well as his *Ode to the West Wind* (1819), which formally consists of five sonnets.

Despite the ubiquity of the sonnet form in the Romantic period, the fragment, as D. F. Rauber contends, can arguably be defined as 'the ultimate romantic form', whose caesura of the text opens new avenues of interpretation (Rauber 1969: 215). Rauber was among the first Romantic scholars to consider the fragment as a distinct genre, but, more recently, critics such as Thomas MacFarland (1981), Marjorie Levinson (1986) and Sophie Thomas (2005, 2008) have also argued that unfinished poems such as Wordsworth's *The Recluse* (1808), Byron's *The Giaour: A Fragment of a Turkish Tale* (1813) and Keats's *The Eve of St. Mark* (1819), among others, have a greater significance for Romantic literary culture than has been previously acknowledged. Dreams, for example, can be considered collages from memory fragments: *Kubla Khan* is significantly subtitled 'A Vision in a

Dream' (indeed, it is an induced dream fragment); *Christabel* is also focused on dreams and visions, and so too is *The Fall of Hyperion: A Dream* (Fermanis 2009: 95–6). These poems do not so much reflect the inability of the poet to finish a poem, but should rather be understood as examples of a genre that directly, and often deliberately, challenges the aesthetic tastes and principles of the age, encouraging the Reader to 'decide by his own feelings genuinely' ('Preface' to *Lyrical Ballads*, 85) through a 'widening speculation' (Keats, *Letters*, I. 281) and 'the regular stepping of imagination toward a Truth' (*Letters*, I. 218). For more detailed case studies on the fragment see both Chapter 6 and the Conclusion to this book.

Conversation and narrative poems, the epic and the ode

More attuned to everyday life and the championing of quotidian language than even the productions of the ballad revival, Coleridge's conversation poems of the middle and late 1790s 'were deliberately not elevated in their language and style' (Ruston 2007: 66), thus conforming to the (somewhat qualified) ideas of simplicity and democratisation celebrated in the 'Preface' to *Lyrical Ballads*. Relying on the freedom of blank verse, these poems celebrate domesticity ('The Nightingale'), personal relationships with wife and child ('Frost at Midnight'), an immersion in an informal and relaxed nature ('This Lime-Tree Bower, my Prison') and, in 'The Eolian Harp', 'the one life within us and abroad' (l. 26), which Coleridge was preparing to share with Sara, hence promoting ideas of sociability and communion. Significant examples of narrative poems include Coleridge's long and unfinished supernatural poem *Christabel* (1798); Walter Scott's reconstruction of historical events in three of his major narrative poems, *The Lay of the Last Minstrel* (1805), *Marmion* (1808) and *Rokeby* (1813); Byron's Oriental tales, such as *The Giaour* (1813), *The Bride of Abydos* (1813), *Lara* (1814) and *The Corsair* (1814); Leigh Hunt's re-visitation of Dante's fifth canto of *Inferno* in *The Story of Rimini* (1816); and Keats's Boccacesque *Isabella and the Pot of Basil* (1818), his supernatural *Lamia* (1819) and the pastoral story of the shepherd *Endymion* (1818). Shelley also experimented with the genre with long poems such as *The Mask of Anarchy* (1822), *The Triumph of Life* (1822) and *The Revolt of Islam* (1818) (the original uncensored version was entitled *Laon and Cythna*).

A long verse narrative on a serious subject and centred on one heroic character, the epic was written in a formal and elevated style, and can be regarded as the 'kind of poetry best suited to inscribe so-called national values' (Pratt 2005: 337). The revival of interest in the epic in the Romantic period evoked some of the heroic splendour of ancient history but it amalgamated these classical elements with romance plots, tropes and themes (O'Neill 2010: 196). According to Harold Bloom, romance in the Romantic period becomes an internalised quest, having as its hero the poet himself, who searches for his own voice, individuality and identity, as in Wordsworth's *Prelude*, which is now widely considered the first modern epic poem in English (Bloom 1969: 526–36). In his 'Prospectus' to *The Recluse* (1799) Wordsworth, in a language consciously echoing Milton's *Paradise Lost* (1667), states his intention to write a philosophical epic, with the 'soul of man' as its subject (l. 28) rather than seeking to 'justify the ways of God to men' (*Paradise Lost*, 1: 26). Some other examples of epic poems in the Romantic period include Blake's exploration of mythology in *Jerusalem* (1804–20); Robert Southey's alternative history of the discovery of America by a Welsh prince in the twelfth century, *Madoc* (1805), and his Indian epic *The Curse of Kehama* (1810); Shelley's revolutionary utopian dream of *Queen Mab* (1813); and John Keats's mythological fragments on the defeat of the Titans by the Olympians: *Hyperion* (1819) and *The Fall of Hyperion* (published 1856).

In *A Glossary of Literary Terms* (1957), M. H. Abrams describes the classical ode of Horace and Pindar as a 'long lyric poem that is serious in subject, elevated in style, and elaborate in its stanzaic structure . . . free to alter in accordance with shifts in subject and mood'. Moving away from these ancient Greek sources, Abrams focuses on the Romantics' re-interpretation of the ode in the form of the 'meditative' or 'sublime' ode, which he argues conveys a much greater sense of self reflexivity than the traditional ode in its 'attempt[s] to solve either a personal emotional problem or a generally human one' (Abrams 1999: 198). According to Stuart Curran, the Romantic ode usually includes a description of a particularised outer scene, an extended mediation which the scene stimulates (which may be a private problem or a universal situation or both) and the occurrence of an insight, vision, resolution or decision, which signals a return to the original scene described but with a new perspective created by the intervening meditation (Curran 2010b: 210). In *The Cambridge Companion to British Romantic Poetry* James Chandler suggests (with a particular focus on Wordsworth's *Ode: Intimations of Immortality from Recollections of Early Childhood* (1807)) that the Romantic ode can be seen as a 'progress poem' (Chandler 2008: 136; 151): that is, as a type of poem which recognises its own evolution, its interconnections with past examples and its new advancement into 'a poetry-of-consciousness, of reflexive subjectivity' (Chandler and McLane 2008: 5). The ode, therefore, ultimately decrees the suitability of poetic experience as an arena not only of personal ('a progress of sentiments') but also of political and philosophical reform ('an improvement in the nation's feeling soul') (Chandler 2008: 143). Suggestive experiments in the field are Shelley's radical message in *Ode to the West Wind* (1819) and his political declarations in *Ode to Naples* (1819) and *Ode to Liberty* (1820), and Keats's great *Odes* of 1819, which can be read as 'progressive' experiments on sculpture and the plastic arts (*Ode on a Grecian Urn*), a bird's song (*Ode to a Nightingale*), erotic love (*Ode to Psyche*), human psychology (*Ode on Indolence*) and transience and synthesis (*To Autumn*).

Satire

Recent scholarly works by Steven E. Jones (2000, 2003), Gary Dyer (2006) and John Strachan (2007) have effectively demonstrated that satire did not die out in the Romantic period; on the contrary, it was astutely used 'to articulate [the poets'] political, moral and literary convictions' (Moore and Strachan 2010: 261). Coleridge's early political newspaper satire, 'Fire, Famine, and Slaughter: a War

Eclogue' (1798), for example, attacks the policies of the younger William Pitt, while 'The Devil's Thoughts' (1799) (written with Southey) focuses on the corruption of Britain. Another significant example of a satirical text is Blake's *The Marriage of Heaven and Hell* (c. 1790–3), in which Blake assaults the hypocrisy of the church by expounding his revolutionary beliefs. Shelley's passionate outbursts in poems such as *The Mask of Anarchy* (1819), written when he was living in 'exile' in Italy, were aimed at addressing the social and political ills of his own country: 'And spoke—sometimes as one who wrote, and thought/ His words might move some heart that heeded not,/ If sent to distant lands' (ll. 286–8). Shelley's depiction of Wordsworth as a political traitor in *Peter Bell the Third* (1819), and his play *Swellfoot the Tyrant* (1820), which highlights the repression that the king of England perpetrates towards his people, are suggestive of the radical resonances of satire. Keats too experimented with the genre in his unfinished satirical fairy tale, *The Cap and Bells* (1819), which is a 'jealous' response to Byron's *Don Juan* (l. 217). The use of the comic, pouncing *ottava rima* in his *Isabella or The Pot of Basil* (1820) contributes to the ironic subtlety that permeates the greedy actions of Isabella's brothers.

The 'king' of political satire in the Romantic period is, without doubt, Lord Byron. His work, as Moore and Strachan have rightly put it, stands as 'the sharpest tip of an iceberg large in size' (Moore and Strachan 2010: 249). His best-known satirical poems are *English Bards and Scotch Reviewers: a Satire* (1809), in which he defended himself with witty irony from the vituperative attacks of *The Edinburgh Review*; *Beppo, A Venetian Story* (1818), a mock-heroic poem in *ottava rima*, whose comedy of love between the sexes gives rise to a series of absurdities and is supposed to shock English social and literary conventions; and *The Vision of Judgement* (1822), which is a parody of Southey's homonymous poem. However, the most successful of Byron's satirical works is, unquestionably, *Don Juan*. In this humorous unfinished 'epic renegade' ('Dedication', l. 5), written in *ottava rima*, Byron attacks, with wit and brilliance, 'all the Lakers in and out of place' ('Dedication', l. 6) and comments on other writers of the age. More importantly, on the pretext of telling the story of Don Juan's love adventures, Byron, in nearly two thousand stanzas, attacks the false respectability and codes of behaviour of the England of his time. His 'Dedication', for example, serves as a vehement attack on Britain's Foreign Secretary Castlereagh, the 'tyrannical butcher of the Irish rebels', and thus reveals his views and judgements of the organisations and values of European society more broadly (Jones 2005: 406).

The resurgence of satire was not confined to the 'Big Six' poets but extended to authors such as Thomas Moore (1779–1852), James Hogg, Robert Burns and female representatives such as Anna Barbauld, Anna Dodsworth (1740–1801), Ann Mary Hamilton, Elizabeth Hands (1746–1815) and Mary Robinson. Romantic-period satire also flourished in other genres as well as poetry such as drama (particularly pantomime), reviews and pamphlets (see the liberal *Edinburgh*, the conservative *Quarterly* and the omnipresent *Anti-Jacobin*), graphical prints and etchings (see James Gillray's *The Plumb-pudding in danger: – or – State Epicures taking un petit Souper* (*William Pitt; Napoléon Bonaparte*) (1805)) and fiction.

Prose – fiction

In 1810, just before Walter Scott and Jane Austen started publishing fiction, Anna Letitia Barbauld edited the colossal fifty-volume *British Novelists* series (1810–20), whose 'Preface' argues for the value of books for both education and pleasure. The series featured the work of twenty-eight novelists, including female authors such as Fanny Burney, Maria Edgeworth and Ann Radcliffe (1764–1823), and was groundbreaking in its recognition of the novel as a serious genre. The diversity and quantity of the works surveyed confirms Corinna Russell's view that 'the Romantic-period novel . . . foregrounds the heteroglossia or multivocal quality' of this literary form (Russell 2005: 377).

The Gothic novel

While reflecting on the 'General Character of the Gothic Literature and Art' (1818), Coleridge claimed that 'the Gothic art is Sublime' and that he is

> filled with devotion and with awe; I am lost to the actualities that surround me, and my whole being expands into the infinite; earth and air, nature and art, all swell up into eternity, and the only sensible impression left, is, 'that I am nothing!'
>
> (cited in Miles 2002: 62)

Coleridge's emphasis on the sublime in this passage reflects the ways in which later Romantic authors adapted and appropriated the works of their Gothic predecessors, whose medieval settings and supernatural atmospheres, extreme emotions (such as excesses of violence and transgressive eroticism) and fascination with the horrors that existed in the old social and political order served as a catalyst for the works that would follow.

Drawing on this older tradition, Romantic-era Gothic novelists reopened the gates of fancy and imagination, which had been closed by Augustan rationalism, thus channelling unconscious or semi-conscious visions, dreams and terrors into fiction. In his groundbreaking *A Philosophical Enquiry into the Origin of Our Ideas of the Sublime and Beautiful* (1757) Burke argues that the sublime is deeply connected to terror, and that whatever is visibly terrible or great in dimension, obscure and mysterious, is always sublime. His theory of 'negative pleasure', or a 'pleasure mixed with pain', became an essential component of the Gothic novel, and although some of these features were found in the Graveyard poetry of Blair and Young, the founding text of the genre is Horace Walpole's (1717–97) *The Castle of Otranto: A Gothic Story* (1764), whose nightmarish vision and labyrinthine passages were inspired by the engravings of the Italian architect Giovanni Battista Piranesi (1720–78) (see the case study in Chapter 5).

Together with Walpole, one of the most significant writers of the period was Ann Radcliffe, who contributed to Gothic fiction with several extremely successful and popular works such as *A Sicilian Romance* (1790), *The Romance of the*

Forest (1791), *The Mysteries of Udolpho* (1794) and *The Italian* (1797), regarded by many as the quintessential examples of Gothic fiction. Like Walpole, Radcliffe's stories are set in distant times and countries (something that Jane Austen's *Northanger Abbey* (1817) would later reject as too 'un-English') and are meant to arouse feelings of terror and suspense. However, unlike Walpole, Radcliffe nearly always finds rational solutions to the mysteries displayed in her books, a legacy of an earlier eighteenth-century rationalism. Nicola Trott is therefore right in suggesting that 'instead of being the work simply of reaction, Gothic writing took part, even if it also took sides, in an *unresolved* argument between rationality and more suggestible and mysterious states of mind' (Trott 2005: 485). Radcliffe's own formula of 'explained' Gothic is itself revisited in her last Gothic novel, *The Italian*, which focuses much more heavily on the psychology of her villain, Schedoni, than it does on the supernatural.

Since Ellen Moers's coinage of the term 'female Gothic' in *Literary Women* (1976), it has become customary to differentiate between two forms of Gothic literature: the male and the female. As Sue Chaplin has pointed out in 'Ann Radcliffe and Romantic-era fiction' (2014), female Gothic often narrates the experiences of women 'denied full juridical subjectivity and subjected to various forms of systematic exploitation, discipline and persecution' (Chaplin 2014: 204). The male Gothic is similarly concerned with the psychology of characters but tends to focus more on the psychopathology of social and institutional repression. William Godwin's *Caleb Williams* (1794), for example, outlines how legal institutions destroy individuals, while the psychological torments faced by the protagonist in Matthew Lewis's *The Monk* (1796) are analogous to 'the most exquisite and insupportable' tortures inflicted by the Spanish Inquisition (see the case study on *The Monk* in Chapter 1). Other examples of note include the sense of confusion and indecision that characterises the beginning of the monster's narration in Mary Shelley's *Frankenstein* (1818); the psychological realism that defines the 'perplexing' and 'tortuous' *Melmoth the Wanderer* (1820) by Charles Robert Maturin (1782–1824) (Botting 1995: 105); and the moral degradation, physical humiliation and self-destruction discussed in James Hogg's *Private Memoirs and Confessions of a Justified Sinner* (1824).

Case study: Mary Shelley, *Frankenstein, or The Modern Prometheus* (1818)

The Gothic novel arguably reached its climax with Mary Shelley's *Franken-stein, or The Modern Prometheus*, written while in Switzerland with her husband, Byron and other friends. The novel develops through a series of letters from a friend of Victor Frankenstein to his sister. The story, which begins on a 'dreary night of November', is one in which Frankenstein is about to 'infuse a spark of being into [a] lifeless thing' (Mary Shelley 2008: 38) and succeeds in creating a living human creature who, as strong and powerful as he is ugly and revolting, eventually turns into a murderer and destroys his own creator. Frankenstein, the 'modern Prometheus', is a manipulator of nature, but his creature initially shows love and generosity towards everybody following the Rousseauian ideal of man as innately benevolent, although his love turns into hatred and violence when he finds himself rejected because of his hideousness. Set in the 1790s, during the years of the French Revolution, when images of monstrosity proliferated in the works of conservative writers such as Burke's *Reflections on the Revolution in France* (1790) (Burke referred to the Revolution as events 'out of nature' (Burke 1968: 92)), Mary Shelley responded by creating a monster, who, despite the terrible things he does, appears to the reader as a profoundly sympathetic being.

The national tale, the historical novel and the novel of manners

The national tale and the historical novel gave expression to a profound anxiety and self-consciousness about the national (and wider) past in the Romantic era. The national tales of Fanny Burney, Maria Edgeworth and Lady Morgan drew on the sentimental novels of the late eighteenth century in their evocation of everyday life, while 'often containing extraneous information about national history, manners, and culture' (Connolly 2015: 221). Although Scott acknowledges his debt to the national tales of Edgeworth and others, he transforms their 'extraneous' historical elements into a 'plot of loss and growth through historical change' (Trumpener 1997: 131) while retaining the details of place, custom and local time that mark the significance of the genre. For this reason, Georg Lukács has famously argued that Walter Scott was the first novelist to truly capture a sense of historical specificity: 'What is lacking in the so-called historical novel before Sir Walter Scott is precisely the specifically historical, that is, the derivation of the individuality of characters from the historical peculiarity of their age' (Lukács 1963: 19). For Lukács, what Scott does more successfully than any other writer in the period is to give human embodiment to historical-social types and therefore to represent the collision of different social trends and historical forces (Lukács 1963: 35).

Scott's strategy of 'embodiment-typification', and his capacity to show how important historical changes affect everyday life, was certainly an influential realisation of the period's intense interest in what is meant to 'be of one's age' (Chandler 1998: 378). In particular, his novels draw heavily on the theme of national identity, where the choice of settings contributes to the formation of national character, as in his Waverley cycle, beginning with *Waverley* (1814) itself, the story of an English family known for its Jacobite sympathies. Set in the reign of George II of England and during the bloody days of 1745, when Charles Edward Stuart was trying to gain the throne of England, Waverley was the first of a trilogy including *Guy Mannering* (1815) and *The Antiquary* (1816), which successfully blended romance with history, history with politics, and past with present, while simultaneously presenting the spiritual growth of a young hero (Robertson 1998: 211–18). *Ivanhoe* (1820), a romance of adventure set in the Middle Ages a century after the

Norman conquest, is Scott's first novel set outside Scotland and in the very distant past. Significantly, in this novel Scott presents the union of actual historical events and imaginary heroes: the hero is not King Richard the Lion-Hearted, but Wilfred of Ivanhoe, an imaginary Saxon nobleman. Other historical novels by Scott include *The Bride of Lammermoor* (1819) (see Chapter 5), *Kenilworth* (1821), *The Fortunes of Nigel* (1822), *Quentin Durward* (1823) and *Woodstock* (1826).

More recently, it has been acknowledged that an overwhelming critical emphasis on Scott has led to the undervaluing and even neglect of earlier and alternative forms of historical fiction – particularly those by influential women writers such as Jane West, Sophia Lee and Charlotte Smith – and the critical focus on Scott has therefore rightly been challenged by scholars such as Ian Duncan (2005) and Fiona Price (2009). Sophia Lee's historical novel *The Recess, or a Tale of Other Times* (1783), for example, features fictional twin daughters of Mary, Queen of Scots by a secret marriage. Similarly, Mary Shelley's *Valperga, or, the Life and Adventures of Castruccio, Prince of Lucca* (1823) is a feminist recasting of Scott's masculinist histories, containing a telling narrative reversal in which the actual historical figure, Castruccio, is reduced to a means to an end while the centre of the history is instead provided by the lives of the two fictional female heroines. As Stuart Curran points out, Shelley adapts Scott's formula of the light and dark heroine but turns it to radically divergent ends, as her polarised heroines embrace and succour each other (even if they both ultimately fail in their attempts at self-determination) (Curran 2003: 103–15).

Jane Austen has long been recognised as the founding representative of the 'novel of manners', or 'domestic novel', a kind of fiction focused on everyday life and events. To use Alfred Lord Tennyson's words, Austen delineated 'the smallness of life to perfection' and reproduced 'novels [which] are perfect works on small scale – beautiful bits of stippling' (cited in Southam 1987: 137). The arrogance of *Blackwood's* attacks on Austen's novels as 'incapable of ever filling that space in the public eye which was filled by [Scott's] massive and masterly pictures' was reproduced in later criticism, which tended to confine her activities to writing 'miniatures' and to isolate her novels from the great historical events of her time (Lewes 1859: 99–113). Yet Austen's work was troubled not only by notions of rank, gender, property, money and social order, but also by historical and political concerns. It is the historical contexts of her novels that have been at the centre of critical attention in the last forty years. As Marilyn Butler has pointed out in her pioneering *Jane Austen and the War of Ideas* (1975), and Claudia Johnson has reiterated in *Women, Politics and the Novel* (1988), Austen's fiction is informed both by the revolutionary context and by the intellectual ideas born out of the French Revolution and Napoleonic Wars. Although 'Austen defended and enlarged a progressive middle ground that had been eaten away by the polarizing polemics born of the 1790s' (Johnson 1988: 196), significantly, novels such as *Pride and Prejudice* (1813), *Sense and Sensibility* (1811) and *Northanger Abbey* (1817) were all in first draft by the 1790s; *Mansfield Park* (1814) is also more 'implicated in the rationale for imperialist expansion than at first sight [it may appear]' (Said 1993: 80–97), as we consider more closely in Chapter 7.

Case study: Jane Austen, *Pride and Prejudice* (1813)

In his poem 'Letter to Lord Byron' of 1936, W. H. Auden, reflecting on Austen's work, firmly declares: 'It makes me most uncomfortable to see/ An English spinster of the middle class/ Describe the amorous effects of 'brass',/ Reveal so frankly and with such sobriety/ The economic basis of society' (ll. 115–19). As these lines suggest, Austen's works can be read not only as narratives of socialisation and domesticity, but also of economic crisis and the value of capital, as implied by the famous opening lines of *Pride and Prejudice*: 'It is a truth universally acknowledged, that a single man in possession of a good fortune, must be in want of a wife' (II. 3). The novel certainly remarks, in exasperation, on the social and economic implications of marriage, but important analogies can be made between the domestic realm of the novel and the historical context of Austen's own time. As Nina Auerbach had argued, the domestic environment in *Pride and Prejudice* merges with the historical when 'in presenting these drawing rooms full of women watching the door and watching each other . . . Jane Austen tells us what an observant, genteel woman has to tell about the Napoleonic Wars: she writes novels about waiting' (Auerbach 1979: 39). Although Austen's references to wars and revolutions often remain indirect, at a remove from guns, smoke and blood (and are therefore very different from Shelley and Byron's depiction of the Peterloo Massacre, for example (see Chapter 1)), *Pride and Prejudice* nonetheless presents traces of the turmoil abroad. As Gillian Russell has pointed out, references to combat and '[t]he hum of wartime, if not the blast or cry of battle, pervades [Austen's] fiction' (Russell 2009: 262). Austen introduces in the novel, for example, the troops in Brighton and the militia in Meryton; and officers like Wickham echo wider concerns about the place of the military in English civil society.

Travel writing

Few readers of Romantic-era writing will fail to be aware of the importance of travel and exploration for the self-fashioning of the Romantic writer. With the development of the practice of the Grand Tour in the eighteenth century, travelling became a rite of passage for the elite classes interrupted only during the Napoleonic Wars. During this wartime period, travel writing proliferated in more local settings, in the colonies and imperial expeditions and in the literary imagination. William Gilpin's *Observations on the River Wye* (1782), for example, discusses local picturesque beauty and was one of the most significant formative influences on writers such as Wordsworth and Coleridge. In *Frankenstein*, Mary Shelley makes the narrator Walton an explorer of the Arctic; Coleridge's Ancient Mariner tells his tale of crime, expiation and redemption in the South

·dy in Chapter 7); and *Kubla Khan* capitalises on the
ʾds.

of the East is also evident in Southey and Byron's
ʾlde Harold's moral and physical pilgrimage through
the equally mysterious settings of Spain, Portugal,
..ıd II), with their glorious pasts and famous monu-
‚ set in central Europe, where 'Self-exil'd Harold wanders
‚ʝ as he visits sites of extraordinary beauty and historical poi-
.ʾaterloo; and the fourth canto, most impressive of all, is set in Italy,
.ature's wild and cruel aspects suit the solitary and melancholy mood of
‚ nero (Cheeke 2003: 95–109). Byron's fascination with Italy was shared by
William Hazlitt, whose *Notes of a Journey from France and Italy* (1826), focus
on the power of art in a period of significant historical and political instability.
Percy and Mary Shelley's *History of a Six Weeks' Tour* (1817) is also a celebration of far-off beauties. Wordsworth too took a walking tour of Europe, which
culminated in *Descriptive Sketches, in Verse, Taken During a Pedestrian Tour in
the Italian, Grison, Swiss, and Savoyard Alps* (1793) and in parts of *The Prelude*, but his travel writing also celebrated 'home' beauties, as in his *Guide to
the Lakes* (1810).

These texts, along with Mary Wollstonecraft's *Letters Written during a Short
Residence in Sweden, Norway, and Denmark* (1796), William Blake's engravings
for John Stedman's *Narrative of a Five Years' Expedition Against the Revolted
Negros of Surinam* (1796), Dorothy Wordsworth's *Recollections of a Tour made in
Scotland* (1803) and Robert Southey's invented *Letters from England by Don
Manuel Alvarez Espriella* (1807), give credence to Charles Batten's claim that
travel books were among the most widely read genre of literature in the period,
second only to novels and romances (Batten 1978: 1). Travel narratives and especially of voyages had, of course, long been popular from the accounts of real
expeditions by Richard Hakluyt (c. 1552–1616) and William Dampier (1651–1715)
to the 'fabulous' or 'fictitious' voyages ironising such accounts by Daniel Defoe
(1660–1731) and Jonathan Swift (1667–1745). Increasingly, however, travel was
not just about seeing new sights and acquiring new information but also about
self-discovery or becoming a new person. The wonder and exoticism of Keats's
traveller 'Silent, upon a peak in Darien' ('On First Looking into Chapman's
Homer', l. 14), the restless, exiled protagonist in *Don Juan* and the studied localism of the travellers in Wordsworth's *Lyrical Ballads* all, in different ways, attest
to the new type of travel and exploration that emerged in the Romantic period.

The experience of self-discovery, so integral to Romantic writing, was fundamental to the new kind of journey that accompanied the idea of travelling for
pleasure or for moral and emotional education, along the lines of the protagonist
of Laurence Sterne's (1713–68) influential *A Sentimental Journey through France
and Italy* (1768). If Barbara Stafford sees Enlightenment travel writing giving way
to a separation between the 'purely entertaining travel book' and the 'instructive
guide' (Stafford 1984: 442) in the Romantic period, Nigel Leask has more recently
argued that Romantic voyaging does not elevate the 'self-consciously literary

strain of travel writing' above other 'discourses of travel', but instead marks 'a critical epistemic threshold in relations between hermeneutic and scientific modes of apprehending the world' (Leask 2002: 51). Romantic travel writing, in other words, could unite science and sentiment, information and experience, empirical and hypothetical forms of knowledge, documentary and speculative types of evidence and subjective and objective styles of writing, deliberately interweaving classificatory, factual and technical language with visual and emotive discourses. Mary Wollstonecraft, for example, is all too aware of the seductions of subjectivity in her Advertisement to *Letters Written during a Short Residence in Sweden, Norway, and Denmark* when she admits that:

> In writing these desultory letters, I found I could not avoid being continually in the first person – 'the little hero of each tale'. I tried to correct this fault, if it be one . . . but in proportion as I arranged my thoughts, my letter, I found, became stiff and affected.
>
> (Wollstonecraft 1987: 63)

As Wollstonecraft's comments suggest, writers of travel narratives were just as aware of the uses of sensibility as those of novels or poetry, and travelogues were often written by practitioners of more than one genre (Pratt 1992: 86–90).

The link between travel narratives and Romantic writing was, therefore, not just metaphorical but also stylistic in nature, as Romantic writers used travel narratives as models, as well as sources, for their own work. The explorative and liminal nature of travel writing made it a particularly important genre for women, allowing them to consider topics political in nature (such as national manners or governments) while simultaneously drawing on traditionally feminine modes and genres of writing. As Elizabeth Bohls and Ian Duncan have pointed out, '[i]t is no accident that travel writing during this time was published more often in the overtly autobiographical forms of journals, diaries, or letters' (Bohls and Duncan 2008: xxiv). This is not, of course, to suggest that women's travel writing was always radical – the propriety of Mariana Starke's (1762–1838) *Letters from Italy* (1800), for example, suggests that she was fully aware of the traditional association of travel with sexual freedom – but rather that travel writing was a hybrid genre particularly suited to the exploration of new types of female subject position.

Prose – non-fiction

The early nineteenth century saw the development of non-fictional prose in multifarious forms, such as the literary review, (auto)biography, essays, memoirs, newspaper and magazine articles, letters and confessions, all of which command equal attention. Many of the authors previously discussed successfully experimented with the genre of non-fiction: works such as Shelley's *Defence of Poetry*, his two pamphlets on Irish affairs dated 1812 (*An Address, to the Irish People* and *Proposals for an Association of Philanthropists*), Wordsworth's 'Preface' to *Lyrical Ballads*, Coleridge's *Biographia Literaria* (and his lectures),

Keats's letters and Dorothy Wordsworth's journals are among the period's most important works of non-fiction. As we have seen in the previous chapter, non-fictional work in the Romantic period was used as an energetic platform for expressing reformist philosophy, as in the utilitarian principles enunciated by Jeremy Bentham's *Introduction to the Principles of Morals and Legislation* (written 1780, published 1789), John Stuart Mill's *Utilitarianism* (published posthumously in 1863), William Godwin's *Enquiry Concerning Political Justice* (1792) and Robert Malthus's *Essay on the Principle of Population* (1798). Moreover, as highlighted in Chapter 1, debates concerning the French Revolution touched on issues such as popular sovereignty, the validity of monarchy, the usefulness of private property, the significance of individual rights and the relationship between religion and politics.

Essays, newspapers, magazines and reviews

The leaders of the new direction of the essay form were Charles Lamb (*Tales from Shakespeare* (1807), *Essays of Elia* (1823)); William Hazlitt (*The Round Table* (1817), *Lectures on the English Poets* (1818), *Table-Talk* (1821–2) and *The Spirit of the Age* (1825)); Leigh Hunt (political essays and reviews); and Thomas De Quincey, whose works include one of the first representations of delinquency in 'On the Knocking at the Gate in Macbeth' (1823), the famously irreverent and sardonic 'On Murder Considered as One of the Fine Arts' (1827), where its author provocatively concentrates on the aestheticisation of crime, and his greatest Gothic tale, 'The Avenger' (1838) (Christie 2005: 435).

Case study: Thomas De Quincey, 'On Murder Considered as One of the Fine Arts' (1827)

In December 1811 in the East End of London seven people from two different families, The Marrs and the Williamsons, were all found with their throats slit. News of the carnage rapidly spread all over the country, generating fear and panic until local authorities imprisoned John Williams, an Irish seaman in his late twenties, who was then mysteriously found dead in his prison cell. To Thomas De Quincey, the details of the investigation were of no interest. What impressed him was the boldness, cruelty and inexplicability of the crimes he attributed solely to Williams, the protagonist of 'On Murder Considered as One of the Fine Arts'. In this 'brilliant exercise in suspense' (Lindop 1981: 379) and sinister irony, De Quincey suggests that 'everything in this world has two handles. Murder, for instance, may be laid hold of by its moral handle . . . and *that*, I confess, is its weak side; or it may also be treated *aesthetically* . . . that is, in relation to good taste' (De Quincey 2006: 10–11). The artistry of crime, or the idea of 'murder for murder's sake' (Morrison in De Quincey 2006: ix), entails notions of sublime terror (the sublime, according to Kant, is that which does 'violence . . . to the imagination' (Kant 2007: 76)) and is directed towards a coterie audience made up of 'Connois-seurs in Murder', who 'profess to be curious in homicide; amateurs and dilettanti in the various modes of carnage; and in short, Murder-Fanciers' (De Quincey 2006: 8). The result is a tightrope between comedy and horror, a Bakhtinian carnivalesque satire of aestheticism, where Williams becomes an artistic genius, who, 'like Aeschylus or Milton in poetry, like Michael Angelo in painting . . . has carried his art to a point of colossal sublimity' (De Quincey 2006: 10).

The explosive growth of the essay and the proliferation of periodicals in the period was increased by the advent of the steam press in 1814. In a period of political instability, war and economic expansion, the newspaper and magazine became indispensable. Significant titles include *The Edinburgh Review* (founded in 1802), *The Quarterly Review* (founded in 1809), *Blackwood's Edinburgh Magazine* (founded in 1817), *The Westminster Review* (founded in 1824) and the more radical and politically aggressive *Examiner* (founded in 1808). These journals, aimed at a cultured and educated middle-class elite, initiated a shift in periodical culture from gentlemanly, well-rounded eighteenth-century periodicals towards dedicated review journals, as well as proliferating a much more vociferous and critical style of reviewing, which often took the form of highly personalised attacks, or what Marilyn Butler has called the 'seductively readable style of 'slashing' criticism' (Butler 2010: 138).

Some of these journals, such as *The Gentleman's Magazine* (founded in 1731), had female counterparts (*The Lady's Magazine* (founded in 1770)). While there had been magazines for ladies since the early eighteenth century, the number of competing titles rapidly increased in the early nineteenth century, with one of the most popular being *La Belle Assemblée* (founded in 1806), which specialised in fashion and contained advertisements for beauty products. Timothy Campbell has shown us the extent to which fashion and, in particular, the cyclical and dated representations of fashionable dress in plates and print (such as the so-called 'dress of the year') helped to make the 'time' of social life newly concrete in the period (Campbell 2013: 188–99). Magazines associated with particular religious groups also began to appear in the early nineteenth century. The Unitarians, the Anabaptists and the Methodists all had their own journals. *The Wesleyan-Methodist Magazine* (founded in 1778), for example, had twice the circulation of *The Edinburgh Review* in the 1810s and 20s. An increase in working-class literacy led to the explosion of radical political periodicals, controlled by the massive sales of the cheap edition of William Cobbett's *Political Register* (founded in 1802). Richard Altick notes that the most successful elite review journal, *The Edinburgh Review*, reached yearly sales of around 13,000 copies, while *Blackwood's*, also considered highly successful, reached 6,000 in 1817. By way of comparison, Cobbett's *Political Register* sold 40–50,000 copies in 1816 (Altick 1957: 392).

Life-writing

The most popular forms of life-writing in the Romantic period are those of the biography and autobiography. Coleridge's *Biographia Literaria* (1817), an interesting blending of letters and biography, is one of the most important texts of Romantic literary theory, where Coleridge, among other things, discusses ideas of primary and secondary imagination and fancy. Romantic biographies, particularly of literary figures, such as the seven-volume *Memoirs of the Life of Sir Walter Scott* (1852) by John Gibson Lockhart, *The Life of Lord Byron* by Thomas Moore (1835), Richard Monckton Milnes's study of Keats, which appeared in 1848, and the Percy Shelley biography by his cousin Thomas Medwin of 1847, all highlight the double structure of retrospection and reflection that lie at the heart of biographical studies. Printers and booksellers also saw the opportunity to market biographies of famous people, often as instructive examples of virtue for readers to follow. Even more significant in explaining the rise of life-writing in the Romantic period are the principles of subjectivity and individualism that are often (but now contentiously) said to define the age. Harding suggests that Romantic self-writing is marked by 'a more individualistic outlook, stressing the *uniqueness* of a person's experience and situation' (Harding 2005: 448). It is the autobiography, in particular, that lends itself to these kinds of subjective and personal agendas. Examples such as *The Autobiography of Leigh Hunt*, which appeared in 1850, together with the publication of Wordsworth's *Prelude or, Growth of a Poet's Mind; An Autobiographical Poem*, demonstrate the significance of the genre as a way of representing the unlimited potential of the individual and his or her feelings.

Jean-Jacques Rousseau's influential *Confessions* (completed 1770, published posthumously in two parts, the first in 1782 and the second in 1789) had a tremendous impact on British Romantic philosophy and literary culture. With its focus on secret desires, fears and introspection, Rousseau's work represents the first real example of modern, secular autobiography and encouraged a new focus on subjectivity and the growth of the mind that was of interest to many Romantic writers. Like Rousseau's *Confessions*, Byron's personal memoirs, unanimously burnt by a group of friends who feared that they would ruin the poet's reputation, attest to the transgressive nature of the confession as a genre. Romantic writers also drew on (and transgressed) narratives of religious conversion, such as the *Confessions* of St Augustine, as in James Hogg's *Private Memoirs and Confessions of a Justified Sinner*. Calvinistic fanaticism and justified crime give way to another form of transgression in Charles Lamb's essay 'Confessions of a Drunkard' (1814). This text is not simply an account of the pleasures of alcohol: by linking the objectivity of the essay form with the subjectivity of the confession, it offers an idea of the pain experienced by addiction (also suggested in Hogarth's engravings of *Beer Lane* and *Gin Lane*). Lamb's essay predates De Quincey's *Confessions of an English Opium-Eater* (1821) by seven years, but the latter offers an extraordinary 'exploration of the subconscious mind through his [De Quincey's] dreams and memories' (Harding 2005: 448) (see the case study in Chapter 7).

As well as encompassing autobiography and biography, the category of life-writing extends to letters, diaries and notebooks. Mary Wollstonecraft's *Letters Written during a Short Residence in Sweden, Norway, and Denmark*; Coleridge's letters to Sara from Germany; Jane Austen's letters to her sister Cassandra; the three editions of Shelley's letters; the surviving epistles of Mary Shelley to her husband, Byron and Trelawny; Byron's letters and journals; Hogg's 'Strange Letter of a Lunatic' (1830); and, above all, Keats's letter-diaries, which contain the cardinal points of his philosophy and poetics, all point to an early nineteenth-century literary culture steeped in intimate and social forms of writing. Keats's letters provide one of the most valuable examples of social exchange in the period: with their fluidity and dialogic nature, the letters are different from confessions or memoirs because they are written with 'an audience in mind' (Mee 2009: xiv, xxxii). If letters were often intended as social forms of dialogue and exchange, Nichola Deane has recently pointed out that letter-writing also embodies 'a potent symbol of popular, articulate, and organised dissent in the period' (Deane 2005: 577), thus establishing the significance of the political letter, as in Helen Maria Williams's *Letters containing a Sketch of the Politics of France* (1795), or in 'the letter intended to have been sent to a gentleman in Paris by the right honourable Edmund Burke' in his *Reflections on the Revolution in France* (1790). As a genre, the political letter combines the verbal command of private accounts with the secrecy of political revelations. Important examples of diaries and notebooks produced in the period are those of Benjamin Robert Haydon (1786–1846), Coleridge and William Godwin. Coleridge's notebooks, of which seventy-two have survived, consist of very disparate themes such as his travels, readings, philosophical and scientific studies, lecture plans and prayers (Perry 2002). Josie Dixon has suggested that Coleridge's notebook accounts 'represent at one level a kind of emotional and intellectual journal' and that they therefore need to be read autobiographically in order to reconsider its author's relationship to internal doubt (Dixon 2002: 77).

Drama

Jean-Jacques Rousseau's *Letter to D'Alembert on the Theatre* [*Lettre à Monsieur D'Alembert sur les spectacles* (1758)], which was written as a negative response to D'Alembert's proposal to open a public theatre in Geneva, interestingly presents two, seemingly contrary, portraits of theatre-goers, one depicting their isolation as they engage with the dramatic 'fables' performed in the playhouse, and the other their promiscuous sociability. Although the majority of Rousseau's lengthy letter focuses on the harmful effects and the lack of societal benefits of this art form, he also recognises that 'the stage is, in general, a painting of the human passions, the original of which is in every heart' (Rousseau 1960: 18). It is Rousseau's emphasis on theatrical emotions that appealed to Romantic writers. For example, Joanna Baillie's 'Introductory Discourse' to *Plays on the Passions* (1798), which strongly influenced Byron, defended and explained her ambitious design to illustrate each of the deepest and strongest desires of the human mind, the 'simple trait of the human heart', 'genuine and true' to nature (Baillie 1832: 14). Performed in London at Drury Lane and Covent Garden – the only two legitimate theatre houses, also designated 'patent' or 'royal' theatres – Baillie's plays were not a theatrical success, but they nonetheless indicate a shift in Romantic drama from external action to the internal drama of the mind. While popular drama in the period usually tended to rely on special visual effects such as *tableaux vivants* and Italian-style scenic spectacles, the Romantic stage's new focus on internalisation – fusing dramatic and lyric modes – preferred reflection over action. To paraphrase Rousseau's words in his *Lettre*, spectators become both spectacles and actors, promoting the internalisation of theatrical relations (Rousseau 1960:18). The theatre was also one of the most important sites for an exploration of the interaction between aesthetic and political concerns. While stage censorship prevented direct allusions to current events, political commentary could nonetheless be displaced into spectacular and spectatorial forms that could potentially reach a large audience. Percy Shelley felt that his theatre, for example, was not only valuable because it was a 'community endeavour' that offered the rewards of a complex 'socialized imagination' (Sperry 1986: 427), but also because it could reach the 'multitude' during the crises of Peterloo and ensuing reforms.

In 1821 Shelley expounded his most profound definition of drama in *A Defence of Poetry*, where he argued that 'so long as it continues to express poetry', drama is 'a prismatic and many-sided mirror, which collects the brightest rays of human nature and divides and reproduces them from the simplicity of these elementary forms' (491). For Shelley, it is drama, in its association with poetry, which is credited with the capacity to 'offer a possible scenario of a wholly transformed world' (O'Neill and Howe 2012: 555). The drama's ability to mirror political and social transformations is particularly evident in the way in which it revisited the subjectivity of the Romantic lyric. One of Shelley's most famous dramas is *The Cenci* (1819), a verse drama inspired by the story of Beatrice Cenci, who, ravished by her father, in desperation has him murdered. With the Licensing Act of 1737 keeping tight censorship over the theatre (the Lord Chamberlain had the power to approve any play before it was staged), the tragedy was rejected because of its 'morally unacceptable incest theme' (Bieri 2008: 137). Conceived as a hymn to a heroic resistance to tyranny, Shelley himself regarded the play as 'perhaps [the most] fearful domestic tragedy which was ever acted on the scene of real life' (cited in Bieri 2008: 138). The French playwright Antonin Artaud in 1935 called *The Cenci* the first example of the 'Theatre of Cruelty'.

At the same time as working on *The Cenci*, Shelley was writing *Prometheus Unbound* (1819), a lyrical and philosophical drama in four acts inspired by Aeschylus' *Prometheus Bound*. The play tells the story of the long struggle between Prometheus (who, like Beatrice Cenci, symbolises man's desire for personal fulfilment and spiritual liberty) and Jupiter (who, like Count Cenci, represents tyranny and oppression). In a letter written in April 1819 to Thomas Love Peacock Shelley argued that *Prometheus Unbound* 'is a drama with characters and mechanisms of a kind yet unattempted' (*Letters*, II. 94), as they, similarly to Baillie's dramatic intent, represent different aspects of the human psyche. Shelley also experimented with different dramatic forms and contexts: *Hellas* (1821), for example, is a lyrical drama inspired by the Greek revolt against the Turkish yoke, in which Shelley innovatively sets out the prospects for European history in terms of conflicts with the Islamic world (ll. 221 ff.).

European history is also explored in Byron's dramatic works. *Marino Faliero* (1820), written when Byron was becoming active in the Carbonari movement in order to support the Italian cause against Austrian usurpation, is based on the life of the Doge of Venice, tragically beheaded for having organised a *coup d'état* with the intention of becoming prince. (Eugène Delacroix and Francesco Hayez's paintings on the execution of Faliero are referred to in Chapter 5.) As Alan Richardson has pointed out, Byron's claim that his own dramatic works were written 'without regard to the stage', but rather for the 'mental theatre of the reader', highlights the usefulness of written texts, which not only allowed him to write works of a much greater length, but also to touch on more sensitive political, ideological and religious ideas than would have been allowed on the licensed stage of the time (Richardson 2004: 136). Writing to Lady Byron on 14 September 1821, Byron explained his new theatrical revolution as follows: 'I am trying an experiment – which is to introduce into our language – the *regular* tragedy – without regard to the stage – which will not admit of it – but merely to the *mental* theatre of the reader' (*Letters and Journals,* VIII. 201). To Byron, the notion of 'mental theatre' seems to mean that the stage on which his dramas will be played out is in the reader's mind (Richardson 2004: 148), but alternatively – or simultaneously – it could mean that the subjects of his dramas are the 'minds' of his characters.

Case study: Lord Byron, *Manfred* (1817)

One of Byron's most significant examples of closet drama is *Manfred, A Dramatic Poem,* the first of several of his plays to enjoy theatrical success in the Romantic period. Concerned to represent ideas more than actions, and 'minds' more than dialogues, Byron stages a tale of mystery and passion, where metaphysical and philosophical elements successfully mingle with Gothic and supernatural representations of a sublime landscape, and where, as Jerome McGann has pointed out, the idea of what Byron calls 'mental theatre' is here 'a drama of the action of Byron's mind as it functions in a poetical . . . mode' (McGann 2002: 193). Act I, Scene II strikes the reader as the deepest example of the theatre of the mind, when Manfred is alone at the top of the Bernese Alps and contemplates the idea of committing suicide in the form of a long soliloquy: 'And you, ye crags, upon whose extreme edge/ I stand . . ./ In dizziness of distance . . ./ I feel the impulse, yet I do not plunge;/ I see the peril, yet do not recede;/ And my brain reels, and yet my foot is firm./ There is a power upon me which withholds/ And makes it my fatality to live (1.2.13–24). This desultory parable of both vacillation and affection towards life completes itself in Manfred's meeting with the father figure of the shepherd, the Chamois Hunter (1.2. 57 ff.), whose intent to guide his flock ends in the physical salvation of Manfred: 'Hold, madman! Though aweary of thy life,/ Stain not our pure vales with thy guilty blood' (1.2.110–1). Just as the Chamois Hunter plunges Manfred back to life, so the figure of the Abbot in the poem is the source of Manfred's realisation that he is his 'own destroyer' (3.4.139), while also attempting to reconcile Manfred with Roman Catholic Christianity. The integrated exploration of crime and death – 'many crimes/ Have made thee –' (3.4.122–3) – ends with release rather than damnation; 'Tis not so difficult to die' (3.4.150). Manfred's last words have been perceptively interpreted by Alan Rawes as 'a final consent in his own being, a "repose" in the flow of his existence, and an openness to whatever his being presents him with – even, paradoxically, death' (Rawes 2004: 125). The final chapter in Manfred's life is thus a journey towards a welcome oblivion: 'He's gone; his soul hath ta'en its earthless flight –/ Whither, I dread to think – but he is gone' (3.4.151–3).

Byron's other attempts at closet drama include *Sardanapalus* (1821), *The Two Foscari* (1821) and *The Deformed Transformed* (1824). He also wrote *The Blues: A Literary Eclogue* (1821) and *The Vision of Judgement* (1822) (see Chapter 3). Other dramatic works written during the Romantic period include Wordsworth's *The Borderers* (written 1795–6, published 1842), where tyranny and its effects are significantly evident in Robert, the protagonist (who provides another example of domestic despotism) and Coleridge's *Osorio* (1797), a melodramatic Gothic tragedy. By telling a parable-like story of crime, punishment and repentance, Coleridge suggestively 'unmasks oppressive ideology by revealing the obvious and submerged constraints on mental freedom' (Purinton 1998: 160). Leigh Hunt's *The Descent of Liberty: A Masque* (1815) celebrates the end of the Napoleonic Wars; and Keats's historical dramas *Otho the Great* and *King Stephen* (both 1819), written in imitation of Elizabethan tragedies, provide examples of Keats's engagement with the genre. Although Romantic-era audiences were unlikely to have seen any of the plays written by canonical Romantic writers, the keen knowledge of practical theatre techniques by Romantic writers such as Baillie, Shelley, Byron and Keats challenges previous understandings of Romantic theatre as exercises in 'closet drama'. While Romantic writers tended to 'put a premium . . . on actions of a specifically verbal sort' (Tucker 2008: 271–2), often focusing on the internal consciousness of their characters in the way described by Byron as 'mental theatre', they were also familiar with stage techniques and were often reviewers of stage productions themselves.

Romantic language

Joanna Baillie's *Plays on the Passions* (1798) argues for the use of an unaffected and artless literary language, as does Wordsworth's 'Preface' to *Lyrical Ballads*, which rejects the artificiality of eighteenth-century poetic diction. The emphasis of the 'Preface' on simplicity echoes Wordsworth's 1800 'Note to "The Thorn"', in which the poet defends repetition against accusations of tautology – 'words in poetry are not symbols but *"things"*, active and efficient' – and maintains the significance of exact repetitions as an indication of passion, 'as beauties of the highest kind' (cited in Wu 2006: 508). The tangible empiricism of the 'Note to "The Thorn"', in its focus on words as 'things' and repetition as a form of passion, is not only at the core of much of the writing of the period, but also calls attention to a differentiation between concrete and abstract language. Wordsworth's emphasis on the 'real language of men' ('Preface' to *Lyrical Ballads,* 57) was part of an anti-aristocratic cultural revolution that included, as we have seen, the ballad revival, the rise of the novel and the increase in women's and workers' literacy and education (see Chapter 1).

Wordsworth's concrete language has been said to demarcate a new beginning in the stylistics of the Romantic period. Until the eighteenth century, literature was thought of as mimetic in function. During the Romantic period it came to be thought of as expressive, as a manifestation of first the artist's sensibility and later of language itself (Abrams 1953: 8–29). This idea is borne out in Wordsworth's attempt 'to follow the fluxes and refluxes of the human mind' and in his emotive and expressive claim that 'all good poetry' takes its origin in 'the spontaneous overflow of powerful feelings', a claim that is nonetheless qualified by the subsequent idea of 'emotion recollected in tranquillity' ('Preface' to *Lyrical Ballads,* 82). (For a more detailed interrogation of this concept, see the Introduction). During the course of this critical shift from imitative to expressive art, charted by M. H. Abrams (1953) in his book *The Mirror* (mimesis) *and the Lamp* (creative imagination, poetic genius, emotional spontaneity), Burke's aesthetic theories of the beautiful and the sublime took on a new importance as a way of searching for a language and terminology to describe and understand those aesthetic feelings that were not adequately accounted for by neoclassical standards of beauty.

Case study: Edmund Burke, *A Philosophical Enquiry into the Origin of Our Ideas of the Sublime and Beautiful* **(1757)**

Among Burke's conditions for sublime perceptions are terror, obscurity, power, vastness, infinity, magnitude (in both organic and inorganic forms), light, colour, sound, suddenness and discontinuity. Sublime language for Burke is purposefully non-descriptive, unclear, full of emotional abstraction and designed to incite the passions of the reader or observer:

> Whatever is fitted in any sort to excite the ideas of pain, and danger, that is to say, whatever is in any sort terrible, or is conversant about

terrible objects, or operates in a manner analogous to terror, is a source of the 'sublime'.

(Burke 2008: 36)

Critics such as Terry Eagleton (1990) and, more recently, Christopher Stokes (2010) have noted the political and ideological aspects of the sublime in Burke's thesis, where the sublime is clearly gendered masculine (strong, powerful, dangerous) and the beautiful feminine (soft, smooth, small, delicate, fecund). The experience of the beautiful, moreover, is a passive, objectified one, very different from the active, experiential, questioning trope of the sublime: 'we love what submits to us ... the smoothness; the softnesses; the easy and insensible swell; the variety of the surface, which is never for the smallest space the same; the deceitful maze, through which the unsteady eye slides giddily' (Burke 2008: 105). For Burke, power itself does not equate to sublimity: for example, oxen and domestic horses are seen as powerful but not sublime. Rather, the type of power involved in the language of the sublime is excessive and non-utilitarian: the wild horse, the lion, the monarch are all sublime precisely because they do not have an easily quantifiable utility value. Burke's ideological rationale for monarchical power, both here and in his later *Reflections on the Revolution in France* (1790), therefore rests on non-utilitarian terms, unapologetically promoting the sublime, secretive and even mystical excesses of power because they do not appeal to reason or utility.

Another text that was influential on British Romantic writers' conceptualisation of the sublime was Immanuel Kant's *Critique of Judgement* (1790), a critical response to Burke's *Philosophical Enquiry*. For both Kant and Burke, the sublime is not so much a positive pleasure but rather a 'negative pleasure', or a feeling loosely related to fear, awe, admiration, agitation, astonishment, delight and respect in the face of a boundless object. As Burke puts it:

The passion caused by the great and sublime in *nature* ... is astonishment: and astonishment is that state of the soul in which all its motions are suspended with some degree of horror. In this case the mind is so entirely filled with its object, that it cannot entertain any other, nor by consequence reason on that object which employs it.

(Burke 2008: 53)

Kant too sees the sublime as engendering a kind of break, cleavage or faculty of 'resistance' within the subject (Kant 2007: 90): on the one hand, the sublime raises 'the energies of the soul and give it strength and courage' (Kant 2007: 262), but, on the other, it can be considered to 'contravene the ends of our power of judgement, to be ill-adapted to our faculty of presentation, and to do violence, as it were, to the imagination' (Kant 2007: 76). Yet what is truly sublime for both Burke and Kant is not the power of nature itself but rather the feeling of intellectual mastery over the blockage or fear such phenomena produced:

> Sublimity therefore does not reside in anything of nature, but only in our mind, in so far as we can become conscious that we are superior to nature within, and therefore also to nature without us (so far as it influences us).
>
> (Kant 2007: 94)

The aesthetic mean or midpoint between the sublime and the beautiful is the picturesque, a word coined by William Gilpin in his groundbreaking *Observations on the River Wye* (1782). The 1801 'Supplement' to Johnson's *Dictionary* suggests that the picturesque is something that pleases the eye and is remarkable for its singularity and ability to strike the imagination with the force of landscape painting (see also Chapter 5). Wordsworth's *Tintern Abbey* (1798), for example, strategically places the focus of its scenes in the Wye valley in between picturesque and sublime descriptions. The poem recalls the poet's first visit to the place, stimulating one of the most distinctive moments of the sublime in the whole of Wordsworth's poetry: 'Nor less, I trust,/ to them I may have owed another gift,/ Of aspect more sublime: that blessed mood/ in which the burden of the mystery' (ll. 36–8); 'I have felt/ a presence that disturbs me with the joy/ Of elevated thoughts; a sense sublime' (ll. 93–5). According to John Barrell, the value of this 'sense sublime' is contrasted with 'the language of sense' (l. 111) – the concrete objects perceived by the senses – which is found in nature and here identified with the concrete language of his sister Dorothy and which opposes what Barrell identifies as Wordsworth's intense abstraction. In other words, by constrasting the abstractions of the sublime (of the narrator) with the concreteness of 'the language of sense' (of Dorothy), the poem moves from physical descriptions of the landscape to ever greater levels of abstraction, as the mind turns back through language to reflect upon itself, generating a sense of sublimity (Barrell 1988: 137–67). Wordsworth's celebrations of the 'solitudes sublime' (l. 484) in 'Crossing the Alps' (from the thirteen-book *Prelude*, Book VI), evocative of Shelley's *Alastor* (1815), is also a depiction of a power that transcends nature and the senses: 'The universal spectacle throughout/ Was shaped for admiration and delight' (ll. 60–1); 'in midst/ Of circumstance most awful and sublime' (ll. 75–6); 'in presence of sublime and lovely forms/ with the adverse principles of pain and joy' (ll. 146–7).

Symbols and symbolic language mark another important aspect of Romantic discourse. The ambition of writers in the period to express the 'inexpressible' through language led to an interest in symbols, as in the work of Charlotte Smith, whose figurative language in *Beachy Head* (published 1807), for example, addresses specific political and social issues. Smith's *Elegiac Sonnets* (1784) influenced the writing of *Lyrical Ballads* and other Romantic works such as Wordsworth's *Prelude*. Coleridge's account of symbolic language is particularly evident in Chapter 13 of *Biographia Literaria*, where he defines both the primary and the secondary imagination as powers 'differing only in *degree*, and in the *mode* of [their] operation', where the primary imagination is 'the living power and the prime agent of all human perception' while the secondary imagination 'dissolves, diffuses, dissipates, in order to recreate' (I: 304). Coleridge's poetry proceeds by what in Chapter 17 of *Biographia Literaria* he defines as 'fixed symbols', which for him represent a more meaningful and substantial form of language than everyday speech. In 'This Lime-Tree Bower My Prison' (1797), for example, the symbolic physical setting, where the imaginative process is enlightened by the presence of the divine sun and 'the last rook' (l. 68), is intended as a symbol of the communion the poet feels with the surrounding landscape.

Conclusion

- Understanding the development of genres and forms in the Romantic period becomes ever more complex as the Romantic literary canon expands: it is the sheer variety of forms and styles, including the invention of hybrid or 'distressed' genres such as 'lyrical ballads', which is perhaps the most striking feature of Romantic-era genre studies.
- Romantic-era writing is characterised by formal and stylistic innovations, as well as by the revival of older forms such as ballads and romances. While poetry has traditionally been seen as the dominant literary form of the period, prose forms and drama have received more attention in recent years. This chapter accordingly investigated a wide variety of literary genres, including diaries, letters and notebooks, which have been marginalised in conventional literary histories.
- Romanticism is often said to be characterised by a shift from mimetic to expressive language. Certainly, Romantic theorists, philosophers and writers attempted to account for those notions of taste that could not be explained by neoclassical understandings of beauty. Burke's and Kant's theories of the sublime and the beautiful aimed to provide a language which could encapsulate the indefinable and infinite feeling of transcending nature and the senses.

3 Romantic groups and associations

> Because I think that individuals acting singly with whatever energy can never effect so much as a society.
>
> Percy Bysshe Shelley, *Proposals for an Association of Philanthropists* (1812)

Overview

This chapter examines the importance of the 'group', 'circle' or 'coterie' as a way of understanding Romantic-era literary production. Its chief argument is that Romantic writers exist not merely or even primarily as distinct or solitary voices but rather as members of a series of self-consciously defined groups. It is therefore important to consider Romantic writing both as a group activity and as a social product. The chapter surveys a variety of different groups in the period, from the Lake School to the Peasant Poets, but it also considers the dynamic and shifting mediations between, within and outside these groups in order to challenge traditional understandings of Romanticism that revolve around paradigms such as the 'Age of the Individual' or the 'Age of Nationalism'. While acknowledging the role that solitary meditation has to play in Romantic-era writing, the chapter undermines the myth of the Romantic writer as a solitary genius, arguing instead that the period is defined by a remarkable sense of sociability, which develops rather than rejects eighteenth-century models of sympathetic identification and engagement in the public sphere.

***

Solitary figures famously populate Romantic writing. In his 'Preface' to *Alastor; or, The Spirit of Solitude* (1815) Percy Bysshe Shelley depicts '[t]he poet's self-centred seclusion' and refers to 'the lasting misery and loneliness of the world' (*Poetry and Prose*: 69–70). His attitude is echoed in Mary Shelley's depiction of the creature in *Frankenstein* (1818), who, when abandoned by his creator, is 'wretched, helpless, and alone' (Mary Shelley 2008: 105). Victor Frankenstein too suffers from a heightened sense of loneliness and isolation: he travels alone to a forlorn Scottish island; and in his many hours of lonely thinking, his sense of guilt and remorse steadily increase. Coleridge's ancient mariner (1798) is 'Alone, alone, all all alone,/ Alone on the wide wide Sea' (ll. 232–3); his monk in *The Mad Monk* (1800), replicated in Caspar David Friedrich's famous paintings *Monk by the Sea* (1809–10) and *Wanderer by the Sea of Fog* (1818), 'feel[s] on earth's uneasy scene,/ Such sorrows as will never cease' (l. 13–14) and 'only ask[s] for peace' (l. 15) when he finds himself overwhelmed by visions and voices. Childe Harold's many solitary hours accompany his pilgrimage across Europe. Wordsworth's speaker in *Daffodils* (1804) famously 'wander[s] lonely as a cloud' (l. 1), relishing 'the bliss of solitude' (l. 12), while his *The Seven Sisters; or The Solitude of Binnorie* (1804) meditatively engages with the sense of loss generated from the political upheaval of the period: 'Their father . . . loved the wars so well./ Sing, mournfully, oh! Mournfully;/ The solitude of Binnorie' (ll. 8–11).

Yet as Jon Mee has rightly argued, 'meditation has a role in sociability . . . it is a preparation of the self for coming before the public' to participate in cultural, political and other debates (Mee 2002: 106). As Mee demonstrates, Romantic writers derived many of their ideas about sociability from Enlightenment philosophers such as Lord Shaftesbury, who conceived of sociability as an innate inclination, 'an absolutely natural propensity' (Mee: 106), and Adam Smith, who, in his *Theory of Moral Sentiments* (1759), saw the act of sympathy as the foundation of civil society (see Chapter 1). In *The Social Contract* (1762) Rousseau theorised that the best way to set up a political community was by forming societies in conjunction with laws working for the common good (Day 1995: 69). Rousseau's ideas were influential in the establishment of a number of new types of association in the eighteenth century, which were not legal, institutional or directed by government. These clubs, assemblies, societies and coffee-houses led to the development of what Jürgen Habermas has called the 'bourgeois public sphere', or the 'sphere of private people coming together as a public' (Habermas 1989: 35; see also Chapter 1). The growing importance and development of the public sphere did not diminish as the nineteenth century progressed, but rather became increasingly politicised and polarised, as reactions to the French Revolution and the Napoleonic Wars radicalised writers and thinkers on all sides of the political spectrum.

As Jeffrey Cox has pointed out, to turn to the group in a period that is conventionally designated as either the 'Age of the Individual' or the 'Age of Nationalism' may seem contrary, but focusing on the group offers us an important means of resisting totalising meta-narratives about Romanticism (Cox 1998: 9; 12). In particular, the myth of the Romantic writer as a solitary genius has increasingly been replaced by a more comprehensive view of an early nineteenth-century literary culture that thrived on a variety of networks, associations, coteries and friendships. Drawing on pioneering scholarship by Marilyn Butler (1981), Jeffrey Cox (1998), Beth Lau (2009), Daisy Hay (2010) and others, this chapter discusses the surprising variety of networks, groups and associations that existed in the Romantic period. Butler, for example, has persuasively described the late eighteenth century as an 'age of remarkable sociability' (Butler 1981: 25), and has revealed the common factors that engaged the efforts of so many creative minds. More recently, Jack Stillinger in his *Multiple Authorship and the Myth of Solitary Genius* (1991) sets out the various stages of collaborative creation behind Romantic works that are usually considered to be single authored. Similarly, Daisy Hay's *Young Romantics* (2010) shatters the myth of the Romantic poet as a private, introspective artist, and focuses instead on the communal existence of an astonishingly youthful circle of writers, journalists, actors and activists centred around the so-called 'Cockney School'. As Hay points out, the designation 'Cockney School' draws attention to more than just geography, bringing into new focus the long neglected importance of Romanticism's middle-class metropolitan roots and thereby undermining traditionally lyric-centred views of the period's literary production (see Introduction).

Some of these ideas are exemplified by the way in which Coleridge worked creatively. When writing to Robert Southey in 1802 about his collaboration with Wordsworth on *Lyrical Ballads* (1798), Coleridge suggested that their project 'arose out of conversations, so frequent, that with few exceptions we could scarcely either of us perhaps positively say, which first started any particular Thought' (Worthen 2001: 31). Other works by Wordsworth – for example, his *Intimations Ode* (1803–6) and *The Prelude* – also derive from dialogues with Coleridge, who is frequently directly addressed in his poems. Coleridge was similarly in dialogue with Southey and Thomas De Quincey; Wordsworth with Charlotte Smith; Smith with Byron; Byron with Percy and Mary Shelley. Shakespeare's idea (re-interpreted by Keats in his *Letters*) that 'The web of our life is of mingled Yarn' (*Letters*, I. 169), suggests that it is only by focusing on a network of human relations that one can conceive and compose the best kind of poetry.

Developing these ideas in her collection of essays *Fellow Romantics* (1998), Beth Lau discusses the ways in which male and female writers of the Romantic period are inextricably related, focusing on how much they mutually inspired, influenced and shaped each other's work. In particular, the collection revisits the relationship between Charlotte Smith and Wordsworth; Mary Robinson and Coleridge; Felicia Hemans and Percy Shelley; and Jane Austen and the 'Big Six' Romantic writers (Wordsworth, Coleridge, Byron, Blake, Shelley and Keats) with the intent of 'emphasising common ground and creative dialogue among them' so that 'Romanticism can be more meaningfully and fundamentally reconceived' (Lau 2009: 1; 8). As Lau points out, in some cases Romantic writers even use the solitary figure as a warning about the hubris of pride and self-love: 'solitary self-assertion is a crime that should and will be punished' and can only be expiated when they connect with individuals and communities (Lau 2009: 86).

Other works, such as Gillian Russell and Clara Tuite's edited volume *Romantic Sociability* (2002), emphasise the significance of friendships and collaborations in British radical culture between 1770 and 1840. William Hazlitt clearly attempts in his essays 'On the Tendency of Sects' (1815) and 'On the Conversation of Authors' (1820) – as, to a lesser extent, does Leigh Hunt in his 1816 *Examiner* article about a 'new school' of poetry – to discuss ideas about human relations that were to find their major fulfilment in Percy Shelley's Godwinian *Proposals for an Association of Philanthropists* (1812):

> I propose an association which shall have for its immediate objects Catholic Emancipation and the Repeal of the Act of Union between Great Britain and Ireland; and grounding on the removal of these grievances, an annihilation or palliation of whatever moral or political evil it may be within the compass of human power to assuage or eradicate.
>
> (Shelley 1970: 36)

While the *Proposals* has a clear political agenda, in that it promotes Shelley's passionate belief in Catholic emancipation and Irish independence, Shelley also asserts the vital importance of the group or association in political and intellectual life, as shown in the epigraph to this chapter, where he contends that 'individuals acting singly with whatever energy can never effect so much as a society' (Shelley 1970: 40). In his other pamphlet on Irish affairs, *Address to the Irish People* (1812), Shelley also discusses societies and 'associations conducted in the spirit of sobriety, regularity, and thought' as perfect conduits 'for the production of happiness, liberty, and virtue', and sets out the principal aims of the association: emancipation, freedom and happiness (O'Brien 2002: 273, 275).

As we shall see, the views of Shelley, Hunt, Hazlitt and other members of the Cockney School were not an isolated case. This chapter surveys a variety of different groups in the Romantic period including the Lake School, the Cockney School, the Holland House Set, the Satanic School, and radical and dissenting circles such as the Warrington Academy, the Della Cruscans and Bluestocking salons. All of these groups attest to the Romantic taste for freely associating coteries, both as a means of acquiring an audience in the vein of earlier manuscript circles and as a way of promoting social and political agendas, where writers, as a group, acquire the Shelleyan role of 'unacknowledged legislators of the world', who give form to human emotional and imaginative life (*A Defence of Poetry* 1821: 508).

The Lake School

The Lake School has been described as the first official literary group of the Romantic period. Its denomination was coined by Francis Jeffrey (1773–1850) in an 1817 review of Coleridge's *Biographia Literaria* (1817), a literary autobiography which reflected on Coleridge's friends and associates such as Robert Southey, William and Dorothy Wordsworth and Thomas de Quincey, all of whom resided in the Lake District. Jeffrey's hostile review focused on the group's perceived vulgarity; in particular, the new subject matter of their poetry, their prosaic language, the elevated role they gave to the imagination, their views of the role and task of the poet, their revolutionary ideas on poetic style, such as their emphasis on simplicity, and the discrepancy between form and content in their work. As we have seen in Chapter 2, all of these ideas were most fully theorised by Wordsworth in his 'Preface' to *Lyrical Ballads*. In his earlier 1802 review of Southey's epic poem

Thalaba the Destroyer (1801), published in *The Edinburgh Review*, Jeffrey popularised and consolidated the belief that 'a *sect* of poets' with 'a splenetic and idle discontent with the existing institutions of society' had settled in the English countryside with Wordsworth 'as one of its chief champions and apostles' (Jeffrey 1802: 63). While Jeffrey accentuates what he perceives to be the Lake School's resistance to social and civil laws, Byron, on the other hand, in his unpublished Dedication to *Don Juan*, criticises the localism and narrowness of the Lake poets 'which makes [him] wish you'd change your lakes for ocean' (ll. 33–40).

Yet such hostility towards the Lake School should not obscure the practice of collaborative writing that lies behind the work of the writers in this group. When Coleridge met Southey in 1794, for example, they intended to emigrate together to America, where, on the banks of the Susquehanna River in central Pennsylvania, they would found a 'Pantisocracy': an idealistic rural community made up of twelve men and twelve women, all of whom enjoyed equal rights, including love, ownership and the abolition of private property (White 2006: 130 ff.). Although Pantisocracy came to nothing, its value rests on its philanthropic principles, which grew out of discourses of friendship and association. In 1795 Coleridge and Southey settled in the Lake District, where Dorothy and William Wordsworth were also residing. Crucially, the rural Lakes represented for them a lifestyle and sense of community similar to that which they had sought in America. In 'Michael' (1800), 'Simon Lee' (1800) and 'The Ruined Cottage' (1798), for example, Wordsworth asserts the voice of the local and pastoral world of human labour, domestic industry and familial bonds (see the case study in Chapter 2).

Hazlitt's backhanded compliment in his lecture 'On the living Poets' (1818) that Wordsworth and Coleridge 'were for bringing poetry back to its primitive simplicity and state of nature' appears to be at work in both writers' rural depictions in *Lyrical Ballads* (Hazlitt 1970: 215), but equally important was their sense of friendship and mutual affection. From 1797 to 1798 Wordsworth and Coleridge spent nearly every day together. Dorothy too was a constant companion in their walks. As Emma Mason has recently pointed out, William's relationship with Dorothy was one of both professional and personal reliance, exemplifying an 'affectionate bond that both inspired and attracted to it figures such as Coleridge, fellow writers Charles Lamb and Thomas De Quincey, and the sisters Mary and Sara Hutchinson' (Mason 2010: 1–2). As Wordsworth reminds us in *Home at Grasmere* (c. 1800–4), notwithstanding 'the quietness/ of this sublime retirement' (ll. 722–3), the Lakes to him and Dorothy represented a highpoint of culture and civilisation, suggesting a strong, symbiotic bond between themselves and place: 'Society is here:/ the true community the noblest Frame/ of many into one incorporate' (ll. 818–28).

The relationship between the Coleridges and the Wordsworths is central to John Worthen's *The Gang* (2001), where he considers the way in which William and Dorothy Wordsworth, Coleridge and the two Hutchinson sisters, Sara and Mary, formed a close-knit group by seeing or writing to each other constantly (particularly between March and July in 1802). Worthen notes that throughout this collaborative period both Wordsworth and Coleridge worked on some of their finest and most familiar poems such as the *Immortality Ode* and *Dejection: An Ode* (1802) respectively. Worthen has rightly argued that both Dorothy and the Hutchinson sisters were involved in Wordsworth and Coleridge's creative processes when transcribing, coping and recopying their work, for posterity or otherwise (Worthen 2001: 33). It was Dorothy who had the most formative influence on the writing of both Coleridge and her brother, and the association of their collective creative ideas represents the culmination of a period of great artistic fertility.

In *Dorothy Wordsworth and Hartley Coleridge: The Poetics of Relationship* (2012) Nicola Healey has more recently investigated Hartley Coleridge and Dorothy Wordsworth's relationships with Wordsworth and Coleridge, and has argued for the originality of Hartley and Dorothy's own work, with a specific focus on the sense of relationship, community, democracy and sociability necessary for establishing authorial autonomy in the shadow of their more famous relatives. Her arguments do not undermine but rather deepen Worthen's recreation of the group's intertwined lives. Indeed, they lived, as Worthen demonstrates, 'in such an extraordinarily intimate way' (Worthen 2001: 5) as to label themselves a 'Gang' (Coleridge, 'A Soliloquy of the Full Moon, she being in a mad Passion' (1802), 1. 27), or 'a circle of borderline, fugitive, family', thus implying the political and radical, as well as the social dimension, of the group's activities (Worthen 2001: 22).

Both Nicholas Roe's *Wordsworth and Coleridge: The Radical Years* (1988) and, more recently, Daniel E. White's *Early Romanticism and Religious Dissent* (2006) suggest that the culture of the Lakers was primarily one of opposition and rebellion, grounded on the poets' political milieu. Both scholars examine Wordsworth's and Coleridge's relations with William Godwin, Joseph Johnson and their circles, and demonstrate how the Lake School was vividly alive to radical issues in metropolitan Britain, rather than simply confining their interests to the mental and physical geography of the Lake District. If White ultimately reads Coleridge's failed collaboration with Southey, Lamb and Wordsworth as one which leads him to question and even dismiss the integrity of the School's experience, he nonetheless challenges the view that the Lake School was simply local or even national in its orientation, arguing that Wordsworth, Coleridge and others evinced a much more cosmopolitan understanding of democracy, liberty and humanity (White 2006: 127). Similarly to the Cockney School gathered around Leigh Hunt, the Lakers preached a political and reformist agenda, demonstrating that they were committed to putting literature in the service of social, cultural and political reform, although they were later seen as apostates: former revolutionaries who became conservatives.

The Cockney School and the Holland House Set

Literary critics have traced the first consistent reference in Britain to the Cockney School to the arrogant 1817 attacks made by *Blackwood's Edinburgh Magazine* on Leigh Hunt and his circle, when Z. famously asserted that 'None of [the Cockneys] are men of genius – none of them are men of solitary meditative habits; they are lecturers of the Surrey Institution [Hazlitt], and the editors for Sunday papers [Hunt, Thelwall], and so forth' (Z. 1818 No. 3, July). In his 1850 *Autobiography* the radical journalist and editor of *The Examiner,* Leigh Hunt, reclaimed the deprecatory term, arguing that 'The Cockney School of Poetry' was 'the most illustrious in England', characterised by members 'born within the sound of Bow Bell' (cited in Cox 1998: 229). The term 'Cockney' was therefore applied to people brought up in the urban atmosphere of the city of London – a significant juxtaposition to the more rural Lake School – but the *Blackwood* attacks referred not only to the spatial location of the group but also to their linguistic characteristics and political affiliations: 'Cockney' connoted the negative characteristics of a certain type of Londoner (common, weak and effeminate) as well as their perceived political force and their unacceptable attitudes towards religion, politics and sexuality.

Both Keats and Shelley belonged to the circle gathered around Hunt at Hampstead, which also included William Hazlitt, Charles Lamb, the painter Benjamin Haydon and the poet John Hamilton Reynolds (1794–1852) among others. In his 1998 study *Poetry and Politics in the Cockney School: Keats, Shelley, Hunt and their Circle*, Jeffrey N. Cox has challenged the traditional image of the Romantic poet as an isolated figure by recreating the social nature of the work of the second generation of Romantics (see, for example, Shelley's dedication of *The Cenci* to Leigh Hunt and of *Adonais* to John Keats), and he has highlighted how their work responded to a particular moment in history: they were, as John Whale has so succinctly put it, 'a loose literary grouping of London liberals' (Whale 2005: 544), which tried to keep the hope for reform and even, perhaps, revolution alive during a period that saw the defeat of Napoleon, the apparent victory of the restored monarchies and the re-establishment of old corrupt systems (Cox 1998: 56).

Case study: John Keats, 'Sleep and Poetry' (1817)

Revisiting Z.'s attacks on Keats as an 'uneducated and flimsy stripling' (Z. 1818: 519–20), Keats's social involvement with the Cockney School's liberal political agenda has received particular attention in recent years from Roe (1997), Cox (1998), Keach (1986), Wu (2001) and others. In particular, William Keach has shown how 'Keats's loose liberal couplets are the stylistic analogue of the loose liberal politics he had imbibed from Hunt' (Keach 1986: 183). In 'Sleep and Poetry', for example, Keats's rhymes rebound with evident freedom as in the following 'unclosed' couplets: 'vacant air/ prying stare' (ll. 31–2); 'infant's force/ rocking horse' (ll. 185–6); 'wretched rule/ taught a school' (ll. 194–5). For Keach, Keats's poetical style, which appears like a game of *bouts-rimés*, can be interpreted, on the one hand, as a political statement, whereby the free versification and reformist language correspond to a liberal political agenda, thus resisting the social and moral constraints attached to eighteenth-century closed couplets. On the other hand, however, Keats's 'stylistic extravagance might appear to be radically anti-political' (Keach 1986: 190) in its tendency to produce lines which seem to be more focused on the aesthetic principles of beauty and pleasure than on politics. Whatever Keats's intention, the effect of the couplets is one that draws attention to both the aesthetics and political connotations of his writing, so that critics such as Z., 'far from being his assassins', ultimately 'played a vital role in nurturing Keats's early promise' (Wu 2001: 50).

The Cockney School also exerted – albeit briefly – its influence in a European context when it attempted to recreate the Hunt circle in Pisa with personalities such as Byron, the Shelleys and Leigh Hunt. If the Cockney School of poetry was predominantly centred on establishing a relationship between style, language and poetry, what is evident in the work of the Pisan Circle – a group of liberal Anglo-Italians, or, as Mary Shelley put it, 'a little nest of singing birds' (cited in Schoina 2009: 140) – is their focus on matters other than 'English' ones. It was not Britishness or nationalism that predominantly preoccupied the circle, but rather notions of biculturalism, Europeanness and ultimately transnational issues. Maria Schoina (2009) rightly argues that the historical importance of the Pisan circle lies in its attempt to establish 'a highly ambivalent bicultural social space, identity, and literacy' (Schoina 2009: 130), while Jeffrey Cox reads the Pisan coterie as a wide community of liberal writers, who aspired, through communal thinking, to cultural and social reforms, as witnessed by the publication of *The Liberal* magazine. The Pisan experience was a fruitful time for some of the British Romantics: Shelley, for example, composed *Adonais* (1821), his 'Preface' to *Hellas* (1821) and *Lines Written among the Euganean Hills* (1819) while in Pisa. Hoping for the political renewal of Italy (and with England firmly in mind), Shelley in the final section of *Euganean Hills* presents a vision of community, previously absent in the poem, between nature and the spirits which populate it: 'All things in that sweet abode/ With its own mild brotherhood' (ll. 368–9), thus suggesting a desire for a harmonious intellectual society. Yet with the precocious deaths of Keats and Shelley, and the ongoing ideological and personal differences between Hunt and Byron, the School gradually ceased to exist in any functioning political or literary sense by the 1830s.

Like the Cockney School, the Holland House Set was a London experience, but unlike the middle-class Cockneys, the Holland Housers gathered in the wealthy surroundings of Kensington. Between 1799 and 1840 the Foxite Whig circle of Holland House presided over by Henry Richard Fox (Lord Holland) (1773–1840) and his wife Elisabeth Vassall Fox (Lady Holland) (1771–1845) was touted by almost everyone who had a serious interest in the politics, science and literature of the day. The significance of Holland House is evident in Thomas Faulkner's *History and Antiquities of Kensington* (1820), which offers a historical account of the 'several royal and illustrious personages' (Faulkner 1820: 113) who resided in the palace, as well as a descriptive catalogue of its collection of pictures. Leigh Hunt's two-volume *The Old Court Suburb* (1855), on the other hand, condemns the physical and intellectual demolition of Holland House, which he interprets as the end of a period of fecund literary enthusiasm. Accounts of Holland House continued to proliferate during the second half of the nineteenth century. Princess Marie Liechtenstein's colossal *Holland House* (1874) offers a detailed exploration of the most famous Whig salon of the age and acknowledges the significance of the circle's intellectual and political legacy. In *The Holland House Circle* (1908) Lloyd Sanders also focuses on a sociability model, but he 'is concerned rather with persons than the place' (Sanders 1908: V) and offers a valuable examination of the men of letters who populated the famous 'salon': from Matthew 'Monk' Lewis to Lord Byron and the discussion surrounding his burnt memoirs (1816) to conversations on Lady Caroline Lamb's (1785–1828) first novel *Glenarvon* (1816) (in which she satirises Holland House after she had fallen out with Lady Holland), as well as noting the presence of Samuel Rogers (1763–1855), Thomas Moore, Walter Scott and several influential European authors such as Ugo Foscolo (1778–1827) and Madame De Staël (1776–1817) (see Chapter 6).

Following the German sociologist Jürgen Habermas's views on the development of bourgeois society, cultural historians today tend to see the (admittedly elite) Holland House salon as critical to the development of a British middle-class public sphere: a relatively socially inclusive space where enlightened and even radical ideas could circulate outside the control of the authorities. As well as being a centre for Whig society and politics, Holland House also had some practical advantages for its affiliates. As a member of the government, Lord Holland had considerable powers of patronage (an accepted fact of political life at the time) and was able to use his influence to put writers in dialogue with politicians and aristocrats (Kelly 2013: 208). The Set officially came to an end upon the death of Lord Holland in 1840 but continued as a social circle throughout the nineteenth and twentieth centuries.

The Satanic School

In the 'Preface' to *A Vision of Judgement* (1821), Robert Southey coined the pejorative designation 'Satanic School' for 'men of diseased hearts and depraved imagination', whose 'monstrous combinations of horrors and mockery, lewdness and impiety' demonstrated a 'satanic spirit of pride', irreverence and irreligion (Southey III: 543–4). While no names were mentioned, Byron presumed that most of the comments were addressed to him and answered Southey in the 'Preface' to his own parody, *The Vision of Judgment* (1821), declaring that the members of the 'supposed' 'Satanic School' 'have done more good, in the charities of life, to their fellow-creatures, in any one year, than Mr Southey has done harm to himself by his absurdities in his whole life' (*Poetical Works*, 6, 310). Byron's *Vision* indirectly alludes to fellow poets such as Blake, Shelley, Keats and Leigh Hunt, whose work was similarly believed to express a licentious dismissal of orthodox views and lifestyles. Southey's reference to a 'Satanic School' thus not only condemns

Byron, but also calls attention to the radical principles of co-operative association affiliated with the Cockney School, to which Shelley, Keats and Hunt belonged.

Informing Southey's criticism are Romantic re-interpretations of Milton's *Paradise Lost* (published 1667): some of the members of the Satanic School were perceived to be advocating a form of rebellion against social and political institutions in their work, where the figure of Satan represented not so much moral culpability but awe-inspiring power and grandeur. In Blake's re-readings of Milton's epic poem Satan is seen as the true hero: his devil in *The Marriage of Heaven and Hell* (1790), for example, seems to favour a positive characterisation of Satan (Werner 1986: 58). One of the features of Southey's misreading of the second generation of Romantic poets is his belief that they worshipped Satanic principles. On the contrary, for Blake in *The Marriage*, Hell and Satan become symbols of liberty, while – in a deliberate reversal of accepted values and dogmas ('Without contraries there is no progression') – Jehovah is seen as a malevolent and envious God (Blake 2008: 34). Heaven is seen in Hell and Hell in Heaven: thus reversed, they can regenerate each other and a marriage can take place.

Many critics have noted that the Romantic age exhibits a resurgent fascination with Satan, who, as Hazlitt put it, was 'the most heroic subject that was ever chosen for a poem' (cited in Schock 2003: 39). Mario Praz in his groundbreaking study, *The Romantic Agony* (1933), successfully highlights the significance of the Romantics' attention to erotic and morbid themes, arguing that the Romantic interest in the persistent linkage of ideas of beauty and death, moral transgression and the creation of the 'fatal woman' and the 'fatal man' all underscore the Satanic traits of their poetics. More recently, Peter Schock's book *Romantic Satanism: Myth and the Historical Moment in Blake, Shelley, and Byron* reads Romantic Satanism as an act of rebellion (Schock 2003: 2). According to Schock, the Romantic emphasis on Satanic freedom grew out of the liberal and radical culture of the 1790s. As Simon Bainbridge has pointed out, Wordsworth and Coleridge associate demonic traits with the Satanic figure of Napoleon (Bainbridge 1995: 131 ff.); and later, Shelley and Byron also call attention to the Satanic aspects of the French general, with the intention, this time, of resurrecting what Schock defines as 'the spirit of Blakean Satanism' (Schock 2003: 79).

Shelley's rejection of traditional Christianity in *The Necessity of Atheism* (1811) is reflected in his essay 'On the Devil, and Devils' (c. 1819), in which he criticises misreadings of the Bible: 'The Christians have turned this Serpent into their Devil, and accommodated the whole story into their new scheme of sin propitiation' (cited in Brewer 1994: 102); and in the 'Preface' to *Prometheus Unbound* (1820), where he outlines the close similarities between Prometheus and the Devil. Byron's Lucifer in *Cain* (1821) similarly displays its author's scepticism towards fixed ideas of good and evil. Lucifer appears as a moral teacher for the protagonist: he teaches Cain the significance of knowledge, love and what he believes is the meaning of life after death. Lucifer's response to Cain's fear of death – dictated by what Lucifer himself calls 'A paradise of ignorance, from which knowledge was barred as a poison' (2.2.101–2) – assures Cain that he will not die (Cardwell 2011: 68–9), as death is only the prelude to another state. Shelley and Byron challenge the idea that the Devil can be considered responsible for all evil. As William Brewer has pointed out, '[i]n removing the Devil from the story of man's fall, Shelley and Byron . . . suggest that man himself, not a demon, is to blame for his expulsion from the Garden of Eden' (Brewer 1994: 103).

Satanic images also proliferate in the writings of Gothic writers: Matthew Lewis's Ambrosio in *The Monk* is a fallen religious figure who consorts with the Devil; James Hogg's Satanic imagination in his *Private Memoirs and Confessions of a Justified Sinner* (1824) opens with a manuscript found beside the body of an uncannily preserved suicide victim; in Mary Shelley's *Frankenstein* (1818) both the creator and the creature invoke Satan. For Victor Frankenstein, Satan appears as 'the fitter emblem of my condition; for often, like him, when I viewed the bliss of my protectors, the bitter gall of envy rose within me' (Mary Shelley 2008: 105). As a modern Prometheus-Satan, Frankenstein challenges the gods with the creation of his monster, and the analogy between Satan and the creator is represented by the making of supernatural and un-human forms. The monster, on the other hand, critically compares his own condition with Satan's: 'Satan had his companions; fellow-devils, to admire and encourage him; but I am solitary and detested' (2008: 105). The notion of Satanism in the Romantic period can therefore be seen as a response to the revolutions of the age: Frankenstein's monster embodies both the difficult landscape of war and revolution abroad and that of political dissent at home, as discussed in the case study of *Frankenstein* in the previous chapter.

The Warrington Academy, the Bluestockings and the Della Cruscans

Another form of sociability in the Romantic period is encapsulated by one of the most prestigious, nonconformist educational institutions of the eighteenth century: the Warrington Academy. Active as a teaching establishment from 1753, the Academy was set up by those who dissented from the Church of England. Warrington itself was a thriving commercial centre, which served as a gateway to the North West, a fact reflected in the finances and enrolment of the young Academy (White 2006: 26 ff.). In his book *Early Romanticism and Religious Dissent* (2006) Daniel E. White focuses on the association of Anna Letitia Barbauld and her father John Aikin (who taught at the Academy from 1758) with the Warrington circle, arguing for the Academy's desire to practice as fully as possible a new style of education based on debates around the unconventional political writings of Godwin, Wollstonecraft, Coleridge and Southey. Other significant members of the Academy circle were Joseph Priestley (1733–1804), William Enfield (1741–97), Thomas Pennant (1726–98) and William Roscoe (1753–1831), whose mutual goal was to introduce more liberal, scientific and utilitarian studies into English education.

Warrington also had a significant role in enhancing the participation of women in ideas and debates in a period in which they were largely excluded from the coffee-houses, taverns and clubs in which the newly emerging public sphere was thriving (Habermas 1989: 62). There is little doubt that Barbauld's most prolific period took place at Warrington, in the environment provided by both the town and the Academy. She studied at home, and composed and circulated her poetry in a communal context at Warrington. Her poems reflect the Academy's commitment to the repeal of the Corporation and Test Acts, attempts to abolish the slave trade and debates over the French Revolution. Although Warrington had closed its doors by 1786, as had most of the other dissenting academies around the country such as Hoxton, Daventry and the New College, the re-evaluation of female roles at the Academy is suggestive of its connections to the later Bluestocking circle associated with Elizabeth Montagu.

During the second half of the eighteenth century the term 'Bluestocking' (capitalised) was used to refer to a small group of intellectual women led by Lady Montagu, whose aim was to promote conversations centred around philanthropic issues, art, literature and publishing ventures, or, as Nicole Pohl and Betty Schellenberg have so succinctly put it, the 'blue stocking doctrine [of] rational conversation' (Pohl and Schellenberg 2005: 2). Despite its strong focus on female members, the designation 'Bluestocking' derived from the naturalist writer Benjamin Stillingfleet (1702–71), whose unique habit of wearing blue stockings while attending Montagu's salons gave the group its name. Among the other male participants in the literary salons were Samuel Johnson (1709–84), the actor David Garrick (1717–79) and the painter Joshua Reynolds (1723–92).

By the 1820s the term 'bluestocking' (un-capitalised) began to refer more loosely to literary or learned women who actively participated in the public sphere. It was used in both a complimentary and uncomplimentary sense. Thomas Moore's comic opera in three acts *M.P.; or The Bluestockings* (1811) and Byron's *The Blues: A Literary Eclogue* (1821), for example, offer parodies of this coterie. Similarly, Thomas De Quincey in his *Autobiography* refers to the group as a 'feeble minority', while William Hazlitt declares them 'the most odious character[s] in society' (cited in Eger 2010: 206). Some of these angry assessments provide, as Elizabeth Eger notes, 'perverse evidence of the bluestockings' eminence' (Eger 2010: 206). Recent scholarship of texts such as Mary Wollstonecraft's novel *Mary: A Fiction* (1788) and her *A Vindication of the Rights of Woman* has attempted to widen and reassess the bluestockings' intervention and reverberation in Romantic circles, both by considering bluestocking sociability and by re-examining their connections with male colleagues and audiences. An example of bluestocking sociability is provided by the female poet Anna Barbauld, who often dined at the house of Elizabeth Montagu in order to observe 'the imposing union of literature and fashion' (cited in Janowitz 2002: 71). Bluestocking women thus played a central role in the cultural and collective transformations of the period, establishing, in particular, the importance of sociability for Romantic cultural activity and identity.

Another group relevant to Romanticism's intellectual and artistic sensibility is the Della Cruscans, an association of late-eighteenth-century expatriate poets living in Florence, who shared radical and liberal ideas and collaborated with a group of like-minded patriotic Tuscan literati. The Della Cruscans' work, as Jerome McGann has noted, was characterised by 'extreme artifice of expression, erotic subject matter, and a theatrical self-consciousness' (McGann 1995: 96). Although the group's name was taken from the Florentine Accademia della Crusca, founded in 1583, whose aim was to purify the Italian language from any foreign inflections, this association of writers, including Robert Merry (1755–98), Bertie Greatheed (1759–1826), William Parsons (1745–1817), Hester Thrale Piozzi (1741–1821) and Mary Robinson, had a very different task in mind than their Florentine predecessors. As John Mee has pointed out, the choice of their name had a political connotation, as it was meant to commemorate the suppression of the liberal Accademia Della Crusca by Duke Leopold of Tuscany in 1783, thus denoting the opposition of the poets to the repressive Tuscan government of the day through a series of poems based on strong symbolism and often obscure imagery (Mee 2002: 104–22). The first poetical production of this literary circle was *The Arno Miscellany* (1784), although *The Florence Miscellany* (1785), which contained several pieces by Italian poets, became the founding document of Della Cruscanism. The Della Cruscan poets also published in two London newspapers, the *World* and the *Oracle*; and it was with the pseudonym 'Della Crusca' that Merry made a name for himself in literary London. *The British Album* (1790) was Merry's passport into the world. It also contained Anna Matilda's (Hannah Cowley) poems and works by fellow writers known as Arley and Benedict.

Case study: Robert Merry, 'To Anna Matilda' (1788)

The opening lines of Merry's poem 'To Anna Matilda', written on 28 October 1788, announce his return to England:

> In VAIN I FLY THEE – 'tis in vain,
> The swift bark bears me o'er the boist'rous main;
> For mid the giant shades that sweep
> The heaving bosom of the deep,
> When mountain-clouds, lash'd by the gale,
> Spread o'er the sun their transient veil,
> THY FORM APPEARS!
>
> (*The British Album*, II, ll. 1–7)

These far-fetched images, telescoped metaphors, hyperbolic phrases and common tropes showcase Della Crusca's formal preoccupations: the poem is a site where his artificiality is most evident and where he appears to privilege language more than content. In the following lines Della Crusca goes on to refer to Anna Matilda's 'burnish'd locks, and smile' (l. 9) and remarks that 'I see thee – and adore the while' (ll. 9–10), while also using explicit sensual images ('For thee my hot sighs stole away' (l. 16)), eccentric mannerisms ('O I live, I live for thee alone' (l. 30)) and extravagant conceits: 'THAT ANNA, AND THAT I, WERE ONE' (l. 52). Theatrical, sentimental and even superficial, 'To Anna Matilda' is representative of the type of poetry created by the very artificial processes that Romanticism is often seen to oppose.

Attacked by Wordsworth in his 'Preface' to *Lyrical Ballads* for 'the triviality and meanness both of thought and language' of their poetical works (Wu 2006: 498), the Della Cruscans were rediscovered in the 1950s and 1960s by scholars such as Edward Bostetter (1956) and William Norman Hargreaves-Mawdsley (1967), who highlighted the importance of the movement and of their work; but it was only with Jerome McGann's 1995 study of Romantic sentimentalism that authors such as Byron, Keats, Shelley and Moore were shown to be indebted to the sentimentalism and ornamental style of this English-Italian coterie.

The Peasant Poets

In contrast to the theatricality and mannerism of the Della Cruscans, some poets of the Romantic period sought to establish a connection with the simplicity of the land and the pleasures of rural life. Many, although not all, of these poets were self-taught or from the labouring classes. While critics tend to associate peasant-pastoral poetry with the 1800s, the first significant example can be found in the work of Scotland's greatest bard, Robert Burns (1759–96), whose aim was to 'valorise the experience of the rural poor', often in local dialect, while retaining a deep moral and political tone (Moore and Strachan 2010: 231). The popularity of the 'Ettrick Shepherd', James Hogg, also indicates a fascination with Scotland's rustic life, as in *The Shepherd's Calendar* (1829), a series of tales reminiscent of John Clare's 1827 collection of the same name, which was inspired by the Scottish poet James Thomson's *The Seasons* (1748) and his depictions of the simple natural world of rural felicity. John Clare (1793–1864), perhaps the best-known example of a labouring-class poet, was himself fascinated by the landscapes of childhood in Bloomfield's *The Farmer's Boy* (1800) (also inspired by Thomson's *The Seasons*), whose celebration of rural traditions and tale of pastoral country life are recounted by the protagonist Giles. Published in the same year as Wordsworth's 'Preface' to *Lyrical Ballads*, *The Farmer's Boy* encapsulates Rousseau's principle of bringing society back to its original simplicity and state of nature. Characteristics of peasant poetry can also be found in *Lyrical Ballads* itself: the attachment of the protagonist in 'Simon Lee, the old Huntsman' to the 'root of an old tree' (l. 84) and 'the tangled root [he] severed' (l. 94), as well as the 'tales . . . Of shepherds, dwellers in the valleys' in 'Michael', exemplify Wordsworth's focus on the importance of local traditions and community in the lives of labouring people.

But if Wordsworth was an educated, even elite, poet writing poetry of truthful simplicity, Clare was a 'Northamptonshire Peasant Poet' (a name conferred on Clare by his shrewd publisher Taylor), who worked as a labourer and whose enthusiastic commitment to locality and particularity, and deliberate decision to include misspellings, rural idioms, regional dialects and missing punctuation in his poems, was a sign of his own experience. The physical, social and moral climate in which Clare was brought up was that of industrialisation and of an accelerated process of enclosure (see also the references to the Scottish 'Clearances' in Chapter 1). Before enclosure, or what Clare scathingly calls 'the fence of ownership' (l. 8) in his poem 'The Mores' (1812), much of the arable land in England was organised in an open-field system so that rights to the use of land were shared between land-owners and commoners. If during the eighteenth century enclosures were regulated by Parliament, in that a separate Act of Enclosure was required by any village that wished to enclose its land, in 1801 the General Enclosure Act enabled any village to enclose its land if three quarters of its landowners agreed. Parliamentary enclosures usually provided commoners with some land in compensation but it was often limited and of poor quality. According to Clare, 'Inclosure came and trampled on the grave/ Of labour's rights and left the poor a slave' ('The Mores', ll. 20–1). Clare compares the 'Unbounded freedom' of the past to the mental and spatial diminution of 'little parcels little minds to please/ With men and flocks imprisoned ill at ease' (ll. 49–50). According to John Goodridge, what preoccupied Clare the most about the enclosure process 'was not economic efficiency' but 'the idea of trespass' of property (Goodridge 2013: 124), 'the betrayal of the land-scape' and 'the politics of exploitation' (Goodridge 2013: 165), with all its moral and civil implications.

Despite Goodridge's claim that Clare's 'political writing was often more oblique' than that of his fellow Romantic poets (Goodridge 2013: 123), for some of his contemporaries Clare's work was too politically sensitive. It was this sensitivity which initiated a troubled relationship with sponsors, with the exception of Lord Radstock, who was not only one of Clare's best friends, but was also sympathetic to the poet's satirical work and bitter attacks on the government's new regulations. The loss of common land created in Clare a strong sense of alienation and dislocation further emphasised by his departure from his home village Helpstone (although he moved only three miles away). 'The Flitting' (1832) is his attempt not only at recording his sense of displacement and isolation from a poetic community that treated him as an outsider or anomaly – 'The Summer like a stranger comes/ I pause and hardly know her face' (ll. 3–4) – but also represents his emphasis on the value of 'littleness' as a celebration of modesty and humility.

Case study: John Clare, 'The Flitting' (1832)

In 'The Flitting' Clare refers to 'natures beautys that inspired/ [his] heart' (ll. 117–18), like the 'sunny streams' (l. 52) and 'the pasture brook' (l. 164), and represents something apparently insignificant like a 'weed' (l. 186 ff.) as a beautiful fragment of the natural world. Clare is a poet of nature, and writes in the voice of one who knows nature intimately; but he refuses to elevate any one of his natural subjects over any other. 'Passions of Sublimity', for Clare, 'Belong to plain and simpler things' (ll. 77–8) such as the little moss that persists when the pomp of ancient tales has long passed away (ll. 80–8). As Mina Gorji pointed out, Clare's use of 'littleness' or 'little things' has a series of complex meanings: 'littleness' and a carefully orchestrated attention to detail is not just a celebration of simplicity, but also a way of asserting 'his refined sensibility, and creat[ing] and express[ing] a familiar intimacy with the world around him' (Gorji 2013: 92). This world, as Paul Hamilton has recently noticed, is recreated in his poetry

> by a ground-up view directly privileging the position from which Clare worked on and saw the land; not a position from which aesthetic proportion was imposed but one obviously subject to the contingencies of up and down, bareness and growth, low and high.
>
> (Hamilton 2014: 236)

The pastoral impulse that Clare so intensely evokes in his poetry is also associated with the theme of childhood memories: 'I dwell on trifles like a child/ I feel as ill becomes a man' (ll. 57–8). 'The Flitting' in this context demonstrates the child's continuing ability to feel at home in his rural landscape in a way that a dislocated adult may not.

Women writers such as the 'Bristol milkmaid' Ann Yearsley (1753–1806), the serving maid Elizabeth Hands, Mary Leapor (1722–46), Mary Collier (1688–1762) and Janet Little (1759–1813) also emphasised the value of rural life with their focus on ploughboys, milkmaids and shepherds. Ann Yearsley, in particular, is well-known for her collection of poems *The Rural Lyre* (1796), which is not only a celebration of domesticity and social and familial bonds, but also engages with issues related to contemporary history, politics and religion. Even earlier, with Hannah More's patronage, and her 'A Poem on the Inhumanity of the Slave Trade' (1788), Yearsley became known to the public for her involvement in social and political issues, situating both her and her patron in what Moore and Strachan call Romanticism's 'sentimental tradition of humanitarian poetry' (Moore and Strachan 2010: 227). Although typically beginning their career in explicit opposition to a critical taste that favoured more traditional and learned forms of poetry, labouring-class poets distinguished themselves by addressing issues beyond those related to agriculture and country landscapes.

Conclusion

- Recent scholarly work has revealed how groups and associations, and the dynamic interactions and mediations between them, are of fundamental significance for a revised understanding of British Romanticism. Rather than relying on the long-standing stereotype of the Romantic poet as a solitary genius, this chapter foregrounded the importance of an early-nineteenth-century literary culture that thrived on a variety of networks, coteries and friendships.
- Romantic groups are sometimes dismissively defined by fellow poets to single out what they considered the worst aspects of their poetry (for example, the Cockneys, the Satanic School, the Bluestockings and the Peasant Poets),

but most groups reclaimed these designations in order to signal the uniqueness or comparative position of the group. The Cockney School, for example, promoted the principle of co-operative 'sociability' not just in its own right but also as a contrast to what it saw as the self-interested introspection of the Lake School. Similarly, the Della Cruscans were deliberately transgressive in their improvisatory style, self-consciously setting themselves up against the emphasis on simplicity favoured by Wordsworth and his circle.

- Traditionally, Romantic scholarship has been strongly gendered and tended to centre predominantly on male groups. More recently a number of critics have argued for a renewed appreciation of sentimental literary forms and of women's contributions to the Romantic movement, focusing, in particular, on the work of the Bluestockings, the Della Cruscans and female labouring-class poets.

4 National, regional and local Romanticism

> '*This* country!' replied the blind man – 'I am of every country in broad Scotland, and a wee bit of England to boot.'
>
> Walter Scott, *Redgauntlet* (1824)

Overview

This chapter explores the development of distinctly national literary agendas in Romantic-era Britain, as well as examining devolutionary approaches to Anglo- or English-centric Romanticism. It focuses, in particular, on so-called 'four nation' studies that question older centre/periphery models of literary production, especially those that locate the driving cultural forces of British Romanticism in England and/or metropolitan London, and define themselves against the supposed exotic 'otherness' of Celtic cultures. The chapter considers each of the four 'nations' – England, Ireland, Scotland and Wales – as separate public spheres or distinctive systems of cultural production rather than merely as peripheral voices, but it also considers the possibility of a more cohesive British national identity following the Acts of Union. The final part of the chapter examines local, regional and other micro-nationalist identities in the context of archipelagic studies, looking, in particular, at West Country Romanticism, while also exploring transnational identities, border crossings and in-between locations such as seas and rivers as a way of further contesting larger nationalisms and territorialisms.

***

The period 1780–1860 is often seen as the age of nascent or emerging European nationhood: not only did Britain, France and Germany experience a new sense of national consolidation, but the period also saw the awakening of many Central European peoples lacking their own nation-states. It has long been acknowledged that Romantic-era literary writing played a significant role in this national awakening, as national identities were imagined in virtual and narrative forms long before they were materially consolidated in political terms, but there has been considerable disagreement about both the origin and nature of the rise of nationhood and nationalism in Europe. Ernest Gellner, for example, sees Western nationhood as an ideological development resulting from internal social changes such as industrialisation, rising literary rates, print technologies and the decline of traditional social and religious elites (Gellner 1983), while Benedict Anderson has argued that the model of the modern nation-state was imported to Europe from the Americas in the nineteenth century (Anderson 1993).

The first part of this chapter considers literary-critical responses to these kinds of debates about the rise of nationhood and nationalism in Britain, exploring, in particular, the impact of 'four nation' approaches, which see England, Ireland, Scotland and Wales as playing distinct but overlapping roles in the creation of a modern Britain. Katie Trumpener's *Bardic Nationalism: The Romantic Novel and the British Empire* (1997), for example, argues for the geographically dispersed production of the nation across the British Empire, and, in particular, for the importance of Ireland and Scotland in generating new forms of cultural nationalism. Although there is little consensus about whether or not a homogeneous pan-British identity existed in the early nineteenth century, Trumpener's argument that British literature was largely constituted through the imitation and appropriation of antiquarian and nationalist literary developments in Scotland and Ireland is now widely accepted among literary scholars.

The second part of the chapter considers the existence (or otherwise) of separate public spheres and national literary agendas in Scotland, Ireland, Wales and England. In relation to Scotland, the chapter examines the importance of the Scottish Enlightenment and a thriving periodical culture in the creation of a distinct Scottish public sphere, as well as considering the relevance of bardic traditions and vernaculars for the development of Scottish Romantic literature. With regard to Ireland, it emphasises the role of antiquarian and philological developments in inventing a proto-modern Ireland with 'Enlightenment credentials' (Gibbons 2009: 183), as well as exploring the impact of debates surrounding Catholic Emancipation and Irish Republicanism on the literature of the period. The focus of the discussion on Wales is similarly on the antiquarian interests emerging from the philological and literary researches of Welsh antiquarians such as Edward Lhuyd (1660–1709) as well as on revivals of Welsh bardic and druidic traditions such as Iolo Morganwg's (1747–1826) adaptations of the eisteddfod.

The localism of English writers such as William Wordsworth and Jane Austen, on the other hand, can be seen as part of a quest for national identity as well as psychic wholeness (Bolton 2006: 123), shoring up a peculiarly English identity centred on a 'green core' or heartland that 'came to stand in metonymic relationship to the nation as a whole' (Joannou 2012: 39). The final part of this chapter examines the importance of regional Romanticisms such as West Country regional cultures in contesting the kind of overarching conceptions of 'Englishness' that works by Austen and Wordsworth imply. The chapter considers these regional studies in the context of archipelagic theory – or the inter-relational study of identities and locales within the British isles – and the role it has played in extending the devolutionary drive of 'four nation' approaches by focusing on transnational borrowings and border crossings. In particular, the chapter considers the importance of in-between locations such as seas and rivers in creating opportunities for shifting national boundaries and fluid identities in Romantic-era writing.

Union, nationhood and the 'four nations'

The Act of Union between England and Scotland in 1707, and between Great Britain and Ireland in 1800, saw the formation of the United Kingdom of Great Britain and Ireland. Following the first Act of Union, Linda Colley has argued that the peoples of the British Isles gradually developed a new and distinct sense of 'Britishness' based largely on their Protestantism and perceived differences from Catholic Europe (Colley 1992: 6, 54) but also on numerous other factors such as the loss of Britain's American colonies after the American Revolutionary War (1775–83), the 'total warfare' and mass conscription of the Napoleonic Wars (1803–15), an emerging 'cult of commerce' and a new emphasis on empire (Colley 1992: 56). Although Colley goes on to account for the political radicalism of the period – in particular, the involvement of working- and middle-class men and women in mass petitioning campaigns for parliamentary reform, the abolition of the slave trade, and Catholic Emancipation (Colley 1992: 372) – her study counters earlier (but still influential) claims by Eric Hobsbawm (1962), E. P. Thompson (1966) and others that the long eighteenth century was characterised more by revolution and radicalism than by stability and citizenship within a larger British nation.

Colley is right in suggesting that the long eighteenth century saw the gradual emergence of a more collective sense of British identity, but it has increasingly been acknowledged that the Acts of Union also brought with them an acknowledgement of regional differences (Stafford 2005: 115), as well as a sense that union was a partial or incomplete project (Brockliss and Eastwood 1997: 1). While Scotland's entry into the Union saw the dissolution of its political autonomy and the increasing anglicisation of its language, the Union also left intact many of the cultural institutions that played a major role in defining a separate Scottish identity and public sphere, such as the Kirk or national religion, the universities, the law and the financial system (Pittock 2008: 19–21). In Wales, too, distinctive cultural and political institutions, such as the Welsh language, either remained strong or were revitalised in the eighteenth century. In Ireland the majority of Irish people saw the Union as a symbol of their oppression by an Anglo-Protestant ascendency. Even in England, identities were divided between city and country, and economic changes gave a new importance to the regional identities of major cities such as Manchester, Bristol and Liverpool (Mitchell 2009: 246–7).

This combination of relative disaffection from the Union and the existence of local and regional identities problematises arguments by Colley and others that Britishness was created by the construction of a homogeneous pan-British identity, which was imposed over or blended with an array of older and more entrenched regional loyalties. As Colin Kidd has pointed out, in Scotland alone various forms of nationalistic Scottishness, Anglophobia and Anglo-Britishness could all co-exist (Kidd 1993: 5). Evan Gottlieb and Juliet Shields have rightly argued that sub- and super-national forms of affiliation were not 'exclusive' or even 'antagonistic phenomena' in a period in which Britishness was 'still under construction' (Gottlieb and Shields 2013:1, 3), but the proliferation (and even intensification) of local and regional identities in Scotland, Ireland and Wales suggests that diversity continued to flourish after the Union. Some historians have even denied that there was a genuine pan-British identity in the period, leading Laurence Brockliss and David Eastwood to convincingly argue that, for most eighteenth-century Britons, the new United Kingdom was a multinational state made up of three or four distinct nations rather than just an amalgam of many regional identities (Brockliss and Eastwood 1997: 2).

In the last twenty years these arguments about the uneven and geographically dispersed rise of British nationhood have taken root in Romantic literary criticism. In part, this has led to an interest in the contribution of regional genres such as the national tale to the rise of a collective sense of British identity (see Chapter 2), but, more often than not, such criticism has seen the emergence of devolutionary or de-centralising approaches, which call into question traditional meanings of 'Britishness' and the primacy given to English literature in critical accounts of the period. 'Four nation' approaches, in particular, have explored the discrete but inter-related literatures, cultures and histories of England, Ireland, Scotland and Wales, thereby subverting Anglo-English, Anglo-centric or centre/periphery understandings of British Romanticism which suggest that the 'mores and manners of metropolitan England' are 'somehow universal' (Gottlieb and Shields 2013: 8).

The idea that British culture in the nineteenth century was made up of four nations rather than one has certainly encouraged a more nuanced understanding of English, Irish, Scottish and Welsh literature. In particular, influential studies by Trumpener, Robert Crawford (1992) and others have resisted or at least disrupted the notion that Scotland, Wales and Ireland can be considered part of a larger 'Celtic periphery', or what Matthew Arnold and others thought of as a 'Celtic fringe' (Kidd 2003: 874). Declan Kiberd (1996) and Christopher Morash (2003), among others, have shown us the extent to which the Celtic countries acted as a repository of all that England wanted to deny or banish, but, as Joep Leerssen has pointed out, the concept of 'the Celt' is more of a construct or ethnonym than a reality, and, as such, carries with it a whole series of cultural and ideological presumptions (Cunliffe 2003: 5; Leerssen 1996: 4). Jane Moore has rightly noted that, historically, the idea of 'the Celt', or 'Celticism', is linked to the cultural revivals that took place in Scotland, Ireland and Wales in the 1770s and 1780s 'as part of the vogue for antiquarianism which saw a coming together of scholars keen to recover ancient Gaelic cultures as evidence of a pre-British source of cultural identity and authority' (Moore 2011: 252). Undoubtedly, there was a shared emphasis in Scotland, Ireland and Wales on the importance of the bard or minstrel as the embodiment of a (lost) national spirit as well as on the idea of the song as a marker of national identity, but a number of scholars have pointed out that it would be a mistake to consider the bardic revivals in Scotland, Ireland and Wales as an expression of a common peripheral identity rather than as more local or regional reactions to a varying set of political, cultural and economic circumstances (Sorensen 2000: 17; Murdoch 1999: 8).

Antiquarian research of the time suggests that there was little consensus about the origins or ethnicity of the Celtic peoples: the Welsh did not always consider themselves 'Celtic', sometimes arguing that they descended from the ancient Britons; the Scots were divided between Dalriadan and Saxon Highlanders; while the Irish claimed to be descended from the ancient Milesians or Phoenicians (Groom 2014: 372). Although antiquarian works such as Sylvester O'Halloran's (1728–1807) *An Introduction to the Study of the Antiquities of Ireland* (1770) and John Pinkerton's (1758–1826) *Enquiry into the History of Scotland* (1814) solidified a regionally based sense of cultural identity by collecting and translating ancient texts from popular and folk cultures, they could also be ambivalent in their political orientation, either performing a number of socially cohesive functions by upholding Unionism or presenting alternative allegiances and genealogies to metropolitan versions of Britishness (Manning 2009: 46). Following the Union, some antiquaries in Scotland, for example, sought to preserve Scottish national feeling and to revive crypto-Catholic sensibilities by retrieving Jacobite songs or by publishing collections in the Scots language, such as Allan Ramsay's *The Ever Green* (1724) and *The Tea-Table Miscellany* (1724–37). In Ireland Charlotte Brooke's (1740–93) *Reliques of Irish Poetry* (1789) performed a similar function, publishing poems in the Gaelic language and arguing for an Irish literary history at least as long as that of England and Scotland.

Collections and histories such as Thomas Percy's *Reliques of Ancient English Poetry* (1765), Thomas Warton's *History of English Poetry* (1774–81) and Joseph Ritson's (1752–1803) *Ancient English Metrical Romances* (1802), on the other hand, can be read as part of 'a cultural project of "nation-building"' (Manning 2009: 52), synthesising a national history from the literary remains of regional cultures. While such works sought to valorise the writing of an earlier, more primitive age, their primitivism paradoxically supported an emergent brand of modern nationalism by attempting to diffuse or homogenise regional difference. The affective power and emotional spontaneity of early English, Scottish, Irish and Welsh songs and ballads therefore not only provided Romantic poets such as Walter Scott, William Wordsworth, Samuel Taylor Coleridge, Thomas Moore and John Keats with a range of alternative rhetorical registers to eighteenth-century neoclassicism (see Chapter 1), as suggested by the prose-like simplicity of *Lyrical Ballads* (1798) and the Gothic medievalism of Keats's *The Eve of St Agnes* (1820), they also uncovered a series of anxieties about the uncertain relationship between Britain and its dependent 'nations' – anxieties about authenticity, identity and the historical past that were played out as much in the literature of the period as they were on the political stage.

Scottish Romanticism

In the last twenty years a renewed critical emphasis on the Scottish Enlightenment and its thinkers (such as David Hume, Lord Kames, Adam Smith and Adam Ferguson) has re-established Scotland as an important eighteenth-century centre of learning. Edinburgh, or the 'Athens of the North', as it was then known, played a key role in the creation of disciplines that are now associated with the formation of modernity, such as moral philosophy, history, the natural or social sciences, law, economics and literature. As the eighteenth century progressed, Scotland's cultural institutions came to rival English ones and even to dominate British intellectual, critical and literary debates: not only was Edinburgh an important publishing centre and the site of the most influential review periodicals of the day such as *The Edinburgh Review* (1802) and *Blackwood's Edinburgh Magazine* (1817) (Morrison and Roberts 2013: 1–22), but Scottish writers also actively sought to make a place for their literature in post-Union Britain. Robert Crawford, for example, has explored Scotland's unique role in the formation of British literary history and identity, which, he argues, was largely generated in Scottish periodical and literary culture (Crawford 1992: 1).

At the same time, Scottish antiquarian scholarship and poetic works such as James Macpherson's Ossianic poems (1761–5) and Walter Scott's *Minstrelsy of the Scottish Border* (1802–3) were concerned to invoke the importance of a 'lost' national past by collecting, conserving, inventing and even, in Macpherson's case, plagiarising and forging popular traditions and oral cultures that were fast fading away under Scotland's insistent modernisation. As fragments of a lost national past, collections of folk songs and other forms of popular culture not only appropriated a plebian culture for an emergent middle class, but they also represented the figure of the Scottish folk hero as a source of national renewal. Ironically, such national myth-making was taking place at the very time that these traditions were being erased from Scottish society. As Ian Duncan has pointed out, the destruction of Highland clan society following the 1745 Jacobite uprising – and the subsequent Clearances or forced eviction and emigration of Highlanders in the 1760s (see Chapter 1) – were part of 'a logic of modernization' that reflected the 'uneven political geography of the country', as symbolised by the 'primitive Highlands' and the 'improving Lowlands' (Duncan 2009: 160–1). The Clearances have been referred to as a form of 'internal colonialism' which deprived native Gaelic culture of political force and prestige (Makdisi 1998: 183), but there were numerous other examples of cultural assimilation in eighteenth-century Scotland, including the introduction of the discipline 'Rhetoric and Belles Lettres' at the University of Edinburgh, which privileged English over the Scots language (Duncan 2009: 164).

Dorothy Wordsworth's (1771–1855) reference to 'half-articulate Gaelic hooting' in her 1803 *Recollections of a Tour Made in Scotland* (1894) suggests that Scots was increasingly seen by outsiders as the barbarous language of a primitive people (Wordsworth 1894: 116). Even in Scotland reviewers urged the 'Heaventaught ploughman' (Henry Mackenzie (1745–1831), cited in Low 1974: 67–8), Robert Burns, to write in English rather than Scots, indicating the heated linguistic debates surrounding the use of Scots in the period. While most educated Scots were bilingual (that is, able to write in either Scots or English), eighteenth-century authors such as Hugh Blair (1718–1800) and James Beattie (1735–1803) tended to write in standard English. The 'vernacular' poets (Robert Fergusson (1750–74), Ramsay and Burns), on the other hand, deliberately wrote in Scots or a Scots–English hybrid as, it has been argued, a 'gesture of support for a denigrated tongue' (McClure 1995: 30). By presenting himself as a 'bardie' and simple farmer of Ayrshire, Burns was able to appropriate a bardic voice, mixing traditional folk subjects with idealised representations of national character in a way that high-lighted their political and subversive potential. In 'A Bard's Epitaph' (1786), dis-cussed in the following case study, Burns combines Scots and English in a form of code-switching that has ambiguous connotations.

Case study: Robert Burns, 'A Bard's Epitaph' (1786)

In 'A Bard's Epitaph' Burns represents himself as a dying but still important national symbol: 'Is there a bard of rustic song,/ Who, noteless, steals the crowds among . . . Is there a man, whose judgement clear/ Can others teach the course to steer' (ll. 7–8, 13–14). In a punning fashion, the bard both 'steals' a position among the crowds and 'steels' that crowd towards 'frater-feeling strong' (ll. 11), or a sense of Scottish national fraternity. Burns sees the bard (and thus himself) as 'a poet whose insights convey a national per-spective and for whom self-expression simultaneously involves cultural definition' (McGuirk 1985: 106). Commenting on his own 'thoughtless follies' (ll. 23), he advises the reader to combine national sentiment with 'prudent, cautious, self-control' (ll. 29). Switching from Scots in the opening stanza – 'Owre blate to seek, owre proud to snool' (l. 3) – to standard English in the final stanza, Burns links self-control with an anglicised voice. This code-switching implies that English prudence is desirable, but the English voice is also linked to the poet's decline and death. As Corey Andrews points out, the final lines of the poem may be seen as ironic in light of Burns's bardic project of national identification, but they also created a suc-cessful model for national unification in which Scotsmen could choose either English or Scots as best suited the moment (Andrews 2004: 331).

Burns's use of both Scots and English challenges the hierarchies set out by a metropolitan norm, and creates a tension between what Murray Pittock calls 'anglopetal' and 'anglofugal' representations of Scotland's place within the British polity (Pittock 2008: 7). There is just such a tension between Scottish and angli-cised speech in James Hogg's *Private Memoirs and Confessions of a Justified Sinner* (1824), where the protagonist's devilish double, Gil Martin, speaks English in what is otherwise a Scots environment, emphasising his lack of local roots and associating English with the veneer of conventional politeness. Similarly, in Scott's novels the heroic grandeur of Fergus McIvor or Rob Roy (who speaks only Scotch Gaelic) and the humble piety of Jeanie Deans in *The Heart of Mid-lothian* (1818) (who speaks Lowland Scots) contrasts strongly with the commercial utili-tarianism of 'anglicised' characters such as William Osbaldistone in *Rob Roy* (1817). On the one hand, the use of the Scots vernacular seems to produce a simple distinction between 'insiders' (Scots) and 'outsiders' (English), but the inclusion of glossaries, appendixes and footnotes in works such as Ramsay's *The Ever-Green* and Scott's 'Scotch' novels also catered for an ever growing commercial, middle-class English readership, for whom vernaculars were commodified and oral culture repackaged (Cronin 2014: 166).

Ian Duncan has suggested that the popularity of Scott's historical novels with the English middle classes was more of a resource than a burden for Scott's contemporaries, convincingly arguing that his success encouraged alternative types of Scottish fiction, which primarily took two forms: comic and sentimental depictions of traditional, rural or small-town settings and manners; and a materialist rather than supernatural version of the Gothic (Duncan 2007: 252, 253). John Galt (1779–1839), for example, wrote historical novels such as *The Entail* (1823) and *Ringan Gilhaize* (1823), but he is better known for his essays on local history such as *Annals of the Parish* (1821) and *The Provost* (1822), which eschew Scott's romance model in favour of annalistic histories of society. Susan Ferrier (1782–1854) too ignored historical romance and wrote national domestic fiction such as *Marriage* (1818) and *The Inheritance* (1824) in the vein of Maria Edgeworth's 'fashionable life' tales, a genre earlier imported into Scotland from Ireland by Elizabeth Hamilton's (1756–1816) *The Cottagers of Glenburnie* (1808) and Mary Brunton's (1778–1818) *Self-Control* (1811). Christian Isobel Johnstone (1781–1857), on the other hand, replaces Scott's Unionist synthesis and Ferrier's conciliatory national tale with the collision between Scottish domestic romance and Irish revolutionary violence in *Clan-Albin* (1815) and *Elizabeth de Bruce* (1827).

Drama also flourished in Romantic-era Scotland, with an explicitly 'national drama' emerging in the 1800s. Joanna Baillie's Scottish-themed tragedy *The Family Legend*, for example, was produced in Edinburgh in 1810, with the help of Scott, as part of an attempt to encourage a national Scottish drama. Scott himself wrote a number of historical plays on the Scottish past, including *Halidon Hill* (1822) and *MacDuff's Cross* (1822), but the numerous dramatic adaptations of his Waverley novels proved more popular with audiences. The more successful of Baillie's plays were not primarily on Scottish subjects: her two-volume collection *Plays on the Passions* (1798, 1801), for example, included *Count Basil* (a tragedy on love) and *De Montford* (a tragedy on hatred). In the long 'Introductory Discourse' to the first volume of *Plays on the Passions* Baillie not only explicated her novel aim of illustrating individually each of the strongest passions of the human mind but also her quarrel with romance and the novel, anticipating Wordsworth's arguments in the 'Preface' to *Lyrical Ballads* when she argues that the authors of contemporary novels have 'represented men and women speaking and acting as men and women never did speak or act' (Baillie 1990: 18).

Despite a surge in Scottish literature in the 1820s, Scotland's literary eminence declined sharply after the 1830s due to the 1825–6 financial crash that depressed the book trade, and transport and financial technologies that brought Edinburgh too close to London to ensure the 'gravitational integrity' of a rival centre, as well as the reform measures which rationalised Scottish institutions along English lines and thus eroded their local autonomy (Duncan 2009:162). Even Scott's 'Scotch' novels, once considered the wonders of their day, were increasingly criticised for the rapidity of their publication and their lack of internal unity. Scott's appeal to a mass readership – the very thing that brought him such fame and financial success in his own lifetime – contributed to later judgments that his novels were more market commodities than literary works (Cronin 2014: 173). Indeed, in bidding farewell to Scotland, Thomas Carlyle's anti-novelistic experiment *Sartor Resartus* (1836) deliberately rejects the reconciliatory tone of Scott's historical novels and dismantles their insistence on the relationship between the national past and national character (Duncan 2007: 309).

Irish Romanticism

Unindustrialised, impoverished and largely Catholic, it has been argued that Ireland had neither the same investment in the Union as Scotland nor the same desire to anglicise its cultural and political institutions (Colley 1992: 322). In a literary sense, too, Ireland has proven to be a more difficult case even than Scotland. Margaret Kelleher has rightly noted that Irish literary history does not readily conform to periodisations such as Romanticism, Victorianism or modernism (Kelleher 2014: 219). Indeed, the relationship between Ireland and Romanticism has, for a long time, seemed 'propositional' rather than 'fixed' (Kelly 2011: 2). In his chapter on Ireland in the seminal collection *Romanticism in National Context* (1988), for example, Tom Dunne repudiates the standard chapter title – 'Romanticism in England', 'Romanticism in Germany', etc. – in favour of a more complex one: 'Haunted by History: Irish Romantic Writing 1800–1850' (Dunne: 1988: 68, cited in Tonra 2013). That Dunne chooses to begin his overview of Irish Romantic writing with the date of the Union says much about the kind of colonial haunting he envisages.

More recently Julia Wright (2014), Claire Connolly (2011), Luke Gibbons (2009), James Chandler (2006) and Ina Ferris (2002), among others, have reclaimed 'Irish Romanticism' as an important and meaningful term (Kelleher: 2014, 219), arguing that the late eighteenth and early nineteenth centuries form a culturally as well as a politically distinct period in Irish history. Working against both the 'gradualist' and 'separatist' tendencies in literary criticism on Romantic Ireland, Connolly rightly notes that 'neither rebellion nor Union provide a neat framing of the period' (Connolly 2011:12), with Irish Romanticism instead requiring reading strategies that are more alert to the contested nature of Irish identity (Connolly 2014: 406–7). For example, many Irish national tales, far from being insular, facilitate the introduction of cosmopolitan Europe into the Irish Romantic periphery through the figure of the traveller or returned exile (Gibbons 2009: 191). Although Joep Leerssen has applied the term 'auto exoticism', or the internalisation of imperial exotic ethnotypes (Leerssen 1996: 29–30), to Sydney Owenson's representation of Ireland in *The Wild Irish Girl* (1806), the novel's heroine, Glorvina, is nonetheless as knowledgeable about circulating Enlightenment debates in mainland Europe as she is proficient on her Irish harp (Gibbons 2009: 182).

More recent readers and critics of Irish Romantic writing have therefore looked beyond postcolonial accounts of the relationship between England and Ireland to acknowledge a more fluid world of cultural exchange, even within the confines of a primarily Anglophone print culture. Leith Davis has rightly noted that the expression of communality was made more difficult in Ireland than in Scotland because the London literary market exerted such a powerful influence over the Irish publishing system (Davis 1993: 12). But while Ireland did not have a thriving indigenous publishing culture like Scotland's, it did have an emerging periodical and review culture in the form of magazines such as the *Dublin Penny Journal* (1832) and the *Dublin University Magazine* (1833), as well as an esteemed antiquarian community, as the work of Charles Vallancey (1721–1812), Sylvester O'Halloran and Charlotte Brooke attests (O'Halloran 2004). Far from being a stagnant backwater, Ireland was modernising in the late eighteenth and early nineteenth centuries; and improving transportation and postal systems not only led to a re-evaluation of Ireland in terms of global power relations but also to a closer bond between Ireland and England (Lloyd 2013).

At the same time, there is no doubt that Irish writing in the period, more strongly even than Scottish or Welsh writing, is 'marked by a sense of grievance' (Connolly 2006: 409) steeped in the country's political turmoil and, in particular, in a series of failed rebellions or revolutions (Kelly 2011: 3). For example, discrimination against Catholics and non-conformists and the suppression of Irish culture by the British administration led to a rebellion by the Society of United Irishmen (aided by the French) in 1798. After the Union, a second rebellion led by Robert Emmet (1778–1803) in 1803 resulted in the hanging of Emmet, Thomas Russell (1767–1803) and fifteen other participants. The Young Ireland republican movement of the 1830s capitalised on the grievances that remained after these failed rebellions, although they would not launch their own abortive uprising until 1848. As Maria Edgeworth famously put it in a letter to her brother in India dated 19 January 1834: 'It is impossible to draw Ireland as she now is in a book of fiction – realities are too strong, party passions are too violent to bear to see, or care to look at their faces in the looking-glass' (cited in Zimmern 1883: 185).

In some ways, then, Ireland and Irish Romanticism could be seen as being 'on a collision course with Britishness and the ideology of empire' (Gibbons 2009: 185), thus signalling its difference from the more pro-Union Scotland and Wales. Certainly, as Jim Kelly has noted, there was scepticism in Ireland towards the kind of 'safe' antiquarian cultural nationalism taking place in Scotland (Kelly 2011: 4). In Charles Maturin's (1782–1824) *The Milesian Chief* (1812), for example, Randall O'Morven, the father of the rebel Connal, questions the political efficacy of cultural nationalism:

> Do you think that poring over an old Irish manuscript, or wandering over these wild shores, listening to an old harp with hardly a string to it will put a potatoe [sic] in your mouth, or give one stone to repair those ruins you live in, or bring back your land to you again?
>
> (Maturin 1812: 1. 66)

Similarly, Glorvina in Owenson's *The Wild Irish Girl* argues that regional Milesian pride is

> fatal to the community at large. It is the source of innumerable disorders, by promoting idleness, and consequently vice. It frequently checks the industry

of the poor, and limits the exertions of the rich, and perhaps is not among the least of those sources whence our national miseries flow.

(Owenson 1806: 118)

Siobhán Kilfeather has rightly noted that from 1798 to 1848 'the terrain of Irish fiction – and of Irish autobiography – is littered with corpses, intact and dismembered, some-times piled so deep one can hardly scramble over them to discover plot or understand characters' (Kilfeather 2004: 54). It is not, therefore, surprising that the romance plots of Walter Scott's historical novels are often ineffectual in their Irish counterparts; for example, in *The Milesian Chief* both of the plot's two love stories are violently sundered by fictional Irish rebellions that recall those of 1798 and 1803, suggesting that 'a private happiness becomes impossible when nations break' (Trumpener 2007: 332). Irish Gothic fiction, in particular, tended to problematise or 'haunt' the politics of unity and reconciliation that underpins the national tale (Killeen 2014: 16–18; Morin 2011: 4). Yet, as Connolly argues, along with these dissident representations of personal and political turmoil came 'persistent calls to mould civil society into a more progressive shape' (Connolly 2006: 408). For example, in Owenson's *The Wild Irish Girl* a young Englishman falls in love with the daughter of the Gaelic family dispossessed by his ancestors, and their marriage alludes to the Union with Great Britain. For Seamus Deane, early nineteenth-century Irish culture is even defined by a gradual accommodation within the Union: it is 'the history of a consolidated effort, frustrated by prejudice but implacable in its direction, to recruit Irish Catholics into the Union with the help of the Irish Catholic Church while appeasing the endless fears and bigotries of the Irish Protestants' (Deane 1997: 20, cited in Connolly 2011: 5).

Deane and Connolly are right in suggesting that reformist literature is equally as prevalent as dissident literature in early nineteenth-century Ireland, even if it largely follows an Anglo-Protestant/Catholic divide. As Connolly notes, the appeal and marketability of *The Wild Irish Girl* formula is evident from publications such as Charles Maturin's *The Wild Irish Boy* (1808), Henrietta Rouviere Mosse's (?–1834) *The Old Irish Baronet: Or, Manners of My Country* (1808) and Elizabeth Plunkett's (1769–1823) *The Exile of Erin* (1808) (Connolly 2006: 415). Maria Edgeworth's regional novels such as *Castle Rackrent* (1800) also project the Irish countryside in reformist terms, presenting a picture of agricultural improvement rather than invoking the nationalist energies that often accompanied descriptions of the sublime landscapes of Irish Gothic fiction, such as Regina Maria Roche's (1764–1845) *Children of the Abbey* (1796) and Maturin's *Melmoth the Wanderer* (1820). John (1798–1842) and Michael Banim's (1796–1874) *Tales, by the O'Hara Family* (1825), on the other hand, emerged from the literary culture of a rising Irish Catholic bourgeoisie and is explicitly concerned with the doubled or split nature of Irish identity.

As Matthew Campbell's magisterial study *Irish Poetry Under the Union, 1801–1924* (2013) suggests, it was not only fiction or the novel that engaged with the heady politics of the period. Thomas Moore's popular Orientalist poem *Lallah Rookh* (1817) for example, sets aspects of the failed Irish rebellions of 1798 and 1803 and debates concerning Catholic Emancipation against a backdrop of eastern exoticism (see Chapter 7). When Lady Holland wittily remarked, 'Mr Moore,

I have not read your "Larry O'Rouke". I don't like Irish stories', she was not far off the mark (cited in Meagher 2009: 243). The 'Iran' of the poem closely echoes 'Erin'; and Hafed and Hinda, the lovers of 'The Fire-Worshippers' section of the poem, can be read as portraits of Robert Emmet and his sweetheart, Sarah Curran (1782–1808) (Kelly 2009: 287–94). Similarly, Moore's best-selling *Irish Melodies* (1808–34) coincided with a period of intense debate about the 'Irish Question' (particularly Catholic Emancipation) in Westminster (see Chapter 1). Performed in drawing rooms and concert halls as well as circulating in print, Moore's nostalgia in these songs is often seen as catering for an English-speaking audience. As early as 1825 William Hazlitt claimed that Moore had frivolously converted 'the wild harp of Erin into a musical snuff-box' (VII. 234), thus muting the radical undertones of his Irish subject matter. But like Moore's prose satires such as *Captain Rock* (1824), which aimed to awaken the British Parliament to the wrongs suffered by Ireland, the *Irish Melodies* have recently been reassessed as political poems, particularly when read in conjunction with Moore's more aggressively political prose, such as his biography of Lord Edward Fitzgerald (1763–98) (1831).

Case study: Thomas Moore, 'O Breathe Not His Name' (1808)

P. J. Mathews has noted that while Thomas Moore aspired to inhabit the sphere of the Anglo-Irish ascendency, he nonetheless harboured a deep resentment towards the injustices that class had inflicted on Catholic Ireland (Mathews 2008: 3). As a friend of Robert Emmet at university, Moore was aware of his own liminal position as both a figure connected with Irish nationalism and a darling of the London drawing room. One of his most celebrated poems from *Irish Melodies*, 'O Breathe Not His Name', famously plays on Emmet's final speech from the dock, where the Irish leader rejects the epitaphs of his contemporaries in favour of a future victory for Ireland: 'When my country takes her place among the nations of the earth, then, and not till then let my epitaph be written'. Drawing on Emmet's injunction to silence, Moore's poem begins: 'Oh breathe not his name, let it sleep in the shade/ Where cold and unhonour'd his relics are laid' (ll. 1–2). As Colleen English has noted, Moore's use of the word 'shade' evokes an image of Emmet's ghost or spirit that is not yet laid to rest but is rather kept alive by the collective mourning of the Irish nation (English 2015: n.p.): 'Sad, silent, and dark, be the tears we shed' (l. 3). Yet far from being a fatalistic and sentimental portrait of Gaelic defeat, Moore's song can be read as gesturing towards a clandestine revolutionary solidarity that draws strength from Emmet's memory: 'And the tear that we shed, though in secret it rolls,/ Shall long keep his memory green in our souls' (ll. 7–8). While other poems in the *Irish Melodies* collection seem to mourn a glorious past that is irrevocably gone – for example, 'Let Erin Remember the Days of Old', ''Tis Gone, and For Ever' and 'Weep On, Weep On' – 'O Breathe Not His Name' paradoxically combines silence with a stirring call to grieve, remember and take action.

> As Leith Davis has astutely argued, while English readers saw Romantic images of Irish defeat, Irish readers could see in Moore's songs their own desire for independence reflected back to them (Davis 1993: 11).

Moore was not, of course, the only Irish poet of note in the period. Mary Tighe (1772–1810) was much admired by Moore and John Keats, and her poem *Psyche, or the Legend of Love* (1805) was a popular success. Mary Leadbeater (1758–1826), too, published a volume of poems in 1808, although she is perhaps better known for prose works such as *Cottage Dialogues among the Irish Peasantry* (1811), *The Landlord's Friend* (1813), *Tales for Cottagers* (1814) and *Lives of the Irish Peasants* (1822). Mary Balfour (1780–1819) provided eight translations for Edward Bunting's (1773–1843) popular *General Collection of Ancient Irish Music* (1809) and in 1810 published her own collection *Hope*, which contains some translations of Gaelic poetry, as well as writing *Kathleen O'Neil: A Grand National Melodrama* (1814). Critical interest in Irish women's poetry, and Irish Romantic poetry more generally, has been heightened by Stephen Behrendt's electronic text-base *Irish Women Poets of the Romantic Period* (2008), as well as by a new recognition that the literary outputs of Romantic Ireland were not limited to national tales and Gothic romances but rather encompassed a much wider range of genres, forms and rhetorical techniques.

Welsh Romanticism

Stuart Mottram and Sarah Prescott have recently drawn attention to the fact that Wales has either been cursorily treated or ignored altogether in 'four nation' scholarship (Mottram and Prescott 2012: 8–9). Jane Aaron concurs that important considerations of the rise of British nationalism, such as Trumpener's *Bardic Nationalism*, often have very little to say about Wales:

> Clearly she [Trumpener] did not find Welsh fictions which suited her argument. She would have had no trouble finding novels located in Wales, but it is certainly more difficult to find ones focusing on the type of aspiring nationhood that she ascribes to the Scottish and Irish fictions of the period.
>
> (Aaron 2007: 11)

Aaron's own work has focused on the Welsh Gothic as an alternative to integrationist national tales, emphasising figures such as the scapegoat, the sin-eater, hell-hounds, druids and Welsh witches. Indeed, many works of the period such as Robert Evans's *The Stranger; or, Llewellyn Family* (1798), J. Morrington's *The Cottage of Merlin Vale* (1809) and Evan Jones's *The Bard; or, the Towers of Morven* (1809) draw on the mythologised Celtic origins of Welsh nationalism in a way suggestive of Welsh 'otherness' rather than national integration.

How, then, should we account for the relative lack of Welsh national tales in the period? Wales was certainly slower than England and Scotland to modernise and industrialise but that does not explain its difference from Romantic-era Ireland, which, despite its relative backwardness and disaffection from the Union, pioneered the national-tale genre that is central to Trumpener's argument about bardic nationalism. While late-eighteenth-century Wales was no political threat to the crown in the way that Ireland was, for much of the eighteenth century it was nonetheless considered more linguistically and culturally 'foreign' than any of the other nations. By the early nineteenth century this had begun to change as Wales was transformed from 'a marginal province into a sector of an imperial economy' (Williams 1985: 173). Indeed, by the 1820s the increasing anglicisation and urbanisation of the Welsh south-east resulted in a dramatic increase in immigration and the growth of an English language print culture, including journals such as *The Cambrian* (1804), the *North Wales Chronicle* (1807) and the *Carmarthen Journal* (1810), which complimented a flourishing Welsh periodical press, including journals such as *Y Clychgrawn* (1793), *Seren Gomer* (1814) and *Y Gwyliedydd* (1823).

Despite the rise of an English-language print culture in Wales, 'Welshness' became ever more celebrated as the eighteenth century progressed. First, there was a revival of interest in Welsh history, language, literature and customs led by members of the new Welsh middle classes in the mid eighteenth century such as the Morris brothers of Anglesey, who founded the Cymmrodorion Society in London in 1751. The groundbreaking work of the scholar-poet Evan Evans (1731–89) and the publication of ancient Welsh poetry in his *Some Specimens of the Ancient Welsh Bards* (1764) also refuelled interest in the Welsh bardic past, as an ever increasing number of folklorists, antiquaries, philologists and lexicographers studied the Welsh language and ancient texts. Evans's Welsh language poetry, published under his bardic title Ieuan Glan Geirionydd, demonstrates an early appreciation of the Welsh mountain landscape and is written in the style of Goronwy Owen (1723–69), who had himself studied traditional bardic metres. Later in the century Augusta Hall (Lady Llanover) (1802–96) publicised the Welsh national costume; and Lady Charlotte Guest (1812–95) translated a corpus of medieval stories published under the title *The Mabinogion* (1838–45).

The revival of antiquarian interest in Welsh history was also reignited by the formation of Welsh societies such as the previously mentioned Cymmrodorion (a social society for Anglo-Welsh) and the Gwynnedigion (a society for the preservation of Welsh language and history), which not only promoted a local enthusiasm for touring old battle sites, but also assisted in raising the standard and status of local eisteddfodau, or festivals of poetry and music. Poets such as Ebenezer Thomas (1802–63) (bardic name of Eben Fardd), John Blackwell (1797–1841) (Alun) and, later, John Robert Pryse (1807–89) (Golyddan) did a great deal to raise the standards of entries to the eisteddfod, as well as to improve the status of traditional forms such as the *englyn unodl* union that had remained popular for centuries. The inventions of Iolo Morganwg also helped to cement the status of the eisteddfod as a national institution devoted to the study of Welsh history, poetry and music. The inventor of the druidic Gorsedd ceremony and the writer of hundreds of 'triads', or bardic aphorisms, ostensibly encapsulating the history and mythology of the Welsh people from pre-Christian times, Iolo's vision of Wales' glorious medieval past was largely based on material he had invented himself (Constantine 2007). In 1792 Iolo founded the Gorsedd Beirdd Ynys Prydain, which was based on the supposed activities of the ancient Celtic druidry, in Primrose Hill, London. In 1795 he returned to Glamorgan to hold his first Gorsedd in his native country, although it was not until 1819 that a Gorsedd ceremony was held after a local eisteddfod in Carmarthen, thus formally associating the Gorsedd with the eisteddfod.

Such efforts to define a positive cultural identity for Wales should not, however, automatically be conflated with expressly nationalist movements or with Welsh separatism. In some cases it is true that the Welsh bardic stance was far from integrationist: when the Welsh antiquary and harpist Edward Jones (1752–1824) published his *Musical and Poetical Relicks of the Welsh Bards* in 1784, for example, his position was not conciliatory but rather formed part of his resistance to English national tradition, deliberately evading the stadialist logic of refinement by invoking an earlier, independent and highly developed national culture (Manning 2009: 63). Yet dual loyalty for Wales and Britain can be seen in the royal patronage of Welsh societies and in some of the topics selected for the eisteddfod. Similarly, when the English-born but Welsh-residing Felicia Hemans (1793–1835) published her 1822 verse collection *Welsh Melodies* with the Denbighshire musician John Parry (1776–1851) (bardic name of Bardd Alaw) she was regarded by her Welsh audience as a 'poet for Wales' writing within the Welsh bardic tradition and its resistance to English conquest and forced colonisation. While some critics find the expansionist rhetoric of empire in some of Hemans's other poems problematic (Wolfson 2001: xvi; see Chapter 7), her *Welsh Melodies* demonstrate the durability of Welsh culture and evince a form of cultural affirmation that is nationalist but not necessarily separatist.

Case study: Felicia Hemans, 'The Hall of Cynddylan' (1822)

The sixteen songs in Felicia Hemans's 1822 collection *Welsh Melodies* are almost entirely set in the distant past and have as their subject early Welsh warriors, with a specific emphasis on the themes of invasion, conquest and exile. For example, the final poem in volume one, 'Chant of the Bards before their Massacre by Edward I', is a resistance poem which celebrates the bards' (mythical) refusal to submit to captivity. Yet despite these dark themes, the melodies are built around the 'recurring trope' of Wales as the refuge of a 'free people who, because they are free, are also rich in patriotic song' (Kelly 2002: 33). The third elegy in the collection, the four-stanza 'The Hall of Cynddylan' ('Stafell Gynddylan'), is a free adaptation of Willam Owen Pughe's (1759–1835) 1792 edition of the ninth-century *Heroic Elegies of Llywarch Hen*, an extract from which is printed (in antiquarian fashion) in a footnote beneath Hemans's own text. The poem is once again dark and mournful – 'The Hall of Cynddylan is voiceless and still,/ The sound of its harpings hath died on the hill!' (ll. 5–6) – but the silence of the hall is expressed in song, thereby celebrating the heroism and sacrifice that led to the 'desolate scene' and the near destruction of the Welsh culture described (ll. 7). As Elizabeth Edwards notes, the *Welsh Melodies* are nearly always studied in the context of 'post-colonial suffering', but Hemans was working within a period of cultural renewal that saw the emergence of a Welsh cultural public sphere, suggesting that her Welsh poems are neither apologies for the British state nor simple expressions of suffering (Edwards 2015: 93). Hemans's hopes for a revived Cambria are complicated by the elegiac context in which they are expressed, but her poems are nonetheless scholarly, archival and antiquarian, seeking to build a new future for Cambria from the Welsh past.

English Romanticism

Despite the popularity of travelogues and Oriental tales in the Romantic period (see Chapters 2 and 7), some writers presented a notion of Englishness that was more local and specific than the cosmopolitanism that appealed to their contemporaries. George Crabbe, John Clare, Jane Austen and William Wordsworth, to name but a few writers, largely set their works within England, and their localism can be seen as a deliberate gesture at a time when questions of 'Englishness' and 'Britishness' were still very much under discussion. To be English, for these authors, is to be rooted in the south of England, as represented by the view of the Hampshire countryside in Jane Austen's *Emma* (1818) (Joannou 2012: 39): 'It was a sweet view – sweet to the eye and the mind. English verdure, English culture, English comfort, seen under a sun bright, without being oppressive' (9. 391). As Jonathan Bate has pointed out in his wider study of eco-consciousness and place, Austen's 'ideal England is one in which social relations and the aesthetic sense . . . are a function of environmental belonging' (Bate 2000: 7). Similarly, Anne Janowitz has referred to Wordsworth's 'naturalized nationalism' (Janowitz 1990:133), while James Garrett has argued that, in works such as *Guide to the Lakes* (1810–35), '[t]he celebration of local variation always presupposed that "true" national character could be abstracted from the local' (Garrett 2008: 8).

The work of Austen and Wordsworth forms part of a more general 'cultural strategy of naturalizing the country, and its local social relations' (Tuite 2002: 100). As Clara Tuite has pointed out, a central component of English or Anglo-British identity was the 'nationalist romance of green England' (Tuite 2002: 150), or what Suvendrini Perera has referred to as 'the invention or reification of a green and rural core, which serves as the touchstone of the truly "English" and distances to the peripheries other cultural groupings such as Wales, Scotland, and Ireland' (Perera 1991: 35). In part, the emphasis of these writers on the English countryside was a rejection of the cultural values of the urban metropolis (Mitchell 2009: 248), but their shared vision of rural England also had the effect of underscoring the importance of local traditions for a distinctive English identity. This is not to suggest that English Romantic writers 'invented' the local or that the Romantic period was the moment in which literary localism originated – indeed, Romantic writers drew heavily on Shakespeare and Marvell (1621–78) – but rather that this was the period in which domestic, local and national identities uniquely intersected in ways that saw the beginnings of a new sense of civic nationhood, as suggested by the following case study of *Mansfield Park* (1814).

Case study: Jane Austen, *Mansfield Park* (1814)

Miranda Burgess has tellingly described Austen's novels as 'English version[s] of British national romance, (Burgess 2000: 156). Like the Gothic romances and national tales that Austen revises, her national romance uses symbolic marriages to unite competing cultures and classes, and to celebrate the English national character. Of all of her novels, *Mansfield Park* is arguably the most concerned with the politics of nationhood. It is no coincidence, as Marilyn Butler has pointed out, that Mansfield Park is located in Northamptonshire, 'the most midland county in the heart of England' (Butler 1990: xiii). In part, setting Mansfield Park in the heart of the English countryside works to bring to the fore Austen's 'anti-metropolitanism', or her 'city-versus-country cultural politics' (Tuite 2002: 149). At the core of the novel, for example, is the contrast between the urban, sophisticated, French-speaking Mary Crawford and the countrified, unassuming Fanny Price. Their battle for Edmund Bertram is much more than just a private battle of the hearts, representing a larger power struggle to establish the core values of an increasingly commercial and industrialised England.

Yet Austen's anti-urban message is only one dimension of the novel's complicated politics, which also invokes questions of nation and nationhood. Katie Trumpener has argued that, unlike writers of the national tale, Austen is alert to the complexities of cultural nationalism, citing Mary's phoney harp-playing as an example of the 'kind of [cultural] imperialism' or cultural appropriation that Austen critiques and resists (Trumpener 2007: 18). Mary's comments regarding the tardy delivery of her harp certainly indicate the superficiality of her engagement with everything the harp represents: 'Guess my surprise when I found that I had been asking the most unreasonable, most impossible thing in the world, had offended all the farmers . . . I was a little embarrassed at first by the sturdy independence of your country customs' (5. 68–9). Fanny immediately recognises the false and performative nature of Mary's harp-playing, which is a form of individualistic self-advertisement rather than a true appreciation of Celtic culture. Yet this criticism of cultural appropriation aside, Clara Tuite argues that Austen's localism ultimately participates in an 'insidious form of English domestic imperialism', which 'homogenizes regional difference' and subsumes it with a larger British national identity (Tuite 2002: 150). As Tuite points out, although *Mansfield Park* is set against Anglo-French colonial rivalry in the Caribbean, here, too, the novel reasserts its Englishness as it posits the need to uphold an 'England outside itself' with William Price's triumphant career as a sailor abroad mirroring his sister's regeneration of the domestic English estate (Tuite 2002: 152).

Archipelagic studies, regional Romanticism and border crossing

'Four nation' approaches work against Romantic self-representations of England as the 'green core' of eighteenth- and early-nineteenth-century Britain. But while such approaches seek to replace a monolithic notion of English or British Romanticism with a more carefully nuanced set of cultural contexts, some critics have argued that such criticism tends either to treat national identities as 'objective and defined' or to promote separatist Scottish, Irish and Welsh Romanticisms rather than relationships *between* nations, regions and locales. The challenge, as Nick Groom has argued, is to 'understand national identities . . . as contingent, elastic, and fugitive, as fluid and interdependent'. For Groom, regional relationships are more entangled and mutually dependent than 'four nation' studies suggest, requiring not so much a reversal of centre/periphery relations as a 'peripherization of the centre' (Groom 2014: 363). Certainly, the relationship between the four nations is one of deep and (sometimes) antagonistic collaboration rather than one of separate spheres. A case in point is Macpherson's Ossianic writing, which in its claims for a separate Scottish national identity both strengthened and elided similar Irish claims by appropriating Irish mythology for its own purposes. In *Fingal* (1762), for example, Macpherson argues against any Irish claim to Ossianic heritage while simultaneously maintaining kinship with the Irish, leading to accusations of plagiarism by Irish antiquarians such as Charles O'Conor (1710–91), O'Halloran and Vallancey (Moore 2014: 92–3).

In order to take into account this kind of cross-fertilisation within the four nations, many scholars now prefer to use J. G. A. Pocock's term 'Atlantic Archipelago', which emerges from Pocock's call in 1975 for a new British history that would stress the interdependence of, and complex interaction between, the archipelago (cited in Kerrigan 2008: 89). Comparative studies of Scottish, Irish and English Romanticism by Fiona Stafford (2000, 2010), Murray Pittock (2008) and David Duff and Catherine Jones (2007) have shown us numerous examples of conscious or unconscious collaboration between regions. Some of these studies, such as Stafford's *Local Attachments: The Province of Poetry* (2010), have even sought to displace or de-naturalise the nation-state as a central category of analysis, focusing instead on the development of, and interaction between, other forms of place and identity. John Kerrigan explains this kind of criticism as shifting attention from 'a locus that has been disproportionately endowed with influence and documentation to sites that are dispersed and more skeletally understood' (Kerrigan 2008: 80).

Archipelagic theory therefore questions older ideas of nationhood by looking at a variety of networks, connections and identities emerging from a set of more complex configurations, ranging from large-scale political union to micro-nationalist regions, including provinces, parishes and villages. There has been an increased interest, for example, in regions such as the West Country (Cornwall, Devon, Dorset and Somerset). While much work on this region to date has focused on book or social history, looking at local or county histories, antiquarianism and topographical writing (Brayshay 1996; Maxted 1982), topo-literary studies such as Simon Trezise's *The West Country as Literary Invention* (2000) and Dafydd Moore's work on West Country writers such as the satirist 'Peter Pindar' (John Wolcot (1738–1819)) and the poet/historian Richard Polwhele (1760–1838) (Moore 2008: 2014) have reconsidered the relationship between literature and the social and spatial history of regions.

This kind of 'new regionalism', as Nicholas Roe calls it (Roe 2010: vii), extends beyond book history and geographical enquires by considering regions as intricate spatial networks in which to trace the ideological contestations of the period. Roe, for example, makes the bold claim that the genuine roots of English Romanticism may lie not so much in the Lake District with the Cumberland poets but rather in the founding figures of a 'Bristol School': Thomas Chatterton (1752–70), Joseph Cottle (1770–1853) and the youthful Wordsworth, Coleridge and Southey (Roe 2010: xiii). Roe's point is not so much that regional studies provide competing paradigms or meta-narratives with which to understand Romanticism, but rather that they provide alternative cultural histories in which authors typically considered 'minor' or 'peripheral' become newly visible as significant contributors to their cultural and historical moments. One such author is the Bristol-based publisher and poet Joseph Cottle, whose own poetry has been overshadowed by his publication of important early works by Wordsworth, Coleridge and Southey while they were resident in Bristol or the nearby Quantocks.

Case study: Joseph Cottle, *Alfred: An Epic Poem in Twenty-Four Books* (1801)

As Richard Cronin has noted, many of Joseph Cottle's poems and collections from *Malvern Hills* (1797) to *Dartmoor, and Other Poems* (1823) evince a kind of local patriotism and civic pride, celebrating the West Country as a 'nation within a nation of which the capital is Cottle's own city of Bristol' (Cronin 2010: 3). In Cottle's epic poem *Alfred*, for example, the king refuses to delay a battle against the Danes while he waits for reinforcement from Mercia, arguing that Wessex must not rely on others but rather be 'Dependent on ourselves!' (Cottle 1801: 9. 273) and 'compensate for each deficiency,/ By her own courage' (9. 241–2). Alfred defends England from the Danes, but Cottle's Alfred is King of Wessex rather than King of England, reflecting a 'defiant provincialism' through which Cottle expresses his distrust of the centralised state (Cronin 2010: 4). Cronin rightly refers to Cottle's epic as a provincial, or 'cottage', epic, calling it an 'incongruous' genre that 'contradicts the values that [he] espouses' (Cronin 2010:10). Even more importantly, he links Cottle's epic to the provincialism of other epics such as Robert Southey's *Joan of Arc* (1796), on which *Alfred* was explicitly modelled. For example, like the rural Joan, Cottle's Alfred spends much of the poem in rural retirement, lodging with a humble cottager and learning from him a simple provincial ethic: ' "Rise betimes,/ "Let thy first thoughts ascent to heavenly things,/ "Be frugal, fear not work, and never drink/ "Aught but this brook' (Cottle 1801: 13. 319–22). And the poet/scholar turned military leader dwells more on the devastation wrought by the Danish invasion than on questions of nationhood or national unity: 'How beat my heart/ When as I pass'd some cottage, roofless, burnt,/ I saw the little garden, still adorn'd (11. 131–3). If, as Cronin suggests, Wordsworth's 'The Ruined Cottage' (1797) was itself modelled in some ways on *Joan of Arc*, we can see emerging in works like *Alfred* a distinct type of West Country Romanticism, which was characterised by anti-war sentiments, a defiant provincialism, a rejection of the centralised state and the advocacy of simple, rural values.

Along with this new scholarly attentiveness to regions and regionalism, Romantic criticism has seen a recent surge of interest in border spaces. Mikhail N. Epstein has described the border as a region of 'transculture', in which a peculiar set of tensions might include a 'state of not-belonging' or a hybrid amalgam of the characteristics of bordering lands (Epstein 1995: 298). As Stafford asks in her essay 'Writing around the Irish Sea' (2013): 'How firmly fixed are the sands of Morecombe Bay, or the waters of the Solway? Where does Scotland stop and Northern Ireland begin? When does Welsh water become English?' (Stafford 2013: 1). Seas and rivers, she argues, are particularly crucial places for identifying not only the relationships between local points or perspectives but also the experience of homelessness. In Walter Scott's *Redgauntlet* (1824), for example, much of the action takes place around and even *in* the Solway (Stafford 2013: 4). As the place where Scotland meets England and north meets south, it is an appropriate location for the kidnapping of Darsie Latimer, the young Englishman brought up in Edinburgh but now seeking his true identity. That Scott considers identity to be a shifting, hybrid thing is clear in the response that the blind Wandering Willie gives to Latimer's question, "Are you of this country?": "*This* country!", replied the blind man, "I am of every country in broad Scotland, and a wee bit of England to boot'" (Scott 1997: 80).

Ever prescient, Scott's own sense of British identity as simultaneously inclusive and exclusive, local and national, whole and fragmented, is crucial to much new work on the inter-relationships between local, national and global identities in the

Romantic period. Collections such as Claire Lamont and Michael Rossington's *Romanticism's Debatable Lands* (2007), Jeffrey Cass and Larry H. Peer's *Romantic Border Crossings* (2008) and Leith Davis, Ian Duncan and Janet Sorensen's *Scotland and the Borders of Romanticism* (2004), for example, not only provide numerous examples of literary hybridity and collaboration across global, national and linguistic borders, but also suggest that the border itself may be a key site for rediscovering a more nuanced, less aggressively polarised (radical/conservative) version of Romanticism. The global implications of these kinds of transnational studies are discussed in more detail in Chapter 7.

Conclusion

- This chapter outlined the rise of distinctly national literary agendas in late-eighteenth- and early-nineteenth-century England, Ireland, Scotland and Wales. It maintained that the four nations should be considered as distinct but inter-related public spheres rather than as peripheral voices, arguing against older centre/periphery models of literary production, which see English Romanticism as the dominant cultural force of the period.
- In relation to Scotland, it considered the relevance of bardic traditions and vernaculars for the development of Scottish Romantic literature. With regard to Ireland, it emphasised the role of antiquarian developments in inventing a proto-modern nation, as well as exploring debates surrounding Irish Republicanism. The focus of the discussion on Wales was similarly on revivals of Welsh bardic and druidic traditions. With regard to England, the chapter suggested that some English writers rejected the cosmopolitanism of their contemporaries in favour of a more local and naturalised nationalism, which reified the rural core of the English countryside.
- Despite considering the four nations as distinct public spheres, the chapter also explored the ways in which they intermingled and collaborated with each other, focusing, in particular, on regional and archipelagic studies, as well as considering the fluid borders of in-between locations such as seas and rivers.

5 Romanticism in the arts

Art may be called the flower of human feeling. It raises itself to the heavens from the most diverse regions of the earth in ever-changing forms.

Wilhelm Heinrich Wackenroder, *Outpourings from the Heart of an Art-Loving Monk* (1797–9)

Overview

This chapter begins with an analysis of the leading visual artists and artworks of the age, both in Britain and abroad, before moving on to assess the significance of landscape and historical painting, as well as examining the sister arts of sculpture and architecture, the popular visual arts of the period and music. In considering these various subjects, the chapter highlights shared links and correspondences between the literary, visual and musical worlds in order to demonstrate that a wider knowledge of the arts of the period is important for a more complete understanding of British and European Romanticism. Mutually informing artworks such as Walter Scott's *The Bride of Lammermoor* (1819) and Gaetano Donizetti's *Lucia di Lammermoor* (1835), as well as the Romantics' interest in ekphrasis and other ways of expressing the visual in words, suggest the need to consider the period's art forms in conjunction rather than in mutually exclusive terms. The chapter argues that such inter-disciplinarity not only reflects the Romantics' own understanding of the ways in which the arts inter-related, but also points to the blind spots in our current critical tendency to separate the literary, visual and musical domains.

***

In an age of revolutions, characterised by historic and irreversible changes, the ideas of freedom, independence and spontaneity profoundly transformed the arts in all their forms. Romantic artists deliberately rejected classical principles in favour of warmth, movement and emotion. William Hogarth's (1697–1764) *Analysis of Beauty* (1753) is, as Ronald Paulson has repeatedly argued (1993, 1997, 2003), a central text in the evolution of eighteenth-century aesthetics and one that sheds much light on the development of visual culture in the Romantic period. Hogarth's insistence that an artist should work directly from nature rather than from classical models, and his idea that what was important about a scene was not its accuracy but its enduring impression, were his chief legacies for the Romantics. Equally influentially, Sir Joshua Reynolds in the 'Fifth Discourse' of his *Discourses on Art* (published 1797) made a compelling claim when he argued that an artist should not look for perfect beauty because otherwise one 'cannot express the passions, all of which produce distortion and deformity, more or less in the most beautiful faces' (cited in Vaughan 1994: 13). Although Reynolds's 'Fifth Discourse' is not explicitly concerned with defining Romantic aesthetics but is rather a re-evaluation of his earlier theory of what constitutes 'truth' in painting, implicit in the text is the sense that the art works of the period embody the imperfections and, ultimately, the weaknesses of the age itself. It is this 'imperfection', Wilhelm Schlegel contends, in contradistinction to Johann Joachim Winckelmann's (1717–68) influential championing of 'calm grandeur and noble simplicity', that is the source of the period's greatness (Breckman 2008: 103).

Reynolds's *Discourses* also consider the hierarchy of genres in painting, ranking the significance of a composition according to its subject matter. As the most 'intellectual' genre (Wright 1997: 3), history painting (including narrative, religious, mythological and allegorical subjects) was considered the highest of all art genres, with portrait, genre (scenes of everyday life), landscape, animal and still life painting following in descending order. Paintings were also differentiated by their purpose, scale, compositional orientation, selection of physical actions and handling of form, colour, light and costume (Wright 1997: 3). The Romantic period greatly increased the status of landscape and genre painting, and also introduced the until then uncategorised 'visionary art' form, exemplified in the work of Henry Fuseli (1741–1825) and Francisco Goya (1746–1828). Although their works varied so widely that Lovejoy's argument for a multiplicity of Romanticisms could well be applied to the visual arts (see Introduction), Romantic-era artists shared at least two fundamental characteristics: creative expression was to them a reflection of the artist's inner feelings; and their work was conceived as a mirror of their own imaginative vision of the world. Romantic artists certainly felt a profound need and desire to debate which medium could best express their new ideals. As far as the visual arts were concerned, painting was considered by Karl Wilheim Friedrich Schlegel in his *General Principles on the Pictorial Arts* (1803) as the most profound way to express the turmoil of the human mind, but debates over the significance of words versus images or the greatness of the literary over the plastic arts were often resolved by synthesis rather than by opposition. Wilhelm Heinrich Wackenroder's (1773–98) sense of art as emotion ('the flower of human feeling'), cited in the epigraph to this chapter, points to the period's unifying understanding of the creative process, whereby art, literature and music walk hand in hand (art's 'ever-changing forms') aspiring to the intercession of God's divine gift (art 'raises itself to the heavens') (cited in Taylor 1987: 133–4).

Romantic scholars have long been interested in the significance of the relationship between word and image, as in Mario Praz's *The Romantic Agony* (1933) and Frank Kermode's *Romantic Image* (1957). More recently the attempt to think about Romantic literature through its relation to the visual is a central feature of Jacqueline Labbe's *Romantic Visualities: Landscape, Gender and Romanticism* (1998). Stephen Cheeke's *Writing for Art: the Aesthetics of Ekphrasis* (2008) also engages with Romantic theorising about the relation of literary texts to the visual arts. Drawing inspiration from these studies, this chapter investigates further the cross-currents between visual culture and the discourse of the visual in the literature of the period. More specifically, it demonstrates that the work of Romantic writers (see, in particular, the pictorialism of Keats's poetry) often engages with the work of artists such as J. M. W. Turner (1775–1851), John Constable (1776–1837) and Samuel Palmer (1805–81). The chapter begins by considering the importance of eighteenth-century art and art theories in the Romantic period, as well as the ways in which the work of Thomas Gainsborough (1727–88), Joseph Wright of Derby (1734–97), Henry Fuseli and Anne-Louis Girodet de Roussy-Trioson (1767–1824) offered influential models for future artists, in particular for the 'landscapists'. Crucially, for Romantic artists, the subjects appropriate for painting had evolved to include sights that excited the imagination and initiated sublime experiences: for example, the subjects of landscape art were often ancient castles, picturesque waterfalls, wild mountains and sublime dreams, initiated either by theoretical, aesthetic and philosophical treatises such as Edmund Burke's *Philosophical Enquiry* (1757) and William Gilpin's *Observations on the River Wye* (1782), or by more tangible experiences such as those of the Grand Tour.

The second half of the chapter considers how British and European artists developed the genre of landscape painting, focusing on Turner's work as the most representative of the period, not only because of his natural subjects but also because of his use of historical and literary themes (see, for example, Turner's response to Byron's work in his painting *Childe Harold's Pilgrimage – Italy* (1823) or *Modern Rome: Campo Vaccino* (1839)). This section also investigates a variety of British and European historical painters and discusses their correspondences and interactions with the development of the historical novel. It addresses as well other forms and ideas of interest during the Romantic period such as Josiah Wedgwood's (1730–95) pottery; the sculptures of Antonio Canova (1757–1822), which – like Keats's poetry – derived inspiration from many sources, including the neoclassical beauties of ancient Greece, while simultaneously celebrating the value of Romantic passions and emotive experiences at the expense of logic and reason; Augustus Pugin's (1812–52) functionalism; and Walpole's artificial Gothic mannerism. The chapter considers, too, the invention and popularity of the period's strategically marketable panoramas, dioramas and phantasmagorias, before going on to argue that music is perhaps the most 'Romantic' of the arts because it enables the composer to probe more deeply into human emotions. This part of the chapter is also concerned to re-evaluate music's relationship with the literary, as in Wordsworth's emphasis on the insufficiency of words in poems such as 'The Solitary Reaper' (1807), and in Keats's *Ode to a Nightingale* (1819), both of which contrast the expressive beauty and power of nature with human art, verbal or musical.

Towards Romanticism

Joseph Wright of Derby's emblematic eighteenth-century portrait of the amateur poet and philosopher *Sir Brooke Boothby* (1781) – who holds a copy of Rousseau's *Confessions* while reclining thoughtfully on the grass – celebrates the union of art and literature, and is the product of both British and European and neoclassical and Romantic influences. Debates about periodisation and definitions of Enlightenment and Romanticism have already been discussed in the Introduction to this book, but it is worth reiterating in this context that in the eighteenth century, when major political and social events were threatening the world's stability, the arts found, on the one hand, a common reassuring language in the absolute certainty of neoclassical models and, on the other, a more exciting, innate mode of expression in the aesthetics of sentimental models. For example, Jacques-Louis David's (1748–1825) idealisation of ancient Greece and Rome, as in his *Oath of the Horatii* (1784–5), dramatically associates past experiences with the Burkean idea of the beautiful, where the aesthetic ideal can translate into ethical and political models. It is David's attention to the morality of the beautiful that gave him the ability to speak a new language to a new audience: not the elite 'men of taste' of the eighteenth century, who used to populate the salons of the *ancien régime*, but a much wider audience, one more intellectually attentive to the development of the history of their own time.

As discussed in Chapter 2, the concept of the sublime is one of the most important developments in eighteenth-century aesthetics. It is fundamental to Fuseli's work, for example, which represented the sublime in art in an autonomous and original way. His visionary art is characterised by exotic forms, and his canvases often find pleasure in terror. *The Nightmare* (1781) is perhaps the best example of Fuseli's visual adaptation of Burke's theories of the sublime. This picture of a young woman dreaming is both topical and subversive, not only in its references to popular images of monstrosity and spectrality in the years just before the French Revolution, but also in making visible the most obscure and dark aspects of dreams and desires. Nightmares, dreams and demonic possessions are also thoroughly documented in the literature of the time. It is often through reverie or dream that fragmentary visions appear to their authors, as in Coleridge's opium-induced *Kubla Khan* (written 1797, published 1816), Thomas De Quincey's *Confessions of an English Opium-Eater* (1821), Byron's uncanny *The Dream* (1816) and 'Darkness' (1816), Keats's *A Dream: After Reading Dante's Episode of Paolo and Francesca* (1820) and Mary Shelley's more Freudian vision in *Frankenstein* (1818).

Mediated or unmediated, dreams helped eighteenth- and nineteenth-century writers and painters alike to explore more closely the relationship between the creative process and sublime visions. Some years before Fuseli's *The Nightmare*, the French painter Anne-Louis Girodet de Roussy-Trioson had already experimented with unconscious manifestations of the mind, as in his *The Sleep of Endymion* (1791) (Figure 5.1). This painting contributes to our understanding of the relationship between the Romantic and the neoclassical in art, as suggested by the following case study.

Figure 5.1 Anne-Louis Girodet de Roussy-Trioson, *The Sleep of Endymion*, oil on canvas, 1791, 198 x 261 cm.

Source: © Musée du Louvre, Paris.

Case study: Anne-Louis Girodet de Roussy-Trioson, *The Sleep of Endymion* (1791), oil on canvas, 198 x 261 cm. Musée du Louvre, Paris

While visiting the French Academy in Rome, Girodet executed this canvas with the intent of representing the young Greek shepherd Endymion in an idealised neoclassical form. Yet the mysterious, sublime and dreamlike atmosphere of the painting hints at an emerging Romantic sensibility, as the enamoured goddess Diana, here shown in the form of a beautiful moonbeam, sits on the body of the sleeping young shepherd. Moreover, Endymion is portrayed in a picturesque scene of laurel, oak, acanthus and myrtle, which is suggestive of Girodet's interest in the aestheticisation of nature, one of the main Romantic preoccupations. Whatever the Academy may have thought of this student's assignment, Girodet imbues neoclassical values with originality and novelty. His departure from David's more rigorous classicism parallels Keats's epic romance *Endymion* (1818) and demonstrates that Romantic ideals are just as capable as classical ones of stimulating literary and artistic activity. William Vaughan reads each of these works somewhat differently, arguing that a defence of classical values and materiality are the focus of Girodet's painting, whereas idealism and transcendentalism are the concerns of Keats's poem (Vaughan 1994: 225–6). Regardless of Girodet's intention, the effect of the painting, as Thomas E. Crow has pointed out, is characterised by its effort to create a vision never before seen', and by its evident duality, which combines the highest expectations of ideal beauty with transports of feeling (Crow 2006: 180).

During the course of the eighteenth century British sensibility became acquainted with another aesthetic category centred on pleasing the eye and intended to reflect a more positive and realistic idea of nature than that of the sublime: that of the picturesque. Recent studies on the picturesque, especially the work of Malcolm Andrews (1989), John Dixon Hunt (1994) and Stephen Copley and Peter Garside (1994), have investigated the literary, artistic, social and cultural history of how we look at landscape. More recently, drawing on metaphors from the visual arts, scholars such as Rosemary Mitchell (2000) and Mark Salber Phillips (2000) have read the picturesque as a historical development, looking particularly at its relationship to historical writing. Walter Scott was one novelist who used visual and painterly imagery to represent history as spectatorial and emotionally affective, as suggested by the comparison of Edward Waverley and the Baron Bradwardine in *Waverley*:

> The Baron, indeed, only cumbered his memory with matters of fact; the cold, dry, hard outlines which history delineates. Edward, on the contrary, loved to fill up and round the sketch with the colouring of a warm and vivid imagination, which gives light and life to the actors and speakers in the drama of past ages. Yet with tastes so opposite, they contributed greatly to each other's amusement. Mr Bradwardine's minute narratives and powerful memory supplied to Waverley fresh subjects of the kind upon which his fancy loved to labour, and opened to him a new mine of incident and character.
>
> (Scott 1986: 57)

Waverley's addition of 'light', 'colour', 'warmth' and 'vividness' to the minute detail and accuracy of the Baron's narratives, characterises Scott's own methodological combination of picturesque and antiquarian representative techniques in his novels.

Interest in the picturesque and the sublime accentuated the desire to tour exotic and foreign sites, as in the experience of the Grand Tour to Europe. Italy's natural beauties, as well as its artistic, historical and archaeological richness – as in the explorations of Herculaneum and Pompeii – attracted artists, intellectuals and men of culture and good taste from all over the world (see, for example, Lord Hamilton's cenacle in Naples). The language of the picturesque also characterises the illustrations of William Gilpin's *Observations on the River Wye* and, in particular, his 'A Picturesque View of Tintern Abbey'. The same goes for Turner's several works on Tintern Abbey (see, for example, *Tintern Abbey: The Crossing and Chancel,*

Looking towards the East Window (1794) and *Tintern Abbey: The Transept* (1794)). These visual representations are an earlier counterpart to Wordsworth's later poem and are suggestive of the artists' fascination with the beauties of the Welsh landscape as well as demonstrating the British Romantic fascination with an 'alternative', more local Grand Tour. As the next section will demonstrate, landscape art in Britain and Europe was strongly influenced by the institution of the Grand Tour, the aesthetic theories of the sublime, the picturesque and the pastoral, which increasingly became a literary and aesthetic means to escape imaginatively from the pressures of industrialisation and urbanisation into an idealised eulogy of the rural.

Romantic painting

Landscape art

Romantic art brought a new dimension to traditional landscape painting, as it was in nature that artists experienced a reflection symbolic of their own emotions. As a creative, pantheistic spontaneous force – both 'destroyer and preserver' (Shelley, *Ode to the West Wind*, l. 14) – nature not only offered a remedy from the pressures of the outside world, but also started to be seen as a potentially politicised entity, as in Shelley's *Ode*. The emphasis placed on nature in the Romantic period may have resulted in a so-called 'cult of landscape', but, as William Vaughan has so perceptively noted, it also gave the genre a new dimension: landscape painting was no longer considered subordinate to historical painting, but, like the latter, it was increasingly seen as capable of representing ennobling events or ideas (Vaughan 1994: 132). Thus, landscape art was not only capable of copying or mimicking nature, but also of producing new impressions and feelings: its status became akin to that of transcendental art, or, to use Coleridge's celebrated phrase, landscape art was able to create that 'willing suspension of disbelief for the moment' (*Biographia Literaria* II. 6) that makes the spectator take an active part in the imaginative process. While there were some 'topographical painters' in the period such as Alexander (1717–86) and John Robert Cozens (1752–97) (who introduced the technique of the watercolour, the lightness of which could seize the subtle shades of the landscape), John Sell Cotman (1782–1842), John Crome (1761–1821), Thomas Girtin (1775–1802) and Richard Wilson (1714–82), the work of painters like John Constable and, even more evidently, J. M. W. Turner reveals the period's new interest in imaginative meditations on landscape.

Constable's work combined a brilliant expertise in painting topographically detailed picturesque and pastoral sceneries with an ability to elicit the more meaningful resonances of such landscapes. This is implicit in the scenarios envisaged by work on his childhood landscape of Suffolk such as *Flatford Mill* (1817), a canvas inspired by Claude Lorrain (1600–82), which portrays a story of calm industriousness by the river Stour. It is both an elegy of working life and a painting of personal nostalgia, as suggested by the image of the young boy and the mill itself (once belonging to the painter's family). The painting can also be read as a reflection on the violent changes and economic recessions that had compromised the countryside of

Constable's youth, in particular the consequences of the mechanisation of farming that followed in the wake of the industrial revolution; the shift of productivity in Britain from cottage industries to manufacture; and the economic decline ensuing from the wars with France, an interest and focus that anticipates the pastoral poetry of John Clare's collection *The Shepherd's Calendar* (1827) (see Chapter 3). In particular, Constable excels in his representation of the 'art of clouds', as demonstrated by John E. Thornes's *John Constable's Skies: A Fusion of Art and Science* (1999) and Edward Morris's *Constable Clouds: Paintings and Cloud Studies by John Constable* (2000). Clouds, as both a physical phenomenon and a metaphorical one, correspond to that inner vision which projects the anxieties and worries of the whole century. Constable's inscrutable and precise use of detail in painting them – for each sketch, for example, he tended to investigate the precise time of the day and the direction of the wind – meant that they became almost more prominent than the human figures portrayed in the foreground of works such as *The Hay Wain* (1821) or *Hadleigh Castle* (1829), where the luminous effects of light and atmosphere accentuate the dramatic and sublime qualities of the scenery.

A detailed attention to the introspective qualities of landscape art is even more evident in the work of J. M. W. Turner, whose paintings can be seen as the culmination of a heightened mood that had been developing in landscape art since the 1770s. In his first exhibited canvas, *Fishermen at the Sea* (1796), Turner reveals his preoccupation with both atmospheric effects and the sublime conflict between man and nature. This is not to suggest that Turner's ideas on landscape art are totally disengaged from the picturesque, but even when the picturesque is invoked it is done so in more subjective terms than that of his contemporaries. A landscape such as *Childe Harold's Pilgrimage – Italy* is a good example of how imagination triumphs over reason, and idealism over actuality, as the place painted is imagined rather than real. When Turner exhibited this canvas at the Royal Academy in 1832 he attached the following lines from Byron's poem in which Harold meditates on the idea of an Italian landscape graced with classical ruins: 'and now, fair Italy!/ Thou art the garden of the world . . ./ Thy wreck a glory, and thy ruin graced/ With an immaculate charm which cannot be defaced' (4. 26). Byron features strongly in Turner's work (see, for example, Figure 5.2): five of his paintings were exhibited at the Royal Academy with lines taken from Byron's poems (Blayney Brown 1992). Similarly, as an illustrator of Walter Scott's *Provincial Antiquities and Picturesque Sceneries of Scotland* (c. 1822–5), Turner's often reinvented landscapes provide new symbolical and metaphorical meaning to well-known sites (Finley 1980).

If picturesque, pastoral and topographical representations had long been the concern of landscape artists, Turner's work is more fully engaged with representing the sublime, as in his sophisticated studies of the contrasts between light and darkness, whether these were representing contemporary events such as his denunciation of water pollution in a late painting such as *Rain, Steam and Speed – The Great Western Railway* (1844) or themes from ancient history, as in his canvases on Carthage or in his numerous shipwreck studies. *Slavers Throwing Overboard the Dead and Dying: Typhon* [sic] *Coming on* (1840) (the *Slave Ship)* (Figure 5.3) powerfully conveys Turner's sublime idea of a disaster at sea in its representation of what Anthony Bailey defines as 'a watery chasm' where '*[a]ll* is about to be

Figure 5.2 J. M. W. Turner, *The Bright Stone of Honour (Ehrenbreitstein) and the Tomb of Marceau, from Byron's 'Childe Harold'*, oil on canvas, 1835, 93 x 123 cm.

Source: © The Ashmolean Museum, Oxford.

Figure 5.3 J. M. W. Turner, *Slavers Throwing Overboard the Dead and Dying, Typhon* [sic] *Coming on*, oil on canvas, 1840, 91 x 122.6 cm.

Source: © The Museum of Fine Arts, Boston: Henry Lillie Pierce Fund.

lost' (Bailey 1998: 360). Although the painting – with its epical narration of the Zong incident of 1781, when 132 slaves were thrown in the open water in order to claim insurance money (see also Chapter 7) – initially appears to be a straight-forward denunciation of the slave trade, it should also be considered as a meditation on the political implications of landscape where, according to Marcus Wood, what counts, is 'anything other than sea and sky' (Wood 2000: 63).

While transcending the naturalism of picturesque or pastoral scenes, *Slavers* contributes to an understanding of Turner's work in apocalyptic terms where rage and fury are made to speak by way of the canvas's colours, as John Ruskin (1819–1900) famously reminds us:

> Purple and blue, the lurid shadows of the hollow breakers are cast upon the sky in lines of blood, girded with condemnation in that fearful hue which signs the sky with horror, and mixes its flaming flood with the sunlight, and, cast far along the desolate heave of the sepulchral waves, incarnadines the multitudinous sea.
> (Ruskin 1903–12: 3. 572–3)

The relationship between social, historical and political spheres remained a dominant preoccupation in Turner's work, especially when it deepened into more sophisticated representations, as shown in the following case study.

Case study: J. M. W. Turner, *The Fighting Temeraire, Tugged to her Last Berth to be Broken Up* (1838), oil on canvas, 90.8 x 122 cm. National Gallery, London. Turner Bequest, 1856.

Turner's specific attention to a calm but symbolically coloured waterscape in *The Fighting Temeraire* (Figure 5.4), or, as he calls the painting, his beloved 'My Darling' (Egerton 1995: 10), artfully combines with other less obvious, but equally significant subjects and themes: the picture's attention to tradition on the one hand and progress on the other; its interest in the old and the new, and birth and death; and, lastly, its delight in flouting the accepted principles of nationalism and patriotism. As Neil MacGregor has rightly remarked, Turner's *Temeraire* was the result of the painter's lifelong, painstaking and 'obsessional study of ships and seas' (cited in Egerton 1995: 9), but it is the blood-red sky – as well as the much discussed 'yellow of the sky'– which, according to John Ruskin (1819–1900), attract the viewer's immediate attention (Ruskin 1903–12: 3. 247). There is little doubt that Turner is creating here an elaborate political polemic, a coloured critique of heroism where the ship embodies the glory of Trafalgar and the sunset sky the death of such valour. Great emotion is also conveyed by the chiaroscuro shades of the 'foul, lurid, red hot malignant smoke' (Egerton 1995: 88), which comes out from the funnel of the tug, reverberating into water and air, while leaving traces of a new era of mechanised progress.

Notwithstanding the artist's clear interest in this 'new age', his riverscape is a representation of the beginning of the end of sail, wooden and oak vessels; and it sets the ground for the onset of the age of steam and iron. It is on the tall, temerarious and gracious *Old Temeraire* – as Ruskin would later refer to it – that Turner focuses his attention with the intent of emphasising her value and strength when compared to the 'little demon' of the new age. The painting can thus be understood as the 'first, strong, almost prophetic idea of smoke, soot, iron, and steam, coming to the front in all naval matters'(Rodner 1997: 52). Simon Schama has read the painting as a representation of 'the whole backstream of British history' (Schama 1995: 361–2): not only had the Temeraire fought under Nelson at the Battle of the Nile in 1798, but seven years later she also served England's heroic cause at Trafalgar. Turner's canvas thus illustrates the painter's desire to portray a certain type of national identity, or, as Dinah Birch has so perceptively put it, English identity becomes 'one of the most powerful currents of feeling in his work' (Birch 1990: 98). Yet this riverscape, which can in some ways be read as 'an essay on patriotism', also identifies the constraints of such an ideal. Interestingly, the scene that Turner captures is that of the Temeraire on her final voyage towards destruction. Birch concludes that the painting's message is that 'military triumphs do not last; ships, like men, are mortal' (Birch 1990: 45). Intriguingly, more evidence of the deconstruction of a victorious past can be perceived by reading the painting as *allos goria*, or 'something said in other terms': the sunset of the man-of-war not only becomes a mirror of the human condition, but it can be argued that her death represents the death of the landscape eco-critically speaking, as air and water pollution was a subject which greatly interested Turner.

Turner's final landscapes took his interest in atmospheric effects to new heights and became instead impressions of reality; shapes were dissolving, spaces stopped being perceptible and colours accentuated their emotional meaning, as in *Shade and Darkness – the Evening of the Deluge* (1843) and its companion piece of the same year, *Light and Colour (Goethe's Theory) – The Morning after the Deluge – Moses Writing the Book of Genesis*. Between 1845 and 1850 Turner was still experimenting with landscape art. Even when representing supposedly placid scenery such as in *Norham Castle* (c. 1845), his radical design is clear: the dissolution of light and colour makes his landscapes ever more remote from reality, sceneries become subordinate to emotions and feelings, and nature resounds with transcendence.

That Turner was the painter who understood most fully the new potential and possibilities of landscape art is beyond question, but he was not, of course, the only landscape painter of note in Romantic-era Britain. George Stubbs (1724–1806) initiated a fascination with animal paintings; Joseph Wright of Derby, who was much admired for his scientific works, as in *An Experiment on a Bird in the*

Figure 5.4 J. M. W. Turner, *The Fighting Temeraire, Tugged to her Last Berth to be Broken Up*, oil on canvas, 1838, 90.8 x 122 cm.

Source: © National Gallery, London. Turner Bequest, 1856.

Air Pump (1768), also showed an interest in animal studies (as well as studies on animals). Richard Parkes Bonington (1802–28) is known for his depictions of the French landscape; John Martin (1789–1854) provides sublime visions of 'apocalyptic darkness . . . a murk of browns and blacks, relieved only by the evil redness of the baleful blood-red sun' (Bradley 2012: 133), as in his Shelleyan *The Last Man* (1849); and Samuel Palmer mingles a Blakean sense of the visionary and the sublime with more pastoral compositions.

If Turner is considered the father of British landscape painting, Caspar David Friedrich is often thought of as his German analogue, whose meditative landscapes, painted in a lucid and meticulous style, hover between a subtle mystical feeling and a sense of melancholy, solitude and estrangement. *Cross in the Mountains* (1808), the ruins of *The Abbey in the Oakwood* (c. 1809) and his later *The Great Reserve* (1832), in their strong faithfulness to natural detail, highlight the pantheistic dimension of the painter's spiritual sentiment. In particular, the spiritualised landscape of Friedrich's Burkean yet Promethean *Monk by the Sea* (c. 1808) is an exploration of the relationship between man and the natural world around him.

Despite the general validity of Stephen Behrendt's recent statement that it is with Romantic art that for the first time humble subjects 'ordinary people, usual people' make their appearance (Behrendt 2005: 62–4), this assertion loses some of its credibility in relation to Romantic landscape art: where people are presented they tend to emphasise the sense of loneliness that comes with the fragility of the human condition, as in the Byronic claim: 'I live not in myself but I become/ Portion of that around me; and to me/ High mountains are a feeling' (*Childe Harold's Pilgrimage*, 3.72. 680–2). In the case of Friedrich's painting the figure of the monk, so hard to crystallise in the wideness of the landscape, enhances the viewer's sense of emptiness as it makes clearer the contrast between human finitude and the infinitude of nature. A monument to the triumph of nature over human aspiration, the infinite space of the landscape serves as an allegory of mankind's need for an eternal, indefinite power. For Friedrich, therefore, the role of art is not the reproduction of a natural reality or even ambience but rather the expression of sublime and universal feelings. Inspired by the teaching of Schelling's 'Nature-Philosophy', he admitted that '[i]t is not the faithful representation of air, water, rocks, and trees, which is the task of the artist, but the reflection of his soul and emotion in these objects' (cited in Sheehan 1989: 333).

The monk, undisturbed and seen from the back while facing the strength of God in nature, returns in other paintings by Friedrich such as the *White Cliffs of Rugen* (1818–19). Monks also feature prominently in the literature of the period, as in Matthew Lewis's *The Monk* (1796) and Coleridge's 'The Mad Monk' (1800). Other paintings by Friedrich have literary references: his famous *Wanderer above the Sea of Fog* (1818) is reminiscent of Byron's *Manfred* standing at the summit of the Bernese Alps (1.2.110 ff.), while his later *Sea of Ice – Wreck of Hope* (1823–4) recalls Captain Robert Walton's expedition to the North Pole in *Frankenstein* (1818). Coleridge also seeks to find in the Pacific Ocean nothing less than the essential principle that governs the 'The land of ice, and of fearful sounds where no living thing was to be seen' in *The Rime of the Ancient Mariner* (1798): 'the ice was here, the ice was there,/ The ice was all around;/ It cracked and growled, and roared and howled/ Like noises in a swound' (ll. 59–62).

The manifestation of the divine in nature is also a key part of Philipp Otto Runge's (1777–1810) work, *The Hülsenbeck Children* (1805–6) and *The Child in the Meadow* (1809) trace the dynamic of a moment of harmony with nature through a child's relationship with God. The importance of the themes of childhood and nature in the literature of the eighteenth and nineteenth centuries is well-known, but its significance for the art world has not yet been adequately explored. An interest in childhood is usually said to originate with Thomas Gainsborough's *The Cottage Door* (1780), where some children play in harmonious relationship with nature and their mother (see also Wordsworth's poems 'We are Seven' and 'The Ruined Cottage' (both 1798)). Gainsborough's *The Cottage Girl with Dog and Pitcher* (c. 1785) and *The Marsham Children* (1787) also consider the idea of innocence in nature. The Romantic idea that the child is best schooled by nature – 'by lakes and sandy shores, beneath the crags/ Of ancient mountain, and beneath the clouds' (ll. 55–6) declared Coleridge in his poem 'Frost at Midnight' (1818), written after the birth of his son Hartley – is also of paramount importance in Wordsworth's 'The Idiot Boy' (1798) and 'Intimations of Immortality' (1807). The landscape art of the period also points to the pervasive influence of Orientalism and exoticism, as in the work of Eugène Delacroix. As the next section of this chapter will demonstrate, exoticism is closely connected to history and historical painting. Napoleon's expedition to Egypt in 1798 and the Greek War of Independence (1821–32), for example, drew attention to the East, thus firing artists' imaginations further afield.

Historical art

All over Europe Romantic artists professed a fascination for history painting: that is, art works characterised by references to past or contemporary historical events, whose main feature – the verisimilitude of the historical fact – became a powerful tool for those who sought to prioritise rules and factuality over imagination and inventiveness. In the visual arts the realism of historical paintings was as much political as it was aesthetic. As discussed earlier in the chapter, the renewed appreciation of history painting was linked to the growth of interest in past cultures and distant lands, such as those of Greece and Rome (see, for example, Jacques-Louis David's *The Oath of the Horatii*, inspired by Livy's historical treaties), as well as to an awareness of Romantic ideals such as liberty and equality, which animated the events and protagonists of the revolutions. It was in this climate that David, who became Napoleon's official painter, began to establish the heroic value of the military leader in artworks such as *Napoleon Crossing the Alps* (also known as *Napoleon at the Saint-Bernard Pass*, 1801) and *The Coronation of Napoleon* (1805–7). However nationalistic David's portraits might now seem, they were intended to promote the celebratory, heroic aspect of Revolutionary France, and became an important reference point for Napoleon's supporters. On the other hand, Antoine-Jean Gros's (1771–1835) *Napoleon Bonaparte Visiting the*

Plague-Stricken in Jaffa (1804), while referencing an episode of Napoleon's campaign in Egypt, shared none of the warlike images of David's painting, but instead portrayed the fearless *exemplum virtutis* (and humanity and kindness) of the French general among images of troops decimated by the plague.

Napoleon's skill as a general and his connection with liberation was an important theme in much of the literature of the time. The third canto of Byron's *Childe Harold's Pilgrimage*, for example, is characterised by what Ian Donnachie and Carmen Lavin call 'the phenomenon of Napoleon and the import of Waterloo' (Donnachie and Lavin 2004: 259), which acquires further importance in light of Byron's own revolutionary ideals in Greece and elsewhere. Following the events of the French Revolution and Napoleon's final defeat at Waterloo, when the Napoleonic censorship was lifted and the Bourbons returned (1814–15), a climate more tolerant towards unrestricted experimentation in the narration and depiction of historical subjects took place (Wright 1997: 1–14). Whereas earlier military paintings such as Benjamin West's (1738–1820) *The Death of General Wolfe* (1770) during the Seven Years' War (1756–63) were characterised by an innovative combination of the conventions of traditional heroic painting (Wolfe's death and the news of his victory in the Battle of Quebec of 1759) and a type of modern realism (contemporary costumes), works such as Scottish artist David Wilkie's (1785–1841) rather satirical celebration of the end of the Napoleonic Wars in *Chelsea Pensioners Reading the Waterloo Dispatch* (1822) and Benjamin Haydon's equally subversive depiction of military authorities in *Chairing the Member* (1828) challenge even more categorically older understandings of history painting. It was, in particular, Wilkie's combination of the detail of genre painting with the heroic idealism of historical painting – his blending of scrupulously accurate subject matter and celebrations of domestic activities in historical settings – which altered nineteenth-century representations of historical art. Indeed, the enthusiasm for contemporary events began to fill the canvases of the age, as in Jean-Louis André Théodore Géricault's (1791–1824) political allegory *The Raft of the Medusa* (1818–19) (Figure 5.5).

Case study: Jean-Louis André Théodore Géricault, *The Raft of the Medusa* (1818–19), oil on canvas, 491 cm × 716 cm, Musée du Louvre, Paris.

For his most ambitious painting, *The Raft of the Medusa*, Géricault was inspired by a tragic event of June 1816: the wreck of a French government ship off the West African coast, largely a result of the ineptitude of the captain, a returned royalist refugee, and of its passengers' desperate struggle to survive. Of the hundred and fifty who embarked on the raft, only fifteen survivors were received on board the brig *Argus* after a number of frantic days in which episodes of cannibalism, mutiny and murder succeeded each other. Géricault's research into the facts of this episode was exceptional.

In order to paint the raft as accurately as possible he read and studied everything he could about the event: he interrogated the survivors; he visited morgues to carefully examine the bodies of the deceased, including the contractions of their limbs, and the different shades created by physical pain and mortal anguish; he travelled by sea to study the effects of the waves and the motions of the wind. Yet Géricault remained hesitant for a long time about which part of the tragedy to translate into canvas. The darkness and suffering of the mutiny episode and the compassionate efforts of the captain of the *Argus* to rescue the survivors, initially considered for inclusion, were eventually replaced with perhaps the tensest and most sublime moment of the calamity: the dramatic cry of those men who, while noticing the ship at the horizon, were unsuccessful in catching her attention.

There are at least fifty preparatory studies (sketches and drawings, watercolours and oils) showing how and why Géricault chose this specific moment of the drama. The painter initially reproduced accurate landscape and scenery details but then concentrated on the agony and pathos of the survivors. Under a dark and cloudy sky filled with tension, the raft remains unbalanced on the waters: agony, here, acquires different connotations in Géricault's rendering of mingled resignation and hope. The man in the foreground, resigned to his fate, places his hand on the corpse of his son; dead bodies and people just about to die float all around; hopeful survivors move their hands in order to be noticed, unsuccessfully, by the ship in the distance. The canvas, which was exhibited at the Paris Salon in 1819, and in London one year later, despite being a mixed success, fired the collective imagination. While it was admired for the strength of its composition and the impeccable realisation of its drama, the dark colours and the lack of order created an overall sense of perplexity. Ruskin's contemporary reading of the painting in *Works*, for example, focuses on the 'gloomy [. . .] subjects' (Ruskin 1903–12: 22. 39) of this 'modern sensational drama', and highlights the effects of the painting's 'evil modernism' (Ruskin 1903–12: 19. 212). Overall, the canvas, despite subverting the role of history painting in its signification of national identity and pride, came to be regarded as a political allegory of what Jules Michelet in 1847 regarded as 'France herself, our whole society is on that raft' (cited in Honour and Fleming 2010: 647). In recent years Albert Alhadeff (2002), Christine Riding (2003; 2013), and Jonathan Miles (2007), among others, have engaged with the social and political implications of the canvas. Riding reads the painting as 'public spectacle and sublime horror as a marketable commodity' (Riding 2003: 71): size and content – as in a panorama – gained important press coverage as a means of compensating for a lack of governmental and private patronage (Riding 2003: 67), thus intensifying the *Medusa*'s significance as a form of both entertainment and propaganda. (A discussion of panorama paintings and systems of patronage appears later in this chapter).

Figure 5.5 Jean-Louis André Théodore Géricault, *The Raft of the Medusa,* oil on canvas, 1818–19, 491 x 716 cm.

Source: © Musée du Louvre, Paris.

If Géricault became known for the conflicted tendencies of his 'realistic imagination', Eugène Delacroix (1798–1863), 'a volcano artistically hidden under a bouquet of flowers' (Baudelaire 1972: 376), found in such conflict the means for an even subtler mastery of his subject matter. *The Barque of Dante* (1822) – painted in response to *The Raft of the Medusa* – demonstrates a deep affinity with the style of Géricault in its depiction of the naked souls of the damned and the Romantic use of intense dark colours. Many of Delacroix's paintings were inspired by literary themes, such as the Byronic orientation of *Death of Sardanapalus* (1827) and *The Shipwreck of Don Juan* (1840), as well as *The Abduction of Rebecca* (1846), which, in its depiction of the scene from Scott's *Ivanhoe* when the Jewish heroine is carried off by two Saracen slaves commanded by the greedy Christian knight Bois-Guilbert, established Delacroix's fame. Delacroix was among the first French painters to explore the works of Romantic writers such as Scott and Byron and to draw illustrations for their books not only in the form of wood engravings but also with mezzotint, aquatints and stipple. He also illustrated eastern subjects, following the lead of British painters, notably his friend Richard Parkes Bonington. Although not directly influenced by one of Byron's poems, a painting such as *The Massacre at Chios* (1824), inspired by a tragic episode of the Greek War of Independence against the victorious Turks, is visibly Byronic in influence. As Vaughan rightly points out: 'Delacroix's own obsession with Greece seems largely to have stemmed from his admiration for Byron and for the poet's part in the Wars of Independence' (Vaughan 1994: 249). Here, the painter has become so absorbed with the confusion and panic of his figures – as when the Turkish knight tries to kill the mother of the woman he has just kidnapped – that he barely manages to check their diverse movements. The painting is impressive in its freedom of expression, its use of brilliant colours and, above all, its fascination with distant lands.

Being focused on scenes far away from home did not preclude Delacroix's interest in French history. As a response to the Revolution of 1830, which saw the ascension of Louis-Philippe to the throne of France, Delacroix famously painted *July 28: Liberty Leading the People* (1830), his most celebrated work, which shows the figure of Liberty – a modern, strong, sensual, bare-breasted Nike – leading the rebellious crowd in turmoil over the pictured corpses. Regarded as a heroic depiction of the Revolution, the painting enhanced Delacroix's political connections, which made possible his travels to Morocco, Algeria, England (where he was acquainted with Constable, Bonington and Turner) and Spain. Although Francisco José de Goya y Lucientes had already been dead for four years when Delacroix visited Spain in 1832, his work had an immense influence on the French painter. Goya himself went to France in exile in 1824, which has made it customary to see him as the father of French Romantic art. The relationship between France and Spain in the years from 1808 until 1814 were of great import for Goya, who was an extraordinary witness to the historical changes of his own generation. In those years Spain, decadent and underdeveloped, was under the French crown of Joseph Bonaparte, arousing a violent, anti-French resistance movement, as expressed in Goya's series of prints *The Disasters of War* (1810–20) and in his oil *The Third of May 1808* (1814), all of which commemorate the resistance of Spanish patriots to Napoleonic troops. When Napoleon was eventually defeated in 1814 and the

Spanish monarchy re-established, the hopes that Goya had pinned on the new King Ferdinand VII were soon dismantled: the monarch abolished the constitution and re-established the Spanish Inquisition (see Chapter 1). The country of the 'usurpers' now, ironically, appeared better than his own, and he left for France under the pretext of finding appropriate medical treatment.

With the exception of *The Parasol* (1777), Goya did not paint pastoral and countryside sceneries or bucolic celebrations in typical Spanish costumes. Most of his works depict subjects from history and literature. Those that are the most modern are often representations either of contemporary violence or of the subconscious. The most progressive and pressing transformation of his pictorial language emerges in his earlier series of etchings entitled *Los Caprichos* (1797–8; published 1799), which contains the famous *The Sleep of Reason Produces Monsters*, and in the visionary strength of the 'Black Paintings' of his home, the Quinta del Sordo (House of the Deaf), including *Saturn Devouring One of his Children* (c. 1820–3). This work, for Nigel Glendinning (1986) and, more recently, Robert Hughes (2003), makes Goya supreme among Romantic artists for the blind power of its representation of bestiality and the fear of usurpation, which is rooted in national history and notions related to the passing of time. Goya's work refuses the lure of absolute models of beauty and instead indulges his strong passion for contrasting shades and colours. In other words, his polemic artistic language denounces, dramatically, the violence, ignorance, superstition and errors of the Establishment. In *The Sleep of Reason Produces Monsters* Goya portrays himself asleep on a desk, graphically showing the way in which reason can be horribly transfigured by irrational impulses.

In Italy, attention to historical and literary subjects characterised much of the work of Francesco Hayez (1791–1882), a Venetian painter living in Milan. Hayez was well acquainted with the local aristocracy, who often commissioned his work. In his *Portrait of Fabrice del Dongo* (at the Battle of Waterloo), mentioned by Stendhal in *The Charterhouse of Parma* (1838) (see Chapter 6), Hayez combined his interest in historical fact with political content and sentimental effusion. As he was also looking for a more extreme kind of literature to excite his imagination, in the late 1860s Hayez shared his contemporaries' fascination with the historical content of Byron's work, in particular the latter's play *Marino Faliero* (1820), whose hero is a noble, proud but liberty-loving Doge, crowned and then decapitated, as revisited in the painter's *The Last Moments of Doge Marin Faliero* (1867). Hayez responded to Byron's work with astonishing vigour, producing a scene that surpassed anything attempted by other Romantic painters (see also Delacroix's *The Execution of the Doge Marino Faliero* (1825–6)). A historical theme was also the main subject of Hayez's most famous work, *The Kiss. Episode of Youth. Costumes of the XIV Century* (1859), which, despite the medieval reference of the title, alluded to the insurrections of the Risorgimento by showing an exile leaving behind the woman he loves. Interpreted as a good omen for the growth of the new nation, the painting reveals more complex historical and political connotations: the colours of the garments of the two youths (blue, red, white and green), for example, recall those of the French and Italian flags; it was in fact thanks to the alliance with France that Italy gained its independence in 1859.

Architecture and sculpture

It was in the field of European architecture and city-planning that the distinctions between the sublime and the beautiful had unprecedented consequences. Western architecture had long been dominated by Greco-Roman models, particularly following the rediscovery of ancient Greek monuments and the antiquities of Pompeii and Herculaneum. But it was in architecture that the attention to planning, awakened by neoclassical sensibilities, was combined with a neo-Gothic focus on the construction of parks and gardens and, within these, with the creation of small temples, false ruins and medieval buildings. The architecture of the Romantic period was therefore characterised by two styles, both of which were rooted in the past: architects and designers imitated either the classical or the Gothic style, re-interpreted in light of modern interests and concerns. More specifically, architecture translated the old principles of regularity and symmetry in diverse and new ways, responding to the widespread fascination for artistic forms distant in time (historicism) and space (exoticism). Batty Langley's *Gothic Architecture: Rules and Proportions* (1742) lauded the return of the Gothic style, which coincided with a fascination with the Middle Ages and the reawakening of religious sentiment, as in Charles Barry and A. W. N. Pugin's Palace of Westminster (Houses of Parliament) (1840–70) and Walpole's villa at Strawberry Hill, which he purchased in 1747.

Case study: Horace Walpole's villa at Strawberry Hill, Twickenham

W. S. Lewis's painstaking edition of the forty-eight volumes of *Horace Walpole's Correspondences* (1937–83) famously narrates the story of the genesis of the first Gothic novel, *The Castle of Otranto* (1764). Inspired by a dream Walpole had while residing at his villa – 'of which all I could recover was, that I had thought myself in an ancient castle . . . and that on the uppermost bannister of a great staircase I saw a gigantic hand in armour'(Walpole 1996: vii) – the novel set the pattern for the aesthetics of space of much of the literature that was to follow. In 1748 Walpole began to 'Gothicise' Strawberry Hill, his villa at Twickenham, which he had just purchased. The villa was an extraordinary mock-antique house (like Walter Scott's home Abbotsford, it was totally artificial), which Walpole intended to transform into a house-museum. He made rooms which looked like chambers in ancient medieval castles or cathedrals in order to delight and possibly deceive the unwary, echoing scenes in *Otranto* where 'the lower part of the castle was hollowed into several intricate cloisters' with 'the door that opened into the cavern' whose 'subterranean regions' appeared like a 'long labyrinth of darkness' (Walpole 1996: 27). William Vaughan rightly suggests that Walpole's 'move was a bold one' (Vaughan 1994: 101), for in creating Strawberry Hill, with its emphasis on irregularity and artificiality, Walpole inspired a new phase of the Gothic revival in both art and literature.

The Strawberry Hill enterprise was not an isolated case. Like Walpole's villa, the house-museum of the architect and collector Sir John Soane in Lincoln's Inn Fields in London (still in existence today) is suggestive of a new type of architectural functionality in its close inter-relation of house, museum and archive, combining elements of monument and mausoleum. Both Walpole and Soane's experiments anticipate Ruskin's concerns in his chapter on 'The Nature of Gothic' (1853) in *The Stones of Venice*, as well as in *The Seven Lamps of Architecture* (1849), where he argues that functionality, in its reflection of the social and political needs of a country, is the most noble aspect of Gothic art. Yet the pattern of the formation of the museum is not solely confined to the social and political implications of functionalism. Stephen Bann reads the expansion of the museum as 'an ideal source for tracing the development of historical discourse and the historical sense in the Romantic epoch'. In other words, the relation between museums and collectors was linked to 'the "historical-mindedness" of their age' and to 'how the sense of the past could be aroused by the display of historical objects' (Bann 1983: 78, 79), suggesting that experiments like Strawberry Hill represent more than a meaningless juxtaposition of armours, furnishings, stained glass and hangings, and instead demonstrate a new kind of materialisation of the past.

Unlike architecture, sculpture in the Romantic period was essentially classical in character and shared most of Winckelmann's ideas about the everlasting qualities of ancient statues, as expressed in his monumental *Thoughts on the Imitation of Greek Works of Art* (1755). The successful archaeological excavations of Herculaneum and Pompeii, and Lord Elgin's marbles shipped from Athens and sold to the British Museum in 1816, not only contributed to the rapid growth of collections of antique sculptures, but also spoke to many Romantic writers. Keats's 1817 sonnet 'On Seeing the Elgin Marbles for the First Time', in particular, shows how powerfully 'each imagined pinnacle and steep' (l. 3) of 'Grecian grandeur' (l. 12) moved his poetic imagination. His other ekphrastic poem on Greek sculpture, written two years later, *Ode on a Grecian Urn* (1819), which was published in January 1820 in the *Annals of Fine Arts*, further debates the relationship between words and the more visual and plastic arts of sculpture and painting, and begins by airing the idea that the visual arts are more eloquent than poetry.

Michael Ferber has argued that 'the urn's only function depends on its sculptured stories and its seeming timelessness' (Ferber 2012: 84), as suggested by the following lines:

> 'Oh Attic shape! Fair attitude! With brede
> Of marble men and maidens overwrought,
> With forest branches and the trodden weed;
> Though, silent form, dost tease us out of thought
> As doth eternity. Cold Pastoral!'

> (ll. 41–5)

Keats, who tries to write a Grecian urn into existence and read it out of its silence, proposes that only words can bring life, warmth and meaning to the sculptured figures on the vase. His work more generally is marked by a fascination with Greece and the Greek sculptural ideal, as is evident in other poems such as *Endymion, Hyperion* (1820) and *Ode to Psyche* (1819). In many of these poems ancient Greek art – born of ancient Greek democracy – represents the youthful spirit of political freedom. Inspired by the same intellectual and classical contexts, the Italian Antonio Canova's work shares Keats's preoccupations with beauty, truth and eternal youth, as in his sculptural rendering of *Endymion* (c. 1819–22) and in the momentous embrace of his *Amor and Psyche* (c. 1788–93), perhaps the most famous of his marble statues. Canova's work, which began a golden age of Romantic sculpture, was frequently imitated across Britain and the rest of Europe, as in the work of the Dane Bertel Thorwaldsen (1770–1844) (see, for example, his 1817 statue of the *Shepherd Boy*, which expresses those Romantic ideals of simplicity and rural life that can also be seen in the work of William Wordsworth, Robert Burns, James Hogg and John Clare). John Flaxman (1755–1826), a close friend of Blake and Canova, also admired the art of ancient Greece. His declarations in favour of the purchase of the Elgin marbles carried considerable weight. Long before Keats's poems on Greece, Flaxman produced an illustrated edition of Homer's *Iliad* (c. 1793). One of the greatest accomplishments of this sculptor was undoubtedly his neoclassical designs for Wedgwood. Flaxman's Wedgwood experience took him to Italy for seven years, where, subsidised by his patrons, he was able to absorb additional classical art, as his replicas of Etruscan and Roman pottery attest. Flaxman's tour of Italy also provided him with inspiration for his funerary monuments, which became his speciality: he raised them to Chatterton in Bristol, Reynolds in St. Paul's Cathedral and to the Corsican patriot Paoli in Westminster Abbey. Funerary monuments in Romantic art offer a visual counterpart to the Graveyard poetry of the day and provide an indication of the growing seriousness with which the idea of memorialisation and the culture of posterity was being taken in the Romantic period (Casaliggi 2012: 46–7).

The artistic marketplace and systems of patronage

Reflecting on issues of patronage and general artistic education in 'An Inquiry Whether the Fine Arts are Promoted by Academies and Public Institutions' (1830), William Hazlitt calls attention to three fundamental concerns: 1) how to offer 'the best models to the student'; 2) the necessity of providing 'immediate emolument and patronage' to the artist; and 3) the value of 'improving the public taste' (Hazlitt 1830: 370–83). Hazlitt's study opened a new direction for the Romantic artistic marketplace, which although still 'immature, and very much in flux' (Eaves 2010: 244) when compared to the literary one, was nonetheless heavily controlled by wealthy patrons and collectors such as George Beaumont (1753–1827) and Josiah Wedgwood, whose strong influence upon both the content and style of formal art ensured that many of the works produced reflected the tastes and preferences of the aristocracy or educated middle classes. By and large, this encouraged a predilection for large-scale pictures and sculptures, as in the case of John Martin's artworks; elevated subject matters as in the historical paintings; and formal portraiture.

Although portraiture and patronage may seem like two distinct topics, they are in fact closely connected: with the development of nationalist sensibilities came more opportunities for portraits of historical characters, artists and writers to be firstly commissioned and then displayed in a public context (Behrendt 2005: 65). No painter was more literary in orientation than Thomas Phillips (1770–1845). An intelligent, perceptive and learned man, quite neglected today, he became the unrivalled master of Romantic portraiture. His portraits of Blake and Byron, for example, commemorate the 'Men of Genius' and 'Men of Power' of the age (Keats, *Letters*, I. 84). In particular, his *Portrait of Lord Byron in Albanian Dress* (c. 1813) celebrates the exotic, historical and adventurous lifestyle of the ultimate Byronic hero (Byron himself), while his *Portrait of Byron* (1814), commissioned by Byron's publisher Murray and painted for the poet's half-sister Augusta Leigh (Figure 5.6), is suggestive of Byron's own obsession with his celebrity status: Byron insisted on wearing open-necked white shirts with large collars and on being painted with very pale skin, dark hair and big red lips. Byron's portraits were so important to him that Walter Scott famously referred to the poet in 1816 as 'the sculpture of a beautiful alabaster vase . . . lighted up from within' (cited in Cochran 2009: 167). Phillips's willingness to appease Byron is suggestive of the endemic commercialisation and standardisation of portraiture and of the direction that the artistic marketplace was taking more generally. Gainsborough, Reynolds, Hazlitt and Palmer,

Figure 5.6 Thomas Phillips, *Portrait of Lord Byron*, oil on canvas, 1814, 91 x 71 cm.
Source: © Nottingham City Museums and Galleries, Newstead Abbey Collection (NA 532).

as well as Hayez, Géricault, Goya and Antoine-Jean Gros, all experimented with portraiture, and some of their work challenges or even destabilises normative portraiture values, as in the case of Géricault's portrayals of the insane, which are striking because of their focus on alienation, and Goya's grotesque portraiture of *Charles IV of Spain and His Family* (1800–1), which, like no other court painting, emphasises with ruthless realism and irony the ugliness and vulgarity of the Spanish royal family.

As state or governmental patronage was much less widespread in Britain than in the rest of Europe, aristocratic patronage had a prominent role in the developments of the arts in Britain. For instance, '[t]he commercial genius of Wedgwood' (Strachan 2007: 26) has been credited with the industrialisation of pottery manufacture in Britain. Wedgwood's understanding of the artistic marketplace was unique; his attitude to it was something like a 'marketing strategy' (Eaves 2010: 244) or business venture; and the fact that he acquired notoriety was largely due to a series of calculated moves which 'cleverly capitalised on the commercial advantages of an international style' (Eaves 2010: 247). In choosing the empires of ancient Rome and Greece for his subjects, he understood the direction in which contemporary public tastes were going. But Wedgwood was also a patron to Flaxman, Wordsworth and Coleridge. Wordsworth, for example, received pecuniary support from Thomas and Josiah Wedgwood Jr, both sons of Josiah Wedgwood; and although the Wedgwood brothers assisted Coleridge more substantially, they also helped fund Wordsworth and Dorothy's travel to Germany in 1798–9. The Wedgwoods, of course, were not the only ones to respond to new directions in the artistic and literary marketplace of Romantic Britain. Notably, Sir George Beaumont, an amateur landscape painter, actor and art collector, offered his support to writers and artists such as Wordsworth, Coleridge, the young Constable and Wilkie. Even though they expressed hesitation over accepting pecuniary support from Beaumont, considering patronage a corrupting influence over art and literature, they all found themselves dependent on the 'influence, support, and friendship' (Matlak 2003: 113) of this generous Tory politician.

The most significant event in Beaumont's life was the founding of the National Gallery in London in 1826, which would become enriched by Beaumont's own fine works of art and bequests, and served as an accompanying venture to the already established Royal Academy. When George III – himself a patron to Benjamin West – founded the Academy in 1768 he was well aware that it would serve to promote the arts in Britain, while at the same time consolidating aesthetic, pedagogical and commercial initiatives. The Academy's supporters hoped that it would encourage a national and specifically British school of painting similar to that of the Italian and French tradition. The role of the Academy was calculated: it promoted nationalism and Britishness through the arts. It was also a place where the spectator-customer could go to annual exhibitions and see the paintings of British artists all in one visit. The Royal Academy, however, only extended its protection and membership to painters and sculptors and purposefully omitted craftsmen (such as engravers), as they were considered copyists rather than original artists. Blake was no exception to this injustice: as he could neither become member of the academy nor exhibit work there, he had to organise his own private exhibition in his brother James's shop. This exhibition was accompanied by a descriptive catalogue, in which Blake openly attacked iconic painters such as Claude Lorrain (1604/5?–82) and Raphael (1483–1520) in light of the denigration engravers had to face. The exhibition was a disaster and the public's negative reaction reinforced the professional difficulties Blake faced in his lifetime.

There were other examples of artistic commercial speculation in Romantic England, such as John Boydell's Shakespeare Gallery – opened in 1789, sold off by lottery and reopened as a self-proclaimed supplement to the Royal Academy – and Fuseli's Milton Gallery, opened a year later. Boydell's exhibition featured paintings by British artists with the aim of promoting historical artworks and engravings, while Fuseli's venture exhibited a series of paintings specifically inspired by the works of Milton. Both ventures were commercial failures. Yet despite their initially unsuccessful results, art galleries and exhibitions had an enormous influence on the art of the age, contributing to the development of a national style suitable to the needs of a consumer society (Calé 2006). Furthermore, the emerging Romantic culture of exhibitions encouraged those examples of Romantic sociability discussed in Chapter 3. Operating as spaces similar to the coffee-houses of the eighteenth century, art galleries not only became sites for many of the debates and controversies of the period, they also emphasised the public's special interest in 'the culture of visibility of the age' (Thomas 2008: 2).

Popular visual arts

The thriving artistic culture of the Romantic period reflects the social interests and conditions of a newly emerging industrial society. In this climate the development of profitable modes of mass entertainment such as panoramas, phantasmagorias and dioramas, to name just a few examples, contributed to the growth of the popular visual arts. In 1787 the Irish painter Robert Barker (1739–1806), while walking on a hill near Edinburgh, started the trend for panoramic paintings, blurring the line where art stopped and where reality began in his 'Panorama of Edinburgh' (1788). A panorama, whose name derives from the Greek 'pan', meaning 'all', and 'horama', meaning 'sight', is an example of how artworks were no less intended for the masses than Wordsworth and Coleridge's ballads. The fascination with illusion and deception in the period brought a new acuity to the genre of panorama, whose imposing Alpine landscapes (see the large-scale paintings of John Martin, for example) or Grand Tour cities or battlefields aimed at revisiting places and moments in memory. As an extensive education was not required to view panoramas, they had a clear impact on mainstream art. Sophie Thomas has rightly remarked that 'the panorama stood, then, at an interesting crossing of high art and popular culture, and offered mass entertainment of a notably precinematic kind' (Thomas 2008: 17).

Despite his distaste for a highly commercialised London (see also Chapter 7), Wordsworth in Book VII of *The Prelude* indicates the extent to which the marketing strategies accompanying the panorama became symbolic of the city itself.

Wordsworth's representation of St. Bartholomew's Fair, as Joel Faflak and Julia Wright perceptively note, 'is often cited not just as an excellent record of a poet's response to the spectacles of the great metropolis . . . but as an indicative catalogue of those spectacles themselves' (Faflak and Wright 2012: 90): 'that ape/ the absolute presence of reality,/ Expressing as in a mirror sea and land' (1805: 7. 248–50). Wordsworth's dexterous oral sketch, which takes the reader through every imaginable visual detail of the fair, is itself a comprehensive word panorama.

Like the panorama, the diorama – a mobile theatre device invented in France by Louis-Jacques-Mandé Daguerre (1787–1851) and Charles Bouton (1781–1853) and first exhibited in London in 1823 – was a form of popular visual entertainment aimed at reproducing 'real' magical illusions. Typical subjects for diorama paintings included Swiss mountain valleys, interiors of Gothic cathedrals and picturesque ruins. There were other artifices to be seen in the period, such as travelling magic-lantern shows (the cosmorama, pleorama and myriorama), but the most significant of all was the overtly Gothic phantasmagoria, which used a modified lantern to project frightening images such as skeletons, demons and ghosts onto walls, smoke or semi-transparent screens. Invented by the Belgian doctor-aeronaut Étienne-Gaspard Robertson (1763–1837) in the late eighteenth century, phantasmagoria was the visual companion to Romanticism's fascination with the sublime and the Gothic (see, for example, Ann Radcliffe and Horace Walpole's work or the collection of German Gothic tales entitled *Fantasmagoriana (Tales of the Dead)* (1812), which inspired Mary Shelley's *Frankenstein* as well as some of Byron's darkest poems). The influence of the popular visual arts is evident in the work of French painters such as Jean-Auguste-Dominique Ingres (1780–1867), Girodet and Géricault, who were highly indebted to this form of art. In particular, the similarities in size between Géricault's *The Raft of the Medusa* and the panorama have been noted (see the case study earlier in this chapter). On the British front, Turner too, in his first naval painting, *Battle of the Nile, at 10 o'clock when the L'Orient Blew Up, from the Station of the Gun Boats between the Battery and Castle of Aboukir* (1799), presents a 'panoramic' view of contemporary history in its depiction of Nelson's sea battle, fought to thwart Bonaparte's strategies against Britain's colonial interests. Like the panorama and diorama, the development of photography by Thomas Wedgwood (1771–1805) and William Henry Fox Talbot (1801–77) in England and by Joseph-Nicéphore Niépce (1765–1833) and Louis-Jacques-Mandé Daguerre in France also made a significant contribution to Romanticism's visual culture: grounded on earlier forms of graphic arts such as painting and print making, photography added optics and chemistry to art production.

Other forms of alternative visual art in the Romantic era include sketches, political cartoons, book illustrations, prints, engravings and etchings. The latter, in particular, were characterised by an innovative accuracy of detail: vegetation, clouds, water and trees captured the viewer's eye like words in a poem. Giovanni Battista Piranesi's etchings of imaginary prisons, *Le Carceri* (1745–61), influenced the work of writers and artists alike. Walpole's *The Castle of Otranto* and Soane's architectural efforts, for example, are indebted to the Italian architect's expertise. By conveying mental oppression and psychological anxiety, Piranesi's etchings successfully present an exaggerated architectural interiority. As we have seen above, the same goes for Francisco Goya's series of etchings *Los Caprichos*, which are inherently marked by a conflict and competition between words and images.

A sense of sublime power is implicit in William Blake's work. Among his crowning achievements as a visual artist (and poet) are his illuminated books such as *Songs of Innocence and of Experience: Shewing the Two Contrary States of the Human Soul* (1794). These works, which also showcase his exceptional technical skills, reflect old medieval manuscript illuminations, yet they also innovatively create relief etchings, where pages were engraved on a steel plate in a reverse mirror image and then printed from copperplate and coloured by hand so that the final result was a unique work of art where '[e]very word and every letter is studied and put into its fit place, the terrific numbers are reserved for the terrific parts, the mild and gentle for the mild and gentle parts, and the prosaic for inferior parts: all are necessary to each other' (Blake 2008: 146).

Case study: William Blake, 'Spring', plate 24 from *Songs of Innocence* (1789), hand-coloured relief etching, watercolour, 19.8 x 12.8 cm, Fitzwilliam Museum, Cambridge – Bridgeman Art Library (CH985826)

Blake's illustrated illumination of 'Spring' (Figure 5.7) acts as a counterpoint to the written word and adds to it an overlay of implication and complication. Although Blake scholarship (in particular, by Eaves *et al.* (1993)) has often insisted on the quasi-independence of text and image in Blake's poetry, in 'Spring' text and image seem particularly inter-related. Blake uses light washes of blue, yellow, pink and green to represent the morning light of Spring. The mother and child's gentle movements towards the sheep in the foreground and the curling lines of the trunk and branches (as well as in the wheat germs below) call the reader's (and viewer's) attention to each of the illustration's figures, highlighting the etching's symbolic references to fertility, abundance and (re)birth. Text and image appeal to all of the reader's senses, describing the arrival of the new season, while evoking the harmony of birdsongs (ll. 5–7), the mute sound of the flute (ll. 1–2) and the innocence of youth (ll. 10–11). In Saree Makdisi's words, the text should be read 'as a charged and dynamic, ever-changing, ever-reconstituted, force field of relations among elements rather than a static, inert, lifeless object' (Makdisi 2015: 14), where nature, childhood, imagination and animality simultaneously co-exist.

Most of Blake's relief etchings take their subjects from the Bible and literary texts – Dante, Shakespeare and Milton were his favourite writers – and reflect the visionary, fantastic and mystical nature of his mind's eye. Totally neglected in

Figure 5.7 William Blake, 'Spring', plate 24 from *Songs of Innocence,* hand-coloured relief etching, watercolour, 1789, 19.8 x 12.8 cm.

Source: © Fitzwilliam Museum, Cambridge – Bridgeman Art Library (CH985826).

his lifetime and known to the public after his disastrous 1809 private exhibition as '[a]n unfortunate lunatic, whose personal inoffensiveness secures him from confinement' (cited in Bentley 1975: 9), he gained notoriety thanks to a group of young artists called the Ancients, led by Samuel Palmer, who made Blake's last years both fecund and amicable.

Romantic music

If the new emphasis in the Romantic visual arts was on the symbolic imagination, in music such suggestiveness could be achieved even more effectively, as melodies and tunes, by transcending descriptiveness, augment their devotion to pure communication, creating 'meaning and significance out of [their] own elements, independent of any attempt to mirror the world outside', an idea which, according to Charles Rosen, becomes 'the model for other arts' (Rosen 2000: 83).

The musician-monk Joseph Berglinger in Wackenroder's *Outpourings from the Heart* provocatively rejects a 'painful earthly striving for words' by implicitly claiming the superiority of musical language over poetry and paintings. For Berglinger – and Wackenroder – it was music that was the true expression of the feelings of the human heart and spoke in the 'language of angels' (cited in Applegate 2005: 58), bringing man closer to an intimation of the divine. The same view was shared by E. T. A. Hoffman, who suggested that music 'is the most romantic of all arts, one might almost say the only one that is genuinely romantic, since its subject-matter is infinity' (cited in Charlton 1989: 33). Both because of its abstract form and its unique ability to reach the masses, music was deemed better able to express examples of the infinite, the indeterminate and the essential.

As discussed in Chapter 2, Romantic writers' engagement with the fragment reflects the insufficiency of language or words to transmit the full content of a message, as in Wordsworth's *Essays on Epitaphs* (1810). In the case of Wordsworth's 'The Solitary Reaper' (1807), although the reaper's song is foreign to the poet, he is able to derive inspiration from it: 'The music in my heart I bore/ Long after it was heard no more' (ll. 31–2). Coleridge's sense of inadequacy is often replaced 'with music loud and long', as in *Kubla Khan* (l. 35). For Shelley, 'music soft, and mild' is seen as a medium capable of capturing intense feelings and fluid sensations: 'That sweetest music, such as spirits of love' (*Prometheus Unbound* 3. 2. 34). Keats's engagement with the 'nocturnal' cry of the nightingale is characterised by 'Dance, and Provençal song, and sunburnt mirth!' (*Ode to a Nightingale*, l. 14), during which the speaker is all ear: 'Darkling, I listen' (l. 51). Robert Burns's songs as well as Thomas Moore's *Irish Melodies* (1808–34) form part of the revival of the ballad associated with Romantic bardic nationalism (see Chapter 4); and the union of the lyric and the ballad in Wordsworth and Coleridge's *Lyrical Ballads* (1798) offers another key example of the interaction between literature and music (Ferber 2012: 124 ff.) (for an analysis of *Lyrical Ballads*, see Chapter 2).

Romanticism's engagement with music has been successfully studied by a number of critics in recent years. Gillen D'Arcy Wood (2010) has investigated the connection between literary and musical culture in the work of Anna Seward, Francis Burney, Wordsworth, Austen and Byron. Siobhàn Donovan and Robin Elliott (2004) focus on German Romantic writers' relationship with music; Harry White's *Music and the Irish Literary Imagination* (2008) offers a seminal account of music as an enduring concern in Irish literature; and Stephen Behrendt argues that 'just as Romantic literature, visual art, and politics worked to democratize society and its attitudes, so did music contribute to the phenomenon' (Behrendt 2005: 75). Drawing on these studies, this section of the chapter will concentrate on Romantic music's connection to art and literature, arguing for the intense collaboration and trans-disciplinarity between the two fields in the period, focusing, in particular, on shared nationalistic themes and the mutual use of ideas relating to freedom, sensuality and creativity.

Romanticism in literature had been well-consolidated for decades before the movement impacted on music. It was instrumental music that better lent itself to the emphasis on feelings and the imagination that characterised the Romantic movement, as in the works of Ludwig van Beethoven (1770–1827), Hector Berlioz (1803–69), Franz Schubert (1797–1828), Franz Liszt (1811–86), Felix Mendelssohn (1809–47) and Frédéric Chopin (1810–49), among others. Other significant forms of Romantic music are opera, choral music (often associated with church songs) and the Lied (or art song). Opera followed different paths in different European countries, but its sourcing of literary works crossed all national boundaries. *Lucia di Lammermoor* by Gaetano Donizetti (1797–1848), for example, is based on Walter Scott's novel *The Bride of Lammermoor*, and Gioacchino Rossini (1792–1868) adapted Scott's *The Lady of the Lake* (1819), *Kenilworth Castle* (1821) and *Ivanhoe* (1820). Berlioz' symphonies *Harold in Italy* (1834) and *The Corsair* (c. 1852) suggest an affinity with Byron's poems, and his overtures to *Rob Roy* (1817) and *Waverley* link his work with Scott's, while Verdi's *Rigoletto* (1851) is inspired by Victor Hugo's play *Le Roi s'amuse* (1832).

Case study: Gaetano Donizetti, *Lucia di Lammermoor* (1835)

Based on Walter Scott's *The Bride of Lammermoor* (1819), Donizetti's *Lucia* strategically links music to the growing interest in historical fiction throughout Romantic-era Europe. The structure and dramatic development of the opera accordingly owe more to Scott and to the British Gothic tradition than to Italian examples. An ancient (and Shakespearean) feud in Lammermoor divides the Protestant Ashtons (Lucia's family) from the Catholic Ravenswoods (Edgardo's family). Lucia, who has fallen in love with Edgardo, the heir of the former Lord of Ravenswood, and whose estates and title Lucia's brother Enrico has usurped, has been forced to marry Lord Arturo Bucklaw, who pledges to restore the Ashtons' prestige. Gothic elements abound in the opera, as in the original text, especially when, in Act 2 Scene 8, the baleful cry of the inhabitants of Lammermoor anticipates the sudden death of a delirious Lucia after she has stubbed her husband to death. By the time Edgardo returns from a diplomatic mission in France the bell is already tolling Lucia's death. In despair he kills himself with a dagger hoping that God will reunite him with the celestial soul of his beloved.

Salvadore Cammarano's (1801–52) libretto strongly re-interprets Edgardo's death: in Scott's novel Edgar mysteriously drowns himself in quicksand near Wolf's Crag to avoid a duel with Colonel Douglas Ashton (Lucy's elder brother), but the death narrated by Cammarano for Donizetti's *Lucia* is more dramatic, ending with Edgardo's last famous words – 'Se divisi fummo in Terra/Ne congiunga il Nume in ciel' ('If we were divided on earth/may God unite us in Heaven') (Act 2, Scene 3) – which give the scene a sombre tone also emphasised by the musical sound of a solo cello. By changing Edgar's original mysterious death into a more 'romantic' ending

where love surpasses human mortality, Cammarano absolutises and spiritu-
alises human relations, thereby challenging the limits dictated by spatio-temporal categories and evincing what William Vaughan defines as 'the
moral feeling of art' (Vaughan 1994: 207) so typical of the age.

Romantic music's connection with the literary world is not confined to contemporary sources: while Richard Wagner's *Faust* (1834) is based on Goethe's tragic
play, others of his masterpieces, such as *Lohengrin* (1850) and *Tristan und Isolde*
(c. 1857–9), draw on ancient Celtic legends. *The Ring of the Nibelung* draws
inspiration from Norse mythology, while Pyotr Ilyich Tchaikovsky's *Romeo and
Juliet* pays tribute to Shakespeare. Wagner's music, like Keats's poetry, is indebted
to the principle of synaesthesia, where the senses of sound, smell, hearing and
sight combine to provide a unifying sense of perception, an idea which was also to
be explored by the Symbolists in the second half of the nineteenth century
(Vaughan 1994: 273).

These examples not only confirm the strong links between music and literature
in the period, they also point to the increasingly nationalistic tastes of their audiences. Giuseppe Verdi's (1813–1901) work, for example, is often associated with
the movement towards Italian independence from Austria and ensuing unification.
Operas such as *Nabucco* (1842) and *La Traviata* (1853) (based on Alexander
Dumas's (1824–95) 1848 novel *The Lady of the Camellias*) are nationalistic in
tone; and his *Aida* (1871) and *Il Trovatore* (1852) draw on Romanticism's fascination with the lure of the exotic in order to reflect on events closer to home. Romanticism's connection with music has also had a substantial impact on twentieth-century
pop and rock lyrics: Coleridge's *The Rime of the Ancient Mariner* was set to music
by Iron Maiden in 1984 and Blake's *Songs* and prophetic books are of interest to
folk artists (Roberts 2007: 100–1). Although Kant, in his *Critique of Aesthetic
Judgement* (section 53), opined that music is the lowest of the fine arts as it only
stimulates the mind through what Wordsworth in *Tintern Abbey* calls 'sensations
sweet' (l. 28), these sensations nonetheless reflect the complexity, ambiguity and
uncertainty of the Romantic age. It was music, Schelling contends, which was 'carried on invisible, almost spiritual wings' (Le Huray and Day 1981: 280) and whose
own silence becomes preferable to real sounds: 'Heard melodies are sweet, but
those unheard/ Are sweeter' (Keats, *Ode on a Grecian Urn*, ll. 11–12).

Conclusion

- This chapter argued that a knowledge of the arts is essential to a more complete understanding of Romantic culture. Developments in the visual arts
  were deeply intertwined with developments in literature, suggesting the trans-
  disciplinarity of nineteenth-century artworks.
- The chapter considered a variety of different art forms and genres, arguing that
  innovations in landscape painting, more than in any other category, exemplified

the notions of individualism and subjectivity typical of the age, as sublime and picturesque views offered an alternative to the neoclassical landscapes of the eighteenth century. Romantic historical art too shifted from a representation of heroic, ideal subjects to a new focus on contemporary events that reveal the ferocity and violence of human nature (as in Géricault and Goya's work), as well as providing new history/genre combinations, which unite the representation of grand events with minute and documentary detail (see the work of Wilkie).

- The artistic marketplace and systems of patronage have traditionally been seen to endorse the values of the middle and upper middle classes, but strategically marketable popular visual arts were developed in the period, such as the panorama and phantasmagoria.
- If sculpture in the period mainly drew its inspiration from classical antiquity, and architecture referenced either functionalism or Gothic mannerism, music was fundamentally reconfigured, with many critics seeing it as the most Romantic of all art forms.

6   European Romanticism

> I am a Citizen of the World – content where I am now – but able to find a country elsewhere.
>
> Byron, 'Letter to John Taaffe, Jr', 12 December 1821

Overview

This chapter examines the history of the Romantic movement in Western Europe, focusing chiefly on shared or trans-European literary, social and aesthetic debates. It presents an overview of German, French, Italian and Spanish literary culture during a period of political and intellectual transitions, but it also draws attention to the transnational connections that made European Romanticism so important for British literary circles and vice-versa. Coleridge's *France: an Ode* (1798), Wordsworth's *On the Convention of Cintra* (1808–9), Byron's *Childe Harold's Pilgrimage* (1812–18) and Shelley's *Lines Written among the Euganean Hills* (1819), to mention just a few important works, not only depict cross-cultural encounters, but also show us social worlds that are deeply interconnected through the shared experiences of the French Revolution and the Napoleonic Wars. While European Romanticism coincided with the rise of nationalism, this chapter argues that such encounters and shared experiences point to a desire for (trans)national connections and affiliations. The chapter's key argument is that it is not nationalism but rather transnationalism that best defines the literary culture of Romantic Europe.

***

Beginning in Germany in the 1770s with the *Sturm und Drang* ('storm and stress') movement, by the 1820s Romanticism had swept through Europe, conquering the French, Italian and Spanish literary worlds. Jean-Jacques Rousseau was revered as the Swiss prophet who preached a return to nature and introduced a confessional literary mode. The young Johann Wolfgang von Goethe (1749–1832) was soon to realise Rousseau's dream of a new type of passionate, emotionally affecting literature in *The Sorrows of Young Werther* (1774). All over Europe the new sensibility permeated cultural and literary phenomena: Ugo Foscolo's translation of Laurence Sterne's *A Sentimental Journey through France and Italy* (1804) is often regarded as the benchmark of Italian Romanticism, but two decades later Alessandro Manzoni (1785–1873), in his letter 'On Romanticism' (1823), more explicitly condemned artistic imitation of the classics and the habitual references to classical mythology. Lord Byron was correct when in 1820 he wrote to Goethe: 'I perceive that in Germany, as well as in Italy, there is a great struggle about what they call *"Classical"* and *"Romantic"* – terms which were not subjects of classification in England, at least when I left it four or five years ago' (cited in Day 1995: 84). Byron perceptively sees Romanticism across Europe as the product of a 'new' literature of intense emotions and infinite desires opposed to the 'old' literature of order and harmony. As already outlined in Chapter 1, this quarrel between classicism and Romanticism occurs during a particularly significant moment in history, associated with the crisis of the Enlightenment, the failure of the French Revolution, the Peninsular and Napoleonic Wars, Napoleon's fall from power and the 1815 Congress of Vienna.

The development of a new Romantic culture throughout Europe highlights some profound links and affinities between various European nation-states: in particular, a shared concern with the modern concept of nationhood; debates about rights, liberty and freedom; and a human longing for infinitude. This chapter argues for the significance of European Romantic ideas and literary works for British literary culture and vice-versa, highlighting notions of cosmopolitanism and transnational links between nations. Although the chapter tends to vindicate both Arthur O. Lovejoy's claim that diversity is a distinctive feature of Romanticism and René Wellek's argument for the essential unity of European Romanticism (see this book's Introduction), it also acknowledges alternative approaches to debates about European Romanticism, which have either replaced a focus on national contexts with a new interest in trans-European phenomena or argued for the exceptionalism of national contexts, such as studies by Remak (1961), Furst (1969), McGann (1983), Parker (1991), Bone (1995) and Ferber (2005). The chapter acknowledges Lilian R. Furst's claim in the second edition of *Romanticism in Perspective: A Comparative Study of Aspects of Romantic Movements in England, France, and Germany* (1979) that 'it is evidently erroneous to compare these Romanticisms as if they were based on an agreed definition, as if they meant the same thing' (Furst 1969: 22), but it also demonstrates that the Romantic authors of Europe are inextricably connected, not only in relation to ideas about nature, the self, the function of art and the artist and the role of imagination, but also in their commitment to political, historical and national causes.

In 1790 Wordsworth made a tour of Europe, which was then followed by several visits to France and Switzerland (some of which were with fellow poet Coleridge); Coleridge and Wordsworth also both visited Germany, and Coleridge – and later Thomas Carlyle – published works introducing German Romantic thought in Britain; Madame de Staël was banned by Napoleon from Paris and went into exile near Geneva in 1803; Byron, Mary and Percy Shelley were also in Geneva in 1816 before moving to Italy, where Byron helped the Italian revolutionaries fight against Austrian dominance in anticipation of his journey to Greece to aid the Greek revolutionaries against the Turkish Empire. Ugo Foscolo, the Greek-Venetian poet, was an advocate of Italian reunification and independence, but served in

Napoleon's army and ended up in exile in London; the French writers François-René de Chateaubriand (1768–1848), Alphonse de Lamartine (1790–1869), Stendhal (1783–1842) and Alfred de Vigny (1797–1863) also all spent many years travelling Europe in the army. It should come as no surprise, therefore, that many of these writers recorded in their writings moments of shared, trans-European social and political anxieties. Works such as Charlotte Smith's novel *Desmond* (1792), the story of a man who journeys through Revolutionary France; Coleridge's *France: an Ode* (1798), in which he initially supports the French Revolution and then explores his feelings of betrayal after the French invasion of Switzerland; *The Prelude* (published 1850), in which Wordsworth expresses his sympathies for the French Revolution; and Byron's tribute to Napoleon in Canto III of *Childe Harold's Pilgrimage* (1816) all record moments of European-wide cultural and political anxiety and are characterised by repeated attempts to define and redefine understandings of European borders and boundaries in response to various revolutions and national struggles across Europe.

Other works of the period are comparative cultural studies. Madame de Staël's novel *Corinne, Or Italy* (1807), for instance, interrogates the differences between the culture of the South (Italy) and that of the North (England), and *On Germany* (1810–13) traces the new Romantic tendencies all over Europe and America. Mary Wollstonecraft's *Letters Written during a Short Residence in Norway and Sweden* (1796) contains thorough observations of these countries, their people and society. Mary Shelley's *Valperga: or, the Life and Adventures of Castruccio, Prince of Lucca* (1823) narrates the fifteenth-century Italian hostilities between the Guelphs and the Ghibellines; and Percy Shelley's *Mont Blanc* (1816) and *Lines Written among The Euganean Hills* (1819) are sublime representations of the Swiss and Italian landscapes. Looking at some significant examples of German (Goethe, Schiller, Tieck, the Schlegels, Novalis), Swiss (Madame de Staël, Rousseau), French (Chateaubriand, Lamartine, Hugo), Italian (Foscolo, Leopardi, Manzoni) and Spanish Romantic authors (Rivas, Zorrilla, José de Espronceda), this chapter argues that if we focus on the ways in which Romantic writers thought of themselves as citizens of the world in the way that Byron did – 'I am a Citizen of the World – content where I am now – but able to find a country elsewhere' (*Letters and Journals*, IX. 78) – then the extent of their interest in developments outside of their own national context becomes clearer. While acknowledging, as Furst and, more recently, Bode have demonstrated, that 'Romanticism varies in its literary aspects from country to country, and that, as a word, it does not have the same meaning everywhere' (Bode 2005: 126), the chapter establishes that cosmopolitanism and the transnational links between nations were just as important to Romantic writers as emergent nationalist tendencies (Wohlgemut 2009).

German Romanticism

Much remarked upon features of the new 'Romantic' sensibility were made evident by *Sturm und Drang* authors Johann Wolfang von Goethe and Friedrich Schiller, as well as by philosophers such as Johann Gottfried Herder (1744–1803), who, although not always considered Romantic in Germany, focused on the role of imagination, the importance of emotions and passions and the significance of freedom. Goethe, 'the pope of poesy' (Prickett 2010: 37), whose *querelle* had in many areas resolved itself in favour of the ancients – 'Classicism is health, Romanticism sickness', he preached – was himself in many ways a Romantic (*Maximen und Reflexionen*, no. 1031). Works such as *Werther* deal with (pre-) Romantic/Ossianic themes of the destruction of love and ensuing suicide, the contrast between the real and the ideal, and overwhelming passions and youthful malaise, while *Wilhelm Meister's Apprenticeship* (1795–6), on the other hand, is a story of ordinary domesticity.

Although a rampant Wertherism and Wilhelmism rapidly spread through Europe, the formal beginning of Romanticism in Germany coincided with the publication of the review journal *Athenaeum* in 1798, on which the Schlegel brothers, the Grimm brothers and poets such as Johann Ludwig Tieck (1773–1853) and Novalis (1772–1801) collaborated. Despite its brief existence, this review outlined and developed the most significant theoretical ideas of the German Romantic School such as the re-affirmation of the concept of *Weltliteratur*, or what Schlegel called in fragment no. 116 'universal poetry' (see the case study in this chapter). If the notion of *Weltliteratur* is fundamental to an understanding of German Romanticism, it is interesting that it coincides with the publication of the more local *Lyrical Ballads* by Wordsworth and Coleridge – in other words, with what some commentators have seen as the literary commencement of British Romanticism (for a revisionist approach see Chapter 1).

As in Britain, two groups of writers can be identified in Germany: the First Generation (Early Romanticism) and the Second Generation (High Romanticism). The authors of the early period such as Tieck, Novalis, Johann Gottfried Herder, Karl Wilheim Friedrich and August Wilhelm Schlegel, Friedrich Schiller, Friedrich Hölderlin, Wilhelm Heinrich Wackenroder and Johann Gottlieb Fichte (1762–1814) were all part of the Berlin-Jena group, an association or school that adopted the cosmopolitan preoccupations and ideals associated with the French Revolution and the Battle of Jena (1806), which, in marking the subjugation of Germany to Napoleon, gave great impulse to German nationalism. While still conscious of a wider European framework, the group were intent on making German Romanticism more 'Germanic'. In the same year the Battle of Jena took place Fichte wrote fourteen lectures known as *Addresses to the German Nation* (1806). With their remarks upon national education, identity and the superiority of the Teutonic race, the lectures pre-empt Percy Shelley's preoccupations in his *Address, to the Irish People* (1812), in which he urges the Irish to fight against the British usurpers.

Susan Bernofsky provides a valuable account of the significance of early Romanticism in Germany, arguing for the central role played by the Schlegel brothers, undoubtedly the two most significant representatives of the Jena group (Bernofsky 2005: 86 ff.). Their writing primarily focuses on the distinction between classical and Romantic poetry, discussed in two groundbreaking works: *Lectures on Dramatic Art and Literature* (delivered in Vienna in 1808 and published in 1809–10) by August Wilhelm Schlegel and *On Old and New Literature*

(1815) by Friedrich Schlegel. Both texts synthesise the aesthetic program of German Romanticism by favouring the modern spirit over the order, serenity and spiritual equilibrium of classical literature. Modern writing, although lacking the harmoniousness of the ancients, contains signs of dissatisfaction and thus the desire to renew and change the world. *Lectures* contains a detailed history of drama; and in his predilection for Shakespeare, who is considered the best advocate of the great passions, Schlegel's work resonates with the dramatic models proposed by Alessandro Manzoni in Italy and Victor Hugo (1802–85) in France. Although the most important part of *Lectures* focuses on drama, Schlegel also argues for a reaffirmation of the culture and values of the Middle Ages and develops ideas about Catholicism and Christian spirituality more generally, which links his work to Coleridgean and Keatsian views on the spiritual significance of art, as well as influencing the development of Spanish Romanticism, as we shall see later in this chapter. Schlegel, like Shelley and Keats after him, considers the positive value of classical culture – Greek, in particular – but he admires the poetry of the Middle Ages as the highest example of human genius for the reasons discussed in the following case study.

Case study: Friedrich Schlegel, *Athenaeum* fragment no. 116 (1798)

One of the most distinctive and much remarked upon texts of German Romanticism is Friedrich Schlegel's *Athenaeum* fragment no. 116, which contains one of the most famous theoretical definition of Romantic poetry:

> Romantic poetry is a progressive, universal poetry . . . It embraces everything that is purely poetic . . . It alone can become . . . an image of the age. . . . It is capable of the highest and most variegated refinement . . . it should forever be becoming and never be perfected. . . . It alone is infinite, just as it alone is free . . . is the only one that is more than a kind, that is, as it were, poetry itself: for in a certain sense all poetry is or should be romantic.
>
> (cited in Breckman 2008: 76–7)

Romantic poetry, for Schlegel, represents a form of progress that is not the material and scientific one typical of Enlightenment and positivist philosophy. The progress of poetry for Schlegel is instead related to a universal notion, towards which poetry aims in its more idealistic form. This kind of progress involves the synthesis of subject and object, sensible and intelligible, the ideal and the real, where Romanticism emerges as the 'progressive', 'universal' projection directed by the regulating idea of a reunification of 'poetry' with life.

Schlegel's assessment of poetry as something all encompassing, which embraces nature, history and society in a kind of eternal development, has palpable resonances with Shelley's equally ideologically driven account of poetic responsibility in his later *A Defence of Poetry* (1821): 'to be a poet is to apprehend the true and the beautiful', where the 'true' and the 'beautiful' are ethically charged concepts (482). The same goes for the chameleon-like qualities of Keats's poet, which are forever changing and progressing: for Keats, the poet is the most 'unpoetical of anything in existence; because he has no Identity – he is continually in[forming] – and filling some other Body' (*Letters*, I. 386–7) (be it a nightingale, a Grecian urn or the Elgin marbles). As in a Vichian *corsi* and *ricorsi* cycle, the poet takes on the character of someone else or some other situation.

Although the emergence of the Jena group is traditionally associated with the theories of the Schlegel brothers, the three great poets of the group were Tieck, Hölderlin and, above all, Novalis. The latter's *Hymns to the Night* (1800), with their emphasis on the loss of a beloved, their desire to overcome the material and to reach the infinite, their spiritual longing to reach God and a general fascination with the theme of death, resonate with the sublime taste of northern European Romantic poetry and, in particular, with Novalis's readings of Edward Young's *Night Thoughts* (1795–7). Among the Early Romantics, Hölderlin has been described as 'the greatest poet of the age' (Bernofsky 2005: 97). Deeply fascinated by the culture of Greece and the Greeks, his poetry is a mixture of epic and drama, but it is with his novel *Hyperion or the Hermit in Greece* (1797–9) that he most fully maintains the glory of the ancient past. In Hyperion's fights against the Turks for the independence of Greece one can see a striking parallelism with Byron's involvement in the Greek cause. Like Hyperion, who fails and becomes a hermit, Byron dies not on the battlefield, as he would have loved, but of fever. Hölderlin shares his love for antiquity and Greek mythology with Keats, whose own unfinished epic fragments, *Hyperion* (1820) and *The Fall of Hyperion* (published 1856), reimagine the French Revolution in a classical context of revolt and defeat. Paul de Man's essay 'Keats and Hölderlin' (1956) indicates the ways in which the work of both writers can be understood in relation to shared philosophical and aesthetic principles, an idea extended in his 'Wordsworth and Hölderlin' (1966) (Gabriel 1989: 116 ff.). The Jena group's connection to British Romanticism is not confined to Hölderlin and his work. Schiller's play *The Robbers* (1782), for example, produced characters who became models for the Romantic self in Ann Radcliffe's Gothic novels (see, in particular, the episode of Ricardo, one of the banditti, in *A Sicilian Romance* (1792)).

The Second Generation of German Romantics – Clemens Brentano (1778–1842), Ludwig Achim von Arnim (1781–1831), Joseph Freiherr von Eichendorff (1788–1857), Adelbert von Chamisso (1781–1838) and Jacob and Wilhelm Grimm (1785–1863, 1786–1859) – were also known as the Heidelberg group (1805–15). Their shared tropes and themes include spiritual turmoil and instability, a search for escape from reality and a refuge in irony, which reveals a bitter consciousness of the limits of human possibility. In particular, E. T. A. Hoffman's oneiric visions, mysterious evocations and fantastical worlds, as in his collection of stories *The Night Pieces* (1817), resonate with the English Graveyard tradition discussed in Chapter 2. They also inspired Charles Nodier's (1781–1844) French Gothic tales of vampires such as *Smarra, or the Demons of the Night* (1821), *Trilby* (1822) and the stage adaptation *The Vampire* (1820) (based on John Polidori's *The Vampyre* (1819)) (see Lokke 2005: 148 ff.).

Significantly involved in the political and social struggles of her time, the work of the Swiss-born Madame de Staël was influential throughout Europe. Her trip to Germany in 1803, where she met Goethe and Schiller in Weimar, awoke her interest in German literature, particularly that of Wilhelm Schlegel. In 1807 she returned to Germany and wrote one of her major works, *De L'Allemagne* (1810–13), a twelve-hundred-page effort. John Claiborne Isbell contends that it was Madame de Staël who 'invented a European [R]omanticism' (Isbell 1994: 4). Her writing attributes to German culture that depth and sincerity of feeling that are proposed as a model for a new European consciousness. While concentrating on the opposition between literature of the north and the south, she also develops the link between classical and Romantic poetry, where the latter is seen as 'a modern, national, Christian and lyrical literature inspired by the restlessness of the age and the exaltation of the I' (*De L'Allemagne* II, 1. 1) (own translation). This work expresses some of the key shared themes of European Romanticism such as anxiety, melancholy and lyric enthusiasm, but, above all, *De L'Allemagne* aims at developing a truly national literature which derives its character and its inspiration from the character and traditions of the people of a country (Moore 2005: 181).

Despite its latent nationalism, *De L'Allemagne* represents a turning point for the development of a European Romantic school (de Staël counted Schiller, Goethe, Schlegel and Byron among her personal friends), if not for its original qualities then certainly for its synthesis of theoretical formulations that developed in Germany at the beginning of the century. German Romanticism was influential in a number of other national contexts, shaping not only the work of British authors such as Keats, Coleridge and Radcliffe, but also writers of the South, including those involved in the development of Italian, Spanish and French Romanticism.

French Romanticism

In the Latin countries the Romantic movement started later than in the northern nations of Germany and Britain. Yet in the period between the Consulate (1799–1804) and the 1848 Revolutions the word 'Romanticism' acquires a momentous status and role in French literature and culture. Its origins lie in a change of sensibility among writers and philosophers of the second half of the eighteenth century up to the fall of the French Empire (1814), whose works consider the horrors of the Revolution, the Napoleonic Wars and the restoration of monarchy. Yet while some French Romantic writing can be seen as a response to national events and sources, it was increasingly understood that these national events had taken on a European-wide significance. *Poetical Meditations* (1820) by Lamartine, and Hugo's *Hernani* (1830) and *The Burgraves* (1843), for example, showcase great French dates and events, but at the same time a new cosmopolitanism was generated by emigration after the Revolution and the transnational encounters of the Napoleonic Wars (see also Chapter 7 on émigré experience). There were also collaborations and borrowings between French and other European writers. Goethe's

Werther (1775) and Sir Walter Scott's novels, for instance, inspired an entire generation of French writers.

The exploration of self-hood that we have already considered in relation to British Romanticism (see Chapter 2) is also one of the main characteristics of French Romanticism and ranges from the '*vague des passions*' (vagueness, uncertainty of sentiment and passion) of Chateaubriand's *The Genius of Christianity; or the Spirit and Beauty of the Christian Religion* (1802) – 'I am nothing; I am only a simple, solitary wanderer . . . It is in the prospect of the sublime scenes of nature that this unknown Being manifests himself to the human heart' (Breckman 2008: 86) – through the '*mal du siècle*' ('the malady of the century') to *The Confession of a Child of the Century* (1836), *Volupté* (1835), and *Indiana* (1832) by De Musset, Sainte-Beuve and George Sand respectively. A host of writers before them such as Rousseau, Étienne Pivert de Senancour (1770–1846) and Benjamin Constant (1767–1830) had recognised for the first time the radical significance of the unique 'I': Chateaubriand's *René* (1802) and *Atala* (1801), Madame de Staël's *Corinne, Or Italy* (1807) and Constant's *Adolphe* (1816) are all spiritual brothers to Byron's *Manfred* and *Childe Harold*, representing the internal embodiment of the quest romance.

Memoirs from Beyond the Grave (1848–50) by Chateaubriand, which he starts writing in 1809 and in which he combines the history of his own ideas and feelings with the history of his time (particularly regarding Napoleon), fascinates the reader with its extraordinary portrayal of a pilgrimage through Central Europe while simultaneously recalling the settings of Byron's *Childe Harold*. René and Harold have much in common. The relationship between Chateaubriand (1768–1848) and Byron has recently been noted by Stephen Minta (2013), Jeffrey N. Cox (2014) and Carla Tuite (2015), whose works have, in particular, highlighted both writers' engagement with the French Revolution and ensuing Napoleonic Wars. Moreover, the very title of Chateaubriand's *Memoirs* resonates with the epic poems of Ossian published by James Macpherson from 1760, and with the Graveyard School and the poetry of Thomas Gray, in particular, whose work Chateaubriand discovered during his stay in London in 1793. Chateaubriand's European focus is also evident in other works such as *An Historical, Political and Moral Essay on Revolutions, Ancient and Modern* (1797, trans. 1815), in which a mythical but occasionally demonic Napoleon acquires the status of the ultimate Romantic icon (Bainbridge 2005: 450 ff.), and *René* (1802), which highlights the relationship between France and Italy, Greece, England, Palestine and Egypt, as well as considering the ruins of the past more generally (see also his *Lettre sur la Campagne Romaine* (1804)). It was not only the landscape of Europe which captured the imagination of Chateaubriand: he had already portrayed exotic scenery in *René* and *Atala*, but it is his *Voyage en Amérique* (1826) (he travelled to America in 1791) which emphasises the lure of exotic and foreign lands while also accentuating man's communion with nature in the manner of the natural poetry of the Lake Poets (for an examination of transatlantic Romanticism see Chapter 7).

As we noted earlier, Germaine de Staël's work offers a cosmopolitan appreciation of the varied cultural contributions of European nationalism, as in *De la*

Littérature: considérée dans ses rapports avec les Institutions Sociales (1800) (henceforth 'On Literature'), which not only examines the influence of religion on literature, but also offers a theory of the progress of literature and civilisation. De Staël's *Corinne: or Italy*, written after her tour of the country in 1804, suggests her admiration for Rome, the Capitol, Vesuvius and numerous churches: the novel glorifies Italy and its art and architecture in a way similar to Cantos III and IV of Byron's *Childe Harold*. It also compares the relationship between the climate, geography, political institutions and art of two different European nations (France and Italy). The cosmopolitanism of French Romanticism is emphasised by another 'Romancier du Moi': Lamartine, whose *Poetical Meditations* – see, in particular, 'The Lake', 'Isolation', 'The Evening', 'Man' (dedicated to Byron), 'Autumn' (reminiscent of Keats) – and *Poetic and Religious Harmonies* (1830) such as 'The Occident' (evocative of Shelley's *Ode to the West Wind*) suggest further links between British and French Romanticism.

Case study: Alphonse de Lamartine, 'Man' from *Poetical Meditations* (1820)

Along with the theme of lost love, in his *Meditations* Lamartine explores the value of the Christian religion. Above all, it is the thought of what is beyond death which haunts him, and he desires, in particular, an eternal life which could compensate for the hardship of the terrestrial one. Lamartinean critics such as Aimée Boutin (2001) have focused on the inter-relation in his meditations of love and religion, arguing that the union of these two themes constitutes the originality of his work. This union is the main focus of his second meditation, 'L'Homme' ('Man'), dedicated to Byron, in which Lamartine engages with the poetic vision of his Romantic predecessor in ways that suggest both attraction and rejection. Lamartine sets the tone of the poem by comparing the sound of Byron's poetry with lightning and wind – 'mixing in the storm with the sound of the torrents!' (ll. 5–6) – while also accentuating a sublime, dark atmosphere and themes of horror: 'The night is your home; horror is your domain' (l. 7). Lamartine's characterisation of Byron in the opening lines is ridden with doubt and moral uncertainty: 'Mysterious spirit, mortal, angel, or demon;/ Whoever you may be, Byron, good or fatal genius' (ll. 2–3). Byron is here apostrophised as a Satanic, adventurous spirit, unrestricted by social constraints: 'Evil is your theatre, and Man is your victim./ Your eye has measured the abyss, like Satan' (ll. 21–4). Here, as in Lamartine's *Life of Lord Byron* of 1865, the British poet lacks the serious-mindedness and religious conscientiousness that Lamartine sees in himself. Yet this focus on Byron's Satanism (see also Chapter 3) is tempered by his admission of Byron's genius: 'It is for truth that supreme God has made your genius' (l. 255). Lamartine believes, as Joanne Wilkes suggests, that Byron 'will use his pre-eminent genius to emulate the melodious choirs of angels and the golden harps of heaven' (Wilkes 2004: 24). The poem, which is essentially about Lamartine's religious turmoil ('Glory to you' – meaning to God – is repeated twenty times in the poem), is also by implication an attempt to argue for the redemptive value of poetry and the poet: 'Man, who remembers the heavens is a felled god' (l. 70). Lamartine once again identifies with Byron in his *Le Dernier Chant du Pèlerinage d'Harold (The Last Canto of Childe Harold's Pilgrimage)* (1825), a poem which, by focusing on divine sentiments such as love and liberty, continues Lamartine's engagement with the decline of the world's major religions.

Other French Romantic writers consolidated the ties between British and French Romanticism. For example, Vigny became, like Byron, a celebrity and was deeply fascinated by the works of British writers. Vigny conquered the public not only with his Scott-like historical novel *Cinq-Mars* (1826), dedicated to Napoleon, but also with his play *Chatterton* (1835), which was based on the life of the young English forger of medieval poetry, Thomas Chatterton. Apart from one trip to England (1838–9), where he met some major figures in British literature and culture (one of the characters in *Chatterton* is called Beckford, a clear tribute to William Beckford, the master of the Gothic novel *Vathek*, composed in French in 1782 and translated into English in 1786), Vigny led the life of a hermit in Paris. His *Poems Antique and Modern* (1826), which were influenced by Byron, Chenier and Chateaubriand, and *The Destinies* (published posthumously in 1864), which contains lyrics such as 'The Bottle in the Sea', 'The Death of the Wolf' and 'The Shepherd's House' (the last of which is evocative of Wordsworth's 'Michael'), focus on notions of selfhood. Mindful of Keats's teaching, the 'Preface' to his 1826 novel *The Fifth of March*, 'Reflexions on Truth in Art', argues for the superiority of art over history and, similarly to Manzoni (discussed later in this chapter), interrogates the boundaries between history and fiction.

References to British Romanticism are also evident in the work of Victor Hugo, whose themes of paternal love, patriotism, happiness and the value of everyday life are reminiscent of some of the ideas in the 'Preface' to *Lyrical Ballads*. At the beginning of his career Hugo travelled to Spain and Italy. When he returned to France he embraced the culture of Romanticism. His ideas and tastes were more fully developed in 1827 with the publication of *Cromwell*, whose 'Preface' constitutes a clear anti-classical manifesto and arguably inaugurates the tradition of French Romantic drama. The literary revolution which Hugo acknowledges in *Hernani* (1830) preceded the Revolution of July, something which the author seems to have foreseen in his 'Preface': 'Romanticism so often ill defined . . . is no more than liberalism in the arts' (Hugo 1968: 3) (own translation). Along with these political concerns, Hugo was also interested in moral questions, particularly the question of evil. *The End of Satan* (published posthumously in 1886), for example, is a work evocative of those of the British Satanic School, with characters such as the Faust-like Manfred and Prometheus. However, as we have seen above, it was Charles Nodier who developed in France the fascination for the Gothic, although the Gothic impulse is also present in the work of Gérard de Nerval (1808–55), who translates Goethe's *Faust* (1808) into English and passionately champions Hoffmann's *Fairy Tales* (1814).

French Romanticism's focus on the relationship between the real and surreal is suggestive of the influence of the work of Coleridge, Blake and Thomas De Quincey, particularly in Hugo's Hegelian/Blakean focus on contrasts. *Odes and Ballads* (1826) seems to be highly influenced by the poems and novels of Walter Scott; *Orientalia* (1829) celebrates Greek literature and culture (as Hemans, Shelley, Byron and others had already done before him); *Hernani* considers the Spanish atmosphere of 'Monts d'Aragon, Galice, Estremadoure!'; while *Contemplations* (1856) (see 'A Villequier') presents a more domestic environment. Hugo also experiments with the epic form in works such as *Castigations* (1853) and *The Legend of the Ages* (1859), with the aim of renovating the supernatural. This idea is an adaption of the Coleridgean concept, discussed in *Biographia Literaria*, of creating a 'willing suspension of disbelief' in order to turn ordinary incidents into extraordinary ones (1983: II. 6). Moreover, in works such as *Light and Shadows* (published 1840), Hugo discusses the function of the poet, who, in a way similar to the ideas about poetic responsibility expounded by Wordsworth and Shelley, was required to civilise, educate, teach and foresee the future. By politicising the figure of the poet, Hugo turns him into a defender of liberal social values. His stress on the poet's role as a prophet is an echo of Shelley's belief in the value and function of poets as 'unacknowledged legislators of the world', as highlighted in *A Defence of Poetry* (1821: 508).

More than anything else, however, Hugo is one of the most significant representatives of French Romanticism for his creation of the French historical (and social) novel. *Les Misérables*, like Sir Walter Scott's *Ivanhoe*, depicts a great epic fresco: the Battle of Waterloo (to which he devotes an entire book of the novel) and the riots of June 1832 (under Louis-Philippe) populate the pages of this *magnum opus*, reflecting the European-wide historical significance of these events: 'Waterloo is not a battle; it is a shift in the world's front' (Hugo 2008: 277). Hugo collected evidence of the battle, visited the fields and, finally, in June 1861 completed the writing of his book. In his poem 'To Victor Hugo' (1877) the poet laureate Alfred Lord Tennyson (1809–92) also focuses on cross-cultural relationships beyond the Channel. Despite his anti-French sympathies, for Tennyson, Hugo remains the 'Stormy Voice of France!' (l. 8), the 'VICTOR in Drama!', the 'Victor in Romance' (l. 1). Together with Hugo, Prosper Mérimée (1803–70), Alexandre Dumas, père (1802–70) and Eugène Sue (1804–57) also experimented with the historical novel. By the 1840s the political and social landscape of France had changed significantly: in 1848 the French Republic had succumbed to internal divisions, the press was closely controlled and its citizens were miserable and unsatisfied. The work of Honoré de Balzac (1799–1850) displays a minute observation of this new reality (similar to Jane Austen's fascination with the details of domestic life, as discussed in Chapter 2). Opposing the idealism of writers such as George Sand, Honoré de Balzac once enthusiastically responded to her: 'You are looking for man as he should be; I take him as he is' (Sand 1991: 923). Balzac was widely perceived to deal with the 'real'. Like Wordsworth and Coleridge (see the 'Preface' to *Lyrical Ballads*), he believed that the task of literature was to draw attention to ordinary human life, to uplift, ennoble and transform humanity while continuing to focus on everyday life. Balzac's epic *The Human Comedy* (1829–48) illuminates the principal traits of French Romanticism in the 1830s, where situations of everyday day life are examined in the context of their relationship with the natural environment.

Henri Beyle (Stendhal), whose works are like portraits of history and society, developed Balzac's emphasis on minute detail into a new kind of psychological realism and acute character analysis. In 1816 Stendhal (and De Musset) travelled from France to Milan, where they met Byron when his friend Polidori was arrested at La Scala by the Austrian troops. The cosmopolitanism of those fervent years is reflected in Stendhal's novels, which portray ardent characters who are full of passion but often victims of the historical moment and the avidity of the establishment. Individualism, energy, strong desires, dangerous lives, pleasures and happiness make the Italian Carbonari an appealing subject of enquiry for Stendhal, as in *The Red and the Black* (1830), which depicts French society and political life in the last years of the Restoration, and *The Charterhouse of Parma* (1839), one part of which is almost entirely dedicated to the Battle of Waterloo. The episode of Fabrice del Dongo at Waterloo reveals the extent to which the hero is in touch with the political events of his own time, but it also discloses how the battle is perceived from the point of view of a novice fighter. Stendhal favoured the psychological over the social and historical, developing a new type of psychological realism that differed substantially from that of the eighteenth-century novel. Stendhal presents a world which is socially fragmented and whose heroes (or anti-heroes) are often outcasts in a modern society.

Similarly to Stendhal, Prosper Mérimée develops Romantic tendencies in his novel *Carmen* (1845) (see also *Colomba* (1840)), where Don Juan is interestingly portrayed as a Byronic hero. The significance of the Spanish world in Mérimée's work, as well as references to Byron, further develops a sense of the period's transnational tendencies. The work of the *enfant terrible* of French Romanticism, Alfred De Musset (1810–57), in particular his *Nights* (1835–7), are mindful of the themes and content of Young's work. De Musset's *Romances of Spain and Italy* (1830) offers a flamboyant and trans-European example of the reach of British Romanticism, while his 'Don Juan' is a tribute to Byron's work. In recent years Jonathan Strauss has examined the shared theme of loss in the poetry of Lamartine, De Musset and De Nerval, suggesting that their works engage, in particular, with the idea of 'incompleteness', which takes the specific form of dejection (loss, bereavement, death). Strauss's observations recall the themes of dejection in British Romantic poetry, especially in the work of Coleridge and Shelley (see *Dejection: An Ode* and 'Stanzas written in Dejection, near Naples' respectively) (Strauss 2005: 192–207). Further links between British and French Romanticism can be seen in the 'art for art's sake' ('l'art pour l'art') of Théophile Gautier (1811–72), whose theory took its inspiration from the aestheticism of Keats and others, and would later have a strong influence on Oscar Wilde. The idea of 'art for art's sake' also characterises Charles Baudelaire's (1821–67) *The Flowers of Evil* (1857), which, significantly, is dedicated to Gautier. Baudelaire's sense of how art aims 'to extract *beauty* from *Evil*' (cited in Blood 1997: 97) also pervades the aesthetic theories of Leconte de Lisle (1818–94) and of the Parnassian movement more generally. Although Baudelaire became famous primarily as an art critic and poet, his collection of essays *Artificial Paradises* (1860), with its focus on drugs as a means of reaching an 'ideal' world, brings to mind Thomas De Quincey's *Confessions of an English Opium-Eater* (1821), *Suspiria de Profundis* (1845) and, more broadly, the work of the Satanic School discussed in Chapter 3. The tradition of the *poète maudit* (the damned poet) embodied in writers such as Novalis, Nerval, Baudelaire and Lautréamont (1846–70), who considered poetry a profoundly transgressive activity, had a deep impact on Western European literature. Intended as a form of rebellion, the poetry of the *maudits* aggressively destabilises social roles and political norms, as in the later work of Paul Verlaine (1844–96), Arthur Rimbaud (1854–91) and Stéphane Mallarmé (1842–98).

Italian Romanticism

The beginnings of Italian Romanticism arguably coincide with the fall of Napoleon in 1814, even though there were several examples of pre-Romantic taste before then, especially in the work of Vittorio Alfieri (1749–1803) and Ugo Foscolo. In 1816 the Milanese newspaper *Biblioteca Italiana* published an article by Madame de Staël in which she invited the Italians to abandon their 'classical' taste in favour of more 'contemporary' foreign standards. As one might expect, the article resulted in a literary battle in which the defenders of the 'new' literature clashed with the defenders of the 'classical' tradition. This polemic between the classicists and the Romantics acquired a wider civil and political meaning. Giovanni Berchet (1783–1851) took part in this debate with his *On 'the Fierce Hunter' and 'Leonora' of G. A. Burger: The Semiserious Letter from Chrysostom to His Son* (1816), which became something close to the manifesto of Italian Romanticism. The letter takes as its starting point the dark sensibility associated with a Germanic taste and literary tradition (particularly its ballads) and investigates the possibility of developing a similar kind of poetry in Italy.

Although, significantly, *Chrysostom* suggests that the classical tradition of poetry is dead, whereas Romanticism poetry is living because the former speaks to the past and the latter to the future – 'Render yourselves coeval with the times in which you live and not with the centuries which have been buried' (cited in Avitabile 1959: 60) – the letter nonetheless repudiates many of the main characteristics of the Romanticism of the North. Not only does Berchet's letter highlight the unsuitability of the Italian language for horrid German and British tastes, it also expresses a distaste for classical mythology and the British Romantic Hellenism of Byron, Keats and Shelley. Nonetheless, similarly to the poetry of Wordsworth and Coleridge, it propounds a popular kind of literature in its polemic against the classical tradition and in its determination to highlight the social meaning of poetry, ideas which are also taken up in the work of Carlo Porta (1775–1821), whose poem in sestets 'Il Romanticismo' (1819), written in Milanese, inaugurated a form of popular literature concerned with the realities of everyday life.

Another instrument propounding the classical/Romantic debate was the Milanese newspaper *Il Conciliatore*, edited by the patriot Silvio Pellico (1789–1854), which strongly focused on anti-Austrian and nationalistic themes. Pietro Garofalo is correct when he suggests that 'a symbiotic relationship with the Risorgimento . . . uniquely characterises Italian Romanticism' (Garofalo 2005: 238). Increasingly, to be 'Romantic' meant to be patriotic and to be 'classical' meant to be on the side of the Austrians, as suggested in the works of some of Italian Romanticism's major representatives: Foscolo, Manzoni and Giacomo Leopardi (1798–1837). Yet while recognising Italian Romanticism's links with a rising nationalism, this part of the chapter also offers a reassessment of its literary climate and focuses on the movement as a 'manifestation of evolving sensibilities while acknowledging both its intellectual debt and its aesthetic innovations with respect to European culture' (Garofalo 2005: 238), especially British Romanticism. Anglo-Italian relations in the Romantic period and the British Romantics' Italian experiences are topics already well explored by many critics, as shown in recent books by Cavaliero (2005), Schoina (2009) and Hay (2010). This section instead focuses on the Italian Romantics' émigré experiences in Britain, as in the case of Foscolo's London sojourn, as part of a complex and qualitative attempt to illuminate bicultural identities. It also identifies the parallelism between the works of Italian and British Romantics, as in the case of Foscolo–Byron, Manzoni–Scott and Leopardi–Keats, in order to demonstrate the significance of cosmopolitanism for the study and development of European Romanticism.

Long a traditional destination for many British artists and tourists on the Grand Tour (see Chapter 5), by the end of the Napoleonic Wars Italy had become, for Byron, the Shelleys, Keats and Leigh Hunt, the land of the picturesque. Depicted by Byron in 1818 in his long, epic poem *Childe Harold's Pilgrimage* as 'the garden of the world' and 'the home of all Art', the country had, in the intervening years under Austrian yoke, lost the gloss of both its liberty and integrity. It nonetheless still appeared breathtakingly beautiful to British observers, to the point that the 'wreck' became 'a glory' and the 'ruin' displayed 'an immaculate charm which cannot be defaced' (*Childe Harold's Pilgrimage* 4. 26. 228–9, 233–4). Italy was, therefore, not just another stop on the Grand Tour for Romantic writers and travellers but also a locus of intellectual reflection and the 'Paradise of Exiles' (Shelley, *Julian and Maddalo*, l. 57). Yet to focus only on Mary Shelley's claim in her poem 'The Choice' that Italy is 'my adopted land, my country, Italy!' (l. 10) is to miss the fact that British culture was as integral to the development of Italian Romanticism as the reverse. This is particularly evident in the work and life of Foscolo, the writer who instigated the so-called 'Italian "anglomania"', or obsessive interest on the part of the Italians in British authors (Parmegiani 2010: 1).

There are several reasons why Foscolo, a Greek-Italian, was exposed to a wider European literature and culture. First, the Venetian Republic during his formative years was particularly receptive towards ideas of transnationalism; second, the translation of *Ossian* into Italian by Melchiorre Cesarotti in 1763–4 ensured that it became an influential text in Italy; and, third, like the French poet Vigny, Foscolo joined the Italian division of Napoleon's army for the cross-Channel invasion of England, following which he lived in London for eleven years. The first significant Romantic Italian-English literary encounter is Foscolo's translation of Laurence Sterne's *A Sentimental Journey through France and Italy*, not only because Sterne's work became available to a larger audience, but also because the translation is a landmark in terms of European cross-cultural sensitivity: an English text depicting a journey through France and Italy is, for the first time, translated from English to Italian. Like Sterne's protagonist, Foscolo was constantly travelling: from Italy to France (in 1806 he met Alessandro Manzoni in Paris and then returned to Milan); from France back to Italy and then Switzerland; and from Switzerland to England. When in England Foscolo was increasingly absorbed in English literature and culture, with a specific focus on eighteenth-century English writers (he was particularly fond of Milton, Gray, Akenside, Thomson, Pope, Swift, Young and Richardson). He planned to write an essay on contemporary British authors (Moore, Scott, Rogers, Crabbe, Southey, Wordsworth, Coleridge, Shelley, Hogg and Byron), but it never came to fruition.

Foscolo's *Sepulchres* (1806), written in response to the 1804 edict of Saint Cloud, which forbade the burial of the dead in marked graves and within the city limits, is not only a picturesque depiction of the Italian fascination with English gardens/ graveyards, but also follows the sublime tradition of Graveyard poetry – in particular, Young's *Nights* and Gray's *Elegy* – neatly capturing the main themes and modes of Foscolo's poetics: the dark aspects of nature; the consolation of love, beauty, faith and hope; and the suffering of exile – or, to put it more simply, life and death.

Case study: Ugo Foscolo, *Sepulchres* (1806)

Foscolo's inspiration for writing this long poem of 295 lines about tombs – especially those of great men such as Michelangelo, Galileo and Machiavelli, buried in the Florentine Church of Santa Croce (ll. 151–212) – came from a conversation he had with fellow poet Ippolito Pindemonte (here his interlocutor). The main themes of the poem include the remembrance and memorialisation of the dead, as well as the importance of the tomb as a locus which moves beyond the material and provides comfort to the living through a 'heaven-sent/ correspondence of such deep affection' (ll. 29–30) that inspires them to noble deeds (ll. 23–40). More specifically, the tomb, with its high civic function, is a testimony to the historical glories and political values of the Greeks who fought and died at Marathon (l. 197 ff.), without whose concrete graves history would be effaced and the grandeur of ancient Greece, the authentic mother of all our civilisation, would seem ephemeral. As Margaret Brose notes, Foscolo's works 'are based on an idealized form of classicism, but the fervor and mode of expression are undeniably Romantic' (Brose 2005: 260). Displaying a Romantic rejection of the materialistic and sensistic philosophy which shaped his initial literary works (ll. 1–22), Foscolo replaces social and physical determinism with individual agency and historical memory, where the dead (both familiar and illustrious) continue living in those who remember them with love and admiration. Foscolo's belief in the immortality of human memory is suggestive of the eternal role of art (Michelangelo), science (Galileo), politics (Machiavelli), poetry and culture (ll. 226–95, 228 ff.): it is the memorialisation of these great men and their work which here serves to rescue Italy from the political and moral degradation into which she has fallen and can generate her rebirth. The message which emanates from the tomb is therefore one of both remembrance and reawakening: poetry in its narration of glories and misadventures, heroisms and sacrifices lasts for eternity and time will never erase what human beings have achieved in fighting for their own ideals.

In an elegantly written polemic against the edict of Saint Cloud, Foscolo designs a kind of synecdoche in which a single historical moment (the edict) stands in for a broader passionate attack on the whole of the Italian Risorgimento: in unifying past (glory), present (corruption) and future (hope) the poem enhances the revolutionary atmosphere of the historical moment. As Mauro Pala has astutely put it, 'politics . . . is here expressed through rhetorical means . . . and provides access to the complex interplay between class, heritage and emerging nationalist consciousness' (Pala 2005: 198). Written by a Greek-Venetian, who always felt the weight of exile (ll. 226–95), this poem is not only a literal journey through the graves but also a metaphorical one through a dismembered Italy, where the topography of exile leads to the life of an outcast. Foscolo's tribute to Englishness is not only evident in his debt to Graveyard poetry and his eulogy of British graveyards, which reflect the strength of a country rich in civil sentiment, where the 'girls who grieve in Britain' (ll. 131–2) have the privilege to pray at the graves of their mothers, it also expatiates on the relationship between the domestic sphere and Foscolo's more direct concern with contemporary British issues such as the battle of Aboukir of 1798 and British women's prayers for the return of Nelson (ll. 133–6). The re-enactment of the battle of Aboukir reflects his anti-Napoleonic sentiments ('who had the captured ship truncated by/ Its tallest mast, and hollowed thence his coffin' (ll. 135–6)). Although for Foscolo himself, an expatriate in exile, the tomb does not offer any consolation (see also *To Zacynthus* – 'My doom/ Is exile and an unwept sepulchre' (ll. 13–14)), he is a poet-prophet who seamlessly combines different aspect of European history: the French Revolution, Napoleon's conquest of Italy, his 'liberation' of Venice and his cession of it to the Austrians and his defeat at Aboukir.

Seen by many as 'the Italian Byron' (Brose 2005: 264), Foscolo's sympathetic insights into British Romantic history and culture are indeed mainly associated with the English poet. Although the two writers never met, their lives have much in common: both were in Switzerland in 1816, both went into voluntary exile, both were engaged in the political turmoil of their own time and both loved Greece. The publication of *Childe Harold's Pilgrimage* marked the literary association of the two writers. Crucially, Byron in the 'Preface' to the fourth canto places Foscolo among the great Italians who 'will secure to the present generation an honourable place in most of the departments of art, science, and belles lettres' (cited in McGann 2008: 147), suggesting the degree to which Byron would later intensify his Italian relations. (Moreover, in 1818 John Cam Hobhouse, the Bristolian politician and memoirist, includes Foscolo's 'Essay on the present literature of Italy' in his *Historical Illustrations of the Fourth Canto of Childe Harold: Containing Dissertations on the Ruins of Rome, and an Essay on Italian Literature).*

Mario Praz has observed that Foscolo can be placed, together with Keats and Hölderlin, '[at] the acme of the late eighteenth – and early nineteenth – century classicism reached within the general framework of Romantic sensitivity' (cited in Parmegiani 2010: 116). The work that is more closely associated with Hölderlin and German Romanticism is Foscolo's confessional novel *The Last Letters of Jacopo Ortis* (1817), whose content can be compared to Goethe's *Werther*. Following the French and English tradition of the eighteenth-century epistolary novel, Ortis contemplates the idea of committing suicide, here intended as the expression of ultimate liberty, a spiritual ideal that fate cannot efface. *Ortis* is a work in which Foscolo essentially internalises the problematic of the human heart, his strong pessimism and his dislike of the Treaty of Campoformio, which is discussed in the opening letter, dated 11 October 1797. Here, a disillusioned Jacopo reflects on the fact that Venice has become Austrian territory: 'The sacrifice of our fatherland has been consummated, everything is lost' (cited in Traversa 2005: 19). In a compelling portrayal of political activism, he is prepared to be imprisoned and to die in his own country (see his beautiful elopement from the Euganean Hills, which Shelley loved). In his self-sacrifice Jacopo is a true Romantic hero, a twin brother to Werther, Chatterton and Manfred.

It was not only Foscolo who demonstrated an interest in the national cause. Following his example, the meaningfulness of past and contemporary history is also key to the work of Manzoni, who, like Wordsworth and Coleridge, was able to understand and translate in writing the advances of his own historical moment by getting nearer to the masses and focusing on everyday life, ordinary people and a common language. In the most important of his theoretical writings, the letter *On Romanticism* to the marquis Cesare d'Azeglio (1823), Manzoni, after having criticised and repudiated the darker aspects of Romanticism, argues that the new literature has to recognise '*reality* as its object, *interest* as its means, and *usefulness* as its purpose' (Prickett 2010: 713–16) (own translation). This new attention to authenticity, reason and the utility of the individual and society points to both the humanitarian and Christian aspects of Manzoni's work: he wishes to use the poetical sense to portray the humblest and deepest affections, as well as the everyday aspects of human existence.

Manzoni's work had an immense patriotic appeal for Italians of the nationalistic Risorgimento period. In his ode *March 1821* (1848), written on the occasion of the Carbonari uprisings of the same year (which he did not publish, but circulated privately), the author exalts the sense of freedom, which he believes can be gained through personal sacrifice. Also of 1821 is the ode *The Fifth of May*, written in commemoration of Napoleon's death. This poem, however, moves far away from the historical event in order to focus, beyond political judgements and resentments ('Was this glory just and true? (l. 31)), on a more human and religious sphere ('He fell, he rose, again was laid' (l. 16)). The poet feels closer to Napoleon, the man and hero, not so much in his moments of glory but in those of fear and despair, dictated by the solitude of his long exile on the island of St Helena. The most striking moment of the ode is when, with Christian devotion, Manzoni perceives a quasi-religious faith in the soul of Napoleon. It is faith, Manzoni believes, which helps 'the greatest man of all ages' to reconcile death with happiness: 'From these weary ashes, though/ Words condemning ban;/ God, who fells and lashes now/ Lifts and soothes again,/ On that lonely dying bed/ Soft His heavenly presence shed' (ll. 102–8).

Like many of his odes, Manzoni's historical novels, such as *The Betrothed* (1827), are structured around the theme of redemption. While the focus of *The Betrothed* is on the author's (as well as his protagonist's) religious maturation through suffering, it nonetheless – following Walter Scott's example in *Waverley* (1814), *Ivanhoe* (1820) and other novels – draws on major historical events of the first half of the seventeenth century, such as the Spanish occupation, while at the same time offering an attack on Austria, which controlled Lombardy at the time the novel was written, as discussed in the following case study.

Case study: Alessandro Manzoni, *The Betrothed* (1827)

Manzoni's *The Betrothed* narrates the adventures of a young couple, Renzo and Lucia, who, forced to leave their hometown to escape the persecution of Don Rodrigo (see the famous 'Farewell, ye mountains' passage in chapter 8), witness wars, moral and physical violence, hunger, pestilence and the plague that strikes Milan in the 1630s. Often using a colloquial or 'living' idiom that he believed could also provide a norm for written language, Manzoni represents life with all of its injustices and sorrows, as in the emotional episode of Cecilia (chapter 34), 'a small child of perhaps nine years of age, dead' after the effects of the plague, and ready to be taken away on a car or carriage by 'a filthy *monatto*' yet deeply loved and mourned by her mother: 'it [the child] was all neatly arranged, with its hair parted on its forehead, and dressed in the purest white, as if those hands of hers [the mother's] had decked it for a party long promised and given as a reward' (Manzoni 1997: 487). The Cecilia episode highlights not only Manzoni's detailed attention to the effects of the plague but also his social and humanitarian account of the feelings of ordinary and humble people. Deeply struck by the oppression of the weak by the strong, he recurs to his deep religious feeling: the characters of Lucia and Father Cristoforo, with their faith in the divine, look for what is good in human existence. While Manzoni differs from Scott in that he offers a deeper psychological insight into his characters and has a greater adherence to history and a greater focus on morality, religion and providence, he owes to British Romanticism his attention to ordinary life and vernacular language, which has clear resonances with Wordsworth and Coleridge's account of poetic responsibility in the 'Preface' to *Lyrical Ballads*.

If Manzoni in the first half of the century was able to interpret and understand the values of the emerging classes, and elaborated a system of literary communication appropriate to them in terms of content and language, Giacomo Leopardi was the Italian Romantic writer best able to come to terms with the other important problematic of the period: the Romantic inner sense or, as Pietro Garofalo has so succinctly put it, 'poetry's contemplation of inner life, of the infinite, of nature' (Garofalo 2005: 251). In his *Discourse of an Italian on Romantic Poetry* (1818), Leopardi approves many of the new Romantic ideals, despite his sometimes explicit recommendation of classical forms and styles. His somewhat ambivalent relationship with the Italian Romantic School was informed by his emphasis on the needs of the humble, his faith in the morality and the teaching of art and his rejection of patriotic propaganda.

Deeply introspective, Leopardi's Romanticism places him closer to the British than the Italian tradition. Like Wordsworth, he believed in the importance of expressing 'emotions recollected in tranquillity', as shown in some of his most famous lyrics such as 'Memories', 'The Solitary Bird' and 'To Silvia' (all published in 1835). Moreover, in his notebook *Zibaldone*, 'a seminal document and comment on Romanticism in Italy' (Garofalo 2005: 251), Leopardi in an entry dated 16 January 1821 offers an example of childhood memories revisited – 'If, as children, we take delight and pleasure in a view, a landscape, a painting, a sound, etc., a story, a description, a fairy tale, a poetic image, a dream, that delight and pleasure is always vague and indefinite' – and suggests that

> The idea that is awakened in us is always indeterminate and limitless, every solace, every pleasure, every expectation, every project, illusion, etc. (indeed, almost every conception), at that age always has something of the infinite about it, and nourishes us and fills our soul in a way that cannot be put into words, even through the smallest objects.
>
> (Leopardi 2013: 283)

More similar to Marcel Proust and James Joyce's epiphanic moments, where a particular situation triggers the poet's imagination and enlivens an experience in people's lives, Leopardi's process of memory differs from Wordsworth's in that it confirms neither restoration nor preservation of past graces and suggests that remembrance is not immune to the transience of time. On the contrary, recollection in Leopardi confirms, rather than compensating for, the losses of time. Leopardi's fascination with simple country life, as detailed in two of his major poems of 1835, 'Saturday Night in the Village' and 'The Calm After the Storm', also links him to some of the British Romantics. In the first poem Leopardi focuses on the theme of expectation (the day before the holiday is the most precious) and underlines the value of real pleasure, which comes from anticipation rather than fulfilment. These ideas suggest a parallel with Keats's *Ode on a Grecian Urn* (1819), where the 'bold lover' will never be able to kiss his paramour.

Leopardi was not only preoccupied with what was happening at home. His work also shows a concern with foreign countries, as we can see, for instance, in his *Dialogue between Nature and an Icelander* (1824) (part of his *Little Moral Works*). The fact that the Icelander is wandering in an unknown region of Africa suggests Leopardi's interest in the cosmopolitan and even global aspects of Romanticism (see Chapter 7), as one can also see in his *Night Song of a Wandering Shepherd of Asia*, discussed below.

Case study: Giacomo Leopardi, *Night Song of a Wandering Shepherd of Asia* (1830)

The image of the shepherd – which brings to mind Wordsworth's 'Michael' and 'Simon Lee' (written 1798, published 1800) – came to Leopardi after reading an 1826 article by a Russian explorer discussing the traditions of the travellers of Asia. In the poem, however, the entire situation has been de-personalised: we are in a faraway and solitary, but unspecified, region of the world. In the symbolic setting of the Asian desert the shepherd's own cosmic meditation arrives at the tragic conclusion that in no matter what form or what condition (human or animal) in 'A day of great ill-omen we are born' (l. 143). The shepherd's doubts, here mindful of 'What Am I?' in the third canto of Byron's *Childe Harold's Pilgrimage* (1816), are suggested not only by his own words but by the silence of the landscape and the flock: 'What are these torches for?/ This never-ending space, and that profound/ endless clear sky? Whatever is the meaning/ of this great solitude? And what am I?' (ll. 85 ff.). Leopardi, as we have seen, was more pessimistic about man's relationship with nature than many of the British Romantics calling it 'evil stepmother' since it appeared to be indifferent to the suffering of human beings. More specifically, the image of the moon in this poem, which is central to the composition, appears detached and indifferent to the shepherd's questions. Nature does not accompany the 'wandering shepherd' in his journey through life, thus emphasising a general feeling of disillusionment.

Spanish Romanticism

Scholars like Diego Saglia have argued that Spanish Romanticism is 'the most national of all', discussing the close symbiosis between the cultural politics of the period and domestic identity (Saglia 1997: 130). More recently Christopher Bode has suggested that 'the situation in Spain resembles that of Italy between the Napoleonic occupation and the *Risorgimento*', thereby questioning whether a national model can adequately explain Spanish Romanticism's international and cosmopolitan aspects (Bode 2005: 132). While acknowledging the importance of Saglia's insights, this section offers an analysis of influences and interchanges between Spain and other European countries, with a particular focus on English-Spanish biculturalism. Despite the fact that many commentators date the beginning of Spanish Romanticism to after 1833, when the king Ferdinand VII died and a liberal political regime was established, Spanish–British encounters were evident in Romantic texts from the beginning of the Peninsular War in 1808 and the ensuing Cadiz Constitution of 1812. Spain featured, for example, in Matthew Lewis's *The Monk* (1796), Ann Radcliffe's *The Italian* (1797), Coleridge's drama *Osorio* (1797) (and its development in *Remorse* (1813)), Godwin's *St Leon* (1799), Wordsworth's pamphlet *On the Convention of Cintra* (1808–9), Hemans's *England and Spain* (1808), Scott's *The Vision of Don Roderick* (1811), Southey's epic *Roderick, The Last of the Goths* (1814), Maturin's *Melmoth The Wanderer* (1820) and William Beckford's travelogue *Letters from Italy with Sketches from Spain and Portugal* (1834). All of these works are concerned with questions of *both* national and transnational identity. Coleridge was absolutely right when in *Biographia Literaria* he self-assuredly wrote: the Spanish cause 'made us all once more Englishmen by at once gratifying and correcting the predilections of both parties' (Coleridge 1983: I. 189). Spanish Romanticism, then, can be seen as an important spatial locus for the British Romantic imagination: its exoticism, ideality and distance, made it, to put it in Friedrich Schlegel's words, 'the very place where the true essence of Romanticism can be determined' (cited in Saglia 1996: 49)

Initially focused upon ideas such as medieval revivalism, Catholicism and cultural nationalism as a way of rejecting Enlightenment rational philosophy and cosmopolitanism (as in the work of the Duque de Rivas and José Zorrilla), Spanish Romanticism subsequently developed into a more destabilising and subversive movement: an 'exaggerated, degraded, execrated Romanticism' similar to the darkness of the British Satanic school, even becoming, with the work of Espronceda (1808–42), Byron-focused (Flitter 2005: 286). These two, seemingly contradictory, aspects of Spanish Romanticism have led to many debates about its limits and importance. According to Edgar Allison Peers's monumental *History of the Romantic Movement in Spain* (1940), Spanish Romanticism arises from a 'popular, traditionalist, and anti-classicist' foundation, fundamentally grounded in neo-Schlegelian and Herderian beliefs (cited in Saglia 1997: 128). According to R. P. Sebold's *Trayectoria del Romanticismo español. Desde la Ilustración hasta Bécquer* (1983), on the other hand, its roots can be traced to the pre-Romantic taste of the late eighteenth century (see authors such as Cadalso, Meléndez Valdés). For Ricardo Navas Ruiz, liberalism is an essential ingredient of the movement, as argued in his *El Romanticismo español* (1990). The impact of transnationalism in the development of Spanish Romanticism is discussed in Fernando Cabo Aseguinolaza's recently published *Historia de la literatura española: 9. El Lugar de la literatura española* (2012), which considers the influence of Spanish Romanticism in Europe and vice versa (as in Lopez Soler's debt to the work of Walter Scott), while also exploring Spanish American literature. Other recent studies include Derek Flitter's argument (1992, 2000, 2005) against depictions of Spanish Romanticism as 'anarchical' and 'subversive' by emphasising its 'restorative, traditionalist, and Christian' roots (Flitter 2005: 276). In particular, Flitter identifies the origins of the movement in the theories of Germanic Romantic thinkers, with a specific focus on Herder's historicism.

German and Spanish Romanticism resemble one another in a number of important ways. The first signs of a German–Spanish inter-relation in the development of Spanish Romanticism are provided by the work of the Hispanicised German Nicolás Böhl de Faber (1770–1836), who in 1814 translated Schlegel's *Lessons on Dramatic Art and Literature*, delivered in Vienna in 1808. These *Lessons* defended the Spanish Golden Age drama and argued for a return to tradition, Spanish nationalism and Catholic thought, thus arousing the inimical feelings of liberals such as José Joaquín de Mora (1783–1864) and José Alcalá Galiano (1843–1919). Schlegel's theorisations on Spanishness, as Saglia has pointed out, are related to the outbreak of the Spanish revolt against Napoleon's invasion and the Peninsular War that followed, thus accentuating the national character of the movement (Saglia 1997: 130). Like Schlegel, Böhl de Faber associated Christianity with a native Romantic tradition in Spain beginning in the Middle Ages, maintaining that neoclassicism constituted an interruption of that tradition (Flitter 1992: 1–22). The focus on nationalism, religion and spirituality was also central, as we have already seen, to Chateaubriand's *The Genius of Christianity*, Foscolo's *Sepulchres* and Manzoni's *The Betrothed*, thus becoming a distinctive factor in a pan-European Romanticism.

Böhl de Faber's role in the development of a pan- or trans-European Romanticism does not solely relate to his fascination with German literary works (although he also read Tieck, Novalis, Goethe and Schiller), but also encompasses his fascination with English Romantic poetry, in particular the work of Burns, Southey and Wordsworth, the latter of whom he saw as 'the leader of the new movement in England, the man who had liberated poetry from pedantic rules' (Flitter 1992: 13). Böhl de Faber is therefore a critical figure, 'an important pioneer' (Flitter 1992: 22), in the development of European transnationalism, as his work not only evinces links with both German and British Romanticism, but also demonstrates the fusion of a Nordic and native tradition in Spanish Romanticism.

The main representative of a prose tradition in Spanish Romanticism is Mariano José de Larra (1809–37), who is mostly remembered for his articles, in which he portrays and criticises the Spanish society of his time. 'Costumbrismo' – the realistic but idealised representation of daily life in Spanish towns and cities, which lies somewhere between journalism and fiction – was also very popular at the time. Mesonero Romanos (1803–82) and Estébanez Calderón (1799–1867) are associated with this genre. One of the first writers to turn 'costumbrismo' into a novel, by introducing action into previously static representations of everyday life, is Fernán Caballero (1796–1877) (pseudonym of Cecilia Böhl de Faber, daughter of Nicolás Böhl de Faber), whose best-known novel, *La Gaviota* (1845–8), while dealing with the dangers of city life, presents an idealised and glamourised Andalucía, thus introducing the recurrent Romantic preoccupation with the dichotomy between the country and the city. In a way similar to other European writers such as Walter Scott and Alessandro Manzoni, Spanish Romanticism also interrogates the value of the past with the historical novels of Enrique Gil y Carrasco (1815–46), Antonio Trueba (1819–89) and Navarro Villoslada (1818–95).

The publication of Ángel de Saavedra's – also known as Duque de Rivas (1791–1865) – *Don Álvaro o la Fuerza del Sino* (1835) marks the beginning of Spanish Romantic drama, which reached its zenith in the 1840s and 1850s with the works of José Zorrilla (1817–93), the most famous playwright of the century and author of *Don Juan Tenorio* (1844). It is in Zorrilla's work that one can see the extension of Byronic themes, most particularly in his exploration of the myth of Don Juan. As Saglia insightfully reminds us, Byron's approach to Spain is a textual one: in *Don Juan*, for example, Spain becomes, both culturally and geographically, the site of many of the distinctive pressures of Romantic culture, in particular the political and social problems of the Napoleonic and post-Napoleonic period (Saglia 1996). Byron's association with Spanish Romanticism is reflected not only in the plays of Romantic Spain but also in its poetry. This is signalled, in particular, by José de Espronceda, whose works and personality were truly Byronic. Referred to as 'the Spanish Byron' (Cochran 2009: 76), his poems reveal not only a fascination with the Romantic taste for 'outcast' pirates and robbers (see his *The Song of the Pirate*, which is reminiscent of Byron's *Lara* and *The Corsair*) and the Ossianic taste of Macpherson, as in 'Óscar y Malvina', but also with the myth of Don Juan in *The Student of Salamanca* (1840), which abounds in Satanic resonances.

Case study: José de Espronceda y Delgado, *The Student of Salamanca* (1840)

A long dramatic poem in four acts set in the Spanish city of Salamanca around the beginning of the seventeenth century, *The Student* was published in 1840 when the Romantic movement had already begun to be challenged by a new type of realist literature in Britain. Yet in its Gothic narration of the Satanic adventures of Don Félix de Montemar – a rakish student led to his death and descent into hell by a phantom after he seduces and abandons the young virgin Elvira and kills her brother Don Diego in a duel – Espronceda references Byron's libertine *Don Juan*. On a first reading it appears as if the poem is just one of the many retellings of this popular tale, but on closer inspection Don Félix is very much a Byronic anti-hero, a 'second Don Juan Tenorio,/ A contemptuous desperado,/ Truculent, reeking bravado,/ Arrogant, spurning the Lord./ Scorn from his eye never absent;/ Irony on his lip lusting,/ Fearing nothing, all entrusting/ To his daring and his sword' (ll. 100–7). Espronceda also draws on Gothic texts when he presents a dark and sublime atmosphere at the start of the poem (Flitter 2005: 288): 'It was late, well after midnight,/ In legend it is explicit,/ When, with earth quietly dreaming,/ Dead men appeared to be living,/ The living corpselike in slumber,/ Enwrapped in thick darkness, grisly' (ll. 1–6). Indeed, Gothic images abound in *The Student*, as when phantoms and witches gather by the church bell around the Gothic castle, paving the way to the imminent catastrophe of Part One:

> A clash of swords, unexpected,
> Strident, sounds; a cry is heard.
> A shriek of death, awful, final.
> Penetrating to the very heart,
> Chilling to the very marrow,
> Causing dread in those who hear.
> The cry of a man pronouncing
> His last farewell to the earth.
>
> (ll. 41–8)

The Gothic atmosphere is also interconnected with the theme of honour (or loss of), which is the focus of much of the poem, as in Elvira's death in Part Two just after having been misused and abandoned by Don Félix. The protagonist of *The Student* has been read as a 'modern existentialist hero in search of an absolute in an absurd universe' (Cardwell 1991: 40). If this is perhaps an over-appreciation of the poem and of its hero, it nonetheless offers a Romantic vision of Spain, which is very much indebted to Byron and the British Gothic tradition.

Through such Don Juanian adventures and Haroldian encounters, Byron became, as Peter Cochran rightly contends, 'the most European of the English so called "Romantic" writers' in that the phenomenon of 'European Byronism' inspired a generation of European writers (Cochran 2009: 67). The popularity of foreign authors such as Schlegel, Scott, Chateaubriand, Ossian and especially Byron strongly influenced the development of Spanish Romanticism, which perhaps more clearly than any of the other national literary histories discussed simultaneously demonstrates the existence of a trans-European Romantic sensibility. Although many critics have argued that Romanticism only began in Spain with the return of political exiles in 1834, the evidence outlined above suggests the existence of a Schlegelian Romantic sensibility in Spain well before the 1830s. Moreover, Spanish Romanticism works within a broad comparative framework across places and countries; and its 'transatlantic empire' (Heinowitz 2010: 21) introduces the idea of global Romanticism, discussed in the next chapter.

Conclusion

- The term 'Romanticism' acquires very different connotations in various European nations: it gains anti-Enlightenment and anti-French resonances in the Germanic countries, where it propels a new kind of nationalist literature. In Italy it has a revolutionary and patriotic flavour as a consequence of the Risorgimento and aspirations to independence. In France the Romantic movement is influenced by the aftermath of the Napoleonic Wars, in Spain by Catholicism and the Peninsular War.

- There is therefore a marked chronological difference in the development of Romanticism in the different European countries discussed: the beginning of Romanticism in Germany coincided with the publication of the *Athenaeum* (1798) by the Schlegel Brothers; in England with the publication of Wordsworth and Coleridge's *Lyrical Ballads* (1798); in Italy with Berchet's *Semiserious Letter* (1816); and in France with Hugo's 'Preface' to *Cromwell* (1827). Romanticism in Spain arguably develops as late as the 1830s, when King Ferdinand VII dies and a liberal political regime is re-established.

- Yet as this chapter made clear, Romanticism can no longer be considered a primarily national phenomenon. The chapter instead highlighted the transnational links between different European nations: Italian Romanticism was in dialogue with French Romanticism, the German with the Spanish, the Spanish with the British and so on.

7   Global Romanticism

Nowadays, national literature doesn't mean much: the age of world literature is beginning, and everybody should contribute to hasten its advent.

Johann Wolfgang von Goethe to Johann Peter Eckermann (1827)

Overview

This chapter explores the ways in which an emerging global consciousness or sense of global synchronicity shaped British Romantic culture, arguing not only that literary Romanticism extends beyond national movements and even beyond the idea of a pan-European Romantic movement, most famously envisaged by René Wellek (see Introduction), but also that thinking about the period in transnational, comparative and global terms can radically change the ways in which we view British and other European Romanticisms. The first part of the chapter considers theories of globalisation and the ways in which they relate to newly revised understandings of Romantic-era nationhood and modernity. The second part of the chapter explores Romantic attitudes towards empire, looking in particular at slavery and abolitionism, exploration and voyaging and migration, transportation and émigré experience. The third part of the chapter considers Romantic Orientalism and postcolonial approaches to Romantic writing, focusing on female writers and on writing on and from British India, while the final part looks at writing on and from the Americas, the Caribbean and the British-controlled southern hemisphere.

***

'Global' and 'globalisation' are words that saturate today's academic discourses, political debates, corporate life and popular culture. But despite – or perhaps even *because* – of their ubiquity, it is easy to forget that they are terms and concepts with a history that is 'embedded in the structure of the world system and in the origins of a global economy' (Ashcroft *et al.* 1998: 112). Keith Hanley and Greg Kucich have reminded us that there were numerous 'sophisticated early articulations' of what we would now call a 'global consciousness' throughout the eighteenth and nineteenth centuries (Hanley and Kucich 2008: 76), including such varied political, economic and cultural ideas as Enlightenment cosmopolitanism; 'rights' discourses such as the 1787 Constitution of the United States of America and the French Declaration of the Rights of Man of 1789; Adam Smith's world-wide systemisation of capital in *The Wealth of Nations* (1776); and Immanuel Kant's articulation of a peace theory and league of nations in his essay *Perpetual Peace* (1795) (Hanley and Kucich 2008: 75). In all of these ways and more, writers and thinkers in the period imagined themselves as citizens of a wider world, and considered their own position in relative, comparative and differential terms.

This chapter begins by considering the history and theory of globalisation before examining the various ways in which a nascent form of globalisation manifested itself in a number of different contexts in the Romantic period, considering topics such as empire, slavery and abolition, travel and exploration, emigration and Orientalism, as well as discussing writing on and from British India, North and South America, the Caribbean and the southern hemisphere. In each case the chapter considers case studies or examples that illuminate the global reach of British Romantic writing as part of a network of correspondences, links and connections between nations, countries and regions rather than only or even primarily as part of a set or series of national literary histories (see Chapter 4). In so doing it not only considers the impact of transnational methodologies on Romantic studies, but also engages with new understandings of Romantic-era nationhood and nationalism, which see the emerging nations of early nineteenth-century Europe not as phenomena to be rejected or transcended by an emphasis on global processes, but rather as the products of these very processes.

Romantic globalisation, nationhood and modernity

Theorists of globalisation tend to explain its emergence in terms of its impact on understandings of time and space, seeing the effects of 'globalizing forces' (Waters 1995: 2) as the 'staggering compression of space and time', which in turn produces 'a de-territorialized sense of instantaneous connection across vast distances and among widely different individuals' (Hanley and Kucich 2008: 78). According to Roland Robertson, the shift in attitudes towards time and space accompanying globalisation results in 'a compression of the world and an intense consciousness of the world as a whole . . . both concrete global interdependence and consciousness of the global whole' (Robertson 1992: 8), requiring the restructuring of 'social relations and imagined communities from local contexts to indefinite spans of time and space' (Giddens 1990: 21). Globalisation can therefore be defined not just as a set of processes which generate 'transcontinental or interregional flows and networks of activity, interaction, and the exercise of power' (Held *et al.* 1999: 16), but also as 'the intensification of worldwide social relations which link distant localities in such a way that local happenings are shaped by events occurring many miles away and vice versa' (Giddens 1990: 64).

A. G. Hopkins has argued that 'archaic' and 'proto-globalisations' occurred prior to 1800, but that 'modern globalisation' has its origins in the emergence of an imperial and global economy in the early nineteenth century (Hopkins 2002: 2), making the Romantic period an important era in the history of globalisation. Imperialism, in particular, created new spaces for cross-border contacts, transnational personal encounters and exchanges and other forms of international mobility. Goethe argued as early as 1827 that national literature was redundant (cited in Moretti 2000: 54; see the epigraph to this chapter), but his keen interest in world literature was driven not just by intellectual curiosity but also by new world markets, as books and other forms of printed material increasingly circulated around the world. It is certainly no coincidence that the tendency to 'think globally' or to project a 'global imaginary' emerged during a time of 'decisive imperial and cross-cultural relations' (Gottlieb 2014: 2–3). As Alan Lester and David Lambert have pointed out, the British Empire was made up of overlapping webs of relationships across different spaces that were entangled while also being clearly distinct (Lester and Lambert 2006: 1–31). Over the course of the nineteenth century growing networks of connections spread across Britain's colonial holdings, not only forging strong regional identities, and affiliations between colonies based on their geographic and cultural distance from a remote metropole (Giles 2014), but also linking England, Ireland, Scotland and Wales with these distant colonies.

Thinking about local and national identity in the period was therefore increasingly framed in more global ways, drawing on Enlightenment anthropological discourses about the uneven development of various ethnic and racial groups, and constructing analogies between nation formation and empire building. Walter Scott's novels *Waverley* (1814) and *Rob Roy* (1821), for example, 'underline the ideological capaciousness of empire' when they famously compare the British victims of encroaching modernity with the conquered peoples of colonial exploitation, such as American Indians and Eskimos (Trumpener 2007: xiii). Miranda Burgess, Evan Gottlieb and others have therefore increasingly rejected the idea of a straightforward separation between nationalism and globalism, arguing that both cultural and civic nationalism, far from being 'modular', grew out of the 'complex, uneven network of exchanges of ideas, people, goods, and money that accompanied the rise of the modern nation state' (Burgess 2009: 95–6). As Burgess has pointed out, nationalism under the conditions of what has been called 'early', 'nascent' or 'first-wave' globalisation is best seen as a 'dynamically fractured' conceptual model, 'pulled against itself by its origins in the debates on transnational political and uneven development *within* the British isles', as well as by its exportation to the British colonies and other spheres of colonial interest (Burgess 2009: 96). Even the very idea of 'Britishness' or 'Englishness' has, as Elizabeth Fay and Alan Richardson contend, become 'internally fractured' because of the 'global implications of Romantic imperialism and colonialism' (Fay and Richardson 1997: i).

For Burgess, the turn of the nineteenth century sees the rise of a new sense of global synchronicity encapsulated by the Romantic national tale (see also Chapters 2 and 4), which she argues is a 'profoundly "civic"' and highly 'fluid, transnational' 'model of the global public sphere [its] writers wished . . . to shape' (Burgess 2009: 93, 94). Richard Maxwell too has maintained that the 'increasing velocity of change' experienced in the Romantic period created what we might call a 'condensation in time', which, in turn, led to 'a kind of conceptual intimacy among the scattered denizens of a transformed world, who now share[d] points of reference as well as conditions of survival' (Maxwell 2000: 425). This sense of global synchronicity is neatly captured by the Irish novelist Maria Edgeworth in a letter to her stepmother of 29 December, 1821 about Scott's new novel, *The Pirate* (1821): 'Thanks to the printing press – the mail coach and the steam packet beyond the gifts of fairies we can all see and hear what each other are doing and do and read the same things nearly at the same time' (cited in Colvin 1971: 303). Edgeworth's letter describes the simultaneity of reading habits in Dublin and London, but it could easily be extended to other areas of colonial and trading interest around the world such as North America, India and the Pacific islands, where books, newspapers, magazines and other forms of printed matter circulated increasingly freely.

If by 1800 it had become conceivable to live in New South Wales, South America or New England and yet feel connected to certain regions or communities thousands of miles away in England or Ireland, it was both the result of changes in technology and changes in historical perspectives, particularly the new idea of history as a mass experience (Anderson 1993: 188). Georg Lukács has described the phenomenon of massification with reference to the Revolutionary and Napoleonic Wars: 'The French Revolution, the revolutionary wars and the rise and fall of Napoleon . . . for the first time made history a *mass experience*, and moreover on a European scale' (Lukács 1963: 25). Extending Lukács's argument, James Chandler has rightly argued that other (more global) forms of massification such as mass conscription, mass travel and mass migration were equally important in generating a wider sense of collective synchronicity in the period (Chandler 1998: 42). Although it is a somewhat nightmarish vision, William Wordsworth's representation of London in Book VII of the 1805 *Prelude* as a 'panoptic simulacrum of the colonial world' (O'Brien 2007: 132) or miniature version of the whole spatial system of empire brilliantly encapsulates the dizzying sense of time/space compression that imperialism, globalisation, modernity and massification collectively produced in early nineteenth-century Britain.

Case study: William Wordsworth, *The Prelude* (written 1805)

For Wordsworth, the space of St Bartholomew's Fair is symbolic of a modern imperial metropolis ('a type not false/ Of what the might City is itself' (7. 696–7)), a site where the turmoil, confusion and alienation of the globalising process is most evident. As a place where social, geographical and racial hierarchies are erased and 'jumbled up together', the fairground (and London more generally) is a terrifying example of the global reach of the British Empire:

> The silver-collared Negro with his timbrel,
> Equestrians, Tumblers, Women, Girls, and Boys,
> Blue-breeched, pink-vested, with high-towering plumes.
> —All moveables of wonder from all parts,

> Are here, Albinos, painted Indians, Dwarfs,
>
> . . .
>
> All out-o'-th'-way, far-fetched, perverted things,
> All freaks of nature, all Promethean thoughts
> Of man; his dulness, madness, and their feats
> All jumbled up together to make up
> This Parliament of Monsters.
>
> (7. 677–81, 688–92)

The ethnically mixed London crowd constantly threatens to turn into a deluge or swarm, combining the English working-class mob with its colonial counterpart in the form of 'out-o'-th'-way, far-fetched, perverted things', resulting in the 'blank confusion' of modernity:

> Oh, blank confusion! and a type not false
> Of what the mighty City is itself
> To all except a Straggler here and there,
> To the whole swarm of its inhabitants;
> An undistinguishable world to men
>
> (7. 696–700)

Wordsworth is unable to map or chart the dizzying array of networks, systems and practices that London encompasses, its 'very unrepresentability' symbolic 'of the abstract space of commodity and capital flows' (Makdisi 1998: 32). Indeed, it is in relation to the global spatio-temporal flows encapsulated by London that Wordsworth subsequently constructs a more stable, recognisable and knowable kind of place in the English countryside: a local 'spot of time' that he can control, map and order (7. 736–41).

Romanticism and empire

Historians and literary scholars of imperial Britain have increasingly categorised the late eighteenth and early nineteenth centuries as a period of scepticism towards empire, arguing that the cultural relativism of figures such as Adam Smith, Edmund Burke and Jeremy Bentham eventually gave way to a new imperialist variant of liberalism, which was driven by a profound sense of European cultural superiority and exemplified in the later thought of John Stuart Mill and Alexis de Tocqueville (1805–59) (see, for example, Pitts 2005). These so-called 'turn to empire' theses have been complemented by revised understandings of the relationship between 'East' and 'West'. Nigel Leask, for example, has questioned colonial paradigms as an adequate way of understanding Romantic writing, deconstructing rigid notions of 'East and West' by arguing that the Romantic period marks a moment of British and wider European colonial vulnerability: not only did Britain lose its colonies in America, but Abyssinia, Egypt, India and Mexico all resisted colonial rule, with varying degrees of success (Leask 2009: 17). The Romantic poet Anna Letitia Barbauld would certainly have agreed with Leask, when she argued in her contentious poem *Eighteen Hundred and Eleven; A Poem* (1812) that the war-mongering British Empire would soon be eclipsed by the republican United States: 'And think'st thou, Britain, still to sit at ease/ An island Queen amidst they subject seas' (Barbauld 1812: ll. 39–40).

Taking into account the fragility of the British Empire in the late eighteenth and early nineteenth centuries enables a new focus on points of cultural contact, communication and connection between Britain and its colonies that differs from traditional postcolonial understandings of the binary relationship between coloniser and colonised. Malcolm Kelsall, for example, has argued that it is not logical to read Romantic writers' relationship to imperialism 'retrospectively from the instantaneous present', thus infusing it with 'the guilt of the post-colonial West' and its politics of 'apologetic retreat' (Kelsall 1998: 245). At the same time, however, this emphasis on British Romantic liberalism has obscured the strong strand of conservative support for British expansionism by Robert Southey, Thomas De Quincey and other contributors to the *Quarterly* and *Annual Reviews*, as well as downplaying the contradictions that exist in the ostensibly anti-colonial writings of Smith, Burke and Bentham, all of whom were at least prepared to envisage a future in which population growth would make Britain's colonies viable and cost-effective (Winch 1965: 147–54).

There is little doubt that the Romantic period was 'a watershed' in British colonial history, 'witnessing a move from a protectionist colonial system . . . to a free-trade empire with a political and moral agenda' (Fulford and Kitson 1998: 3) that encouraged 'a new spirit of enlightened trusteeship' (Leask 2009: 271) towards indigenous religious, moral and political systems. But the debate over empire was not confined to Whig and radical voices. Southey's veneration of Anglicanism in his essays against Catholic Emancipation, for example, flowed not so much from his own personal faith as from his political conviction that a national church was central to British liberty at home and control abroad (Eastwood 1989: 284). The growing commitment of many commentators to British colonial expansion was similarly motivated by a desire to extend the benefits of a liberal British civilisation to other countries. While some abolitionists, such as Anthony Benezet (1713–84) in his *Some Historical Account of Guinea* (1772), represented natives as noble savages living a pastoral life until interrupted by Europeans, most writers in the period (regardless of their attitude towards slavery) looked forward to their eventual Christianisation and civilisation.

Some scholars have even found Romantic discourse to be complicit in a new kind of racism, citing the emphasis on blood, soil and climate in some Romantic-era abolitionist literature (Young 1995: 42; Anderson 1993: 60), although others characterise late-eighteenth- and early-nineteenth-century attitudes towards Africa, the Orient and elsewhere as more open-minded than the aggressive biological racism of the Victorian period (Brantlinger 1988: 217). Yet the rhetoric of British liberality and civility was troubled by a number of factors: for one thing, the repression and corruption of the Pitt government had resulted in a number of voluntary emigrations as well as the flight of radicals to America and elsewhere, suggesting that the mother country was herself plagued with economic and moral concerns. As we have seen in Chapter 3, the British political situation prompted Coleridge, Wordsworth and Southey, for example, to envisage the possibility of a utopian society in America that they called 'Pantisocracy'. For another thing, slavery was increasingly seen as incompatible with the aims and objectives of a civilised nation-state. The question of internal and external forms of slavery – from the suffering of African plantation slaves and those on slaver ships (see, for example, J. M. W. Turner's painting of the *Slave Ship* discussed in Chapter 5) to the plight of white child chimney sweeps and female governesses – made the issue of abolition one of the most pressing concerns in late-eighteenth- and early-nineteenth-century Britain.

Slavery and abolitionism

Having been declared unconstitutional in Britain by Lord Mansfield's (1705–93) anti-slavery ruling of 1772, completely abolishing slavery at home and in the colonies was seen by abolitionists as an important step in restoring British prestige against the lost American colonies, which, in continuing to practise slavery in the face of their Constitution, were considered hypocrites of the worst kind. Anti-slavery discourse also acted as one of the few forms of opposition to Pitt's government after the passing of the Gagging Acts in December 1795 (see Chapter 1). John Thelwall's novel *The Daughter of Adoption* (1801), for example, considers the slave rebellions of 1791–1804 in French St Dominigue (now Haiti) as comparable to the author's own experiences of persecution as a radical in Britain. Despite focusing on a French colony, the novel does not allow the reader to forget about British colonialism: 'O Jamaica! Jamaica! Thou island of abominations and horrors! What inconceivable cruelties are there with which those who insult our national virtue by calling themselves English planters have not polluted thee!' (Thelwall 2013: 170). Like William Earle's *Obi; or, The History of Three-Fingered Jack* (1800) and Leonora Sansay's (1773–?) *Secret History; or, The Horrors of St. Domingo* (1808), Thelwall's novel suggests the significance of the Haitian Revolution as the first successful anti-colonial slave rebellion against European powers, even if, as Peter Kitson argues, the text reproduces stereotypes of black sexuality and fails 'to fashion an appropriate textual iconography for the suffering of the slaves' (Kitson 2010: 120–38).

Other abolitionists also saw slavery as a forum for wider political concerns. For Evangelical abolitionists such as Hannah More, Mary Butt Sherwood (1775–1851) and William Wilberforce (1759–1833), abolitionism was part of a larger attempt to morally reform the British ruling classes. However, the inter-relationship of abolitionism and other political and economic concerns could be problematic. As Deirdre Coleman has pointed out, the ideology of anti-slavery was sometimes closely allied to that of colonisation and imperialism (Coleman 1994: 342). In *Romantic Colonization and British Anti-Slavery* (2005) Coleman draws on David

Brion Davis' *The Problem of Slavery in the Age of Revolution* (1975) to provocatively argue that many of the leading anti-slavery campaigners, including Dr John
Fothergill (1712–80) and Dr John Coakley Lettsom (1774–1815), were less concerned with how emancipated slaves might express their capacity for freedom than
with devising substitute schemes for slave labour (Coleman 2005: 5). Thomas
Clarkson's (1760–1846) *Essay on the Impolicy of the African Slave Trade* (1788) –
one of the sources for Coleridge's famous 'Lecture on the Slave Trade' to Bristol
and West Country dissenters in 1795 – argued, for example, that it would be preferable to colonise and commercialise Africa for commodities like sugar and cotton
than to export enslaved Africans to the West Indies for the same purpose.

This dovetailing of abolitionist and imperial thinking led to a number of contradictory and ambiguous positions in Romantic-era writing, some of which are encapsulated in Jane Austen's novel *Mansfield Park* (1814). On the one hand, the novel's
silences concerning the Bertram family's dependence on slaves in the West Indian
colony of Antigua do not diminish Austen's support for the abolition of the slave
trade. Indeed, Coleman has rightly pointed to the novel's critique of the indolence
and luxury of Lady Bertram languishing with her pug on the sofa at Mansfield,
combining the traits of the English woman with the features of the West Indian plan-
tation-owner's wife (Coleman 1994: 354), a female 'type' also rebuked more explicitly in Anna Letitia Barbauld's 'Epistle to Lord Wilberforce' (1791): 'Lo! where
reclin'd, pale Beauty courts the breeze,/ Diffus'd on sofas of voluptuous ease;/ With
anxious awe, her menial train around,/ Catch her faint whispers of half-utter'd
sound' (Barbauld 1792: ll. 58–61). At the same time, however, the novel's rejection
of absenteeism, whether at home in England or in the colonies, is suggestive of
Austen's continued commitment to British expansionism (Leask 2009: 271).

More generally, women's writing about slavery, and in particular their analogies
between their own disenfranchised state and that of black slaves, tended to perpet-
uate racial hierarchies that suggested the superiority of white women to black
people (Coleman 1994: 342). Hannah More's prose tract *The White Slave Trade.
Hints towards framing a Bill for the Abolition of the White Female Slave Trade, in
the cities of London and Westminster* (1792), for example, argues for the importance of abolishing slavery at home, a slavery that involved the wives, mothers and
daughters of the abolitionists themselves, in a way that totally elides black experiences. In Austen's *Emma* (1818) Jane Fairfax too insinuates that the English
governess suffers as much as African slaves:

> 'I did not mean, I was not thinking of the slave-trade,' replied Jane; 'governess-
> trade, I assure you, was all that I had in view; widely different certainly as to
> the guilt of those who carry it on; but as to the greater misery of the victims,
> I do not know where it lies.'
>
> (5. 325)

Similarly, in Mary Robinson's 1796 novel *Angelina* the heroine's father, Sir Edward
Clarendon, is both a West Indian slave owner and a tyrannical parent, who attempts
to barter his daughter for social advancement.

Alan Richardson's excellent analysis of Robert Southey's attempt to reproduce a radical Enlightenment critique of slavery in his 'Poems Concerning the Slave Trade' (1794–8), especially the six sonnets published in his 1797 *Poems*, draws out other ambiguities in abolitionist appeals, arguing that Southey 'founders on his apparent inability to represent a black subject without setting off the negative associations with blackness' (Richardson 1998: 143). For example, while Southey celebrates the Haitian Revolution in 'To the Genius of Africa' (1797), he increasingly turns to the heroic portrayal of white subjects in his 1810 verses on Lord Grenville (1759–1834), who saw the final passing of abolitionist legislation in 1806–7. Grenville becomes a symbol of British liberty and justice, as Southey envisions the entire African continent filled with gratitude for Grenville and England, just as, conversely, Barbauld rebukes an ungrateful England in her 'Epistle to Lord Wilberforce' on Parliament's rejection of his bill to end the slave trade.

Brycchan Carey has shown us the extent to which both anti- and pro-slavery writers in the period engaged with sentimental discourses surrounding the representation of suffering (Carey 2005), but the emphasis in Romantic-era writing on either the inhumanity of the white slaver or the genius of the white abolitionist is suggestive of the elision of the actual experiences of slaves. One exception is Olaudah Equiano's (1745–97) *Interesting Narrative or the Life of Olaudah Equiano* of 1789, which can perhaps best be described as an example of what Mary Louise Pratt calls 'auto-ethnography', whereby a colonised or enslaved subject undertakes to represent themselves in ways that engage with the colonisers' or enslavers' own terms (Pratt 1992: 7): not only does Equiano find that he is increasingly at ease with the European culture he initially deems so terrifying, professing a desire to 'imbibe' and 'imitate' the English culture in which he is immersed (Equiano 2001: 93), but he also uses his narrative to position himself politically in debates about slavery and the abolitionist cause in England.

Case study: Olaudah Equiano, *The Interesting Narrative or the Life of Olaudah Equiano* (1789)

Olaudah Equiano (Gustavus Vassa) was born in what is today Nigeria and kidnapped with his sister by slave traders headed for the West Indies at the age of 11. Volume one of the *Interesting Narrative* begins with a description of Equiano's native African culture, outlining customs, manners and religious practices, and pointing to the biological similarities between Africans and Christian Europeans: 'Let the polished and haughty European recollect that his ancestors were once, like the Africans, uncivilized, and even barbarous. Did Nature make them inferior to their sons? And should they too have been made slaves?' (Equiano 2001: 63). Equiano's journey into slavery begins when he is abducted from his village and subsequently finds himself on board a slaver ship:

I was not long suffered to indulge my grief; I was soon put down under the decks . . . I became so sick and low that I was not able to eat, not had I the least desire to taste anything. I now wished for the last friend, Death, to relieve me.

(Equiano 2001: 70–1)

The descriptions of the desperate conditions, extreme hardships and brutal treatment suffered by the author at the hands of the European slavers are punctuated by his wonder at new sights and experiences, but such wonder only serves to further illuminate the inhumanity of the white slavers. As Deirdre Coleman has rightly pointed out, the ultimate effect of Equiano's narrative is to produce a reversal of black and white binaries, so that it is the English that are savage and irrational rather than enslaved black people (Coleman 1994: 348), an oppositional strategy particularly evident when Equiano describes his fear that the white English sailors with their 'horrible looks, red faces, and long hair' were going to eat him (Equiano 2001: 70).

With support from the British abolitionist movement, Parliament enacted the Slave Trade Act in 1807, ending the transatlantic trade as carried out by British mercantile ships, but slavery in the colonies continued. Revolts and insurrections, such as the 'Baptist War' in Jamaica in 1832, helped to expedite the end of slavery (Craton 1983). The Slavery Abolition Act, passed in 1833, abolished slavery in the British Empire on 1 August 1834 (with the exception of St Helena, Ceylon and the territories administered by the East India Company) in return for monetary compensation to plantation owners. Children under six were completely freed but other slaves became apprentices until full freedom was granted in 1838.

Travel and exploration

As the travel narrative as a genre has been extensively discussed in Chapter 2, this section will instead consider the wider cultural significance of travel to remote geographic zones in the period. The Romantic interest in primitive cultures and the ensuing valorisation of various forms of cultural primitivism show us an eighteenth- and early-nineteenth-century British public consumed with desire for images of its distant 'others'. Curiosity, as Nigel Leask has reminded us, has both negative and positive connotations, promoting the desire for travel and knowledge, on the one hand, but also encouraging the commodification of wonderment or astonishment for economic gain, on the other hand (Leask 2002). The descriptive images of African women's sexual practices in James Bruce's (1730–94) *Travels to Discover the Source of the Nile* (1790), for example, made him seem to some a voyeur or 'curioso'. Similarly, some of the descriptions and engraved images of torture and bondage in John Gabriel Stedman's (1744–97) *Narrative of a Five Years' Expedition Against the Revolted Negroes of Surinam* (1796) have been deemed 'colonial pornography' (Wood 2002: 234).

Leask has noted the way in which curiosity increasingly gave way to 'bourgeois utility' following the inauguration of an official British 'exploration establishment' marked by the foundation of the African Association in 1788 (Leask 2002: 273). Mary Louise Pratt too has argued that the turn from navigational discovery to interior exploration coincided with a shift in European 'planetary consciousness' towards a utilitarian global classificatory project based on a Linnaean model that sought to systematise and explain, as well as appropriate, the natural landscapes of the New World (Pratt 1992: 11). Despite an official rhetoric of enlightened cosmopolitanism, international scientific expeditions became one of the most important instruments of European expansionism in the second half of the eighteenth century: mapping the earth's surface was inextricably linked to an ever-expanding search for commercially exploitable resources, territorial surveillance and administrative control, coinciding with a new territorial phase of global market capitalism (Pratt 1992: 9).

Romantic writing on voyages and interior exploration often simultaneously displays both the empiricism and systemisation that was the aim of scientific travel and the inevitable physical and moral conflicts provoked by colonial incursions and encounters with other peoples at different or uneven stages of development. The literature of shipwreck and maritime disaster had an especially important influence on Romantic representations of exploration. Connected with the tradition of spiritual autobiography, the figure of the suffering mariner had always had strong links with religious conventions, but the associations between maritime suffering and spiritual revelation were complicated by the rise of more empiricist modes of travel writing in the eighteenth century (Thompson 2007: 59–106). Samuel Taylor Coleridge's *Rime of the Ancient Mariner* (1798) is a text that perfectly encapsulates the interaction of spiritual and material suffering with imperial exploitation, and is suggestive of the ways in which wonder or curiosity about the New World could be fetishised and commodified.

Case study: Samuel Taylor Coleridge, *The Rime of the Ancient Mariner* (1798)

The main plot line of Coleridge's *The Rime of the Ancient Mariner* is based on the actions of a sailor, Simon Hatley (1685–?), who shot down an albatross while on a maritime expedition, as recorded in Captain George Shelvocke's (1675–1742) *Voyage Round the World by Way of the Great South Sea* (1726). Several commentators have accordingly claimed that the guilt the mariner feels after shooting the albatross might be a displacement of a more general guilt experienced by Western maritime nations for their treatment of native colonial cultures (McKusick 1993: 106; Ebbatson 1972: 198). Yet, as Debbie Lee has rightly pointed out, the albatross is just one possible symbol or emblem of guilt in the poem (Lee 2004: 57). What slows the ship is not so much the lack of wind or the navigational disaster at the South Pole, but rather the outbreak of death and disease, with accompanying symptoms such as tongues 'withered at the root' and 'choked with soot', 'throat unslaked, with black lips baked' and eyes 'glazed' (ll. 132, 134, 151, 140). As Lee argues, these symptoms suggest that the crew fall prey to the kinds of deaths from malaria, leprosy and yellow fever that awaited British seamen voyaging into tropical zones (Lee 2004: 56–7). More general images of rot, filth, disease and decay join these images of colonial diseases, as Coleridge turns the natural causes of these epidemics into more mysterious moral ones: 'the very deeps did rot: O Christ . . ./ Yea, slimy things did crawl with legs/ Upon the slimy sea' (ll. 119, 121–2). The poem specifically links this rot to the death of the mariner's shipmates, associating the ruination of the natural world with the ruination of the shipmen and, more generally, with the destruction of the British national body: 'I looked upon the rotting sea,/ And drew my eyes away;/ I looked upon the ghastly deck,/ And there the dead men lay' (ll. 234–7).

Patrick J. Keane has traced many of the poem's symbols and images to sources in debates on abolition and slavery, arguing that both the ship that the mariner sails on and the ghostly spectre ship encountered by the crew may be slaver ships (Keane 1994: 146). Lee has also persuasively argued that Coleridge links the disease of slavery to the destruction of individual bodies, following abolitionists such as Thomas Clarkson, who maintained that the slave trade was insupportable because of the diseases to which slaver crews were exposed (Lee 2004: 57). The poem can therefore be seen as a radical critique of imperialism in that it debunks the myth of the maritime hero by showing the actual physical state of the mariners on their homecoming. But, arguably, *The Rime* is less an attack on colonial expansion than on the fate of British sailors and their families, as well as on the unrealistic expectations of the British public. The feverish mariner could be seen either as a representative of the ruined British shipman rotting on the ship's deck or as a symbol of the fever of the British imagination, always thirsting for new tales of discovery and adventure: the 'uncertain hour' when 'agony returns;/ And till my ghastly tale is told/ This heart within me burns' (ll. 575–7).

Migration, penal colonies and émigré experience

Travel in the Romantic period was not always occasioned by discovery, exploration and adventure, but also by migration of both the voluntary and the involuntary kind. Forced to find an alternative location to which to transport its convicts after American independence, Britain turned to the newly discovered lands of Australia, particularly New South Wales, claimed for Britain by James Cook (1728–79) on a voyage to the Pacific in 1770. In 1778 Joseph Banks (1743–1820) reported on the suitability of Botany Bay for a new penal settlement, and in 1788 the first shipment of convicts arrived in Australia, with tens of thousands of people subsequently being transported to New South Wales and Van Diemen's Land. Along with penal colonies, white settler communities were also encouraged and established voluntarily in Australia, South Africa (in particular, in the Eastern Cape Colony), Canada and elsewhere, largely because British resettlement in these regions was seen as preferable to continuing emigration to the now independent United States (see Chapter 1). As Karen O'Brien has pointed out, most colonial emigrants were from Scotland, Ireland and Wales, and were therefore 'themselves the victims of an ongoing, internal imperial process of disinheritance, political oppression and clearance' (O'Brien 2007: 126). Moreover, English, Irish, Scottish and Welsh immigrants were often settled separately, reflecting internal ethnic divisions within Britain. There were thus clear links between the migrations to colonies in the Americas, Africa, Australia and the South Seas and the internal 'othering' of a newly unionised Britain (see Chapter 4).

O'Brien has pointed to the 'imaginative investment' by British Romantic writers in white settler colonies overseas (O'Brien 2007: 121), particularly between 1790 and 1830, when emigration was largely seen as an outlet for the country's poor and more generally as a response to the concerns about poverty and population growth expressed in tracts such as Robert Malthus's *Essay on the Principles of Population* (1798) (see the case study in Chapter 1). Although radicals tended to oppose emigration on the grounds that it undermined the imperatives for social reform in Britain, more conservative commentators, such as Southey in his article 'On the State of the Poor' (1812), saw emigration both as a means of dealing with demographic issues such as surplus population and as an opportunity to export British culture, as well as a massive national investment opportunity in the form of new markets (Coleman 2005: 123). In Southey's epic poem *Madoc* (1805), for example, images of darkness are associated with the monarchies of Europe, whereas the beginnings of a new dawn is imagined in America: 'soon would I/ Behold that other world, where yonder sun/ Speeds now, to dawn in glory!' (3. 650–7). The poem initially imagines a group of medieval Welshmen discovering America, but Madoc's goal quickly becomes imperialist in orientation, and he faces the disintegration of his own utopian vision as he is forced either to control native populations or expel them (Bolton 2006: 125). Southey's earlier *Botany Bay Eclogues* (1794) are similarly suggestive of idealistic transferrals of white European ideologies abroad, but they are more concerned with the victims of unjust social circumstances than later works such as *Madoc*.

Case study: Robert Southey, *Botany Bay Eclogues* (1794)

In Southey's five eclogues each of the speakers, conversing or soliloquising during a different time of the day (morning, noon, evening, night), has been transported for life to the penal colony of Botany Bay, New South Wales. Reflecting on their past actions, the speakers illuminate the injustices of English society and, in particular, the English legal system: Elinor (morning), the sole female speaker, for example, has sunk into prostitution after the death of her father; Humphrey and William (noon) have been condemned for the crimes of theft and shooting partridges respectively; John, Samuel and Richard (evening) have been ruined in the army and navy; and Frederic (night) has been transported for poaching, even though it was to avoid starvation. Each speaker considers him or herself an exile or outcast from England. Playing on the theme of exile traditionally present in Virgil's classical eclogues, but seeking to invert the traditional values of the epic form (Bainbridge 2003: 83), Southey uses the 'savage' and 'joyless' shores of Botany Bay in order to condemn the social injustice of 'angry England':

> Welcome ye savage lands, ye barbarous climes,
> Where angry England sends her outcast sons—
> I hail your joyless shores! my weary bark
> Long tempest-tost on Life's inclement sea,
> Here hails her haven! welcomes the drear scene,
> The marshy plain, the briar-entangled wood,
> And all the perils of a world unknown.
>
> (ll. 51–7)

However, he also depicts an idealised land of natural beauty and opportunity, uncorrupted by European civilisation:

> Welcome, wilderness,
> Nature's domain! for here, as yet unknown
> The comforts and the crimes of polish'd life,
> Nature benignly gives to all enough,
> Denies to all superfluity.
>
> (ll. 73–7)

Australia is savage, wild and uncivilised, but it is also a place where the 'comforts and the crimes of polish'd life' are 'as yet unknown', making it unclear whether the Australian landscape is meant to be redemptive or whether it will cause criminals to repent because of its harshness (Brantlinger 1998: 111). The poem suggests that the convicts are privileged to see a natural environment in its original state, untouched by human hands, and implies that, through hard work and mutual endeavor, an idyllic version of British civilisation can be replicated or recreated in the colonies.

Migration (forced or otherwise) did not, of course, only occur from Britain to its colonies or former colonies. There were also a growing number of immigrants to Britain after the French Revolution. Conservatives tended to use the émigrés to highlight Britain's liberty and freedom as a liberal place of refuge from anarchy and terror, whereas radicals and progressives used the émigré position to critique British injustices against minority groups and warmongering. Interestingly, émigré experience was particularly resonant in women's writing of the period. This is not to suggest that émigré experience was confined to women or that only women wrote about émigrés, but rather that émigré experience was used by women to reflect their sense of shared disenfranchisement with other groups in early-nineteenth-century society. Adriana Craciun has argued that French émigrés arriving in Britain after the 1790s counteracted an 'intensifying nationalism' with new forms of cosmo-politanism (Craciun 2007: 169). Charlotte Smith's four-volume novel *Marchmont* (1796), for example, rejects national boundaries in favour of imagined communi-ties of transnational sympathy: 'Thrown by misfortune from the bosom of my country, I early learned to be a Citizen of the World. – In what obscure corner of it . . . . shall *I* ever find a quiet asylum?' (Smith 1796: 4. 101). Yet as the above quotation suggests, Smith's cosmopolitan ideal of the citizen of the world is double-edged, suggesting both freedom and exile, an ambiguity she also pursues in her earlier poem on émigré experiences, *The Emigrants* (1793), discussed in the following case study.

Case study: Charlotte Smith, *The Emigrants* (1793)

Book 1 of Charlotte Smith's long poem *The Emigrants* is set in November 1792, just before King Louis XVI's execution and England's declaration of war on France. The emigrants of Smith's title wander along the English coast, haunted by the violence of the French Revolution (Wolfson 2000: 516); but as Smith makes clear in Book 2 of the poem, set six months later in April 1793, her sympathy is universal rather than national in its orienta-tion, extending to all on the 'suffering globe' (Smith 1793: 2. 422). Even more importantly, for Smith the suffering of exiles is potentially instructive to the current powers of England:

> Ye venal, worthless hirelings of a Court!
> Ye pamper'd Parasites! whom Britons pay
> For forging fetters for them; rather here
> Study a lesson that concerns ye much;
> And, trembling, learn, that if oppress'd too long,
> The raging multitude, to madness stung,
> Will turn on their oppressors; and, no more
> By sounding titles and parading forms
> Bound like tame victims, will redress themselves!
>
> (1. 329–37)

Smith thus parallels the fate of the émigrés with the British victims of state violence and injustice. Moreover, the experience of the French aristocratic emigrants offers a 'lesson' to their English counterparts: if they continue to oppress the common citizens of England then these citizens will become a 'raging multitude', which will no longer be quieted by the usual forms of aristocratic power (e.g. 'sounding titles and parading forms'). In Book 2 of the poem Smith shifts her focus from national injustice to a gendered critique of war, conflating revolutionary and gender politics by focusing on the plight of widows and orphans: 'A wretched Woman, pale and breathless, flies!/ And, gazing round her, listens to the sound/ Of hostile footsteps' (2. 258–60). This combination of the personal and the political is suggestive of Smith's understanding of the ways in which the individual – particularly the individual female – is caught up in larger ideological and political systems.

Orientalism and the East

Following the loss of its American colonies in 1783, Britain sought to establish a so-called 'second empire', shifting its attention away from the Americas and towards Asia, the Pacific and Africa. The East India Company drove the expansion of the British Empire in the East. British control over India was virtually complete after the French Revolutionary Wars, but Britain also expanded its territory outside of India via the eviction of Napoleon from Egypt (1799), the capture of Java from the Netherlands (1811), the acquisition of Singapore (1819) and Malacca (1824) and the defeat of Burma (1826). Other areas in the East were described as part of Britain's 'informal' empire because of profitable trade links or monopolies: for example, Britain was engaged in a profitable yet illegal opium export trade to China from the 1730s, which led to the First Opium War between Britain and China from 1840–2.

The Orient held a widespread fascination both for Romantic writers and reading audiences. Between 1798 and 1817 several writers responded to the public's demand for settings in Asia, North Africa and the Caucasus: Walter Savage Landor (1775–1864) began the craze with *Gebir* (1798), followed by Robert Southey's *Thalaba the Destroyer* (1801) and *The Curse of Kehama* (1810), as well as Byron's best-selling Oriental tales *The Giaour* (1813), *The Corsair* (1814) and *Lara* (1814), Percy Shelley's *Alastor* (1815) and Thomas Moore's *Lalla Rookh* (1817). Moore's *Lalla Rookh* and Byron's Oriental tales, in particular, were hugely popular, selling over 250,000 copies. The early-nineteenth-century literary market was certainly in the throes of a mania for Orientalist writing but, as John Regan has pointed out, poets and critics also debated the question of how to versify an Oriental subject matter that was both 'hugely attractive and largely unpalatable to British readerships' (Regan 2014: 85). The annotating tendency in Oriental poetry of the period underlines the fact that poets and historians looking to the East were preoccupied with counteracting the 'counterfactual excesses' of their Eastern sources – a preoccupation that manifested itself in the compilation of errata (Regan 2014: 86). In *Thalaba*, for example, Southey describes how 'all the skill I might possess in the art of poetry was required to counterbalance the disadvantage of a mythology . . . which would appear monstrous if its deformities were not kept out of sight' (4. 4).

Southey's concern to discipline and dominate his Eastern sources is suggestive of Edward Said's famous argument that 'Orientalism is a Western style for dominating, restructuring, and having authority over the Orient' so as to systematically discipline, 'manage – and even produce – the Orient' (Said 1977: 3). Drawing on the work of Michel Foucault and his association of knowledge and power, Said's primary argument is not only that the West constructed or created the East, but also that the Orient and other regions fulfilled Europe's need for psychological, social and political centering, so that 'European culture gained in strength and identity by setting itself off against the Orient as a sort of surrogate and even underground self' (Said 1977: 3). The East thereby became the repository of those characteristics that the West itself did not acknowledge (sensuality, decadence, violence, etc.) and could map onto other locations, such as the East Indies, Africa and Latin America. This was a point not lost on writers of the time. In *The Missionary: An Indian Tale* (1811), for example, the attraction of the Irish writer Sidney Owenson's seventeenth-century Portuguese missionary, Hilarion, to the Indian prophetess, Luxima, results in her excommunication and eventual death, underscoring Owenson's belief that it is the Indian colonial subject – and, by analogy, the Irish colonial subject – who suffers the consequences of Portuguese/British intervention into indigenous belief systems.

Other texts considered the impact of British imperialism and colonialism on the English subject and national body. Thomas De Quincey's quasi-autobiographical *Confessions of an English Opium-Eater* (1821), for example, can be read as an attempted inoculation against infection and disease from the East (Barrell 1991: 109), but his apologia for opium is also an apologia for imperialism, a means of displacing domestic anxieties onto the Oriental 'other' (Leask 1992: 171). De Quincey's focus on China, Malaysia and other East Asian sites as scenes of 'horror' is relatively rare in Romantic-era writing, and China in particular has been neglected as a site for the British Romantic imagination, although this neglect has recently been rectified by Peter Kitson's excellent *Forging Romantic China: Sino-British Cultural Exchange, 1760–1840* (2014).

Case study: Thomas De Quincey, *Confessions of an English Opium-Eater* (1821)

In De Quincey's account of a wandering Malay's visit to his cottage in Grasmere, a servant girl, Barbara, informs De Quincey that there is 'a sort of demon below, whom she clearly imagined my art could exorcise from the house' (De Quincey 1998: 56). As Nigel Leask points out, De Quincey 'mobilizes the full armoury of racial discrimination' in the 'telling confrontation' between the pure English servant girl and the Oriental 'other' (Leask 1992: 210):

> The beautiful English faced of the girl, and its exquisite fairness, together with her erect and independent attitude, contrasted with the sallow and bilious skin of the Malay, enameled or veneered with mahogany by marine air, his small, fierce, restless eyes, thin lips, slavish gestures and adorations.
>
> (De Quincey 1998: 56)

Unable to lay his hands on a Malay dictionary, De Quincey addresses the Malay in some lines from the *Iliad*, which is the nearest approximation to an Oriental language he can muster. To address the Malay in Greek, ostensibly an act of welcome and friendship, points to the elitism of Western culture and civilisation. De Quincey's (potentially lethal) gift of opium to the Malay is a similarly ambiguous one. De Quincey assumes that the Malay, by virtue of his Eastern descent, is an opium eater, an assumption built on very shaky foundations of fact, given that Britain introduced the opium trade to China and elsewhere.

In a merging of external and internal fears, the Malay subsequently moves from reality to dream in a section of the text entitled 'The Pains of Opium': 'The Malay has been a fearful enemy for months' (De Quincey 1998: 72). In the opium dream initiated by the Malay's visit De Quincey sees India, Egypt and China merge into a mass of snakes, crocodiles, pagodas, reeds and mud (De Quincey 1998: 73). Taking on multiple identities ('I was the priest, I was the idol'), De Quincey is unable to maintain any hierarchical distinction between his Eastern and Western selves (De Quincey 1998: 74). This hybridity is terrifying, as he becomes smeared with the 'Nilotic mud', buried in coffins and incarcerated in pyramids (De Quincey 1998: 74). The European self-presence is overwhelmed by the terror of cultural miscegenation: the horrid alien other is revealed as the double of his own consciousness, ultimately symbolised by the leering head of the crocodile. Thus the opium dream reveals De Quincey's discovery that his is a hybrid identity: his relationship with an imaginary East, like that of an imperial power with its colonial dependencies, is a relation of interdependence and can no longer be thought of in terms of a safe transaction between self and other, even the qualified selfhood of the text's title.

As the case study of De Quincey's *Confessions* suggests, Romantic scholarship on the East has called into question Said's formulation of a historically unified Western attitude towards the East, pointing not only to a range of colonial encounters and subject positions but also to the ambivalences of these encounters. As Paul Hamilton has pointed out, while the initial presentation of Conrad's pirate company in Byron's *The Corsair* 'unproblematically maps a sublime sense of self on to imperial politics' – 'O'er the glad waters of the dark blue sea,/ Our thoughts are boundless, and our souls are free,/ Far as the breeze can bear, the billows foam,/

Survey our empire, and behold our home' (1. 1–4) – Conrad the Greek eventually becomes ensnared by Gulnare, the eastern 'homicide', who rescues him from imprisonment by murdering Pasha Seyd (Hamilton 2014: 234). In throwing off the restraints of femininity (despite it being the compromised femininity of the harem) and rescuing the hero, Gulnare effectively emasculates and Orientalises Conrad, suggesting the ambivalent results of colonial encounters with the East: 'His latest virtue then had joined the rest' (3. 548).

Female writers and the East

Female writers and travellers from Mary Wortley Montagu (1689–1762) to Harriet Martineau established an alternative, gender-specific discourse on the East that both collaborated in the ideologies of European colonialism and also entered into complex negotiations with it (Melman 1992: 2). Montagu in her *Letters from the Levant or Turkish Embassy Letters* (1763), for example, represents the intimate, private female space of the harem, hitherto represented as the locus of exotic sex and masculine desire, as a humanised haven associated with sexual liberty for women. Female Victorian writers, on the other hand, remade the harem in the image of the middle-class home, where women's privacy and morality could be exercised, thereby familiarising and domesticating the Orient (Mills 2005: 3; Melman 1992: 316). Some of the ambiguities of the female writing position – in particular the reification of domesticity – are captured in the following case study of Felicia Hemans's 1829 poem 'The Traveller at the Source of the Nile'.

Case study: Felicia Hemans, 'The Traveller at the Source of the Nile' (1829)

If Hemans was considered *the* representative female writer or poetess of the period by influential critics such as Francis Jeffrey and William Gifford, she nonetheless chooses a masculine subject position in her popular discovery poem: 'The Traveller at the Source of the Nile'. Like its companion piece 'The Flower of the Desert' (based on an episode in Mungo Park's (1771–1806) *Travels in the Interior Districts of Africa* (1799)), 'The Traveller' is concerned with a British male explorer in North East Africa. Hemans draws on a passage in James Bruce's *Travels to Discover the Source of the Nile* (1790), in which its author portrays a complex moment of sublime discovery when he claims that the Fountains of Gish are the source of the Nile. Focusing on her traveller's subsequently troubled reflections more than on his initial triumph or '[t]he rapture of the conqueror's mood' (l. 13), Hemans hints at the emptiness of imperial rhetoric:

> Night came with stars:- across his soul
> There swept a sudden change;

E'en at the pilgrim's glorious goal
A shadow dark and strange
Breathed from the thought, so swift to fall
O'er triumph's hour – *and is this all?*

(ll. 19–24)

Imperial conquest and the masculine self-aggrandisement initially displayed in the familiar 'monarch-of-all-I-survey' trope quickly give way to domestic reminiscences of home and hearth ('His childhood haunts of play' (l. 32)), abandoning the traveller's glory for nostalgic tenderness:

Where was the glow of power and pride?
The spirit born to roam?
His alter'd heart within him died
With yearnings for his home!
All vainly struggling to repress
That gush of painful tenderness.

(ll. 43–8)

In replacing masculine glory with female tenderness and global ties with domestic priorities, Hemans attempts to transform the value placed on familiar domestic contexts. In some ways therefore she could be said to define a new space for self-empowerment and identity based on the more local ties of family and domesticity. But, as Nigel Leask points out, it would be a mistake to read this poem solely or even primarily as a gender-oriented critique of masculine exploration or British imperialism. Instead, he argues that Hemans defines 'a newly conjugal imperial subject based on sentimental ties of nostalgia and kinship' (Leask 2009: 290). This was an imperial model later exploited by Benjamin Disraeli, Rudyard Kipling and others as Britain's colonial power expanded in the later nineteenth century.

British India

Not all Romantic-era writing on the East can or should be read as an apology for empire. Jenny Sharpe argues that 'in the historical example of India', for example, '*sympathy* and *identity* are equally constitutive of Orientalist discourse as *hostility* and *alterity*' (Sharpe 1993: 38). Javed Majeed too has shown that at the beginning of the nineteenth century attitudes towards India were riven between William Jones (1746–94) and Warren Hasting's (1732–1818) 'Orientalist' view of India, which valued Indian culture and tradition, and the 'Anglicist', utilitarian or evangelical view, encapsulated in James Mill's *History of British India* (1822), that India should be governed by English law and administrative systems (Majeed 1992: 3–4; see also Bolton 2006: 200). Despite his increasing conservatism, Jones, for example, did not simply impose a colonialist discourse and rhetoric on India, but also partially fostered Indian nationalism by assisting in the process of liberating its writings from Brahma control and facilitating what became known as the 'Bengal Renaissance' (Franklin 2011: 272; Mukherjee 1968: 3).

Hastings, as the Governor of Bengal and director of the East India Company, also believed in allowing for Indian cultural and political autonomy. Yet by the end of the eighteenth century there were growing fears that the East India Company was becoming despotic towards the 40 million Indians living under its rule. Edmund Burke's impeachment of Hastings in 1788 on charges of corruption partly stemmed from concerns about protecting India from the East India Company, but also highlighted his belief in Britain's responsibility to improve, transform and advance its Indian subjects. Burke's speeches leading up to the trial of Hastings from 1788–95 may be suggestive of colonial guilt, but Burke was not an anti-colonialist: he instead argued for a different and more effective colonial policy than that executed by Hastings and others. The dissolution of the East India Company in 1858 and the assumption of direct imperial control of India under the British Raj saw the zenith of such ambitions, ushering in a new period of 'high' empire, as Britain consolidated its hold on its colonies.

More recently, several scholars of British India have extended their studies to local and indigenous writing in the period, recognising that we need literary studies that do not view the East primarily as an abstraction, reflection and projection of British or other European imaginations. Anthologies and bibliographical surveys of Indian writing in the eighteenth and nineteenth centuries are now copious, but there has also been an increased critical interest in indigenous (especially East Indian) writing in British India, such as Dan White's *From Little London to Little Bengal: Religion, Print, and Modernity in Early British India, 1793–1835* (2013), Daniel Sanjiv Roberts's 'Dark Interpretations: Romanticism's Ambiguous Legacy in India' (2012), Rosinka Chaudhuri's *Derozio, Poet of India* (2008) and forthcoming monographs by Manu Samriti Chander and Humberto Garcia. These studies seek to replace binary divisions between 'metropole' and 'periphery' by arguing that identities in British India were often formulated across national and proto-national boundaries (White 2013: 110). White's study, in particular, focuses on the fluidity of print cultures in a period of colonialism and imperialism, looking not only at periodicals but also at missionary education and the establishment of mixed-race schools such as Drummond's Academy in Calcutta.

The example of the poet and political activist Henry Louis Vivien Derozio (1809–31) indicates the ways in which colonial immigration could have a profound impact on local culture in Bengal and elsewhere. The son of an English and a Portuguese settler, the Calcutta-born Derozio attended Drummond's, where he was exposed to the work of Romantic writers such as Keats, Byron and Shelley. Despite being of European descent, Derozio was passionately attached to Bengal and is considered one of the first nationalist poets of Modern India: 'My Country! In the days of Glory Past/ A beauteous halo circled round thy brow/ And worshiped as deity thou wast' (*To India – My Native Land* (1828), ll. 1–3). In 1826 Derozio joined the staff of Hindu College, established by the Bengali editor and educationalist

Raja Rammohum Roy (1772–1833) (White 2013: 114). Derozio's students were known as 'Derozians' and his teachings inspired the 'Young Bengal Movement', which formed part of the religious and social advances of the Hindu community during the nineteenth-century Bengal Renaissance. The literary writing of this extraordinary renaissance, and its interaction with various other forms of colonial writing, including European settler and metropolitan writing, is only now receiving the recognition it deserves in accounts of the literary culture of British India.

America, the Caribbean and the southern hemisphere

North America: the United States and Canada

Fiona Robertson has pointed to the ways in which the marginalisation of transatlantic crossings in accounts of British history after the loss of the American colonies is echoed in their marginalisation in literary history (Robertson 2014: 246). In *America: A Prophecy* (1793), for example, William Blake reimagines the American War of Independence, but there is a disconcerting elision of America at the end of the poem, as the narrative of revolution re-crosses the Atlantic to France and European revolutionary discourse. Similarly, scholarly analyses of the Romantic period in Britain continue to associate its beginnings with the French Revolution in 1789, ignoring the fact 'that for the writers of Wordsworth's immediate generation – those born in and around 1770 – the actual war taking place during their childhood was the War of Independence' (Robertson 2014: 249; see also Introduction). This, Robertson astutely argues, overlooks the ways in which the French Revolution was, for British observers, secondary both to Britain's 'Glorious' Revolution of 1688 and the less glorious loss of the American colonies.

Paul Giles too has convincingly argued that the American Revolutionary War was a defining moment in the Anglo-American relationship, generating a more profound and protracted influence on both nations than has generally been allowed (Giles 2001: 1–2). North America's cultural and political achievements after the American Revolution certainly aroused a number of anxieties in Britain, the central one being whether the centre of civilisation might eventually shift westward from Europe to America. James Chandler has demonstrated that levels of anti-American sentiment were high from 1815–30, and that fears were aroused by issues such as the new American constitution, the Napoleonic Wars, emigration and an increased literary competitiveness between Britain and America. All of these things, he argues, 'brought a new America newly into focus in Britain', although it was not until after the wars with France had ended that 'America watching' became a 'British national hobby' (Chandler 1998: 447, 453). John Keats's long journal letters written to his brother and sister-in-law in America after they had emigrated, for example, not only manifest a desire to discover what life in America is like, but also attempt to situate America within a wider context of historical and cultural improvement:

> Dilke . . . pleases himself with the idea that America will be the country to take up the human intellect where England leaves off – I differ there with him

greatly – A country like the united states whose greatest Men are Franklins
and Washingtons will never do that.

(*Letters*, I, 397)

Keats primarily dismisses Washington and Franklin (1706–90) because of their
attitude to financial gain, representing America as a place of cultural materialism
in its privileging of politicians over poets and pragmatism over the imagination.

The celebrated Irish poet Thomas Moore was similarly disappointed in what he
perceived as the materialism, cultural barrenness and political hypocrisy of the
infant republic (Moore 2011: 79). After travelling extensively through America
and Canada in the summer and autumn of 1804, Moore published verses denigrat-
ing America, the Democratic-Republican party and Thomas Jefferson (1743–1826),
whose alleged affair with a black slave he famously describes in 'Epistle VII' of
his *Epistles, Odes, and Other Poems* (1806): 'The weary statesman for repose hath
fled/ From halls of council to his negro's shed/ Where blest he woos some black
Aspasia's grace/ And dreams of freedom in his slave's embrace!' (Moore 1806: ll.
7–10). A repeated theme in Moore's writing on the United States are his observations on slavery: 'Who can, with patience, for a moment see/ The medley mass of
pride and misery,/ Of whips and charters, manacles and rights,/ Of slaving blacks
and democratic whites' ('Epistle VI', Moore 1806: ll. 139–42). Moore's writing
on Canada, on the other hand, emphasises the sublime beauty of the Canadian
landscape in comparison to the wretchedness of American cities (Moore 2011: 84).
Moore's criticisms of the United States and his preference for Canada provoked
outrage in America, but they were part of a wider attempt to curtail the appeal of the
fledging republic for British emigrants, as evident in poems such as Wordsworth's
'Ruth' (written 1800).

Case study: William Wordsworth, 'Ruth: Or the Influences of Nature' (1800)

Karen O'Brien has rightly suggested that many of Wordsworth's poems are
unsuccessful attempts at emigration or failures to settle, associated meta-
phorically with the unsettled life and mind of the American savage-settler
(O'Brien 2007: 129–30). In 'Ruth: Or the Influences of Nature', from the
1800 *Lyrical Ballads*, the faithless 'youth from Georgia's shore' (l. 19) who
abandons Ruth is liked to a native Indian ('with Indian blood you deem him
sprung' (l. 25)), emboldened by the freedoms of the American victory and
imbued with a kind of rootless desire to roam (ll. 19–20). Ruth learns of
America only vicariously through the tales of this youth. In his depiction of
America, Wordsworth drew on popular travel narratives such as Jonathan
Carver's (1710–80) *Travels Through the Interior Parts of North America*
(1778), William Bartram's (1739–1823) *Travels in Florida* (1791) and
Samuel Hearne's (1745–92) *Journey from Hudson's Bay to the Northern*

Ocean (1795) (Bolton 2006: 120). Wordsworth thus borrows the trope of discovery from these narratives and applies it to his own familiar Lake District, highlighting the exotic and picturesque descriptions of the American landscape in Bartram and other travel narratives, but using it to warn against exciting fantasies of other lands. The unbalancing effect of the American climate, for example, is obvious, leading to moral failing in the youth (ll. 145–56): 'The slave of low desires' (l. 153). As Carol Bolton argues, Wordsworth's message is that identity and self-possession rely on being 'content at home' (Bolton 2006: 123). The place to explore is the familiar – one's own world – as Ruth initially does in the Quantocks as a child. 'Ruth' is a response to contemporary idealisations of colonial life in America, suggesting that such visions are literary creations that elide the realities and pragmatic anxieties of settler life in America.

While not all commentators were against emigration to America, even radical and liberal supporters of America such as Leigh Hunt were unwilling to concede American superiority in the arts and sciences. Surprisingly, this was a view echoed by some Americans themselves, suggesting the 'amorphousness' both of the new republic's territorial and political status, and 'parallel uncertainties about the status and authority of American discourse' (Giles 2012: 1). As Richard Cronin has argued, the extraordinary success in Britain of Washington Irving's (1783–1859) *Sketch Book* (1819), for example, should be understood in the context of Anglo-American relations. In his 'Account of Himself' Irving (writing as Geoffrey Crayon) explains that he travelled to Europe in search of places and people possessed of a historical depth that somehow made them more substantial than the people and places of America (Cronin 2014: 169). The ironic geographic displacement and transnational impetus of the *Sketch Book* – Irving subverts metropolitan versions of the travel narrative by having the American Crayon explore the curiosities of Europe rather than the other way round – cemented Irving's reputation in Britain and the rest of Europe, but there is also something profoundly nationalist about Irving's writing, particularly the ambivalence towards the imperialism that founded the American colonies displayed in works such as his *History of the Life and Voyages of Christopher Columbus* (1828).

More obviously than Irving, James Fenimore Cooper (1789–1851) attempted to create a native tradition of American letters that could rival British literary history. Cooper was one of the first American novelists to include African, African American and Native American characters in his works. Native Americans, in particular, have central roles in his so-called 'Leatherstocking Tales'. However, his treatment of Native Americans in captivity narratives such as *The Wept of Wish-ton-Wish* (1829) is ambivalent, reflecting the tenuous relationship between frontier settlers and Native Americans also considered in Thomas Campbell's (1777–1844) popular poem *Gertrude of Wyoming* (1809), which treats the massacre of 300 American Revolutionaries at the hands of Loyalists and their Iroquois allies on

3 July, 1778. The most famous of Cooper's novels, *The Last of the Mohicans* (1826), similarly considers the complex interactions and inter-relationships between Europeans and Indians in the context of a war, as discussed in the following case study.

Case study: James Fenimore Cooper, *The Last of the Mohicans; A Narrative of 1757* (1826)

Cooper's *The Last of the Mohicans* is a historical novel set in 1757 during the Seven Years' War, when France and Britain competed for control of North America with the help of various Indian allies. The war between colonial powers is therefore complicated by a series of conflicts between coloniser and colonised, as attacks on the British and their Mohican allies by the Hurons re-stage and mirror the larger colonial war. Here, as in other novels, Cooper provides contrasting pairs of native characters in order to emphasise their potential for both good and evil. The character of Magua, for example, is almost devoid of redeeming qualities, whereas Chingachgook is the noble and courageous chief of the Mohicans. But while Cooper populated his novels with native Americans, he had little direct knowledge of Indian culture, and his presentation of the natives, as well as the structuring of his novels, owes much to the work of Walter Scott (Crawford 1992: 182). The depth of the debt that Romantic-era American literary culture owes to Scottish modes and concepts is clear in the extent to which Cooper's America is 'Scotticized' (Crawford 1992: 186; see also Manning 2002). Like Scott's *Waverley* (1814), *The Last of the Mohicans* is a memorialisation of a culture Cooper sees as vanishing: 'The pale-faces are the masters of the earth, and the time of the redmen has not yet come again. My day has been too long.' (Cooper 1826: 3. 295) But, even more than *Waverley*, this is a novel as much about global changes as it is about national heritage; and unlike Scott's historical novels, the conclusion of *The Last of the Mohicans* is about loss rather than conciliation or resolution. The union of Cora and Uncas, which would have symbolised the resolution of conflicts between the British and Native Americans, does not take place and the novel ends instead with Alice mourning Cora's death. Whether or not Cora's death is the result of Cooper's unease with the problematic race dynamics of a union between European and Indian, the novel ultimately denies the reader both a romantic and a national resolution (Camden 2010: 119). Even this most 'national' of American novelists is therefore bound up in the complex inheritances of British colonialism and the worldwide cultural changes that it produced.

Despite a traditional scholarly focus on white settler writers such as Cooper, Catherine Maria Sedgewick (1789–1867) and Henry Wadsworth Longfellow (1807–82), transatlantic Romanticism has recently been more successful in challenging the Eurocentric focus of Romantic studies by considering the writing of indigenous peoples in studies such as Tim Fulford's *Romantic Indians* (2006) and Kate Flint's *The Transatlantic Indian 1776–1930* (2008). Drawing on Paul Gilroy's pioneering *The Black Atlantic: Modernity and Double Consciousness* (1995) in their claims for a 'Red' or 'Indian' Atlantic, both studies emphasise the fluidity of national and cultural identity, arguing that Indian identity was constructed both by European projections and by Indian subversions of these stereotypes and ciphers. As these studies have demonstrated, missionary schooling meant that much early-nineteenth-century literature authored by Native American Indians was written in English. The Ojbwe writer George Copway (1818–69), for example, demonstrated a fascination with the works of Burns, Byron, Scott and Southey (Hutchings and Wright 2011: 8). Yet the influence was not all one-sided: Copway, William Apess (1789–1839) and other Indian writers combined emerging European literary genres like confessions and the novel with oral tales and myths, creating new hybrid forms whose impact on British and European literary culture is only now being fully acknowledged.

South America

There was a significant interest in the Romantic-era in the discovery, conquest and colonisation of South America by the Spanish and Portuguese, as exemplified by the popularity of Helen Maria William's *Peru* (1786), Joel Barlow's (1754–1812) *The Vision of Columbus* (1787), John Thelwall's play *The Incas* (1792), R. B. Sheridan's (1751–1816) adaptation of August von Koetzebue's (1776–1819) *Pizarro* (1799) for the London stage and William Lisle Bowle's (1762–1850) *The Missionary* (1811–13), among other works. Recent criticism of transatlantic Romanticism has suggested that it focuses too narrowly on North America, overlooking not only these works but also Britian's material stakes in slavery in places like the West Indies and, in particular, its 1806 attempt to colonise territories in Spanish America. Scholarly studies on South America have accordingly tended to shift the focus from the United States to Britain's 'crisis of empire', with Spain acting as a focal point for Britain's own questions about colonial ideology and its practices. As Juan Sánchez has pointed out, '[t]he collapse of Britain's transatalantic empire and Spain's central role in producing it had cultivated deep-seated anti-Spanish sentiments' (Sánchez 2007: 174). Spain and Portugal were therefore increasingly represented as foils for an alternative, more benign British colonial policy.

Arguments in favour of Spanish American emancipation by James Mill, Jeremy Bentham and others, for example, opened a new space for Britain to represent itself as a liberal empire, which would abolish the twin evils of slavery and trade monopoly so inherent to the corrupt Spanish and Portuguese regimes. Mill's essay on the 'Emancipation of Spanish America' in *The Edinburgh Review* for 1809 echoes *Libertadores* such as Francisco de Miranda (1750–1816) in arguing that the emancipation of Spanish America was as worthy a cause as the abolition of slavery. Such arguments raise the global dimension of conceptions of personal freedom by considering freedom not in relation to the French Revolution but rather in relation to the emancipation of slaves and Spanish colonists. Yet while the colonial policies of Spain and Portugal came under ever increasing scrutiny in Britain, condemnation of Spanish and Portuguese rapacity could function in multiple ways, offering either a more generalised indictment of European and British colonial violence or a means of deflecting criticism from Britain and thus of endorsing British global expansion.

Poems like Williams's *Peru* have been read as anti-imperialist condemnations of Spanish rapacity, which function as a more generalised indictment of European and British colonial violence. But as Sánchez points out, Williams's focus on the so-called 'Black Legend' of the Spanish conquest of America could also been seen as a way of deflecting criticism away from Britain and of endorsing British global expansion, resulting in what Mary Louise Pratt has defined as an 'anti-conquest' narrative, which seeks to assert innocence at the same time as asserting European hegemony (Sánchez 2007: 173; Pratt 1992: 39). Although Thelwall's *Incas* rewrites the sixteenth-century Spanish conquest of the Inca empire with a victory of the natives over the Spaniards, most commentators were as pro-British as they were anti-Spanish. In *A Tale of Paraguay* (1825), for example, Southey implicitly presents Britain as a benign, paternalistic power, which could distinguish itself from the genocides of Spain and Portugal by zealously exporting a superior Protestant culture to the Americas. Similarly in his three-volume *History of Brazil* (1810–19) he champions the Portuguese settlers over their European counterparts as the settlers gradually align themselves with ostensibly British colonial practices rather than Iberian ones.

The Carribbean and the British-controlled southern hemisphere

Scholarly work on the Caribbean, the West Indies and Africa has unsurprisingly tended to focus on writing by African slaves, such as the work of Mary Prince (1788–c.1833), a slave living in the West Indies, and Juan Francisco Manzano (1797–1854), a slave living in Cuba, as well as considering the memoirs, autobiographies, anti-slavery tracts and fictional works of African and African-heritage writers living in Britain such as Ukawsaw Gronniosaw (c.1705–75), Ignatius Sancho (c.1729–80), Ottobah Cugoano (c.1757–c.1791), John Jea (1773–?) and Olaudah Equiano. Studies on slavery and abolition have been discussed above, but there have also been significant recent contributions to the literature of the British Caribbean, such as Karinna Williamson's *Contrary Voices: Representations of Indian Slavery, 1657–1834* (2008), James H. Basker's *Amazing Grace: An Anthology of Poems about Slavery, 1660–1810* (2005), Alan Richardson and Debbie Lee's *Early Black British Writing* (2004) and Vincent Carretta's *Unchained Voices: An Anthology of Black Authors in the English-Speaking World of the Eighteenth Century* (1996), some of which include non-English writing in various patois. The works collected in these anthologies have revealed the extent to which black writers were at the forefront of illuminating not only the political and personal abuses of empire (see the case study of Equiano earlier in this chapter), but also the psychological relationships at the heart of imperialism. They have also illuminated the vitality, complexity and hybrity of black and African culture in the period, which, as Gilroy has pointed out, is suggestive of the dynamic nature of ethnic, racial and national identities more generally (Gilroy 1995).

As the wealth of literature by West Indian and African immigrants demonstrates, immigration both to and from Britain played an enormously important role in spreading and generating new ideas and literary forms. Shared and emotive British settler identity in spheres of British colonial influence such as the Cape Colony and New South Wales suggest that such communities not only faced a variety of threats (real and imagined), but also forged their own literary identities in ways that were quite different from that of their mother country. It is therefore often argued that Romanticism did not take place in the southern hemisphere. In *Australian Poetry: Romanticism and Negativity* (1996), for example, Paul Kane claims that while Australian writers did not have a 'native, original tradition of poetry against which to set themselves or test their strength' the very 'absences of romanticism, or the failure of imaginative strength in Australian poetry, has nevertheless determined the way poets in Australia have written about nature' (Kane 1996: 5; see also Coleman and Otto 1992).

Certainly, the influence of Romanticism in Australia and elsewhere in the southern hemisphere was not simple or direct, but the idea that British settlers created an early version of antipodean realism in opposition to literary Romanticism rests on outdated 'interiority' models of Romanticism (see Introduction). For example, writers in Australia, New Zealand and South Africa produced their own versions of the 'national tale' (see Chapters 2 and 4) such as Henry Savery's (1791–1842) *Quintus Servington* (1830–1), the anonymous *Makanna; Or the Land of the Savage* (1834), Edward Augustus Kendall's (c.1776–1842) *The English Boy at the Cape* (1835), William Howitt's (1792–1879) *A Boy's Adventures in the Wilds of Australia* (1855), Henry Kingsley's (1830–76) *Geoffrey Hamlyn* (1859), Charles Rowcroft's (1798–1856) *Tales of the Colonies* (1843), Catherine Helen Spence's (1825–1910) *Clara Morison* (1854) and *Tender and True* (1856), and Henry Butler Stoney's (1816–94) *Tanaki: A Tale of the War* (1861). All too often these colonial versions of the national tale are dismissed as 'ripping yarns' rather than as serious explorations of nationhood or attempts to record vernacular language (a project central to Romantic discourse more generally).

The Gothic novel also flourished in the southern hemisphere. Unlike the national tale, which tended to celebrate local experience, the antipodean Gothic novel, like its metropolitan counterpart, was concerned with difference, distance and displacement (Otto 2005; Turcotte 1998). It is therefore unsurprising that many Gothic romances produced in Australia, New Zealand and South Africa are set in Britain and Ireland, referring to the colonies only indirectly and at distance: see, for examples, the Irish-Australian Anna Maria Bunn's (1808–89) *The Guardian: A Tale* (1838) and Mary Fortune's (c. 1833–c.1910) *The White Maniac: A Doctor's Tale* (1867). Lyric and narrative poetry that can be described as 'Romantic' was also produced in the southern hemisphere, most notably lyric representations of marginalised groups such as convicts, Australian Aboriginals and New Zealand Maori communities, and local or regional ballads such as Thomas Pringle's

(1789–1834) collection *African Sketches* (1834) (Johnson: 2012). More recent studies on the writing produced in late-eighteenth and early- to mid-nineteenth-century Australia, South Africa and New Zealand have therefore questioned the idea that its relationship to Romanticism was necessarily or inevitably one of absence or belatedness, particularly in relation to representations of landscape and indigenous populations (Landsdown 2009: 120).

Conclusion

• This chapter argued that modern globalisation is not a novelty nor an unprecedented, radical departure from prior modes of global and transnational thinking but rather a continuation and escalation of previous practices surrounding the emergence of capitalism and imperialism. This makes the Romantic period a central one for understanding and observing the emergence of various global phenomena, including the compression of space and time, and a new consciousness of the world as a synchronic, global whole.

• Imperialism and colonialism, in particular, created the conditions for cross-border contacts, transnational personal encounters and exchanges and other forms of global mobility, affecting the way in which national identity was formed and understood. The chapter argued not only that cultural and civic nationalism grew out of geopolitical exchanges of goods, people, print and ideas surrounding the rise of the modern nation-state but also that the process of national 'othering' was mirrored in the process of colonial 'othering'.

• The Romantic period is often considered a relatively benign moment in British imperial and colonial history. Certainly, there was an intense interest in the political and moral ramifications of Britain's imperial ambitions, particularly surrounding slavery, but the period also saw a commitment to promoting British culture abroad. In considering writing on empire, slavery, travel, exploration and migration, the chapter drew on postcolonial theory in order to highlight the ambiguous attitude of British Romantic writers to internal, European and colonial 'others'.

• When considering writing on and from different regions such as India, the United States, South America and Australia, the chapter emphasised studies that use global, comparative and transnational approaches in order to demonstrate the importance of connections, interactions and transculturations between different nations, groups and communities.

Conclusion

Legacies of Romanticism

> The Romantic is . . . an element of poetry which may be more or less dominant or recessive, but never entirely absent.
>
> Friedrich Schlegel, from 'Letter about the Novel' (1799)

Overview

As a conclusion to the book, this chapter not only demonstrates how Romanticism influenced the literature of the nineteenth, twentieth and twenty-first centuries, but also shows how the writing of the Romantic era speaks to significant social, cultural and political concerns in our own time. Starting with an analysis of the process and meaning of posterity, the chapter moves on to argue for the value of specific Romantic legacies such as the role of the artist; fragmentation and stream of consciousness; the languages of the sublime, memory and revelation; the development of neo-Romantic movements such as the Apocalyptics and the Regionalists; the significance of Romantic understandings of history for our own contemporary culture; and the role of the Romantic genius in an age of mass celebrity. The chapter concludes with a reflection on how the Romantic 'cult of posterity' functions throughout both modern and postmodern literature, as well as in the writing of the present day.

***

In a letter to Thomas Moore dated 27 August 1822, Lord Byron suggestively concludes his extended description of Percy Bysshe Shelley's cremation of only a few days earlier with the following words: 'All of Shelley was consumed, except his *heart*, which would not take the flame, and is now preserved in spirits of wine' (*Letters and Journals*, IX. 197). Byron notes that Shelley's heart was eventually wrapped in a manuscript version of *Adonais* (1821), Shelley's own lament for the untimely death of John Keats and his greatest elegy to neglected poetic genius. Despite the contested and highly mythologised nature of this episode, the story of Shelley's unconsumed heart ('*Cor Cordium*', or 'Heart of Hearts', reads the inscription on his grave) is central to Romantic ideas regarding legacy and posterity: if the heart of the poet survives, it stands as a symbol of his or her continued poetic energy and potency. In her recent group biography *Young Romantics: The Shelleys, Byron and Other Tangled Lives* (2010) (see Chapter 3) Daisy Hay narrates the episode of Shelley's death and burial in a chapter entitled 'Future', in which she argues, following Andrew Bennett (1999), that the Romantics introduced a new tradition of writing aimed at a future rather than a current audience (Hay 2010: 247 ff.). This so-called Romantic 'cult of posterity' also permeates artistic representations of the period, as demonstrated by the 1889 painting by the French artist Louis Édouard Paul Fournier (1857–1917) *The Funeral of Shelley* (Figure 8.1), which – notwithstanding the factual inaccuracy of the composition (for example, Edward Trelawny (1792–1881), Leigh Hunt and Lord Byron, depicted on the far left, were not present at the scene, nor was Mary Shelley, here kneeling in the background) – is a good example of the extent to which Shelley was writing (and Fournier was painting) for posterity. Not only does the painting speak to the inter-relationship between literary and visual culture, and between British and European Romanticisms, but it can also be read as a narrative bridge that simultaneously evokes past memories (the death of Shelley) and projects present and future anxieties (Shelley's memorialisation and afterlife).

Andrew Bennett insightfully proposes that it is posterity, rather than immediate fame, which 'validates the poet' (Bennett 1999: 2). Our highest praise for any poem is still, as he points out, 'to say that it will last, that it will live on, in the future' (Bennett 1999: 4). As the Romantics themselves argued, the body is of little consequence: what matters is the legacy of the writer's work itself as a reflection of 'the spirit of the age', a spirit that still endures today in our own intense social, religious, and political upheavals; in our celebration of originality and genius; in the continued belief in political emancipation and the need for self-determination; and, as Shelley put it in his 'Preface' to *The Revolt of Islam* (1818), in 'the tempests which have shaken the age in which we live' (ll. 5–6), in our desire for 'liberty and justice'

Figure 8.1 Louis Édouard Paul Fournier, *The Funeral of Shelley*, oil on canvas, 1889, 129.5 x 213.4 cm.

Source: © Walker Art Gallery, National Museums Liverpool.

and in our residual 'faith and hope . . . which neither violence nor misrepresentation nor prejudice can ever totally extinguish among mankind' (ll. 11–13) (Shelley 2000: 32). Shelley was all too aware that his prophetic voice was addressing future generations. As a visionary and utopian poet offering images of a world enslaved in the present but liberated in the future, the messages of his radical texts such as *The Revolt of Islam* and *The Mask of Anarchy* (1819) are recognisable both in the Islamic terrorist attacks which have swept across the Western world since 11 September 2001 (Madrid, 2004; London, 2005; Glasgow, 2007; Stockholm, 2010; Toulouse, 2012; Paris, 2015; Brussels, 2016) and in our collective responses to them.

This chapter is not only concerned with an investigation of the various ways in which Romanticism has influenced the literary cultures of the nineteenth and twentieth centuries, as there are already many significant studies on the matter – see, in particular, Carmen Casaliggi and Paul March-Russell's recent *Legacies of Romanticism: Literature, Culture, Aesthetics* (2012), which is the first study to survey this long history of indebtedness in both the nineteenth and twentieth centuries – but also argues that Romanticism speaks to the political and cultural questions of our own time. In the epigraph to this chapter Friedrich Schlegel rightly recognises that the Romantic imagination is something that is 'never entirely absent' (cited in Wheeler 1984: 78). Yet the 'legacy' that Romanticism bestows upon successive literatures not only suggests continuity, but also the re-evaluation and re-interpretation of its own agenda. As Casaliggi and March-Russell have argued, Romanticism's legacy 'privileges future reception over current tastes and leaves unresolved contradictions in its wake concerning the nature of the author, the relationship to the audience, and the worth of the literary text' (Casaliggi and March-Russell 2012: 5).

Victorian, modernist and postmodernist aesthetics

Romanticism's legacy in the Victorian period is the territory charted by Richard Cronin's *Romantic Victorians* (2002), John Beer's *Romantic Consciousness: Blake to Mary Shelley* (2003a), Lene Østermark-Johansen's *Romantic Generations: Text, Authority and Posterity in British Romanticism* (2003), Joel Faflak and Julia M. Wright's *Nervous Reactions: Victorian Recollections of Romanticism* (2004) and Andrew Radford and Mark Sandy's *Romantic Echoes in the Victorian Era* (2008). From these many excellent studies it emerges that Romanticism continued to play a prominent role in the mid-Victorian period (1830–70), when imperial and technological power was at its strongest, but when the inheritance of Romantic ideas were also at its most pressing. Romantic traces and influences can be linked to a wide range of Victorian writers, such as Robert Browning (1812–89) and Alfred Tennyson, who sought to develop Romantic preoccupations with idealism, time, memory and history. Even the championing of realism, as, for example, in the works of George Eliot (1819–80), Dante Gabriel Rossetti (1828–82) and John Ruskin, can be seen as a negotiation with Romanticism: that is, as an aesthetic development that could accommodate and contain Romantic expressions of passion and self-will.

Romantic legacies also figure prominently in Victorian and Edwardian art history and theory. Vivian de Sola Pinto has insightfully argued that Victorian and Edwardian poetry was 'full of imitations of romantic nature poetry, which bear much the same relation to the poetry of Wordsworth and Keats as that which the landscapes of contemporary academicians bore to those of Turner and Constable' (De Sola Pinto 1967: 116). The inter-relationship between word and image, which is effectively captured in the ekphrastic poems of William Blake and John Keats, as well as in the poems appended to artworks of the period by J. M. W. Turner and others, extends into Victorian discourses surrounding art, most notably in the work of Oscar Wilde (1854–1900), John Ruskin and Walter Pater (1839–94). In an interview published in the *St James's Gazette* of 8 January, 1895, when Wilde was asked whether he had been influenced by any of his predecessors, he not only praised the ekphrastic work of fellow Victorian writers, but also suggested the prominent role of Romantic poets for his writing: 'setting aside the prose and poetry of the Greek and Latin authors, the only writers who have influenced me are Keats, Flaubert and Walter Pater' (cited in Raby 1988: 16). Of the authors mentioned by Wilde, it is the ongoing influence of Keats which best emphasises how the plasticity attributed by August Schlegel to Romantic literature continues in post-Romantic writing (Casaliggi and March-Russell 2012: 6).

Recent studies have also begun to explore the significance of Romantic legacies in a comparative British and American context, particularly in the literature of the twentieth century, as in Edward Larrissy's *Romanticism and Postmodernism* (1999), Andrew Bennett's influential *Romantic Poets and the Culture of Posterity* (1999), Eberhard Alsen's *The New Romanticism* (2000), John Beer's *Post-Romantic Consciousness: Dickens to Plath* (2003b), Michael O'Neill's *The All-Sustaining Air: Romantic Legacies and Renewals in British, American, and Irish Poetry since 1900* (2007), Damian Walford Davies and Richard Marggraf Turley's *The Monstrous Debt: Modalities of Romantic Influences in Twentieth-Century Literature* (2006), Alexandra Harris's *Romantic Moderns: English Writers, Artists and the Imagination: from Virginia Woolf to John Piper* (2010), and Mark Sandy's *Romantic Presences in the Twentieth Century* (2013). The re-evaluation of Romantic aesthetic theory in the period 1870–1920 is evident in the values of the Decadent, or 'art for art's sake' movement, which is, at once, a reassertion of Romantic traditions and a prefiguration of modernist self-reflexivity. Romanticism also shapes D. H. Lawrence's (1885–1930) essentially Romantic theme of the conflict between the natural and the so-called civilised world in novels such as *The Rainbow* (1915) and its sequel *Women in Love* (1920). Even 'high' modernism (1920–60) can be interpreted as part of a dialectical response to the Romantic legacy; for example, the defence of neoclassical values by T. S. Eliot (1888–1965) and Ezra Pound (1885–1972) actively situates Romanticism as the antithesis that underpins the dialectic of modernism.

Modernist responses to Romantic literature tend, therefore, to articulate a tension between the veneration of past models, on the one hand, and apparent disavowal, on the other. James Joyce's (1882–1941) *A Portrait of the Artist as a Young Man* (1916) charts the writer's formative experience and the development and growing expertise of the artist. His protagonist, Stephen Dedalus – a surname which recalls the master craftsman of classical mythology – epitomises the achievement of classical art.

While celebrating Romanticism's responses to classicism, as in the plasticity of Keats and the Hellenism of Shelley, Joyce also aims to convert the philistine Irish to the cult of beauty inherited from the Greeks. In a similar vein, the (neo-Romantic) literary and artistic avant-gardes of Imagism, Cubism, Futurism, Expressionism, Dadaism and Vorticism, although ambivalent to both classicism and Romanticism, never fully managed to erase, as Friedrich Schlegel anticipated, their debt to both. In particular, the idea of spontaneity ('all good poetry is the spontaneous overflow of powerful feelings' ('Preface' to *Lyrical Ballads,* 62)) not only informs the work of such important late nineteenth-century writers as Henry James (1843–1916), but also paves the way for modernism's focus on mental processes, as in, for example, the new technique of stream of consciousness, influenced by the work of philosophers such as the French Henri-Louis Bergson (1859–1941) and the American William James (1842–1910). As John Worthen has argued, '[t]he Romantic period is to us a site of vivid experience lying at the threshold of our own era and which for that reason has become fascinating to us'. Worthen goes on to reinforce the point that the Romantics 'seem to be having experiences very much as we do' in that 'they are fascinated by the ways their minds work', so much so that 'some of Coleridge's notebook entries resemble stream-of-consciousness fiction, while some of Dorothy's journal entries are compressed poetry' (Worthen 2001: 13).

There is therefore a formative dialogue between the theorisation and development of the stream-of-consciousness technique and the Romantic fragment form, as a site for disjointed images of the infinite, oxymoronically 'complete in itself' (cited in Rosen 1995: 48), totally balanced and yet unstable. As discussed in Chapter 3, the fragmentation of Coleridge's *Kubla Khan* (1797) is the result of a vision-induced dream of pain and disease: when this vision, along with the poet's inspiration and imagination, vanishes, only the fragment survives. Arguably, the stream-of-consciousness novels of Marcel Proust (1871–1922), James Joyce and Virginia Woolf (1882–1941) are a re-visitation of this Romantic genre and its modes of representation in their conception of time as a flowing continuity of separate fragments enlivened in a character's mind through memories, dreams, associations of ideas, sensations and intuitions. Romantic literature can also be regarded as a precursor of the process of medialisation in recent cinematic devices, such as montage, flashbacks, fade-outs, slow-ups, etc., which visually translate the main aspects of fragmentation and which are used to depict the motion of one's consciousness, such as the interior monologue (the instrument used to translate the psychic phenomenon of stream of consciousness into words).

Case study: James Joyce, *Ulysses* (1922), from episode 8 ('Lestrygonians')

Part of episode 8 of Joyce's *Ulysses* depicts Mr. Bloom standing in front of a shop window in Nassau Street, in the centre of Dublin, where a long sequence of fragmented thought and associations of ideas cross his mind. Bloom's train of thought is made up of seventeen segments (or fragments) which are connected with six different subjects (1. Yeates and Son; 2. Sinclair; 3. Glasses; 4. Germans; 5. Lost-property office; 6. Farmer's daughter) in an unbroken Alphian river-like flow:

> He crossed at Nassau street corner and stood before the window of Yeates and Son, pricing the field glasses. Or will I drop into old Harris's and have a chat with young Sinclair? Wellmannered fellow. Probably at his lunch. Must get those old glasses of mine set right. Goerz lenses, six guineas. Germans making their way everywhere. Sell on easy terms to capture trade. Undercutting. Might chance on a pair in the railway lost property office. Astonishing the things people leave behind in trains and cloak rooms. What do they be thinking about? Women too. Incredible. Last year travelling to Ennis had to pick up that farmer's daughter's bag and hand it to her at Limerick junction. Unclaimed money too. There's a little watch up there on the roof of the bank to test those glasses by.
>
> (*Ulysses* 158)

The intricacy of these fragments is suggestive of Bloom's subtle train of thought, which requires some exertion from the reader: confused and ill-arranged, the extract moves from the outside to the inside of the character; and the reader witnesses changes in verb tenses and frequent elisions of words, often accompanied by grammatical mistakes, which reinforce abstruse meanings. Joyce's creation of this new kind of 'dream language', in itself a mixture of existing and invented words with a disordered syntax and inaccurate punctuation, is an experiment in the realm of the conscious and unconscious mind. Christopher A. Strathman rightly calls this new language an example of 'what remains unthought in thinking' (Strathman 2006: 3).

Friedrich Schlegel, in the well-known *Athenaeum* fragment 206, offers a definition of the Romantic fragment, which he sees as 'a little work of art, complete in itself and separated from the rest of the universe like a hedgehog' (cited in Rosen 1995: 48). Although 'separated from the rest of the universe' in their naturally disordered, yet patterned, sequence of thoughts and feelings, Joyce's segments crop up in the individual mind uncensored – or incompletely censored – by rational control and thus are 'complete' in themselves. In this way such moments are very similar to Coleridge's dream vision in the fragment *Kubla Khan*. Opium-induced or otherwise, Joyce's stream of consciousness, dependent on fragments of words and sentences, represents a significant attempt to reconfigure the Romantic fragment form. *A Portrait of the Artist as a Young Man* (1916), *Finnegans Wake* (1939) and *Stephen Hero* (published posthumously in 1944) are all novels which can be appreciated as fragments or, as Jorge Luis Borges put it in his 'Fragment of Joyce' (1941), through Joyce's 'multitudinous diversity of styles', or his 'gifted omnipotence of the word' (Borges 2000: 220–1).

Through his stream-of-consciousness technique Joyce produced an unconventional post-Romantic prose that nonetheless re-discovers the sublimity of the epiphanic moment by engaging with Edmund Burke's views on the sublime and the beautiful (see Chapter 3), as well as imbuing his work with a confessional, quasi-religious tone, as in fragment IX from *Shine* and *Dark* (c. 1900, published 1992): 'Told Sublimely in the language/ Which the shining angels knew' (ll. 1–2). Joyce's association of the sublime with religious epiphany is centred around his preoccupations both with the poet's former and present selves, and with future encounters with the spiritual world: 'only, when the heart is peaceful,/ when the soul is moved to love,/ May we hearken to those voices/ Starry singing from above' (ll. 7–10) (*Poems and Exiles*, 61). There is something both Blakean and Shelleyan in Joyce's confessional and epiphanic tone, but Joyce also captures in his work the 'renovating virtue' (*Prelude*, 1. 10) of Wordsworth's 'spots of time', which, as Gabrielle McIntire and others have recently demonstrated, can be seen as instances of epiphanic revelations (McIntire 2008: 166). Wordsworth's 'spots of time' also resonate in Woolf's 'moments of being', which occur when one receives an emotional blow analogous to a physical shock that disrupts the ordinary flow of perception (see, for example, the second part of *To the Lighthouse* (1927), which is entitled 'Time Passes') (Sim 2010: 137 ff.).

The sublime and memory, as re-worked by (post)modernist sensibilities, are both powerful legacies of the Romantics. After 1960, in particular, Romanticism is rehabilitated and reconfigured by postmodern and postcolonial literature, both as a reassessment of the modernist movement and as a way of rethinking the imperial contexts that underpin the Romantic legacy (see the examples in the section later in this chapter on 'Romanticism, history and postcolonialism'). The way in which post-Romantic writers engage with what is terrifying, awe-inspiring and inherently magnificent can be seen in Jean-François Lyotard's postmodern adaptation of the Romantic sublime, which attempts to express the 'inexpressible' or 'unpresentable' (Tabbi (1995) and Larrissy (1999)), and in the postmodern reconfiguration of the Gothic (Wallace and Smith (2009)), which revisits the dark images of the fragmented self and the horrors of the historical moment in works of science fiction, horror and fantasy such as William Gibson's cyberpunk novel *Neuromancer* (1984). Gothic tyrants, imprisoned innocents, dangerous secrets, labyrinthine spaces, artificial intelligences and the cyborg-like villains of the post-human era make their appearance in dystopian surroundings, where the matrix (the film *The Matrix* (1999) drew inspiration from Gibson's novel) is presented as a sublime place, a kind of electronic Eden where the fallen 'meat' of the body is surrendered to the 'bodiless exultation' of cyberspace (Di Tommaso 2014: 489). 'Neuro', the nervous system and the novelty of the creative genius, merge with the romance of the narrative plot in a way that suggests the emergence of a 'new' Romantic legacy.

Neo-Romanticism

In the 1940s the Romantic tradition in Britain underwent an extraordinary renaissance not only in literature but in the other arts as well. Prose works by Kenneth

Clark (1903–83) and Herbert Read (1893–1968) attempted to recover the freshness and naturalness of Wordsworth's theme of lost innocence, often as a result of a vanished contact with nature; and the British landscapes of Paul Nash (1889–1946), John Piper (1903–92), Graham Sutherland (1903–80) and, later, John Craxton (1922–2009) became central to a new nostalgic Palmerian and Turnerian pastoral vision, which was broadly concerned with the sublimity of individual psychic states rather than with faithful representations of the landscape. Piper's interest in the sublime is evident, for example, in his paintings of bombed churches and wartime ruins (Hockenhull 2012: 179–97).

The so-called 'neo-Romantic' movement found its ultimate literary expression in the writings of the Apocalypse group of wartime poets, which included Dylan Thomas (1914–53). Many writers in this group drew on the sublimity of John Martin's apocalyptic landscapes, in which cataclysms are rendered on huge canvases with a painstaking attention to details (see Chapter 5). The Apocalyptic poets highlighted the importance of heightened subjectivity and the related Romantic notions of suffering and destruction. The Romantic inheritance also flourishes – albeit with certain ruptures and divisions – in the work of 1950s writers such as Thom Gunn (1929–2004) and Kingsley Amis (1922–1995), when they promote a return to compact, well-made poetry, which is readily understandable. In aiming for concrete and truthful representations in language and images, neo-Romanticism implicitly relied upon ideas of naturalness and spontaneity that are reminiscent of Wordsworth's theory and practice in *Lyrical Ballads* (see Chapter 2).

The work of the 'Regionalists' in the 1960s and 1970s, which was centred on various provincial cities, can be read in parallel with the discussion of regionalism in Chapter 4. Poets such as Roy Fisher (1930–) (Birmingham), Adrian Henri (1932–2000) (Liverpool), Jon Silkin (1930–97) (Newcastle) and Seamus Heaney (1939–2013) (Belfast) developed a distinctly local literary agenda, while also concentrating on common themes such as the relationship between the young and their local environment, idealism and disillusionment and the search for identity. Seamus Heaney's negotiation with the legacies of Romanticism – particularly with the work of John Clare and William Wordsworth – can be read as a reconsideration of the Romantic poets' relationship with nature as one of symbiosis, force and identity. As Edward Larrissy has recently suggested, it is Clare, in particular, through his attention to the rhythm of regional vernacular that accentuates Heaney's own poetic excavation of Northern Ireland's tangled heritage and territorialism (Larrissy 2012: 105–16).

Growing out of these neo-Romantic interests in landscape and the picturesque, the rise of ecocriticism and environmental studies, as evidenced by thinkers such as Jonathan Bate, Greg Garrard and Kate Soper, is another of Romanticism's legacies (see Introduction). As Tim Morton has put it, 'eco-criticism is another version of Romanticism's rage against the machine, a refusal to engage the present moment. Like imperialism, ecocriticism produces a vision of the text as a pristine wilderness of pure meaning' (Morton 2005: 704). Romanticism's focus on nature, animal rights, organicism and pantheism has served as a template for contemporary nature-versus-science debates. In Mary Shelley's *Frankenstein* (1818), for example, the monster may appear to be unnatural and transgressive, but his speech is human and suggests that the relationship between nature and science must be constantly questioned.

Romanticism, history and postcolonialism

Some sections of this book examined New Historicist practices (see, in particular, the Introduction). Other sections focused on the Romantics' own historical self-consciousness and the development of the historical novel (see Chapter 2). Despite Stephen Dedalus's affirmation that 'history . . . is a nightmare from which I am trying to awake' (*Ulysses* 34), history and its meanings are significant preoccupations in modernist and postmodernist writing, not only in the work of Joyce and Woolf but also in war poetry and writing on the Holocaust, as in *Austerlitz* (2001) and *Campo Santo* (published posthumously in 2003) by W. G. Sebald (1944–2001), where questions of nationhood and identity are challenged by the legacies of the past (Tabbi 2012: 260–74). As Andrew Bennett has so succinctly put it, 'Romanticism survives as history' (Bennett 1999: 1). In light of this claim, W. B. Yeats's preoccupation with loss in *September 1913* (1913) – 'Romantic Ireland's dead and gone' (ll. 7, 15, 23, 31) – loses validity. Romantic Ireland is not dead after all, but rather lives on through the memory and commemoration of the Irish Separatist leaders: O'Leary (ll. 8, 16, 24, 32), Fitzgerald, Emmet and Tone (ll. 20–1) (see Chapter 4), whom, from their graves, will bring about re-readings of their actions (Bornstein 2006: 19–35).

Within the historical context a re-thinking of capitalism, industrialisation, consumerism, colonialism, imperialism and modernity also emerges as one of the most influential of Romanticism's legacies. In *Romantic Imperialism: Universal Empire and the Culture of Modernity* (1998) Saree Makdisi suggests that 'Romanticism can be partly understood as a diverse and heterogeneous series of engagements with modernization' (Makdisi 1998: 6) and that, in its resistance to modernity, Romanticism simultaneously advocates a continuity 'with the beginnings of modernization and persists alongside it to the end' (Makdisi 1998: 10). As discussed in Chapter 7, Romanticism, in marking the beginning of modernity and hence newly revised understandings of time and space, also relates to the phenomenon of globalisation. With its interest in the colonial subject in texts like Byron's *Corsair* (1814) and Mary Shelley's *Frankenstein* – in the latter the monster is seen as racially other and distinctively non-European, as is the figure of Safie, the Christian Arab – the Romantic aesthetic emerges as both 'other' and Eurocentric. While Romanticism is implicated in a Western imperial imagination, in which works such as those of Joseph Conrad (1857–1924), Rudyard Kipling (1865–1936) and E. M. Forster (1879–1970) (see especially *A Passage to India* (1924)) continue to explore Romanticism's fascination with 'otherness' and exoticism, Romantic writing also contains self-critiques of imperial control and colonial otherness (see the unwitting hybridity of Thomas De Quincey's identity in *Confessions of an English Opium-Eater* (1821) discussed in Chapter 7).

Romanticism, alienation and celebrity culture

Like Romantic literature, twentieth-century writing often evinces a strong sense of dissatisfaction with socio-political conditions. Frustration, inadequacy, anger and, above all, 'alienation', which William Vaughan argues is one of Romanticism's greatest legacies (Vaughan 1994: 266), appear in the enduring iconography of the transgressive and rebellious genius. The idea of the rebellious genius makes itself felt in the work of writers such as the 'Angry Young Men' (the new *poètes maudits*) of the 1950s, whose writing voiced the frustration and disillusionment of the post-war generation, or, in an age of mass celebrity, in the music of performers such as Jim Morrison (1943–71) and Freddy Mercury (1946–91), who, besides attacking the establishment, also promoted the development of new libertarian and permissive ideas that permeated the 1968 revolts and the ideals of rebel groups such as skinheads, punks and rockers.

The Romantic era is also the site of an emergent and recognisably modern celebrity culture, where the lives and work of artists and actresses such as Gioacchino Rossini and Sarah Siddons (1755–1831), and sporting personalities such as Daniel Mendoza, were followed and celebrated. It is Lord Byron, in particular, with his good looks, extreme lifestyle and redefinition of the role of the poet, who is considered the first modern celebrity and victim of early fandom. Tom Mole (2007), for example, has investigated the role that Byron has played in the development of a modern celebrity culture, as well as considering the ways in which the industries of printing and publishing were fundamental to the creation of that culture (see also Mole 2009). New media such as film have continued the preoccupation with Romantic culture. Jerrold E. Hogle has noted that adaptations in new media have 'produced a dazzling variety and a troubling portrait gallery at worst', whereby adaptations of Mary Shelley's *Frankenstein*, Jane Austen's popular novels and contemporary Romantic film biographies (see *Pandaemonium* (2000); *Becoming Jane* (2007); *Bright Star* (2009); *Desperate Romantics* (2009)) depict the Romantics 'as simultaneously inspiring creators, on the one hand, and eccentric monsters, on the other' (Hogle 2005: 631). While the Romantics and their writing are often deliberately distorted and misrepresented in such adaptations, they nonetheless survive in the popular imagination and in our contemporary culture. The legacies of Romanticism are therefore not only suggestive of Schlegel's idea in the epigraph to this Conclusion that the Romantic aesthetic will 'never be completely absent' but also of Novalis's 1798 claim that 'the world must be romanticized': to romanticise the world is to give 'the common a higher meaning, the everyday, a mysterious semblance, the known, the dignity of the unknown, the finite, the appearance of the infinite' (cited in Rommel 2004: 226).

Conclusion

- This chapter has sketched out the extent to which Romanticism has preconditioned contemporary developments in art, literature, philosophy and popular culture, profoundly shaping creative work throughout the late nineteenth, twentieth and twenty-first centuries, both in Britain and abroad. The legacies and shaping influences of Romanticism suggest that literary history should not be considered simply in teleological terms. Rather than seeing an antagonism between Romanticism and Victorianism/modernism/postmodernism, the chapter argued for a relationship of reconfiguration and negotiation, as Romanticism was adopted, reinvented and questioned by later literary movements.

- The chapter pointed to the importance of some specific legacies such as 1) the role of the Romantic artist; 2) the ongoing valorisation of spontaneity and originality; 3) the languages of the sublime, memory and revelation; 4) the development of neo-Romantic movements such as the Apocalyptics and the Regionalists; 5) the value of history and memory; and 6) the enduring iconography of the rebellious genius.

- Individual writers responded to, and were affected by, Romanticism in different ways: modernist and postmodernist authors developed complex debts to the Romantic tradition, as in the case study of Joyce, but even when opposing the Romantic consciousness they bring into being a dialectical connection with it.

- The chapter concluded by mentioning one of the most controversial legacies of Romanticism: its relationship with an emerging celebrity culture, and thus the extent to which literary value can be assimilated to the commodification of culture in the form of contemporary social and media studies (as well as discourses of fan culture).

Guide to further reading

Introduction: Romanticism and its discontents

As the Introduction is largely concerned with debates and issues surrounding periodisation and the construction of literary history, some general reflections on literary history seem in order:

Besserman, Lawrence (ed.) (1996) *The Challenge of Periodization: Old Paradigms and New Perspectives*, New York: Garland.

Brown, Marshall (ed.) (1995) *The Uses of Literary History*, Durham, NC: Duke University Press.

Perkins, David (1992) *Is Literary History Possible?* Baltimore, MD: Johns Hopkins University Press.

—. (ed.) (1991) *Theoretical Issues in Literary History*, Cambridge, MA: Harvard University Press.

For essays more specifically on Romantic literary history and disputes concerning periodisation, see the following:

McGann, Jerome J. (1996) "Rethinking Romanticism", in Lawrence Besserman (ed.) *The Challenge of Periodization: Old Paradigm and New Perspectives*, New York: Garland, 161–78.

Parker, Mark (1991) "Measure and Countermeasure: The Lovejoy-Wellek Debate and Romantic Periodization", in David Perkins (ed.) *Theoretical Issues in Literary History*, Cambridge MA: Harvard University Press, 227–48.

Siskin, Clifford (2009) "The Problem of Periodization: Enlightenment, Romanticism, and the Fate of System", in James Chandler (ed.) *The Cambridge History of English Romantic Literature*, Cambridge: Cambridge University Press, 101–26.

As examples of the traditional 'internalised' mode of understanding Romanticism, the following studies remain insightful:

Abrams, M. H. (1971) *Natural Supernaturalism: Tradition and Revolution in Romantic Literature*, New York: W. W. Norton.

—. (1953) *The Mirror and the Lamp: Romantic Theory and the Critical Tradition*, Oxford: Oxford University Press.

Frye, Northrop (1968) *A Study of English Romanticism: English Literature and its Background, 1760–1830*, New York: Random House.

For seminal revisionary studies of the Romantic period, see:

Butler, Marilyn (1981) *Romantics, Rebels and Reactionaries: English Literature and its Background, 1760–1830*, New York and Oxford: Oxford University Press.

McGann, Jerome (1983) *The Romantic Ideology*, Chicago, IL: University of Chicago Press.

Siskin, Clifford (1988) *The Historicity of Romantic Discourse*, New York and Oxford: Oxford University Press.

Recommended works setting out critical concepts and theoretical/methodological approaches include:

Favret, Mary and Nicola J. Watson (eds.) (1994) *At the Limits of Romanticism: Essays in Cultural, Feminist, and Materialist Criticism*, Bloomington, IN: Indiana University Press.

Hogle, Jerrold E. (2010) "Romanticism and the 'Schools' of Criticism and Theory", in Stuart Curran (ed.) *The Cambridge Companion to British Romanticism*, Cambridge: Cambridge University Press, 1–33.

O'Neill, Michael and Mark Sandy (eds.) (2005) *Romanticism: Critical Concepts in Literary and Cultural Studies*, New York and London: Routledge.

Chapter 1: Contexts of Romanticism

There are a daunting number of studies of eighteenth- and early-nineteenth-century British history, including studies of political history, intellectual history, constitutional history, economic history, military and naval history, cultural history, social history, women's history, imperial history, gender history and the history of religion. Good introductory works on the history, politics and philosophies of the long eighteenth century include:

Hunt, T. L. (2008) *Defining John Bull: Political Culture and National Identity in Late Georgian England*, Aldershot: Ashgate.

Marshall, P. J. and Alaine Low (eds.) (1998) *The Oxford History of the British Empire: Vol. II: The Eighteenth Century*, Oxford: Oxford University Press.

O'Gorman, Frank (1997) *The Long Eighteenth Century: British Political and Social History* 1688–1832, London: Arnold.

Porter, Roy (2000) *Enlightenment: Britain and the Creation of the Modern World*, London: Allen Lane.

Thompson, E. P. (1966) *The Making of the English Working Classes*, New York: Vintage.

The specific areas covered in this chapter are too numerous to be individually addressed, but for recommended edited collections on Romanticism that cover a wide range of ideas, events and contexts, see the following:

Chandler, James (ed.) (2009) *The Cambridge History of English Romanticism*, Cambridge: Cambridge University Press.

Curran, Stuart (ed.) (1993) *The Cambridge Companion to British Romanticism*, Cambridge: Cambridge University Press.

McCalman, Iain (ed.) (2001) *An Oxford Companion to the Romantic Age: British Culture 1776–1832*, Oxford: Oxford University Press.

Chapter 2: Romantic forms, genres and language

There are many individual and collective studies devoted to the treatment of formal developments in Romantic poetry, the novel, drama and non-fiction. Examples are given below:

Bradley, Arthur and Alan Rawes (eds.) (2003) *Romantic Biography*, Aldershot: Ashgate.

Chandler, James and Maureen McLane (eds.) (2008) *The Cambridge Companion to British Romantic Poetry,* Cambridge: Cambridge University Press.

Cox, Philip (1996) *Gender, Genre and Romantic Poets*, Manchester: Manchester University Press.

Duff, David (2009) *Romanticism and the Uses of Genre*, Oxford: Oxford University Press.

Keach, William (2004) *Arbitrary Power: Romanticism, Language and Politics*, Princeton: Princeton University Press.

Leask, Nigel (2002) *Curiosity and the Aesthetics of Travel Writing, 1770–1840: 'From an Antique Land'*, Oxford: Oxford University Press.

Rawes, Alan (ed.) (2007) *Romanticism and Form*, Basingstoke: Palgrave Macmillan.

Roe, Nicholas (ed.) (2005) *Romanticism: An Oxford Guide*, New York: Oxford University Press, 273–591.

Strachan, John (2007) *Advertising and Satirical Culture in the Romantic Period*, Cambridge: Cambridge University Press, 2007.

Wu, Duncan (ed.) (1998) *A Companion to Romanticism*, Oxford: Blackwell, 323–84.

Chapter 3: Romantic groups and associations

There are some general studies on the Lake School, the Satanic School, the Cockney School and the Bluestockings, as well as studies focusing on the careers of particularly prominent members of these movements. There is, by comparison, very little scholarship available on the Holland House Set and the Della Cruscans. Examples of some influential general studies are listed below:

Butler, Marilyn (1981) *Romantics, Rebels and Reactionaries: English Literature and its Background, 1760–1830*, New York and Oxford: Oxford University Press.

Cox, Jeffrey N. (1998) *Poetry and Politics in the Cockney School: Keats, Shelley, Hunt and their Circle*, Cambridge: Cambridge University Press.

Eger, Elizabeth (2010) *Bluestockings: Women of Reason from Enlightenment to Romanticism*, Basingstoke: Palgrave Macmillan.

Hay, Daisy (2010) *Young Romantics: The Shelleys, Byron and Other Tangled Lives*, London: Bloomsbury.

Kelly, Linda (2013) *Holland House: A History of London's Most Celebrated Salon*, London: I. B. Tauris.

Lau, Beth (ed.) (2009) *Fellow Romantics: Male and Female British Writers, 1790–1835*, Aldershot: Ashgate.

McGann, Jerome J. (1995) "The Literary World of the English Della Cruscans", in Elaine Scarry (ed.), *Fins de Siècle: English Poetry in 1590, 1690, 1790, 1890, 1990*, Baltimore, MD: Johns Hopkins University Press, 95–122.

Pohl, Nicole and Betty A. Schellenberg (eds.) (2005) *Reconsidering the Bluestockings*, Berkeley, CA: University of California Press.

Roe, Nicholas (1997) *John Keats and the Culture of Dissent*, Oxford: Clarendon Press.

—. (1988) *Wordsworth and Coleridge: The Radical Years*, Oxford: Clarendon Press.

Russell, Gillian and Clara Tuite (eds.) (2002) *Romantic Sociability: Social Networks and Literary Culture in Britain 1770–1840*, Cambridge: Cambridge University Press.

Schock, Peter (2003) *Romantic Satanism: Myth and the Historical Moment in Blake, Shelley, and Byron*, Basingstoke: Palgrave Macmillan.

Schoina, Maria (2009) *Romantic "Anglo-Italians": Configurations of Identity in Byron, the Shelleys, and the Pisan Circle*, Aldershot: Ashgate.

White, Daniel E. (2006) *Early Romanticism and Religious Dissent*, Cambridge: Cambridge University Press.

Worthen, John (2001) *The Gang: Coleridge, the Hutchinsons and the Wordsworths in 1802*, New Haven, CT: Yale University Press.

Chapter 4: National, regional, and local Romanticism

As discussed in this chapter, the rise of nationhood and nationalism in late-eighteenth and nineteenth-century Britain has been hotly debated by a number of historians, some of whom have argued against the existence of a homogenous pan-British identity in the period. Useful studies of the rise of nationalism in Britain and Western Europe include the following:

Gellner, Ernst (1983) *Nations and Nationalism*, Ithaca, NY: Cornell University Press.
Kidd, Colin (1999) *British Identities before Nationalism: Ethnicity and Nationhood in the Atlantic World, 1600–1800*, Cambridge: Cambridge University Press.
Newman, Gerald (1987) *The Rise of English Nationalism: A Cultural History, 1740–1830*, New York: St Martin's Press.

It is useful to read these historical studies alongside works more specifically on the development of 'British' literature and the rise of literary nationalism in Britain, such as:

Crawford, Robert (1992) *Devolving English Literature*, Oxford: Oxford University Press.
Kidd, Colin (1993) *Subverting Scotland's Past: Scottish Whig Historians and the Creation of an Anglo-British Identity, 1689-c.1830*, Cambridge: Cambridge University Press.
Trumpener, Katie (2007) *Bardic Nationalism: The Romantic Novel and the British Empire*, Princeton, NJ: Princeton University Press.

There are numerous works on the 'four nations', many of which argue for the importance of antiquarian developments in Scotland, Ireland and Wales in generating new forms of 'Britishness'. The following essays are recommended as useful starting points:

Connolly, Claire (2006) "Irish Romanticism, 1800–1830", in Margaret Kelleher and Phillip O'Leary (eds.) *The Cambridge History of Irish Literature*, Cambridge: Cambridge University Press, I. 407–48.
Duncan, Ian (2009) "Edinburgh and Lowland Scotland", in James Chandler (ed.) *The Cambridge History of English Romantic Literature*, Cambridge: Cambridge University Press, 159–81.
Stafford, Fiona (2005) "England, Ireland, Scotland, Wales", in Nicholas Roe (ed.) *Romanticism: An Oxford Guide*, New York: Oxford University Press, 114–25.

For studies on comparative, regional, archipelagic and transnational Romanticism, see the following:

Lamont, Claire and Michael Rossington (eds.) (2007) *Romanticism's Debatable Lands*, Basingstoke: Palgrave Macmillan.
Roe, Nicholas (ed.) (2010) *English Romantic Writers and the West Country*, Basingstoke: Palgrave Macmillan.
Stafford, Fiona (2010) *Local Attachments: The Province of Poetry*, Oxford: Oxford University Press.

Chapter 5: Romanticism in the arts

For comprehensive illustrated surveys of both British and European Romantic art, see the following:

Blayney Brown, David (2001) *Romanticism: Art and Ideas*, London: Phaidon.
Noon, Patrick, Stephen Bann, David Blayney Brown, Rachel Meredith, Christine Riding and Marie Watteau (2003) *From Constable to Delacroix: British Art and the French Romantics*, exh. cat., London: Tate Gallery Publishing.

Vaughan, William (1999) *British Painting: the Golden Age from Hogarth to Turner*, London: Thames and Hudson.

—. (1994) *Romanticism and Art*, London: Thames and Hudson.

The following are some of the most useful interdisciplinary studies of the ways in which the visual arts, music, literature and history inter-relate, especially in England and France:

Behrendt, Stephen C. (2005) "The visual arts and music", in Nicholas Roe (ed.) *Romanticism: An Oxford Guide*, New York: Oxford University Press, 62–76.

Heffernan, James A (1985) *The Re-Creation of Landscape: A Study of Wordsworth, Coleridge, Constable and Turner*; Hanover, NH and London: University Press of New England.

Labbe, Jacqueline M. (1998) *Romantic Visualities: Landscape, Gender, and Romanticism*, Hampshire and London: Macmillan Press.

Mitchell, Rosemary (2000) *Picturing the Past: English History in Text and Image, 1830–1870*, Oxford: Oxford University Press.

Paulson, Ronald (1982) *Literary Landscape: Turner and Constable*, New Haven, CT: Yale University Press.

Thomas, Sophie (2008) *Romanticism and Visuality: Fragments, History, Spectacle*, London and New York: Routledge.

For more specific studies on historical painting and Romantic history, see:

Rodner, William S. (1997) *J. M. W. Turner, Romantic Painter of the Industrial Revolution*, Berkeley, CA and London: University of California Press.

Wood, Marcus (2000) *Blind Memory: Visual Representation of Slavery in England and America 1790–1865*, Manchester and New York: Manchester University Press.

Wright, Beth S. (1997) *Painting and History during the French Restoration: Abandoned by the Past*, Cambridge: Cambridge University Press.

For a comprehensive study on British Romantic music, see:

Temperley, Nicholas (ed.) (1981) *Music in Britain: The Romantic Age 1800–1914*, London: Athlone Press.

Chapter 6: European Romanticism

Details about European Romanticism are available from general studies which describe its major social, intellectual, political and cultural developments. Examples include the following:

Breckman, Warren (2007) *European Romanticism: A Brief History with Documents*, Boston and New York: Bedford/St. Martin's.

Ferber, Michael (2005) *A Companion to European Romanticism*, Oxford: Blackwell.

Hamilton, Paul (2013) *Realpoetik: European Romanticism and Literary Politics*, Oxford: Oxford University Press.

Hoffmeister, Gerhart (ed.) (1990) *European Romanticism: Literary Cross-Currents, Modes, and Models*, Detroit: Wayne State University Press.

Isbell, Claiborne J. (1994) *The Birth of European Romanticism: Truth and Propaganda in Staël's 'De L'Allemagne', 1810–1813*, Cambridge: Cambridge University Press.

McClanahan, Clarence E. (1990) *European Romanticism: Literary Societies, Poets, and Poetry*, Oxford: Peter Lang.

Prickett, Stephen (2010) *European Romanticism: A Reader*, London: Continuum.

Wohlgemut, Esther (2009) *Romantic Cosmopolitanism*, Basingstoke: Palgrave Macmillan.

Chapter 7: Global Romanticism

There are numerous studies on globalisation but the ones of greatest relevance to readers of this book are those that more fully consider the history or origins of globalisation and concepts such as 'early' or 'first-wave' globalisation:

Hopkins, A. G. (ed.) (2002) *Globalization in World History*, London: Random House.
Waters, Malcolm (1995) *Globalization*, London and New York: Routledge.

More specific studies on Romanticism, modernity and globalisation include:

Gottlieb, Evan (2014) *Romantic Globalism*, Columbus, OH: Ohio University Press.
Hanley, Keith and Greg Kucich (eds.) (2008) *Nineteenth-Century Worlds: Global Formations Past and Present*, London and New York: Routledge.
Otto, Peter (2011) *Multiplying Worlds: Romanticism, Modernity, and the Emergence of Virtual Reality*, New York: Oxford University Press.

Romanticism and empire has long been a topic of extensive study and there are many fruitful results, but the following books remain excellent starting points:

Coleman, Deirdre (2005) *Romantic Colonization and British Anti-Slavery*, Cambridge: Cambridge University Press.
Fulford, Tim and Peter Kitson (eds.) (1998) *Romanticism and Colonialism: Writing and Empire, 1780–1830*, Cambridge: Cambridge University Press.
Leask, Nigel (1992) *British Romantic Writers and the East: Anxieties of Empire*, Cambridge: Cambridge University Press.

For the most innovative transnational work on writing produced in India, America and other British or former British colonies, see:

Giles, Paul (2012) *The Global Remapping of American Literature*, Princeton, NJ: Princeton University Press.
Gilroy, Paul (1995) *The Black Atlantic: Modernity and Double Consciousness*, Cambridge, MA: Harvard University Press.
White, Dan (2013) *From Little London to Little Bengal: Religion, Print, and Modernity in Early British India, 1793–1835*, Baltimore, MD: Johns Hopkins University Press.

Conclusion: Legacies of Romanticism

The legacies of Romanticism has recently been a topic of scholarly interest and there are several studies that examine this long history of indebtedness. Romanticism's legacies in the Victorian period are examined in the following studies:

Cronin, Richard (2002) *Romantic Victorians: English Literature, 1824–1840*, Basingstoke and New York: Palgrave Macmillan.
Faflak, Joel and Julia M. Wright (eds.) (2004) *Nervous Reactions: Victorian Recollections of Romanticism*, Albany: State University of New York Press.
Radford, Andrew and Mark Sandy (eds.) (2008) *Romantic Echoes in the Victorian Era*, Aldershot: Ashgate.

Romanticism's legacies in the twentieth and twentieth-first centuries are examined in the following excellent studies:

Larrissy, Edward (ed.) (1999) *Romanticism and Postmodernism,* Cambridge: Cambridge University Press.

O'Neill, Michael (2007) *The All-Sustaining Air: Romantic Legacies and Renewals in British, American, and Irish Poetry since 1900,* Oxford: Oxford University Press.

Sandy, Mark (ed.) (2012) *Romantic Presences in the Twentieth Century,* Aldershot: Ashgate.

Walford Davies, Damian and Richard Marggraf Turley (eds.) (2006) *The Monstrous Debt: Modalities of Romantic Influences in Twentieth-Century Literature,* Detroit, MI: Wayne State University Press.

The following study is the first to survey the legacies of Romanticism in both nineteenth and twentieth-century culture and covers areas such as the Gothic, Victorianism, modernism, postmodernism and postcolonialism.

Casaliggi, Carmen and Paul March-Russell (eds.) (2012) *Legacies of Romanticism: Literature, Culture, Aesthetics,* New York and London: Routledge.

For more specific studies on Romanticism and the 'cult of posterity', see:

Bennett, Andrew (1999) *Romantic Poets and the Culture of Posterity,* Cambridge: Cambridge University Press.

Østermark-Johansen, Lene (2003) *Romantic Generations: Text, Authority and Posterity in British Romanticism,* Copenhagen: Museum Tusculanum Press.

Bibliography

Introduction: Romanticism and its discontents

Abrams, M. H. (1971a) *The Mirror and the Lamp: Romantic Theory and the Critical Tradition*, Oxford: Oxford University Press.

—. (1971b) *Natural Supernaturalism: Tradition and Revolution in Romantic Literature*, New York: W. W. Norton.

—. (1963) "English Romanticism: The Spirit of the Age", in Northrop Frye (ed.) *Romanticism Reconsidered: English Institute Papers*, New York: Columbia University Press, 26–72.

Armstrong, Isobel (1995) "The Gush of the Feminine: How Can we Read Women's Poetry of the Romantic Period", in Paula R. Feldman and Theresa M. Kelley (eds.) *Romantic Women Writers: Voices and Countervoices*, Hanover, NH: University Press of New England, 13–32.

Babbitt, Irving (1919) *Rousseau and Romanticism*, Boston and New York: Houghton Mifflin.

Barrell, John (2000) *Imagining the King's Death: Figurative Treason, Fantasies of Regicide, 1793–1795*, Oxford: Oxford University Press.

Bate, Jonathan (1996) "Living with the Weather", *Studies in Romanticism* 35: 431–47.

—. (1991) *Romantic Ecology: Wordsworth and the Environmental Tradition*, London and New York: Routledge.

Bloom, Harold (ed.) (1979) *Deconstruction and Criticism*, New York: Seabury.

—. (1970) "The Internalization of Quest-Romance", in Harold Bloom (ed.) *Romanticism and Consciousness: Essays in Criticism*, New York: W. W. Norton. 3–24.

Bode, Christopher (1992) "Romanticism and Deconstruction: Distant Relations and Elective Affinities", in Gunther Blaicher and Michael Gassenmeier (eds.) *Romantic Continuities*, Essen: Verl. Die Blaue Eule, 131–59.

Brown, Marshall (1993) "Enlightenment and Romanticism", in Stuart Curran (ed.) *The Cambridge Companion to British Romanticism*, Cambridge: Cambridge University Press, 25–47.

—. (1991) *Preromanticism*, Stanford, CA: Stanford University Press.

Burstein, Miriam (2004) *Narrating Women's History in Britain, 1770–1902*, Aldershot: Ashgate.

Butler, Marilyn (1989) "Repossessing the Past: The Case for an Open Literary History", in Marjorie Levinson *et al.* (eds.) *Rethinking Historicism: Critical Readings in Romantic History*, London: Blackwell, 64–84.

—. (1988) "Romanticism in England", in Roy Porter and Mikulás Teich (eds.) *Romanticism in National Context*, Cambridge: Cambridge University Press, 37–67.

—. (1981) *Romantics, Rebels and Reactionaries: English Literature and its Background, 1760–1830*, New York: Oxford University Press.

Canuel, Mark (2002) *Religion, Toleration and British Writing, 1790–1830*, Cambridge: Cambridge University Press.

Caudwell, Christopher (1937) *Illusion and Reality*, London: Macmillan.

Chandler, James K. (2009) "Introduction", in *The Cambridge History of English Romantic Literature*, Cambridge: Cambridge University Press, 1–10.

—. (1998) *England in 1819: The Politics of Literary Culture and the Case of Romantic Historicism*, Chicago, IL and London: University of Chicago Press.

Cox, Phillip (1996) *Gender, Genre, and the Romantic Poets: An Introduction*, Manchester: Manchester University Press.

Craciun, Adriana (2005) *British Women Writers and the French Revolution: Citizens of the World*, London: Palgrave.

Cronin, Richard (2002) *Romantic Victorians: English Literature, 1824–1840*, Basingstoke and New York: Palgrave Macmillan.

Culler, A. Dwight (ed.) (1961) *Poetry and Criticism of Matthew Arnold*, Boston: Houghton Mifflin.

Curran, Stuart (1988) "The I Altered", in Anne K. Mellor (ed.) *Romanticism and Feminism*, Bloomington, IN: Indiana University Press, 185–207.

De Man, Paul (1984) *The Rhetoric of Romanticism*, New York: Columbia University Press.

Duncan, Ian, with Leith Davis and Janet Sorensen (2004) "Introduction", in Leith Davis, Ian Duncan and Janet Sorensen (eds.) *Scotland and the Borders of Romanticism*, Cambridge: Cambridge University Press, 1–19.

Eastwood, David (1989) "Robert Southey and the Intellectual Origins of Romantic Conservatism", *English Historical Review* 104: 308–31.

Eichner, Hans (1972) "Introduction", in Hans Eichner (ed.) *"Romantic" and its Cognates: The European History of a Word*, Toronto: University of Toronto Press, 3–16.

Favret, Mary A. (1993) *Romantic Correspondence: Women, Politics and the Fiction of Letters*, Cambridge: Cambridge University Press.

Galperin, William and Susan Wolfson (1997) "'Romanticism' in Crisis: The Romantic Century", *Romantic Circles*, accessed 20 May 2015: http://www.rc.umd.edu/reference/misc/confarchive/crisis/crisisa.html

Garrard, Greg (2004) *Ecocriticism*, London and New York: Routledge.

—. (1996) "Radical Pastoral?", *Studies in Romanticism* 35.3: 449–65.

Gilmartin, Kevin (2007) *Writing Against Revolution: Literary Conservatism in Britain 1790–1832*, New York: Cambridge University Press.

Grange, William (2011) *Historical Dictionary of German Literature to 1945*, Lanham, MA: Scarecrow Press.

Hamilton, Paul (2003) *Historicism*, 2nd ed., London and New York: Routledge.

Hutchings, Kevin (2007) "Ecocriticism in British Romantic Studies", *Literature Compass* 4/1: 172–202.

Immerwahr, Raymond (1972) "'Romantic' and its Cognates in England, Germany and France before 1790", in Hans Eichner (ed.) *"Romantic" and its Cognates: The European History of a Word*, Toronto: University of Toronto Press, 17–97.

Isbell, John (2004) "Romantic Disavowals of Romanticism, 1800–1830", in Steven P. Sondrup and Virgil Nemoianu (eds.) *Nonfictional Romantic Prose: Extending the Borders*, Amsterdam: John Benjamins, 37–57.

Jacobus, Mary (1989) *Romanticism, Writing, and Sexual Difference*, Oxford: Clarendon Press.

Janowitz, Anne (1998) *Lyric and Labour in the Romantic Tradition*, New York: Cambridge University Press.

Kasmer, Kisa (2012) *Novel Histories: British Women Writing History, 1760–1830*, Madison, WI: Fairleigh Dickinson University Press.

Kelley, Theresa (2011) "Introduction", in Theresa Kelley (ed.) *Romantic Frictions, Romantic Circles*, accessed 22 May 2015: http://www.rc.umd.edu/praxis/frictions/HTML/praxis.2011. kelley.html.

Kelly, Gary (1993) *Women, Writing, and Revolution, 1790–1827*, Oxford: Clarendon Press.

Klancher, Jon (1989) "English Romanticism and Cultural Production", in H. Aram Veeser (ed.) *The New Historicism*, New York and London: Routledge, 77–88.

Kroeber, Karl (1995) *Ecological Literary Criticism: Romantic Imagining and the Biology of Mind*, New York: Columbia University Press.

Kucich, Greg (2014) 'The History Girls': Charlotte Smith's *History of England* and the Politics of Women's Educational History", in Porscha Fermanis and John Regan (eds.) *Rethinking British Romantic History, 1770–1845*, Oxford: Oxford University Press, 35–53.

Langbaum, Robert (1957) *The Poetry of Experience: The Dramatic Monologue in Modern Literary Tradition*, New York: Random House.

Levinson, Marjorie (1986) *Wordsworth's Great Period Poems*, Cambridge: Cambridge University Press.

Liu, Alan (1989) *Wordsworth: The Sense of History*, Stanford, CA: Stanford University Press.

——. (1988) "Review of *Wordsworth's History Imagination: The Poetry of Displacement* by David Simpson", in *The Wordsworth Circle* 19.4: 172–82.

London, April (2006) *Literary History Writing, 1770–1820*, Basingstoke: Palgrave Macmillan.

Looser, Devoney (2000) *British Women Writers and the Writing of History, 1670–1820*, Baltimore, MD: Johns Hopkins University Press.

Lovejoy, Arthur O. (1924) "On the Discrimination of Romanticisms", *PMLA* 39: 229–53.

Lucas, John (1982) *Romantic to Modern Literature: Essays and Ideas of Culture, 1750–1900*, Totowa, NJ: Barnes & Noble.

McFarland, Thomas (1992) *William Wordsworth: Intensity and Achievement*, Oxford: Clarendon Press.

McGann, Jerome (2002) *Byron and Romanticism*, ed. James Soderholm, Cambridge: Cambridge University Press.

——. (1983) *The Romantic Ideology*, Chicago, IL: University of Chicago Press.

McKusick, James C. (2000) *Green Writing: Romanticism and Ecology*, New York: Palgrave/ St Martin's Press.

McLane, Maureen (2000) *Romanticism and the Human Sciences: Poetry, Population, and the Discourse of the Species*, Cambridge: Cambridge University Press.

Makdisi, Saree (1998) *Romantic Imperialism: Universal Empire and the Culture of Modernity*, Cambridge: Cambridge University Press.

Mellor, Anne K. (1993) *Romanticism and Gender*, New York and London: Routledge.

——. (1990) "Why Women Didn't Like Romanticism", in Gene W. Ruoff (ed.) *The Romantics and Us: Essays on Literature and Culture*, New Brunswick, NJ: Rutgers University Press, 274–87.

Miller, J. Hillis (1979) "On Edge: The Crossways of Contemporary Criticism", *Bulletin of the American Academy of Arts and Sciences*, 32: 13–32.

Moore, Jane (2011) "Celtic Romantic Poetry: Scotland, Ireland, Wales", in Charles Mahoney (ed.) *A Companion to Romantic Poetry*, Chichester: Wiley Blackwell, 251–67.

Nietzsche, Friedrich (1968) *The Will to Power*, trans. Walter Kaufmann and R. J. Hollingdale, ed. Walter Kaufmann, New York: Vintage Press.

Nussbaum, Felicity A. (ed.) (2003) *The Global Eighteenth Century*, Baltimore, MD: Johns Hopkins University Press.

O'Brien, Karen (1997) *Narratives of Enlightenment: Cosmopolitan History from Voltaire to Gibbon*, Cambridge: Cambridge University Press.

Oerlemans, Onno (2004) *Romanticism and the Materiality of Nature*, Toronto: University of Toronto Press.

O'Neill, Michael (1995) "'When This Warm Scribe My Hand': Writing and History in *Hyperion* and *The Fall of Hyperion*", in Nicholas Roe (ed.) *Keats and History*, Cambridge: Cambridge University Press, 143–64.

Parker, Mark (1991) "Measure and Countermeasure: The Lovejoy-Wellek Debate and Romantic Periodization", in David Perkins (ed.) *Theoretical Issues in Literary History*, Cambridge, MA: Harvard University Press, 227–48.

Phillips, Mark Salber (2000) *Society and Sentiment: Genres of Historical Writing in Britain, 1740–1820*, Princeton, NJ: Princeton University Press.

Pittock, Murray (2008) *Scottish and Irish Romanticism*, Oxford: Oxford University Press.

Price, Fiona (2009) *Revolutions in Taste 1773–1818: Women Writers and the Aesthetics of Romanticism*, Aldershot: Ashgate.

Reider, John (1997) "The Institutional Overdetermination of the Concept of Romanticism", *The Yale Journal of Criticism* 10.1: 145–163.

Rigby, Kate (2004) *Topographies of the Sacred: The Poetics of Place in European Romanticism*, Charlottesville, VA: University of Virginia Press.

Robertson, Fiona (2014) "Historical Fiction and the Fractured Atlantic", in Porscha Fermanis and John Regan (eds.) *Rethinking British Romantic History, 1770–184*, Oxford: Oxford University Press, 246–70.

Ross, Marlon (1989) *The Contours of Masculine Desire*, Oxford: Oxford University Press.

Russell, Gillian (2013) "'Who's afraid for William Wordsworth?': Some Thoughts on 'Romanticism' in 2012", *Australian Humanities Review* 54: 66–80.

Sales, Roger (1983) *English Literature in History, 1780–1830: Pastoral and Politics*, New York: St. Martin's Press.

Schmidt, James (2006) "What Enlightenment Was, What it Still Might Be, and Why Kant May Have Been Right After All", *American Behavioral Scientist* 49.5: 651–55.

Schmitt, Carl (1919) *Politische Romantik,* Berlin: Duncker and Humblot.

Simpson, David (1987) *Wordsworth's Historical Imagination: The Poetry of Displacement*, New York: Methuen.

Siskin, Clifford (2009) "The Problem of Periodization: Enlightenment, Romanticism, and the Fate of System", in James Chandler (ed.) *The Cambridge History of English Romantic Literature*, Cambridge: Cambridge University Press, 101–26.

—. (1988) *The Historicity of Romantic Discourse*, New York: Oxford University Press.

—. and William Warner (2011) "If This Is Enlightenment Then What Is Romanticism?", *European Romantic Review* 22.3: 281–91.

Spivak, Gayatri Chakravorty (1981) "Sex and History in *The Prelude* (1805): Books Nine to Thirteen", *Texas Studies in Literature and Language* 23: 324–60.

Spongberg, Mary (2002) *Writing Women's History since the Renaissance*, London: Palgrave Macmillan.

Thompson, E. P. (1966) *The Making of the English Working Classes*, New York: Vintage.

Veeser, H. Aram (1989) *The New Historicism*, London and New York: Routledge.

Walford Davies, Damian (2009) "Introduction", in Damian Walford Davies (ed.) *Romanticism, History, Historicism: Essays on an Orthodoxy*, New York and London: Routledge, 1–13.

Watkins, Daniel P. (1996) *Sexual Power in British Romantic Poetry*, Gainsville, FL: University Press of Florida.

—. (1993) *A Materialist Critique of English Romantic Drama*, Gainsville, FL: University Press of Florida.

Whalley, George (1972) "England Romantic-Romanticism", in Hans Eichner (ed.) *"Romantic" and its Cognates: The European History of a Word*, Toronto: University of Toronto Press, 157–262.

Wellek, René (1963) *Concepts of Criticism*, New Haven, CT: Yale University Press.

—. (1955) *History of Modern Criticism: 1750–1950*, Vol. 2: *The Romantic Age*, New Haven, CT: Yale University Press.

—. (1949) "The Concept of Romanticism in Literary History", *Comparative Literature* 1: 1–23, 147–72.

Williams, Raymond (1976) *Keywords: A Vocabulary of Culture and Society*, New York: Oxford University Press.

—. (1958/1987) *Culture and Society, 1780–1950*, London: Chatto and Windus.

Wolfson, Susan J. (2006) *Borderlines: The Shiftings of Gender in British Romanticism*, Stanford, CA: Stanford University Press.

Worrall, David (2006) *Theatric Revolution: Drama, Censorship and Romantic Period Subcultures 1773–1832*, Oxford: Oxford University Press.

Chapter 1: Contexts of Romanticism

Abrams, M. H. (1971) *Natural Supernaturalism: Tradition and Revolt in Romantic Literature*, New York: Norton.

—. and Geoffrey Galt Harpham (2012) *A Glossary of Literary Terms*, 10th ed., Wadsworth: Cenage Learning.

Ammerman, David (1976) "The British Constitution and the American Revolution: A Failure of Precedent", *William and Mary Law Review* 17.3: 473–501.

Anon (1795) *The Cabinet. By A Society of Gentlemen*, 3 vols, Norwich: J. March.

Bainbridge, Simon (2003) *British Poetry and the Revolutionary and Napoleonic Wars*, Oxford: Oxford University Press.

—. (1995) *Napoleon and English Romanticism*, Cambridge: Cambridge University Press.

Beckett, J. V. (1986) *The Aristocracy in England 1660–1914*, New York: Basil Blackwell.

Bennett, Betty T. (1976) *British War Poetry in the Age of Romanticism: 1793–1815*, New York: Garland.

Bentham, Jeremy (1776) *A Fragment on Government*, London: T. Payne.

Black, Jeremy (2005) *Culture in Eighteenth-Century England: A Subject for Taste*, London: Hambledon and London.

Brewer, John (2009) "Sentiment and Sensibility", in James Chandler (ed.) *The Cambridge History of English Romantic Literature*, Cambridge: Cambridge University Press, 21–44.

Budge, Gavin (ed.) (2007) "Introduction: Empiricism, Romanticism, and the Politics of Common Sense", in *Romantic Empiricism: Poetics and the Philosophy of Common Sense, 1780–1830*, Cranbury, NJ: Associated University Presses, 11–39.

Burke, Edmund (1790/1986) *Reflections on the Revolution in France*, ed. C. C. O'Brien, London: Penguin.

Butler, Marilyn (ed.) (1984) *Burke, Paine, Godwin, and the Revolution Controversy*, Cambridge: Cambridge University Press.

—. (1981) *Romantics, Rebels and Reactionaries: English Literature and Its Background, 1760–1830*, Oxford and New York: Oxford University Press.

Cannon, John (1984) *Aristocratic Century: The Peerage of Eighteenth-Century England*, New York: Cambridge University Press.

Canuel, Mark (2002) *Religion, Toleration and British Writing, 1790–1830*, Cambridge: Cambridge University Press.

Carlson, Julie (2009) "Theatre, Performance, and Urban Spectacle", in James Chandler (ed.) *The Cambridge History of English Romantic Literature*, Cambridge: Cambridge University Press, 490–506.

Chandler, James K. (1998) *England in 1819: The Politics of Literary Culture and the Case of Romantic Historicism*, Chicago, IL: University of Chicago Press.

Claeys, Gregory (1995) "Introduction", in Gregory Claeys (ed.) *Radicalism and Reform: Responses to Burke 1790–1791*, Vol. 1 of *Political Writings of the 1790s*, 8 vols, London: Pickering and Chatto.

Clark, J. C. D. (1985) *English Society, 1688–1832: Ideology, Social Structure and Political Practice*, Cambridge: Cambridge University Press.

Connolly, Claire (2015) "Sea Crossings, Scale and the Imprint of Colonial Infrastructure from Swift to Edgeworth", unpublished Conference Paper, BARS Conference 2015, "Romantic Imprints".

Craton, Michael (1983) *Testing the Chains: Resistance to Slavery in the British West Indies*, Ithaca, NY: Cornell University Press.

Dick, Alex (2013) *Romanticism and the Gold Standard: Money, Literature, and Economic Debate in Britain 1790–1830*, Basingstoke: Palgrave Macmillan.

Eagleton, Terry (1984) *The Function of Criticism*, London: Verso.

Elfenbein, Andrew (1999) *Romantic Genius: The Prehistory of a Homosexual Role*, New York: Columbia University Press.

Evans, Eric J. (1996) *The Forging of the Modern State: Early Industrial Britain, 1783–1870*, Harlow: Pearson.

—. (1983) *The Great Reform Act of 1832*, London: Methuen & Co.

Fairer, David (1998) "Introduction", in *Thomas Warton's 'History of English Poetry'*, 4 vols, New York and London: Routledge.

Favret, Mary A. (2010) *War at a Distance: Romanticism and the Making of Modern Wartime*, Princeton, NJ: Princeton University Press.

Foucault, Michel (1978), *The History of Sexuality: An Introduction*, Vol. 1, trans. Robert Hurley, London: Allen Lane.

Fulford, Tim (2002) *Romanticism and Millenarianism*, New York and Basingstoke: Palgrave.

—. (1999) *Romanticism and Masculinity: Gender, Politics, and Poetics in the Writings of Burke, Coleridge, Cobbett, Wordsworth, De Quincey, and Hazlitt*, Basingstoke: Macmillan.

Gallagher, Catherine (2006) *The Body Economic: Life, Death, and Sensation in Political Economy and the Victorian Novel*, Princeton, NJ: Princeton University Press.

Gay, Peter (1977) *The Enlightenment: The Rise of Modern Paganism*, New York: Norton.

Gilmartin, Kevin M. (1996) *Print Politics: The Press and Radical Opposition in Early Nineteenth-Century England*, Cambridge: Cambridge University Press.

Golinski, Jan (2009) "The Literature of the New Sciences", in James Chandler (ed.) *The Cambridge History of English Romantic Literature*, Cambridge: Cambridge University Press, 527–52.

—. (1992) *Science as a Public Culture: Chemistry and Enlightenment in Britain, 1760–1820*, New York: Cambridge University Press.

Goode, Mike (2009) *Sentimental Masculinity and the Rise of History, 1790–1890*, Cambridge: Cambridge University Press.

Habermas, Jürgen (1989) *The Structural Transformation of the Public Sphere: An Inquiry into a Category of Bourgeois Society*, trans. Thomas Burger, Cambridge, MA: MIT Press.

Hamilton, Paul (2007) *Coleridge and German Philosophy: The Poet in the Land of Logic*, London: Continuum.

Henderson, Andrea (2008) *Romanticism and the Painful Pleasures of Modern Life*, Cambridge: Cambridge University Press.

Heringman, Noah (2004) *Romantic Rocks, Aesthetic Geology*, Ithaca and London: Cornell University Press.

—. (ed.) (2003) *Romantic Science: The Literary Forms of Natural History*, Albany, NY: State University of New York Press.

Hunt, Leigh (1818) *The Examiner*, 20 September, London.

—. (1818) *The Examiner*, 1 March, London.

—. (1817) *The Examiner*, 28 December, London.

—. (1817) *The Examiner*, 21 December, London.

—. (1816) *The Examiner*, 22 August, London.

—. (1815) The *Examiner*, 10 December, London.

Janowitz, Anne (1998) *Lyric and Labour in the Romantic Tradition*, Cambridge: Cambridge University Press.

Jarvis, Robin (1997) *Romantic Writing and Pedestrian Travel*, London: Macmillan.

Johns, Adrian (2009) "Changes in the World of Publishing", in James Chandler (ed.) *The Cambridge History of English Romantic Literature*, Cambridge: Cambridge University Press, 377–402.

Johnson, Claudia L. (1995) *Equivocal Beings: Politics, Gender and Sentimentality in the 1790s – Wollstonecraft, Radcliffe, Burney and Austen*, Chicago, IL: University of Chicago Press.

Keen, Paul (2009) "'With an Industry Incredible': Politics, Writing, and the Public Sphere", in Jon Klancher (ed.) *The Concise Companion to the Romantic Age*, Chicester: Wiley-Blackwell, 99–117.

Kennedy, Catriona (2013) *Narratives of the Revolutionary and Napoleonic Wars: Military and Civilian Experience in Britain and Ireland*, Basingstoke: Palgrave Macmillan.

Klancher, Jon (1987) *The Making of English Reading Audiences, 1790–1832*, Madison, WI: University of Wisconsin Press.

Langan, Celeste (1995) *Romantic Vagrancy: Wordsworth and the Simulation of Freedom*, Cambridge: Cambridge University Press.

Langford, Paul (1989) *A Polite and Commercial People: England 1727–1783*, Oxford: Oxford University Press.

Lewis, Matthew (1796/1973) *The Monk*, ed. Howard Anderson, London: Oxford University Press.

Lloyd, Nicola (2013) "Canals, Commerce and Sympathy in Sydney Owenson's *O'Donnel*", unpublished Conference Paper, BARS Conference 2013, "Romantic Imports and Exports".

McCalman, Ian (1988) *Radical Underworld: Prophets, Revolutionaries and Pornographers in London, 1795–1840*, Cambridge: Cambridge University Press.

McKendrick, Neil, John Brewer and J. H. Plumb (eds.) (1982) *The Birth of a Consumer Society: The Commercialization of Eighteenth-Century England*, Bloomington, IN: University of Indiana Press.

Makdisi, Saree (1998) *Romantic Imperialism: Universal Empire and the Culture of Modernity*, Cambridge: Cambridge University Press.

Malthus, Robert (1798) *An Essay on the Principle of Population*, London: J. Johnson.

Mee, Jon (2003) *Romanticism, Enthusiasm and Regulation: Poetics and the Policing of Culture in the Romantic Period*, Oxford: Oxford University Press.

—. (1992) *Dangerous Enthusiasm: William Blake and the Culture of Radicalism in the 1790s*, Oxford: Oxford University Press.

Milnes, Tim (2010) *The Truth About Romanticism: Pragmatism and Idealism in Keats, Shelley, and Coleridge*, Cambridge: Cambridge University Press.

Mudge, Gavin (2001) "Romanticism, Materialism, and the Origins of Modern Pornography", in *Romanticism and Sexuality, Romanticism on the Net*: 23, accessed 10 May 2009: http://www.erudit.org/revue/ron/2001/v/n23/005988ar.html

Murphy, Paul Thomas (1994) *Towards a Working-Class Canon: Literary Criticism in British Working-Class Periodicals, 1816–1858*, Columbus, OH: Ohio State University Press.

Nattrass Leonora (1995), *William Cobbett: The Politics of Style*, Cambridge: Cambridge University Press.

O'Rourke, Michael and David Collings (2004) "Introduction: Queer Romanticisms: Past, Present, and Future", in Michael O'Rourke and David Collings (eds.) *Queer Romanticism, Romanticism on the Net*: 36–7, accessed 5 May 2015: https://www.erudit.org/revue/ron/2005/v/n36-37/011132ar.html

Outhwaite, R. B. (1995) *Clandestine Marriage in England, 1500–1850*, Rio Grande, OH: Hambledon Press.

Paulson, Ronald (1983) *Representations of Revolution, 1789–1820*, New Haven, CT: Yale University Press.

Paley, Morton D. (1978) *William Blake*, Oxford: Phaidon.

Plotz, Judith (2001) *Romanticism and the Vocation of Childhood*, New York: Palgrave Macmillan.

Poovey, Mary (2008) *Genres of the Credit Economy: Mediating Value in Eighteenth- and Nineteenth-Century Britain*, Chicago, IL: University of Chicago Press.

Porter, Roy (2000) *Enlightenment: Britain and the Creation of the Modern World*, London: Allen Lane.

Probert, Rebecca (2009) *Marriage Law and Practice in the Long Eighteenth Century: A Reassessment*, Cambridge: Cambridge University Press.

Ramsay, Thomas (1774) "To the Lovers of Natural History", *Scots Magazine* 34: 174–5.

Roston, Murray (1965) *Prophet and Poet: The Bible and the Growth of Romanticism*, Evanston, IL: Northwestern University Press.

Russell, Gillian and Neil Ramsey (eds.) (2015) *Tracing War in British Enlightenment and Romantic Culture*, Basingstoke: Palgrave Macmillan.

Ruston, Sharon (2005) *Shelley and Vitality*, New York and Basingstoke: Palgrave Macmillan.

Ryan, Robert M. (1997) *The Romantic Reformation: Religious Politics in English Literature, 1789–1824*, Cambridge: Cambridge University Press.

—. (1976) *Keats: The Religious Sense*, Princeton, NJ: Princeton University Press.

Scrivener, Michael (ed.) (1992) *Poetry and Reform: Periodical Verse from the English Democratic Press, 1792–1824*, Detroit, MI: Wayne State University Press.

Sha, Richard C. (2008) *Perverse Romanticism: Aesthetics and Sexuality in Britain, 1750–1832*, Baltimore, MD: Johns Hopkins University Press.

—. (2001) "Romanticism and Sexuality – A Special issue of *Romanticism on the Net*", *Romanticism on the Net*: 23, accessed 10 May 2015: http://www.erudit.org/revue/ron/2001/v/n23/005994ar.html

Shaw, Phillip (2002) *Waterloo and the Romantic Imagination*, Basingstoke: Palgrave Macmillan.

Smith, Adam (1759) *The Theory of Moral Sentiments*, London: A. Millar.

Southey, Robert (1823) *The History of the Peninsular War*, 3 vols, London: J. Murray.

St. Clair, William (2004) *The Reading Nation in the Romantic Period*, Cambridge: Cambridge University Press.

Swan, Beth (1997) *Fictions of Law: An Investigation of Eighteenth-Century English Fiction*, Frankfurt: Peter Lang.

Thompson, E. P. (1966) *The Making of the English Working Classes*, New York: Vintage.

Verhoeven, Will (2013) *Americomania and the French Revolution Debate in Britain, 1789–1802*, Cambridge: Cambridge University Press.

Watkins, Daniel P. (1996) *Sexual Power in British Romantic Poetry*, Gainesville, FL: University Press of Florida.

Weintraub, Stanley (2005) *Iron Tears: America's Battle for Freedom, Britain's Quagmire, 1775–83*, New York: Simon & Schuster.

Williams, Helen Maria (1790) *Letters Written in France in the Summer of 1790*, London: E. Newbery.

Wollstonecraft, Mary (1790/1993) *A Vindication of the Rights of Man*, in Janet Todd (ed.) *The Political Writings of Mary Wollstonecraft*, London: William Pickering.

Wood, Marcus (2005) *Radical Satire and Print Culture, 1790–1822*, Oxford: Clarendon Press.

Wood, Paul (2004) "Introduction: Stepping out of Merton's Shadow", in P. Wood (ed.) *Science and Dissent in England, 1688–1945*, Aldershot: Ashgate, 1–18.

Worrall, David (1992) *Radical Culture: Discourse, Resistance and Surveillance, 1790–1820*, Hemel Hempstead: Harvester-Wheatsheaf.

Chapter 2: Romantic forms, genres and language

Abrams, M. H. (1999) *A Glossary of Literary Terms*, 6th ed., London: Cornell University Press.

—. (1953) *The Mirror and the Lamp*, New York: Norton.

Alker, Sharon-Ruth and Holly Faith Nelson (eds.) (2009) *James Hogg and the Literary Marketplace: Scottish Romanticism and the Working Class Author*, Aldershot: Ashgate.

Altick, Richard D. (1957) *The English Common Reader: A Social History of the Mass Reading Public, 1800–1900*, Chicago, IL: University of Chicago Press.

Auden, W. H. (1937) "Letter to Lord Byron", in *Letters from Iceland*, London: Faber and Faber.

Auerbach, Nina (1979) *Communities of Women: An Idea in Fiction*, Cambridge, MA: Harvard University Press.

Baillie, Joanna (1832) *The Complete Poetical Works*, Philadelphia: Carey & Lea.

Baines, Paul and Edward Burns (eds.) (2000) *Five Romantic Plays 1768–1821*, Oxford: Oxford World's Classics.

Barrell, John (1988) "The Uses of Dorothy: 'The Language of Sense' in 'Tintern Abbey'", in *Poetry, Language and Politics*, Manchester: Manchester University Press, 137–67.

Bates, Catherine (ed.) (2010) *The Cambridge Companion to the Epic*, Cambridge: Cambridge University Press.

Batten, Charles (1978) *Pleasurable Instruction: Form and Convention in Eighteenth-Century Travel Literature*, Berkeley, CA: University of California Press.

Bautz, Annika (2007) *The Reception of Jane Austen and Walter Scott: A Comparative Longitudinal Study*, London: Continuum.

Bewell, Alan (1989) *Wordsworth and the Enlightenment: Nature, Man, and Society in the Experimental Poetry*, New Haven, CT and London: Yale University Press.

Bieri, James (2008) *Percy Bysshe Shelley: A Biography*, Baltimore, MD: Johns Hopkins University Press.

Black, Jeremy (2001) *The English Press, 1621–1841*, Sutton: The History Press.

Blair, Robert (1982) *"The Grave" Illustrated by William Blake: A Study with Facsimile*, eds. Robert N. Essick and Morton D. Paley, London: Scolar Press.

—. (1743/1797) *The Grave*, Manchester: G. Nicholson.

Bloom, Harold (1969) "The Internalization of *Quest Romance*", *The Yale Review* 58: 526–36.

Bohls, Elizabeth A. and Ian Duncan (eds.) (2008) *Travel Writing 1700–1830: An Anthology*, Oxford: Oxford World's Classics.

Botting, Fred (1995) *Gothic*, London and New York: Routledge.

Bradley, Arthur and Alan Rawes (eds.) (2003) *Romantic Biography*, Aldershot: Ashgate.

Burke, Edmund (1757/2008) *A Philosophical Enquiry into the Origin of our Ideas of the Sublime and Beautiful*, ed. Adam Phillips, Oxford: Oxford University Press.

—. (1968) *Reflections on the Revolution in France*, ed. C. Cruise O'Brien, Harmondsworth: Penguin.

Burroughs, Catherine B. (ed.) (2000) *Women in British Romantic Theatre: Drama, Performance and Society, 1790–1840*, Cambridge: Cambridge University Press.

Butler, Marilyn (2010) "Culture's Medium: The Role of the Review", in Stuart Curran (ed.). *The Cambridge Companion to British Romanticism*, 2nd ed., Cambridge: Cambridge University Press, 127–52.

—. (1975) *Jane Austen and the War of Ideas*, Oxford: Clarendon Press.

Campbell, Timothy (2013) "Fashion, Microcosm, and Romantic Historical Distance", in Mark Salber Phillips *et al.* (eds.) *Rethinking Historical Distance*, Basingstoke: Palgrave Macmillan.

Carlson, Julie (1994) *In the Theatre of Romanticism*, Cambridge: Cambridge University Press.

Cave, Richard Allen (ed.) (1987) *The Romantic Theatre: An International Symposium*, Totowa, NJ: Barnes & Noble, 1987.

Chandler, James (2008) "Wordsworth's Great Ode: Romanticism and the Progress of Poetry", in James Chandler and Maureen McLane (eds.) *The Cambridge Companion to British Romantic Poetry*, Cambridge: Cambridge University Press, 136–154.

—. (1998) *England 1819: the Politics of Literary Culture and the Case of Romantic Historicism*, Chicago, IL and London: University of Chicago Press.

—. (1984) *Wordsworth's Second Nature: A Study of the Poetry and Politics*, Chicago, IL and London: University of Chicago Press.

Chandler, James and Maureen McLane (eds.) (2008) *The Cambridge Companion to British Romantic Poetry*, Cambridge: Cambridge University Press.

Chaplin, Sue (2014) "Ann Radcliffe and Romantic-era Fiction", in Dale Townshend and Angela Wright (eds.) *Ann Radcliffe, Romanticism and the Gothic*, Cambridge: Cambridge University Press, 203–18.

Cheeke, Stephen (2003) *Byron and Place: History, Translation, Nostalgia*, Basingstoke: Palgrave Macmillan.

Christie, William (2005) "Essays, newspapers, and magazines", in Nicholas Roe (ed.) *Romanticism: An Oxford Guide*, Oxford: Oxford University Press, 426–44.

Clery, Emma (1995) *The Rise of Supernatural Fiction, 1762–1800*, Cambridge: Cambridge University Press.

Connolly, Claire (2015) "The National Tale", in Peter Garside and Karen O'Brien (eds.) *The Oxford History of the Novel in English: English and British Fiction 1750–1820*, Vol. 2, Oxford: Oxford University Press, 216–33.

Cox, Jeffrey and Michael Gamer (eds.) (2003) *The Broadview Anthology of Romantic Drama*, Ontario: Broadview.

Cox, Philip (1996) *Gender, Genre and Romantic Poets*, Manchester: Manchester University Press.

Curran, Stuart (ed.) (2010a) *The Cambridge Companion to British Romanticism*, Cambridge: Cambridge University Press.

—. (2010b) "Romantic poetry: Why and Wherefore?", in Stuart Curran (ed.) *The Cambridge Companion to British Romanticism*, Cambridge: Cambridge University Press, 209–28.

—. (2003) "Valperga", in Esther Schor (ed.) *The Cambridge Companion to Mary Shelley*, Cambridge: Cambridge University Press, 103–15.

—. (1986) *Poetic Form and British Romanticism*, Oxford: Oxford University Press.

De Quincey, Thomas (2006) *On Murder*, ed. Robert Morrison, Oxford: Oxford University Press.

Deane, Nichola (2005) "Letters, journals, and diaries", in Nicholas Roe (ed.) *Romanticism: An Oxford Guide*, Oxford: Oxford University Press, 574–89.

Dixon, Josie (2002) "The Notebooks", in Lucy Newlyn (ed.) *The Cambridge Companion to Coleridge*, Cambridge: Cambridge University Press, 75–88.

Duff, David (2009) *Romanticism and the Uses of Genre*, Oxford: Oxford University Press.

—. (1994) *Romance and Revolution: Shelley and the Politics of a Genre*, Cambridge: Cambridge University Press.

Duncan, Ian (2009) "Fanaticism and Enlightenment in *Confessions of a Justified Sinner*", in Sharon-Ruth Alker and Holly Faith Nelson (eds.) *James Hogg and the Literary Marketplace: Scottish Romanticism and the Working-Class Author*, Aldershot: Ashgate, 57–70.

—. (2005) *Modern Romance and Transformation of the Novel*, Cambridge: Cambridge University Press.

Dyer, Gary (2006) *British Satire and the Politics of Style, 1789–1832*, Cambridge: Cambridge University Press.

Eagleton, Terry (1990) *The Ideology of the Aesthetics*, Oxford: Wiley-Blackwell.

Fairer, David (2005) "The Sonnet", in Nicholas Roe (ed.) *Romanticism: An Oxford Guide*, Oxford: Oxford University Press, 292–309.

Fermanis, Porscha (2009) *John Keats and the Ideas of the Enlightenment*, Edinburgh: Edinburgh University Press.

Fischer, Hermann (1991) *Romantic Verse Narrative: The History of a Genre*, trans. Sue Bollans, Cambridge and New York: Cambridge University Press.

Fulford, Tim (1996) *Landscape, Liberty, and Authority: Poetry, Criticism, and Politics from Thomson to Wordsworth*, Cambridge: Cambridge University Press.

Gay, Penny (2002) *Jane Austen and the Theatre*, Cambridge: Cambridge University Press.

Harding, Anthony (2005) "Biography and Autobiography", in Nicholas Roe (ed.), *Romanticism: An Oxford Guide*, Oxford: Oxford University Press, 445–62.

Higgins, David (2005) *Romantic Genius and the Literary Magazine: Biography, Celebrity, Politics*, London and New York: Routledge.

Hilton, Nelson (1998) "William Blake, *Songs of Innocence and of Experience*", in Duncan W (ed.) *A Companion to Romanticism*. Oxford: Blackwell, 103–12.

Hoagwood, Terence A. and Daniel P. Watkins (eds.) (1998) *British Romantic Drama: Historical and Critical Essays*, Cranbury, NJ and London: Associated University Presses, 1998.

Holmes, Richard (1987) "Introduction", in Mary Wollstonecraft, *A Short Residence in Sweden, Norway and Denmark and Memoirs of the Author of A Vindication of the Rights of Woman*, London: Penguin, 21–6.

Janowitz, Anne (2004) *Women Romantic Poets: Anna Barbauld and Mary Robinson*, Devon: Northcote House.

Jarvis, Simon (2007) *Wordsworth's Philosophic Song*, Cambridge: Cambridge University Press.

Johnson, Claudia (1988) *Women, Politics and the Novel*, Chicago, IL: University of Chicago Press.

Jones, Steven E. (2005) "Satire", in Nicholas Roe (ed.) *Romanticism: An Oxford Guide*. Oxford: Oxford University Press, 390–408.

—. (ed.) (2003) *The Satiric Eye: Forms of Satire in the Romantic Period*, Basingstoke: Palgrave.

—. (2000) *Satire and Romanticism*, New York: St. Martin's Press.

Kant, Immanuel (1952/2007) *Critique of Judgement*, ed. Nicholas Walker, Oxford: Oxford University Press.

Keach, William (2010) "Romanticism and Language", in Stuart Curran (ed.) *The Cambridge Companion to British Romanticism*, Cambridge: Cambridge University Press, 103–26.

—. (2004) *Arbitrary Power: Romanticism, Language and Politics*, Princeton: Princeton University Press.

Kelly, Gary (2010) "Romantic fiction", in Stuart Curran (ed.) *The Cambridge Companion to British Romanticism*, Cambridge: Cambridge University Press, 187–208.

Labbe, Jacqueline M. (2000) *The Romantic Paradox: Love, Violence, and the Uses of Romance 1760–1830*, Basingstoke: Palgrave Macmillan.

Leask, Nigel (2002) *Curiosity and the Aesthetics of Travel Writing, 1770–1840: 'From an Antique Land'*, Oxford: Oxford University Press.

Levin, Susan M. (1998) *The Romantic Art of Confession: De Quincey, Musset, Sand, Lamb, Hogg, Frémy, Soulié, Janin*, London: Camden House.

Levinson, Marjorie (1986) *The Romantic Fragment Poem: A Critique of a Form*, Chapel Hill, NC: The University of North Carolina Press.

Lewes, G. H. (1859) "The Novels of Jane Austen", *Blackwood's Edinburgh Magazine*, 86 (July): 99–113.

Lindop, Grevel (1981) *The Opium-Eater: A Life of Thomas De Quincey*, London: J. M. Dent.

Lukács, Georg (1937/1963) *The Historical Novel*, trans. Hannah and Stanley Mitchel, Boston: Beacon Press.

MacFarland, Thomas (1981) *Romanticism and the Forms of Ruin: Wordsworth, Coleridge, and Modalities of Fragmentation*, Princeton, NJ: Princeton University Press.

McGann, Jerome J. (2002) *Byron and Romanticism*, ed. James Soderholm, Cambridge: Cambridge University Press.

McNeill, Fiona (2006) "Ballads", in David Scott Kastan (ed.) *The Oxford Encyclopedia of British Literature*, Oxford: Oxford University Press, 114–18.

Mee, Jon (2009) "Introduction", in *John Keats: Selected Letters*, ed. Robert Gittings, Oxford and New York: Oxford University Press, xiii–xxxiii.

Miles, Robert (2002) *Gothic Writing, 1750–1820: A Genealogy*, 2nd ed., Manchester: Manchester University Press.

Milton, John (2008) *Paradise Lost*, ed. Stephen Orgel and Jonathan Goldberg, Oxford and New York: Oxford University Press.

Moers, Ellen (1976) *Literary Women: the Great Writers*, Oxford: Oxford University Press.

Moore, Jane and John Strachan (2010) *Key Concepts in Romantic Literature*, Basingstoke: Palgrave Macmillan.

O'Neill, Michael (2010) "Romantic re-appropriations of the epic", in Catherine Bates (ed.) (2010) *The Cambridge Companion to the Epic*, Cambridge: Cambridge University Press, 193–210.

O'Neill, Michael and Anthony Howe (eds.) (2012) *The Oxford Handbook of Percy Bysshe Shelley*, Oxford: Oxford University Press.

Parker, Mark (2001) *Literary Magazines and British Romanticism*, Cambridge: Cambridge University Press.

Parker, Reeve (2011) *Romantic Tragedies: The Dark Employments of Wordsworth, Coleridge, and Shelley*, Cambridge: Cambridge University Press.

Percy, Thomas (1866) *Reliques of Ancient English Poetry Consisting of Old Heroic Ballads, Songs, and Other Pieces of Our Earlier Poets; Together with Some Few of Later Date*, Vol. 1, Leipzig: Bernhard Tauchnitz.

Perry, Seamus (ed.) (2002) *Coleridge's Notebooks: A Selection*, Oxford and New York: Oxford University Press.

Poplawski, Paul (ed.) (2007) *English Literature in Context*, Cambridge: Cambridge University Press.

Pratt, Lynda (2005) "Epic", in Nicholas Roe (ed.), *Romanticism: An Oxford Guide*, Oxford: Oxford University Press, 332–49.

Pratt, Mary Louise (1992) *Imperial Eyes: Travel Writing and Transculturation*, New York and London: Routledge.

Price, Fiona (2009) *Revolutions in Taste, 1773–1818: Women Writers and the Aesthetics of Romanticism*, Aldershot: Ashgate.

Punter, David (2000) *The Blackwell Companion to the Gothic*, Oxford: Blackwell.

Purinton, Marjean D. (1998) "The English Pamphlet War of the 1790s and Coleridge's *Osorio*", in Terence A. Hoagwood and Daniel P. Watkins (eds.) *British Romantic Drama: Historical and Critical Essays*, Cranbury, NJ and London: Associated University Presses, 159–81.

Rajan, Tilottama and Julia Wright (eds.) (1998) *Romanticism, History and the Possibilities of Genre: Re-forming Literature 1789–1837*, Cambridge: Cambridge University Press.

Rauber, D. F. (1969) "The Fragment as a Romantic Form", *Modern Language Quarterly* 30. 2: 212–21.

Rawes, Alan (2004) "1816–17: *Childe Harold* III and *Manfred*", in Drummond Bone (ed.) *The Cambridge Companion to Byron*, Cambridge: Cambridge University Press, 118–32.

Reed, Arden (1984) *Romanticism and Language*, Ithaca, NY and London: Cornell University Press.

Richardson, Alan (2010) *The Neural Sublime: Cognitive Theories and Romantic Texts*, Baltimore, MD: Johns Hopkins University Press.

—. (2004) "Byron and the Theatre", in Drummond Bone (ed.) *The Cambridge Companion to Byron*, Cambridge: Cambridge University Press, 133–50

Robertson, Fiona (1998) "Walter Scott, *Waverley*", in Duncan Wu (ed.) *A Companion to Romanticism*, Oxford: Blackwell, 211–18.

Roe, Nicholas (ed.) (2005) *Romanticism: An Oxford Guide*, Oxford: Oxford University Press.

Rousseau, Jean-Jacques (1960) *Politics and the Arts. Letter to Mr D'Alembert on the Theatre*, trans. and ed. Allan Bloom, Ithaca, NY: Cornell University Press.

Russell, Corinna (2005) "The Novel", in Nicholas Roe (ed.) *Romanticism: An Oxford Guide*, Oxford: Oxford University Press, 368–89.

Russell, Gillian (2009) "The Army, the Navy, and the Napoleonic Wars", in Claudia Johnson and Clara Tuite (eds.) *A Companion to Jane Austen*, Oxford: Wiley-Blackwell, 261–71.

Ruston, Sharon (2007) *Romanticism*, London and New York: Continuum.

Said, Edward W. (1993) "Jane Austen and Empire", in *Culture and Imperialism*, London: Chatto and Windus, 95–115.

Saglia, Diego (2000) *Poetic Castles in Spain: British Romanticism and Figurations of Iberia*, Amsterdam and Atlanta, GA: Rodopi.

Schoenfield, Mark (2009) *British Periodicals and Romantic Identity*, Basingstoke: Palgrave Macmillan.

Scott, Walter (1986) *Waverley*, ed. Claire Lamont, Oxford: Oxford University Press.

Sheats, Paul D. (2005) "Lyric", in Nicholas Roe (ed.) *Romanticism: An Oxford Guide*, Oxford: Oxford University Press, 310–31.

Shelley, Mary (2008) *Frankenstein: The 1818 Text*, ed. Marilyn Butler, Oxford and New York: Oxford University Press.

Southam B. C. (ed.) (1987) *Jane Austen: The Critical Heritage, Vol. II: 1870–1940*, London: Routledge & Kegan Paul; Totowa, NJ: Barnes and Noble.

Sperry, Stuart M. (1986) "The Ethical Politics of Shelley's *The Cenci*", *Studies in Romanticism* 25: 411–27.

Stafford, Barbara (1984) *Voyage into Substance: Art, Science, Nature and the Illustrated Travel Account, 1760–1840*, Cambridge, MA and London: MIT Press.

Stafford, Fiona (2012) *Reading Romantic Poetry*, Oxford: Wiley-Blackwell.

—. (2010) *Local Attachments: The Province of Poetry*, Oxford: Oxford University Press.

Stelzig, Eugene L. (2009) *Romantic Autobiography in England*, Aldershot: Ashgate.

Steward, Susan (2008) "Romantic meter and form", in James Chandler and Maureen McLane (eds.) *The Cambridge Companion to British Romantic Poetry*, Cambridge: Cambridge University Press, 53–75.

—. (1991) "Notes on Distressed Genres", in *Journal of American Folkore* 104: 5–31.

Stokes, Christopher (2010) *Coleridge, Language and the Sublime: From Transcendence to Finitude*, Basingstoke: Palgrave Macmillan.

Strachan, John (2007) *Advertising and Satirical Culture in the Romantic Period*, Cambridge: Cambridge University Press.

—. and Steven E. Jones (eds.) (2003) *British Satire 1785–1840*, 5 vols, London: Pickering and Chatto.

Stuart, David (2011) *Romantic Magazines and Metropolitan Literary Culture*, Basingstoke: Palgrave.

Thomas, Sophie (2008) *Romanticism and Visuality: Fragments, History, Spectacle*, London and New York: Routledge.

—. (2005) "The Fragment", in Nicholas Roe (ed.) *Romanticism: An Oxford Guide*, Oxford: Oxford University Press, 502–20.

—. (2002) "The Return of the Fragment: 'Christabel' and the Uncanny", *Bucknell Review* 45. 2: 51–73.

Trott, Nicola (2005) "Gothic", in Nicholas Roe (ed.) *Romanticism: An Oxford Guide*, Oxford: Oxford University Press, 482–501.

Trumpener, Katie (1997) *Bardic Nationalism: The Romantic Novel and the British Empire*, Princeton, NJ: Princeton University Press.

Tucker, Herbert F. (2008) *Epic: Britain's Heroic Muse, 1790–1910*, New York: Oxford University Press.

Wallace, Miriam L. (ed.) (2009) *Enlightening Romanticism, Romancing the Enlightenment: British Novels from 1750 to 1832*, Aldershot: Ashgate.

Whale, John (2005) "Non-fictional Prose", in Nicholas Roe (ed.) *Romanticism: An Oxford Guide*, Oxford: Oxford University Press, 538–54.

Wollstonecraft, Mary (1796/1987) *Letters Written during a Short Residence in Sweden, Norway, and Denmark*, ed. Richard Holmes, London: Penguin.

Woodbery, Bonnie (2008) "Charles Lamb's 'Confessions of a Drunkard': Constructing Subjectivity through Context", *Nineteenth Century Contexts*, 22.3: 357–90.

Wu, Duncan (2006) *Romanticism: an Anthology*, 3rd ed., Oxford: Blackwell.

—. (ed.) (1998) *A Companion to Romanticism*, Oxford: Blackwell.

—. (ed.) (1995) *Romanticism: A Critical Reader*, Oxford: Blackwell.

Chapter 3: Romantic groups and associations

Bainbridge, Simon (1995) *Napoleon and English Romanticism*, Cambridge: Cambridge University Press.

Bostetter, Edward E. (1956) "The Original Della Cruscans and the Florence Miscellany", *The Huntington Library Quarterly* 19.3: 277–300.

Braithwaite, Helen (2003) *Romanticism, Publishing and Dissent: Joseph Johnson and the Cause of Liberty*, Basingstoke: Palgrave Macmillan.

Brewer, William Dean (1994) *The Shelley–Byron Conversation*, Gainesville, FL: University Press of Florida.

Broadhead, Alex (2010) "The Della Cruscans: A Survey of Criticism and Resources, 1956–2009", *Literature Compass* 7: 577–85.

Burroughs, Catherine B. (1997) *Closet Stages: Joanna Baillie and the Theatre Theory of British Romantic Women Writers*, Philadelphia, PA: University of Pennsylvania Press.

Butler, Marilyn (1981) *Romantics, Rebels and Reactionaries: English Literature and its Background 1760–1830*, Oxford and New York: Oxford University Press.

Cardwell, Richard A. (2011) "'A Continuance of Enduring Thought': Byron's Metaphysical Journey", in Peter Cochran (ed.) *Byron's Religions*, Newcastle: Cambridge Scholars Publishing, 46–73.

Carlson, Julie A. (1994) *In the Theatre of Romanticism: Coleridge, Nationalism, Women*, Cambridge: Cambridge University Press.

Cline, C. L. (1952) *Byron, Shelley, and their Pisan Circle*, Cambridge, MA: Harvard University Press.

Connell, Philip (2005) *Romanticism, Economics and the Question of 'Culture'*, Oxford: Oxford University Press.

Cox, Jeffrey N. (1998) *Poetry and Politics in the Cockney School: Keats, Shelley, Hunt and their Circle*, Cambridge: Cambridge University Press.

Crisafulli, Lilla Maria and Cecilia Pietropoli (eds.) (2007) *Romantic Women Poets: Genre and Gender*, New York: Rodopi.

Curreli, Mario and Anthony Johnson (eds.) (1998) *Paradise of Exiles: Shelley and Byron in Pisa*, Pisa: ETS.

Day, Aidan (1995) *Romanticism*, London and New York: Routledge.

Eger, Elizabeth (2010) *Bluestockings: Women of Reason from Enlightenment to Romanticism*, Basingstoke: Palgrave Macmillan.

—. *et al.* (eds.) (1999) *Bluestocking Feminism: Writings of the Bluestocking Circle, 1738–1785*, 6 vols, London: Pickering and Chatto.

Faulkner, Thomas (1820) *History and Antiquities of Kensington*, London: Payne and Foss.

Gilmartin, Kevin (2007) *Writing Against Revolution: Literary Conservatism in Britain, 1790–1832*, Cambridge: Cambridge University Press.

Goodridge, John (2013) *John Clare and Community*, Cambridge: Cambridge University Press.

Goodridge, John and Bridget Keegan (2004) "John Clare and the traditions of labouring-class verse", in Thomas Keymer and Jon Mee (eds.) *The Cambridge Companion to English Literature 1740–1830*, Cambridge: Cambridge University Press, 280–95.

Gorji, Mina (2013) "John Clare and the Triumph of Little Things", in Kirstie Blair and Mina Gorji (eds.) *Class and Canon: Constructing Labouring-Class Poetry and Poetics, 1780–1900*, Basingstoke: Palgrave Macmillan, 77–94.

Guest, Harriet (2000) *Small Change: Women, Learning, Patriotism, 1750–1810*, Chicago, IL and London: University of Chicago Press.

Habermas, Jürgen (1989) *The Structural Transformation of the Public Sphere: An Enquiry into the Category of Bourgeois Society*, trans. Thomas Burger with the assistance of Frederick Lawrence, Cambridge, MA: MIT Press.

Hamilton, Paul (2014) "Byron, Clare, and Poetic Historiography", in Porscha Fermanis and John Regan (eds.) *Rethinking British Romantic History 1780–1840*, Oxford: Oxford University Press, 223–45.

Harcstark Myers, Sylvia (1990) *The Bluestocking Circle: Women, Friendship, and the Life of the Mind in Eighteenth-Century England*, Oxford: Clarendon Press.

Hargreaves-Mawdsley, William Norman (1967) *The English Della Cruscans and their Time, 1783–1828*, The Hague: Martinus Nijhoff.

Hay, Daisy (2010) *Young Romantics: The Shelleys, Byron and Other Tangled Lives*, London: Bloomsbury.

Hazlitt, William (1970) "On the Living Poets", in Ronald Blythe (ed.) *William Hazlitt: Selected Writings*, London: Penguin, 215–18.

Healey, Nicola (2012) *Dorothy Wordsworth and Hartley Coleridge: The Poetics of Relationship*, Basingstoke: Palgrave Macmillan.

Heller, Deborah (1998) "Bluestocking Salons and the Public Sphere", *Eighteenth-Century Life* 22: 59–82.

James, Felicity and Ian Inkster (2011) *Religious Dissent and the Aikin-Barbauld Circle, 1740–1860*, Cambridge: Cambridge University Press.

Janowitz, Anne (2002) "Amiable and radical sociability: Anna Barbauld's 'free familiar conversation'", in Gillian Russell and Clara Tuite (eds.) *Romantic Sociability: Social Networks and Literary Culture in Britain 1770–1840*, Cambridge: Cambridge University Press, 62–81.

Jeffrey, Francis (1802) "Review of Southey, *Thalaba the Destroyer: A metrical Romance*", *Edinburgh Review* 1.1 (October): 63–4.

Jones, Kathleen (2000) *A Passionate Sisterhood: Women of the Wordsworth Circle*, Basingstoke: Palgrave Macmillan.

Keach, William (1986) "Cockney Couplets: Keats and the Politics of Style", *Studies in Romanticism* 25: 182–96.

Kelly, Gary (2005) "Clara Reeve, Provincial Bluestocking: From the Old Whigs to the Modern Liberal State", in Nicole Pohl and Betty A. Schellenberg (eds.) *Reconsidering the Bluestockings*, Berkeley, CA: University of California Press, 105–25.

Kelly, Linda (2013) *Holland House: A History of London's Most Celebrated Salon*, London: I. B. Tauris.

Knowles, Claire (2009) *Sensibility and Female Poetic Tradition, 1780–1860: The Legacy of Charlotte Smith*, Aldershot: Ashgate.

Labbe, Jacqueline M. (2000) "The Anthologized Romance of Della Crusca and Anna Matilda", *Romanticism on the Net* 18, accessed 15 May 2015: http://www.erudit.org/revue/ron/2005/v/n38-39/011666ar.html7.

Lau, Beth (ed.) (2009) *Fellow Romantics. Male and Female British Writers, 1790–1835*, Aldershot: Ashgate.

Lucas, John (1998) "John Clare, *The Shepherd's Calendar*", in Duncan Wu (ed.) *A Companion to Romanticism*, Oxford: Blackwell, 301–12.

Marshall, William H. (1960) *Byron, Shelley, Hunt and the Liberal*, Philadelphia, PA University of Pennsylvania Press.

Mason, Emma (2010) *The Cambridge Introduction to William Wordsworth*, Cambridge: Cambridge University Press.

Matlack, Richard E. (1997) *The Poetry of Relationship: The Wordsworths and Coleridge, 1797–1800*, New York: St. Martin's Press.

McGann, Jerome J. (1998) *The Poetics of Sensibility. A Revolution in Literary Style*, Oxford: Oxford University Press.

—. (1995) "The Literary World of the English Della Cruscans", in Elaine Scarry (ed.), *Fins de Siècle: English Poetry in 1590, 1690, 1790, 1890, 1990*, Baltimore, MD: John Hopkins University Press, 95–22.

McKusick, James (1994) "Beyond the Visionary Company: John Clare's resistance to Romanticism", in Hugh Haugthon *et al.* (ed.) *John Clare in Context*, Cambridge: Cambridge University Press, 221–237.

Mee, Jon (2009) "Introduction", in Robert Gittings (ed.) *John Keats: Selected Letters*, New York: Oxford University Press, xiii–xxxiii.

—. (2002) "'Reciprocal expressions of kindness': Robert Merry, Della Cruscanism, and the limits of sociability", in Gillian Russell and Clara Tuite (eds.) *Romantic Sociability: Social Networks and Literary Culture in Britain 1770–1840*, Cambridge: Cambridge University Press, 104–22.

—. (1992) *Dangerous Enthusiasm: William Blake and the Culture of Radicalism in the 1790s*, Oxford: Oxford University Press.

Merry, Robert (1790) *The British Album*, 2 vols, 2nd ed., London: John Bell.

Metzger, Lore (1993) "Satanic School", in Alex Preminger and T. V. F. Brogan (eds.) *The New Princeton Encyclopedia of Poetry and Poetics*, Princeton, NJ: Princeton University Press, 1114.

Moore, Jane and John Strachan (2010) *Key Concepts in Romantic Literature*, Basingstoke: Palgrave Macmillan.

Newlyn, Lucy (2001) *Paradise Lost and the Romantic Reader*, Oxford: Oxford University Press.

O'Brien, Paul (2002) *Shelley and Revolutionary Ireland*, London and Dublin: Redwords.

Pohl, Nicole and Betty A. Schellenberg (eds.) (2005) *Reconsidering the Bluestockings*, Berkeley, CA: University of California Press.

Praz, Mario (1933) *The Romantic Agony*, trans. Angus Davidson, London: Humphrey Milford.

Robinson, Jane (2009) *Bluestockings: The Remarkable Story of the First Women to Fight for an Education*, London: Penguin.

Roe, Nicholas (1997) *John Keats and the Culture of Dissent*, Oxford: Clarendon Press.

—. (1988) *Wordsworth and Coleridge: The Radical Years*, Oxford: Clarendon Press.

Rossetti Angeli, Helen (1911) *Shelley and his Friends in Italy*, London: Methuen.

Russell Gillian and Clara Tuite (eds.) (2002) *Romantic Sociability: Social Networks and Literary Culture in Britain 1770–1840*, Cambridge: Cambridge University Press.

Sanders, Lloyd Charles (1908) *The Holland House Circle*, London: Methuen.

Schock, Peter (2003) *Romantic Satanism: Myth and the Historical Moment in Blake, Shelley, and Byron*, Basingstoke: Palgrave Macmillan.

Schoina, Maria (2009) *Romantic "Anglo-Italians": Configurations of Identity in Byron, the Shelleys, and the Pisan Circle*, Aldershot: Ashgate.

Shelley, Percy Bysshe (1970) *Political Writings, including "A Defence of Poetry"*, ed. Roland A. Duerksen, New York: Appleton-Century-Crofts.

St. Clair, William (1989) *The Godwins and the Shelleys: The Biography of a Family*, New York: Norton.

Stillinger, Jack (1991) *Multiple Authorship and the Myth of Solitary Genius*, Oxford and New York: Oxford University Press.

Werner, Bette Charlene (1986) *Blake's Vision of the Poetry of Milton*, Lewisburg, PA: Bucknell University Press.

Whale, John (2005) "Non-fictional Prose", in Nicholas Roe (ed.) *Romanticism: An Oxford Guide*, Oxford: Oxford University Press, 538–54.

White, Daniel E. (2006) *Early Romanticism and Religious Dissent*, Cambridge: Cambridge University Press.

Wolfson, Susan (2010) *Romantic Interactions: Social Beings at the Turns of Literary Action*, Baltimore, MD: Johns Hopkins University Press.

Worthen, John (2001) *The Gang: Coleridge, the Hutchinsons and the Wordsworths in 1802*, New Haven, CT: Yale University Press.

Wu, Duncan (2001) "Keats and the '*Cockney School*'", in Susan J. Wolfson (ed.) *The Cambridge Companion to Keats*, Cambridge: Cambridge University Press, 37–52.

Z. (1818) "On the Cockney School of Poetry, no. 4", *Blackwood's Edinburgh Magazine* 3: 519–24.

Chapter 4: National, regional and local Romanticism

Aaron, Jane (2007) *Nineteenth-Century Women's Writing in Wales: Nation, Gender and Identity*, Cardiff: University of Wales Press.

Anderson, Benedict (1993) *Imagined Communities, Reflections on the Origin and Spread of Nationalism*, London and New York: Verso.

Andrews, Corey (2004) *Literary Nationalism in Eighteenth-Century Club Poetry*, Lampeter, Wales: Edwin Mellen Press.

Baillie, Joanna (1798/1990) *A Series of Plays, 1798*, ed. Jonathan Wordsworth, Oxford and New York: Woodstock Books.

Bate, Jonathan (2000) *The Song of the Earth*, London: Picador.

Behrendt, Stephen (ed.) (2008) *Irish Women Poets of the Romantic Period*, Alexandria, VA: Alexander Street Press.

Bolton, Carol (2006) "'Green Savannahs' or 'savage lands': Wordsworth's and Southey's Romantic America", in Lynda Pratt (ed.) *Robert Southey and the Contexts of English Romanticism*, Aldershot: Ashgate, 115–32.

Brayshay, Mark (ed.) (1996) *Topographical Writers in South-West England*, Exeter: University of Exeter Press.

Brockliss, Laurence and David Eastwood (1997) "Introduction", in Laurence Brockliss and David Eastwood (eds.) *A Union of Multiple Identities: The British Isles, c.1759–c.1850*, Manchester: Manchester University Press, 1–8.

Burgess, Miranda J. (2000) *British Fiction and the Production of Social Order, 1740–1830*. Cambridge: Cambridge University Press.

Butler, Marilyn (1990) *Jane Austen and the War of Ideas*, Oxford: Clarendon Press.

Campbell, Matthew (2013) *Irish Poetry Under the Union, 1801–1924*, Cambridge: Cambridge University Press.

Carruthers, Gerard and Alan Rawes (eds.) (2003) *English Romanticism and the Celtic World*, Cambridge: Cambridge University Press.

Cass, Jeffrey and Larry H. Peer (eds.) (2008) *Romantic Border Crossings*, Aldershot: Ashgate.

Chandler, James (2006) "A Discipline in Shifting Perspective: Why We Need Irish Studies", *Field Day Review* 2: 19–39.

Colley, Linda (1992) *Britons: Forging the Nation 1707–1837*, New Haven, CT: Yale University Press.

Connolly, Claire (2014) "A Bookish History of Irish Romanticism", in Porscha Fermanis and John Regan (eds.) *Rethinking British Romantic History, 1770–1845*, Oxford: Oxford University Press, 271–96.

—. (2011) *A Cultural History of the Irish Novel, 1790–1829,* Cambridge: Cambridge University Press.

—. (2006) "Irish Romanticism, 1800–1830", in Margaret Kelleher and Phillip O'Leary (eds.) *Cambridge History of Irish Literature*, Vol. 1, Cambridge: Cambridge University Press, 407–48.

Constantine, Mary-Ann (2007) *The Truth Against the World: Iolo Morganwg and Romantic Forgery*, Cardiff: University of Wales Press.

Cottle, Joseph (1801) *Alfred: An Epic Poem in Twenty-Four Books*, London: Longman and Rees.

Crawford, Robert (1992) *Devolving English Literature*, Oxford: Oxford University Press.

Cronin, Richard (2014) "Magazines, *Don Juan*, and the Scotch novels: Deep and Shallow Time in the Regency", in Porscha Fermanis and John Regan (eds.) *Rethinking British Romantic History, 1770–1845*, Oxford: Oxford University Press, 165–78.

—. (2010) "Joseph Cottle and West-Country Romanticism", in Nicholas Roe (ed.) *English Romantic Writers and the West Country*, Basingstoke: Palgrave Macmillan, 65–78.

Cunliffe, Barry (2003) *The Celts: A Very Short Introduction*, Oxford: Oxford University Press.

Davis, Leith, Ian Duncan and Janet Sorensen (eds.) (2004) *Scotland and the Borders of Romanticism*, Cambridge: Cambridge University Press.

—. (1993) "Irish Bards and English Consumers: Thomas Moore's 'Irish Melodies' and the Colonized Nation", *Ariel* 24: 7–25.

Deane, Seamus (1997) *Strange Country: Modernity and Nationhood in Irish Writing Since 1790*, Oxford: Oxford University Press.

Duff, David and Catherine Jones (eds.) (2007) *Scotland, Ireland and the Romantic Aesthetic*, Lewisburg, PA: Bucknell University Press.

Duncan, Ian (2009) "Edinburgh and Lowland Scotland", in James Chandler (ed.) *The Cambridge History of English Romantic Literature*, Cambridge: Cambridge University Press, 159–81.

—. (2007) *Scott's Shadow: The Novel in Romantic Edinburgh*, Princeton, NJ: Princeton University Press.

Dunne, Tom (1988) "Haunted by History: Irish Romantic Writing, 1800–1850", in Roy Porter and Mikulas Teich (eds.) *Romanticism in National Context*, Cambridge: Cambridge University Press, 68–91.

Edwards, Elizabeth (2015) "'Lonely and Voiceless Your Halls Must Remain': Romantic-Era National Song and Felicia Hemans's *Welsh Melodies* (1822)", *Journal for Eighteenth-Century Studies* 38.1: 83–97.

English, Colleen (2015) "Writing the Dead: Elegies and Irish Nationalism", unpublished PhD Thesis, University College Dublin.

Epstein, Mikhail N. (1995) *After the Future: The Paradoxes of Postmodernism and Contemporary Russian Culture*, trans. A. M. Pogacar, Amherst, MA: University of Massachusetts Press.

Ferris, Ina (2002) *The Romantic National Tale and the Question of Ireland*, Cambridge: Cambridge University Press.

Garrett, James M. (2008) *Wordsworth and the Writing of the Nation*, Aldershot: Ashgate.

Gellner, Ernest (1983) *Nations and Nationalism*, Ithaca, NY: Cornell University Press.

Gibbons, Luke (2009) "Romantic Ireland: 1750–1845", in James Chandler (ed.) *The Cambridge History of English Romantic Literature*, Cambridge: Cambridge University Press, 182–203.

Gottlieb, Evan, and Juliet Shields (2013) "Introduction", in Evan Gottlieb and Juliet Shields (eds.) *Representing Place in British Literature and Culture, 1660–1830: From Local to Global*, Burlington, VT and Farnham: Ashgate, 1–14.

Groom, Nick (2014) "Gothic and Celtic Revivals: Antiquity and the Archipelago", in Robert Demaria Jr, Heesok Chang, and Samantha Zacher (eds.) *A Companion to British Literature, Volume III, Eighteenth Century Literature, 1660–1837*, Chichester: Wiley-Blackwell, 361–79.

Hobsbawm, Eric (1962) *The Age of Revolution: Europe 1789–1848*, Preston: Abacus Press.

Janowitz, Anne (1990) *England's Ruins: Poetic Purpose and the National Landscape*, Oxford: Blackwell.

Joannou, Maroula (2012) "'England's Jane': The Legacy of Jane Austen in the Fiction of Barbara Pym, Dodie Smith and Elizabeth Taylor", in Gillian Dow and Clare Hanson (eds.) *Uses of Austen: Jane's Afterlives*, Basingstoke: Palgrave Macmillan, 37–58.

Kelleher, Margaret (2014) "Irish Literary Culture in English", in Alvin Jackson (ed.) *The Oxford Handbook of Modern Irish History*, Oxford: Oxford University Press, 214–31.

Kelly, Gary (2002) "Introduction", in Gary Kelly (ed.) *Felicia Hemans: Selected Poems, Prose and Letters*, Peterborough: Broadview Press, 15–85.

Kelly, Jim (2011) "Introduction", in Jim Kelly (ed.) *Ireland and Romanticism: Publics, Nations and Scenes of Cultural Production*, Basingstoke: Palgrave Macmillan, 1–10.

Kelly, Ronin (2009) *Bard of Erin: The Life of Thomas Moore*, Dublin: Penguin.

Kerrigan, John (2008) *Archipelagic English: Literature, History, and Politics, 1603–1707*, Oxford: Oxford University Press.

Kiberd, Declan (1996) *Inventing Ireland: The Literature of the Modern Nation*, London: Vintage.

Kidd, Colin (2003) "Race, Empire, and the Limits of Nineteenth-Century Scottish Nationhood", *The Historical Journal* 46.4: 873–92.

—. (1993) *Subverting Scotland's Past: Scottish Whig Historians and the Creation of an Anglo-British Identity, 1689-c.1830*, Cambridge: Cambridge University Press.

Kilfeather, Siobhán (2004) "Terrific Register: The Gothicization of Atrocity in Irish Romanticism", *Boundary 2* 31.1: 49–71.

Killeen, Jarlath (2014) *The Emergence of Irish Gothic Fiction*, Edinburgh: Edinburgh University Press.

Lamont, Claire and Michael Rossington (eds.) (2007) *Romanticism's Debatable Lands*, Basingstoke: Palgrave Macmillan.

Leerssen, Joep (1996) *Remembrance and Imagination: Patterns in the Historical and Literary Representation of Ireland in the Nineteenth Century*, Cork: Cork University Press.

Lloyd, Nicola (2013) "Canals, Commerce and Sympathy in Sydney Owenson's *O'Donnel*", unpublished Conference Paper, BARS Conference 2013, "Romantic Imports and Exports".

Low, Donald A. (ed.) (1974) *Robert Burns: The Critical Heritage*, London: Routledge.

McClure, Derrick J. (1995) *Scots and Its Literature*, Amsterdam, John Benjamins.

McGuirk, Carol (1985) *Robert Burns and the Sentimental Era*, Athens, GA: University of Georgia Press.

Mackenzie, Henry (1786) "Review of the Kilmarnock edition", *The Lounger* 97 (9 Dec)., rpt. Donald A. Low (ed.) (1974) *Robert Burns: The Critical Heritage*, London: Routledge, 67–8.

Makdisi, Saree (1998) *Romantic Imperialism: Universal Empire and the Culture of Modernity*, New York and Cambridge: Cambridge University Press.

Manning, Susan (2009) "Antiquarianism, Balladry, and the Rehabilitation of Romance", in James Chandler (ed.) *The Cambridge History of English Romantic Literature*, Cambridge: Cambridge University Press, 45–70.

Mathews, P. J. (2008) "Doing Something Irish': From Thomas Moore to Riverdance", *UCD Scholarcast*, Series 1 (Spring): http://www.ucd.ie/scholarcast/transcripts/Doing_Something_Irish.pdf.

Maturin, Charles (1812) *The Milesian Chief: A Romance*, 4 vols, London: H. Colburn.

Maxted, Ian (1982) *South West England*, Bury St. Edmond's, Suffolk: Library Association, Public Library Group.

Meagher, Shelley (2009) "Thomas Moore, Ireland, and Islam", in Monika Class and Terry F. Robinson (eds.) *Transnational England: Home and Abroad, 1780–1860*, Newcastle upon Tyne: Cambridge Scholars, 233–48.

Mitchell, W. J. T. (2009) "Country Matters", in James Chandler (ed.) *The Cambridge History of English Romantic Literature*, Cambridge: Cambridge University Press, 246–70.

Moore, Jane (2011) "Celtic Romantic Poetry: Scotland, Ireland, Wales", in Charles Mahoney (ed.) *A Companion to Romantic Poetry*, Chichester: Wiley Blackwell, 251–67.

Moore, Dafydd (2014) "'Caledonian Plagiary': The Role and Meaning of Ireland in the *Poems of Ossian*", in Ben Dew and Fiona Price (eds.) *Historical Writing in Britain, 1688–1830: Visions of History*, Basingstoke: Palgrave Macmillan, 92–108.

—. (2013) "'Too Frivolous to Interest the Public': Walter Scott, Richard Polwhele and Archipelagic Correspondence", *Romantik: Journal for the Study of Romanticisms* 2: 103–26.

—. (2008) "Devolving Romanticism: Nation, Region and the Case of Devon and Cornwall", *Literature Compass* 5.5: 949–63.

Morash, Christopher (2003) "The Time is Out of Joint (O Cursèd Spite!): Towards a Definition of a Supernatural Narrative", in Bruce Stewart (ed.) *That Other World: The Supernatural and the Fantastic in Irish Literature and its Contexts*, Gerrards Cross: Colin Smythe, 123–43.

Morin, Christina (2011) *Charles Robert Maturin and the Haunting of Irish Romantic Fiction*, Manchester: Manchester University Press.

Morrison, Robert and Daniel S. Roberts (2013) "Introduction", in Robert Morrison and Daniel S. Roberts (eds.) *Romanticism and Blackwood's Magazine*, Basingstoke: Palgrave Macmillan, 1–22.

Mottram, Stuart and Sarah Prescott (2012) "Introduction", in Stuart Mottram and Sarah Prescott (eds.) *Writing Wales, from the Renaissance to Romanticism*, Farnham: Ashgate.

Murdoch, A. (1999) *British Identities Before Nationalism: Ethnicity and Nationhood in the Atlantic World*, Edinburgh: Edinburgh University Press.

O'Halloran, Claire (2004) *Golden Ages and Barbarous Nations: Antiquarianism and Cultural Politics in Eighteenth-Century Ireland, c. 1750–1800*, Cork: Cork University Press.

Owenson, Sydney (1806) *The Wild Irish Girl: A National Tale*, London: Richard Phillips.

Perera, Suvendrini (1991) *Reaches of Empire: The English Novel from Edgeworth to Dickens*, New York: Columbia University Press.

Pittock, Murray (2011) "Introduction", in Murray Pittock (ed.) *The Edinburgh Companion to Scottish Romanticism*, Edinburgh: Edinburgh University Press, 1–12.

—. (2008) *Scottish and Irish Romanticism*, Oxford: Oxford University Press.

Roe, Nicholas (2010) "Introduction", in Nicholas Roe (ed.) *English Romantic Writers and the West Country*, Basingstoke: Palgrave Macmillan, 1–14.

Scott, Walter (1997) *Redgauntlet. A Tale of the Eighteenth Century*, ed. G. A. M. Wood, Edinburgh: Edinburgh University Press.

Sorensen, Janet (2000) *The Grammar of Empire in Eighteenth-Century British Writing*, Cambridge: Cambridge University Press.

Stafford, Fiona (2013) "Writing around the Irish Sea: Inlets, Outlets, Firths and Mouths", *UCD Scholarcast*, Series 7 (Spring): http://www.ucd.ie/scholarcast/transcripts/Scholarcast31_transcript.pdf

—. (2010) *Local Attachments: The Province of Poetry*, Oxford: Oxford University Press.

—. (2005) "England, Ireland, Scotland, Wales", in Nicholas Roe (ed.) *Romanticism: An Oxford Guide*, Oxford and New York: Oxford University Press, 114–25.

—. (2000) *Starting Lines in Scottish, Irish, and English Poetry: From Burns to Heaney*, Oxford: Oxford University Press.

Thompson, E. P. (1966) *The Making of the English Working Classes*, New York: Vintage.

Tonra, Justin (2013) "Review of Jim Kelly, *Ireland and Romanticism: Publics, Nations and Scenes of Cultural Production* (Basingstoke: Palgrave Macmillan, 2011)", *Romantic Textualities* 21, accessed 24 April 2015: *http://www.romtext.org.uk/reviews/rt21_r08/*

Trezise, Simon (2000) *The West Country as Literary Invention: Putting Fiction in its Place*, Exeter: University of Exeter Press.

Trumpener, Katie (2007) *Bardic Nationalism: The Romantic Novel and the British Empire*, Princeton: Princeton University Press.

Tuite, Clara (2002) *Romantic Austen: Sexual Politics and the Literary Canon*, Cambridge: Cambridge University Press.

Williams, Gwyn A. (1985) *When Was Wales? A History of the Welsh*, London: Penguin.

Wolfson, Susan J. "Introduction" (2001), in *Felicia Hemans: Selected Poems, Letters, Reception Materials*, ed. Susan J. Wolfson, Princeton, NJ and Oxford: Princeton University Press, xiii–xxxi.

Wordsworth, Dorothy (1894) *Recollections of a Tour Made in Scotland A.D. 1803*, 3rd ed., ed. J. C. Shairp, Edinburgh.

Wright, Julia M. (2014) *Representing the National Landscape in Irish Romanticism*, Syracuse, NY: Syracuse University Press.

Zimmern, Helen (1883) *Maria Edgeworth*, London: W. H. Allen.

Chapter 5: Romanticism in the arts

Alhadeff, Albert (2002) *The Raft of the Medusa: Géricault, Art, and Race*, Munich: Prestel.

Andrews, Malcolm (1989) *The Search for the Picturesque: Landscape Aesthetics and Tourism in Britain 1760–1800*, Stanford, CA: Stanford University Press.

Applegate, Celia (2005) *Bach in Berlin: Nation and Culture in Mendelssohn's Revival of the St. Matthew Passion*, Ithaca, NY: Cornell University Press.

Bailey, Anthony (1998) *Standing in the Sun: A Life of J. M. W. Turner*, London: Pimlico.

Bann, Stephen (1983) *The Clothing of Clio: A Study of the Representation of History in Nineteenth-Century Britain and France*, Cambridge: Cambridge University Press.

Baudelaire, Charles (1972) *Selected Writings on Art and Artists*, trans. P. E. Charvet, Cambridge: Cambridge University Press.

Behrendt, Stephen C. (2005) "The visual arts and music", in Nicholas Roe (ed.) *Romanticism: An Oxford Guide*, Oxford: Oxford University Press, 62–76.

Bentley, Gerald Eades (ed.) (1975) *William Blake: The Critical Heritage*, London: Routledge.

Birch, Dinah (1990) *Ruskin on Turner*, London: Cassell.

Blayney Brown, David (2001) *Romanticism: Art and Ideas*, London: Phaidon.

—. (1992) *Turner and Byron*, London: Tate Gallery Publishing.

Bradley, Matthew (2012) "Pole to Pole: Romantic Apocalypse at the Victorian Fin de Siècle", in Carmen Casaliggi and Paul March-Russell (eds.) *Legacies of Romanticism: Literature, Culture, Aesthetics*, New York and London: Routledge, 130–44.

Breckman, Warren (2008) *European Romanticism: A Brief History with Documents*, Boston and New York: Bedford/St. Martin's Press.

Calé, Luisa (2006) *Henry Fuseli's Milton Gallery: 'Turning Readers into Spectators'*, Oxford: Oxford University Press.

—. and Patrizia Di Bello (eds.) (2010) *Illustrations, Optics and Objects in Nineteenth-Century Literary and Visual Cultures*, Basingstoke: Palgrave Macmillan.

Casaliggi, Carmen (2012) "Ruskin's Keats: *A Joy for Ever (and its Price in the Market)*, 'The Mystery of Life and its Arts', and the Resonance of the Severn Circle", in Carmen Casaliggi and Paul March-Russell (eds.) *Legacies of Romanticism: Literature, Culture, Aesthetics*, New York and London: Routledge, 31–51.

Charlton, David (ed.) (1989) *E. A. T. Hoffman's Musical Writings: Kreisleriana, The Poet and the Composer, Music Criticism*, trans. Martyn Clarke, Cambridge: Cambridge University Press.

Cheeke, Stephen (2008) *Writing for Art: The Aesthetics of Ekphrasis*, Manchester: Manchester University Press.

Cochran, Peter (2009) *"Romanticism" – and Byron*, Newcastle: Cambridge Scholars Publishing.

Copley, Stephen and Peter Garside (eds.) (1994) *The Politics of the Picturesque: Literature, Landscape and Aesthetics since 1770*, Cambridge: Cambridge University Press.

Crow, Thomas E. (2006) *Emulation. David, Drouais, and Girodet in the Art of Revolutionary France*, New Haven, CT and London: Yale University Press.

Donnachie, Ian and Carmen Lavin (eds.) (2004) *From Enlightenment to Romanticism*, Anthology II, Manchester: Manchester University Press.

Donovan, Siobhàn and Robin Elliott (eds.) (2004) *Music and Literature in German Romanticism*, Rochester, NY: Boydell & Brewer.

Downie, Louise (2008) *Romantics in the Channel Islands*, St Helier, Jersey: Jersey Heritage Trust.

Eaves, Morris (2010) "The Sister Arts in British Romanticism", in Stuart Curran (ed.) *The Cambridge Companion to British Romanticism*, 2nd ed., Cambridge: Cambridge University Press, 229–61.

—, Robert N. Essick and Joseph Viscomi (eds.) (1993) *William Blake: The Early Illuminated Books*, Vol. 3, Princeton, NJ: Princeton University Press.

Egerton, Judy (1995) *Turner: The Fighting Téméraire*, with a technical examination of the painting by Martin Wyld and Ashok Roy, London: National Gallery.

Ellis, Markman (2008) "Spectacles within doors: panoramas of London in the 1790s", in *Romanticism* 14.2: 133–48.

Faflak, Joel and Julia M. Wright (eds.) (2012) *A Handbook of Romanticism Studies*, Chichester: Wiley-Blackwell.

Ferber, Michael (2012) *The Cambridge Introduction to British Romantic Poetry*, Cambridge: Cambridge University Press.

Finley, Gerald (1980) *Landscapes of Memory: Turner as Illustrator to Scott*, London: Scolar Press.

Glendinning, Nigel (1986) "Goya's Country House in Madrid: The Quinta del Sordo", *Apollo* 123: 102–9.

Griffin, Dustin H. (1996) *Literary Patronage in England 1650–1800*, Cambridge: Cambridge University Press.

Hazlitt, William (1830) "Enquiry Whether the Fine Arts are Promoted by Academies and Public Institutions", in James Northcote, *The Life of Titian: with Anecdotes of the Distinguished Persons of his Time*, 2 vols, London: Colburn and Bentley, ii. 370–83.

Hilton, Nelson (1998) "William Blake, Songs of Innocence and of Experience", in Duncan Wu (ed.) *A Companion to Romanticism*, Oxford: Blackwell, 103–12.

Honour, Hugh and John Fleming (2010) *The Visual Arts: A History*, 7th ed., Upper Saddle River, NJ: Prentice Hall.

Hughes, Robert (2003) *Goya*, London: The Harvill Press.

Hunt, John Dixon (1994) *Gardens and the Picturesque: Studies in the History of Landscape Architecture*, Cambridge, MA and London: MIT Press.

Jones, Jennifer (2006) "Absorbing Hesitation: Wordsworth and the theory of Panorama", *Studies in Romanticism*, 45.3: 357–75.

Kermode, Frank (1957) *Romantic Image*, London and New York: Routledge & Kegan Paul.

Labbe, Jacqueline M. (1998) *Romantic Visualities: Landscape, Gender, and Romanticism*, Hampshire and London: Macmillan Press.

Le Huray, Peter and James Day (1981) *Music and Aesthetics in the Eighteenth and Early-Nineteenth Centuries*, Cambridge: Cambridge University Press.

Loyrette, Henri *et al.* (2008) *Nineteenth Century French Art: From Romanticism to Impressionism, Post-Impressionism, and Art Nouveau*, Paris: Flammarion.

Makdisi, Saree (2015) *Reading William Blake*, Cambridge: Cambridge University Press.

Matlak Richard E. (2003) *Deep Distresses: William Wordsworth, John Wordsworth, Sir George Beaumont 1800–1808*, Newark, DE and London: University of Delaware Press.

Miles, Jonathan (2007) *The Wreck of the Medusa: The Most Famous Sea Disaster of the Nineteenth Century*, New York: Grove.

Mitchell, Rosemary (2000) *Picturing the Past: English History in Text and Image, 1830–1870*, Oxford: Oxford University Press.

Morris, Edward (ed.) (2000) *Constable's Clouds: Paintings and Cloud Studies by John Constable*, exh. cat., Edinburgh: National Galleries of Scotland.

Paulson, Ronald (2003) *Hogarth's Harlot: Sacred Parody in Enlightenment England*, Baltimore, MD: Johns Hopkins University Press.

—. (1997) "Introduction", in William Hogarth, *The Analysis of Beauty* ed. Ronald Paulson, New Haven, CT: Yale University Press, xvii–lxii.

—. (1993) *Hogarth: Art and Politics 1750–1764*, 3 vols, Cambridge: The Lutterworth Press.

Phillips, Mark Salber (2000) *Society and Sentiment: Genres of Historical Writing in Britain, 1740–1820*, Princeton, NJ: Princeton University Press.

Praz, Mario (1933) *The Romantic Agony*, trans. Angus Davidson, London: Humphrey Milford.

Riding, Christine (2003) "The Raft of the Medusa in England: Audience and Context", in Patrick Noon *et al.* (eds.) *Constable to Delacroix: British Art and the French Romantics*, exh. cat., London: Tate Gallery Publishing, 66–73.

Roberts, Jonathan (2007) *William Blake's Poetry*, London: Continuum.

Rodner, William S. (1997) *J. M. W. Turner, Romantic Painter of the Industrial Revolution*, Berkeley, CA and London: University of California Press.

Rosen, Charles (2000) *Romantic Poets, Critics, and other Madmen*, Cambridge, MA: Harvard University Press.

Ruskin, John (1903–12) *The Works of John Ruskin*, 39 vols, ed. E.T. Cook and A. Wedderburn, London: George Allen.

Schama, Simon (1995) *Landscape and Memory*, London: Harper Collins.

Scott, Walter (1986) *Waverley*, ed. Claire Lamont, Oxford: Oxford University Press.

Sheehan, James J. (1989) *German History 1770–1866*, Oxford: Oxford University Press.

Strachan, John (2007) *Advertising and Satirical Culture in the Romantic Period*, Cambridge: Cambridge University Press.

Taylor, Joshua Charles (ed.) (1987) *Nineteenth-Century Theories of Art*, Berkeley and Los Angeles, CA: University of California Press.

Thomas, Sophie (2008) *Romanticism and Visuality: Fragments, History, Spectacle*, New York and London: Routledge.

Thornbury, Walter (1970) *The Life of J. M. W. Turner, RA: founded on letters and papers furnished by his friends and fellow-academicians*, London: Ward Lock Reprints.

Thornes, John E. (1999) *John Constable's Skies: A Fusion of Art and Science*, Birmingham: Birmingham University Press.

Vatalaro, Paul (2013) *Shelley's Music: Fantasy, Authority, and the Object Voice*, Basingstoke: Palgrave Macmillan.

Vaughan, William (1994) *Romanticism and Art*, London: Thames and Hudson.

Viagrande, Riccardo (2005) *Musica e Poesia Arti Sorelle*, Monza: Casa Musicale Eco.

Walpole, Horace (1996) *The Castle of Otranto: A Gothic Story*, ed. W. S. Lewis, Oxford: Oxford University Press.

Warner, Marina (2006) *Phantasmagoria: Spirit Visions, Metaphors, and Media into the Twentieth-First Century*, Oxford and New York: Oxford University Press.

White, Harry (2008) *Music and the Irish Literary Imagination*, Oxford and New York: Oxford University Press.

Wood, Gillen D'Arcy (2010) *Romanticism and Music Culture in Britain, 1770–1840: Virtue and Virtuosity*, Cambridge: Cambridge University Press.

Wood, Marcus (2000) *Blind Memory: Visual Representations of Slavery in England and America 1790–1865*, Manchester and New York: Manchester University Press.

Wright, Beth S. (1997) *Painting and History during the French Restoration: Abandoned by the Past*, Cambridge: Cambridge University Press.

Wurth, Kiene B. (2009) *The Musically Sublime: Indeterminacy, Infinity, Irresolvability*, Bronx, NY: Fordham University Press.

Chapter 6: European Romanticism

Appleby, Carol (2008) *German Romantic Poetry: Goethe, Novalis, Heine, Hölderlin*, Maidstone: Crescent Moon Publishing.

Avitabile, Grazia (1959) *The Controversy on Romanticism in Italy: First Phase 1816–1823*, New York: S. F. Vanni.

Bainbridge, Simon (2005) "Napoleon and European Romanticism", in Michael Ferber (ed.) *A Companion to European Romanticism*, Oxford: Blackwell Publishing, 450–66.

Bandiera, Laura and Diego Saglia (eds.) (2005) *British Romanticism and Italian Literature: Translating, Reviewing, Rewriting*, Amsterdam and New York: Rodopi.

Bernofsky, Susan (2005) "The Infinite Imagination: Early Romanticism in Germany", in Michael Ferber (ed.) *A Companion to European Romanticism*, Oxford: Blackwell Publishing, 86–100.

Blood, Susan (1997) *Baudelaire and the Aesthetics of Bad Faith*, Stanford, CA: Stanford University Press.

Bode, Christopher (2005) "Europe", in Nicholas Roe (ed.) *Romanticism: An Oxford Guide*, Oxford: Oxford University Press, 126–36.

Bone, Drummond (1995) "The Question of a European Romanticism", in John Beer (ed.) *Questioning Romanticism*, Baltimore, MD: Johns Hopkins University Press, 123–32.

Boutin, Aimée (2001) *Maternal Echoes: The Poetry of Marceline Desbordes-Valmore and Alphonse de Lamartine*, Newark, DE: University of Delaware Press.

Breckman, Warren (2008) *European Romanticism: A Brief History with Documents*, New York and Bedford: St. Martin's Press.

Brose, Margaret (2005) "Ugo Foscolo and Giacomo Leopardi: Italy's Classical Romantics", in Michael Ferber (ed.) *A Companion to European Romanticism*, Oxford: Blackwell Publishing, 256–76.

Cabo Aseguinolaza, Fernando (2012) *Historia de la Literatura Española 9. El Lugar de la Literatura Española*, dir. José-Carlos Mainer, Barcelona: Crítica.

Cardwell, Richard A. (2004) *The Reception of Byron in Europe*, London: Continuum.

—. (1991) "Introduction", in José de Espronceda, *The Student of Salamanca – El Estudiante de Salamanca*, trans. C. K. Davies, Warminster: Aris and Phillips, 1–40.

Cavaliero, Roderick (2005) *Italia Romantica: English Romantics and Italian Freedom*, London and New York: I. B. Tauris.

Cerretani, Gianni (2004) *John Keats and Giacomo Leopardi: A Comparative Study*, unpublished PhD Thesis, University of Liverpool (BL: DXN087331).

Clark, Steve and Tristanne Connolly (eds.) (2015) *British Romanticism in European Perspective: Into the Eurozone*, Basingstoke: Palgrave Macmillan.

Cochran, Peter (2009) *"Romanticism" – and Byron*, Newcastle: Cambridge Scholars Publishing.

Cox, Jeffrey N. (2014) *Romanticism in the Shadows of War*, Cambridge: Cambridge University Press.

Day, Aidan (1995) *Romanticim*, London and New York: Routledge.

De Man, Paul (1956) "Keats and Hölderlin", in *Comparative Literature* 8.1: 28–45.

Easterhammer, Angela (2000) *The Romantic Performative: Language and Action in British and German Romanticism*, Stanford, CA: Stanford University Press.

Espronceda, José de (1991) *The Student of Salamanca – El Estudiante de Salamanca*, trans. C. K. Davies, Introduction and Notes by Richard A. Cardwell, Warminster: Aris and Phillips.

Ferber, Michael (2010) *Romanticism: A Very Short Introduction*, Oxford: Oxford University Press.

—. (2005) *A Companion to European Romanticism*, Oxford: Blackwell Publishing.

Flitter, Derek (2005) "Spanish Romanticism", in Michael Ferber (ed.) *A Companion to European Romanticism*, Oxford: Blackwell Publishing, 276–92.

—. (2000) "Ideological Uses of Romantic Theory in Spain", in Carol Tully (ed.) *Romantik and Romance: Cultural Interanimation in European Romanticism*, Glasgow: Strathclyde, 79–107.

—. (1992) *Spanish Romantic Literary Theory and Criticism*, Cambridge: Cambridge University Press.

Foscolo, Ugo (2009) *Sepulchres*, trans. J. G. Nicholls, London: Oneworld Classics.

Furst, Lilian R. (1969) *Romanticism in Perspective: A Comparative Study of Aspects of the Romantic Movements in England, France and Germany*, London: Macmillan.

Gabriel, Norbert (1989) "Paul de Man on Hölderlin", in Herman and Humbeeck (eds.) *Discontinuities: Essays on Paul de Man*, Amsterdam: Rodopi, 11–132.

Garofalo, Piero (2005) "Romantic Poetics in an Italian Context", in Michael Ferber (ed.) *A Companion to European Romanticism*, Oxford: Blackwell Publishing, 238–55.

Hamilton, Paul (2013) *Realpoetik: European Romanticism and Literary Politics*, Oxford: Oxford University Press.

Hay, Daisy (2010) *Young Romantics: The Shelleys, Byron and Other Tangled Lives*, London: Bloomsbury.

Heinowitz, Rebecca Cole (2010) *Spanish America and British Romanticism, 1777–1826: Rewriting Conquest*, Edinburgh: Edinburgh University Press.

Hoffmeister, Gerhart (ed.) (1990) *European Romanticism: Literary Cross-Currents, Modes, and Models*, Detroit, MI: Wayne State University Press.

Holland, Jocelyn (2009) *German Romanticism and Science: The Procreative Poetics of Goethe, Novalis, and Ritter*, London and New York, Routledge.

Hugo, Victor (2008) *Les Misérables*, trans. Julie Rose, London: Vintage Books.

—. (1968) *Hernani*, ed. Herbert F. Collins, London: Macmillan.

Isbell, John Claiborne (1994) *The Birth of European Romanticism: Truth and Propaganda in Staël's De L'Allemagne 1810–1813*, Cambridge: Cambridge University Press.

Jackson, John E. (1999) *Mémoire et subjectivité romantiques: Rousseau, Hölderlin, Chateaubriand, Nerval, Coleridge, Baudelaire, Wagner*, Paris: J. Corti.

Lamartine, Alphonse de (1993) *Poetical Meditations / Méditations Poétiques*, trans. and introd. Gervase Hittle, Lewiston, NY: The Edwin Mellen Press.

Leopardi, Giacomo (2013) *Zibaldone*, ed. Michael Caesar and Franco D'Intino, New York: Farrar, Straus and Giroux.

—. (2008) *Canti*, trans. J. G. Nicholls, London: Oneworld Classics.

Lokke, Kari (2005) "The Romantic Fairy Tale", in Michael Ferber (ed.) *A Companion to European Romanticism*, Oxford: Blackwell Publishing, 138–56.

McClanahan, Clarence E. (1990) *European Romanticism: Literary Societies, Poets, and Poetry*, Oxford: Peter Lang.

McGann, Jerome J. (2008) *Lord Byron: The Major Works*, Oxford: Oxford University Press.

—. (1983) *The Romantic Ideology*, Chicago, IL: University of Chicago Press.

Manzoni, Alessandro (1997) *The Betrothed and History of the Column of Infamy*, ed. David Forgacs and Matthew Reynolds, London: J. M. Dent.

—. (1904) *The Sacred Hymns [Gl'Inni Sacri] and the Napoleonic Ode [Il Cinque Maggio]*, trans. Rev. Joel Foote Bingham, London: Henry Frowde.

Minta, Stephen (2013) *"Atala and Childe Harold's Pilgrimage I and II"*, in Peter Cochran (ed.) *Byron and Latin Culture. Selected Proceedings of the 37th International Byron Society Conference*, Newcastle: Cambridge Scholars Publishing, 316–32.

Moore, Fabienne (2005) "Early French Romanticism", in Michael Ferber (ed.) *A Companion to European Romanticism*, Oxford: Blackwell Publishing, 172–91.

Navas Ruiz, Ricardo (1990) *El Romanticismo Español*, 4th ed., Madrid: Cátedra.

Pala, Mauro (2005) "Facets of the *Risorgimento*: The Debate on the Classical Heritage from Byron's *Childe Harold* to Leopardi's *Canzone ad Angelo Mai*", in Laura Bandiera and Diego Saglia (eds.) *British Romanticism and Italian Literature: Translating, Reviewing, Rewriting*, Amsterdam and New York: Rodopi, 193–208.

Parker, Mark (1991) "Measure and Countermeasure: The Lovejoy-Wellek Debate and Romantic Periodization", in David Perkins (ed.) *Theoretical Issues in Literary History*, Cambridge, MA: Harvard University Press, 227–47.

Parmegiani, Sandra (2010) *Ugo Foscolo and English Culture*, Oxford: Legenda.

Peers, Edgar Allison (1940) *A History of the Romantic Movement in Spain*, Cambridge: Cambridge University Press.

Prasad, Pratima (2009) *Colonialism, Race, and the French Romantic Imagination*, London and New York: Routledge.

Prickett, Stephen (2010) *European Romanticism: A Reader*, London: Continuum.

Remak, Henri H. H. (1961) "West European Romanticism: Definition and Scope", in Newton P. Stallknecht and Horst Frenk (eds.) *Comparative Literature: Method and Perspective*, Carbondale, IL: Southern Illinois University Press, 223–59.

Rigby, Kate (2004) *Topographies of the Sacred: The Poetics of Place in European Romanticism*, Charlottesville, VI and London: University of Virginia Press.

Saglia, Diego (2000) *Poetic Castles in Spain: British Romanticism and Figurations of Iberia*, Amsterdam: Rodopi.

—. (1997) "'The True Essence of Romanticism': Romantic Theories of Spain and the Question Of Spanish Romanticism", *Tesserae* 3.2: 127–45.

—. (1996) *Byron and Spain – Itinerary in the Writing of Place*, Lewinston, NY: Edwin Mellen Press.

Sand, George (1991) *Story of my Life: The Autobiography of George Sand*, ed. Thelma Jurgrau, Albany, NY: State University of New York Press.

Schoina, Maria (2009) *Romantic "Anglo-Italians": Configurations of Identity in Byron, the Shelleys, and the Pisan Circle*, Aldershot: Ashgate.

Sebold, Russell P. (1983) *Trayectoria del Romanticismo español. Desde la Ilustración hasta Bécquer*, Barcelona: Crítica.

Shelley, Mary (1972) *The Choice: A Poem on Shelley's Death*, Folcroft, PA: Folcroft Library Editions.

Staël, Madame de (Anne-Louise-Germaine) (1958–60) *De L'Allemagne, 1810–13*, ed. Simone Balayé, Paris: Garnier-Flammarion.

Strauss, Jonathan (2005) "The Poetry of Loss: Lamartine, Musset, and Nerval", in Michael Ferber (ed.) *A Companion to European Romanticism*, Oxford: Blackwell Publishing, 192–207.

Travers, Martin (ed.) (2001) *European Literature from Romanticism to Postmodernism*, London: Continuum.

Traversa, Vincenzo (ed. and trans.) (2005) *Three Italian Epistolary Novels: Foscolo, De Meis, Piovene*, Oxford and New York: Peter Lang.

Tuite, Clara (2014) *Lord Byron and Scandalous Celebrity*, Cambridge: Cambridge University Press.

Wiley, Michael (2009) *Romantic Migrations: Local, National, and Transnational Dispositions*, Basingstoke: Palgrave Macmillan, 2008.

Wilkes, Joanne (2004) "'Infernal Magnetism': Byron and Nineteenth-Century French Readers", in Richard A. Cardwell (ed.) *The Reception of Byron in Europe Vol. 1: Southern Europe, France and Romania*, London and New York: Continuum, 11–31.

—. (1999) *Lord Byron and Madame de Staël: Born for Opposition*, Basingstoke: Palgrave Macmillan.

Wohlgemut, Esther (2009) *Romantic Cosmopolitanism*, Basingstoke: Palgrave Macmillan.

Chapter 7: Global Romanticism

Anderson, Benedict (1993) *Imagined Communities, Reflections on the Origin and Spread of Nationalism*, London and New York: Verso.

Ashcroft, Bill, Gareth Griffiths and Helen Tiffin (1998) *Key Concepts in Post-Colonial Studies*, London and New York: Routledge.

Bainbridge, Simon (2003) *British Poetry and the Revolutionary and Napoleonic Wars: Visions of Conflict*, Oxford: Oxford University Press.

Barbauld, Anna Letitia (1812) *Eighteen Hundred and Eleven: A Poem*, London: J. Johnson & Co.

—. (1792) *Major Works: Poems*, London: J. Johnson.

Barrell, John (1991) *The Infection of Thomas De Quincey: A Psychopathology of Imperialism*, New Haven, CT: Yale University Press.

Basker, James H. (ed.) (2005) *Amazing Grace: An Anthology of Poems about Slavery, 1660–1810*, New Haven, CT: Yale University Press.

Bewell, Alan (1999) *Romanticism and Colonial Disease*, Baltimore, MD: Johns Hopkins University Press.

Bolton, Carol (2006) "'Green Savannahs' or 'savage lands': Wordsworth's and Southey's Romantic America", in Lynda Pratt (ed.) *Robert Southey and the Contexts of English Romanticism*, Aldershot: Ashgate.

Brantlinger, Patrick (1988) *Rule of Darkness: British Literature and Imperialism, 1830–1900*, Ithaca, NY: Cornell University Press, 1988.

Burgess, Miranda (2009) "Nationalisms in Romantic Britain and Ireland: Culture, Politics, and the Global", in Jon Klancher (ed.) *A Concise Companion to the Romantic Age*, Oxford: Blackwell, 95–6.

Camden, Jennifer (2010) *Secondary Heroines in Nineteenth-Century British and American Novels*, Aldershot: Ashgate.

Carey, Brycchan (2005) *British Abolitionism and the Rhetoric of Sensibility: Writing, Sentiment and Slavery, 1760–1807*, Basingstoke: Palgrave Macmillan.

Carretta, Vincent (ed.) (1996) *Unchained Voices: An Anthology of Black Authors in the English-Speaking World of the Eighteenth Century*, Lexington, KT: University Press of Kentucky.

Chandler, James K. (1998) *England in 1819: The Politics of Literary Culture and the Case of Romantic Historicism*, Chicago, IL: University of Chicago Press.

Chaudhuri, Rosinka (ed.) (2008) *Derozio, Poet of India: The Definitive Edition*, Oxford: Oxford University Press.

Coleman, Deirdre (2005) *Romantic Colonization and British Anti-Slavery*, Cambridge: Cambridge University Press.

—. (1994) "Conspicuous Consumption: White Abolitionism and English Women's Protest Writing in the 1790s", *English Literary History* 61.2: 341–62.

—. and Peter Otto (eds.) (1992) *Imagining Romanticism: Essays on English and Australian Romanticisms*, West Cornwall, CT: Locust Hill Press.

Colvin, Christina (ed.) (1971) *Maria Edgeworth: Letters from England, 1813–1833*, Oxford: Clarendon Press.

Cooper, James Fenimore (1826) *The Last of the Mohicans; A Narrative of 1757*, 3 vols, London: John Miller.

Craciun, Adriana (2007) "Citizens of the World: Émigrés, Romantic Cosmopolitanism, and Charlotte Smith", *Nineteenth-Century Contexts: An Interdisciplinary Journal* 29.2–3: 169–85.

Crawford, Robert (1992) *Devolving English Literature*, Oxford: Oxford University Press.

Davis, David Brion (1975) *The Problem of Slavery in the Age of Revolution, 1770–1823*, Oxford: Oxford University Press, 1975.

De Quincey, Thomas (1998) *Confessions of an English Opium-Eater and Other Writings*, ed. Grevel Lindop, Oxford: Oxford University Press.

Eastwood, David (1989) "Robert Southey and the Intellectual Origins of Romantic Conservatism", *English Historical Review* 104 (1989): 308–31.

Ebbatson, J. R. (1972) "Coleridge's Mariner and the Rights of Man", *Studies in Romanticism* 11: 171–206.

Edgeworth, Maria (1971) *Maria Edgeworth: Letters from England, 1813–1833*, ed. Christina Colvin, Oxford: Clarendon Press.

Equiano, Olaudah (2001) *Interesting Narrative or the Life of Olaudah Equiano* (1789), ed. Angelo Costanzo, Peterborough: Broadview.

Fay, Elizabeth, and Alan Richardson (eds.) (1997) "British Romanticism: Global Crossings", *European Romantic Review* 8.2: i–x.

Flint, Kate (2009) *The Transatlantic Indian, 1776–1930*, Princeton, NJ: Princeton University Press.

Franklin, Michael (2011) *Orientalist Jones: Sir William Jones, Poet, Lawyer, and Linguist, 1746–1794*, Oxford: Oxford University Press.

Fulford, Tim (2006) *Romantic Indians: Native Americans, British Literature, and Transatlantic Culture 1756–1830*, Oxford: Oxford University Press.

Fulford, Tim and Peter J. Kitson (eds.) (1998) "Romanticism and colonialism: texts, contexts, issues", in Tim Fulford and Peter Kitson (eds.) *Romanticism and Colonialism: Writing and Empire, 1780–1830*, Cambridge: Cambridge University Press, 1–12.

Giddens, Anthony (1990) *The Consequences of Modernity*, Stanford, CA: Stanford University Press.

Giles, Paul (2014) *Antipodean America: Australia and the Constitution of U.S. Literature*, Oxford: Oxford University Press.

—. (2012) *The Global Remapping of American Literature*, Princeton, NJ: Princeton University Press.

—. (2001) *Transatlantic Insurrections: British Culture and the Formation of American Literature, 1730–1860*, Philadelphia, PA: University of Pennsylvania Press.

Gilroy, Paul (1995) *The Black Atlantic: Modernity and Double Consciousness*, Cambridge, MA: Harvard University Press.

Gottlieb, Evan (2014) *Romantic Globalism*, Columbus, OH: Ohio University Press.

Hamilton, Paul (2014) "Byron, Clare, and Poetic Historiography", in Porscha Fermanis and John Regan (eds.) *Rethinking British Romantic History, 1770–1840*, Oxford: Oxford University Press, 223–45.

Hanley, Keith and Greg Kucich (2008) "Introduction: Global Formations and Recalcitrances", in Keith Hanley and Greg Kucich (eds.) *Nineteenth-Century Worlds: Global Formations Past and Present*, London and New York: Routledge, 1–16.

Held, David, Anthony McGrew, David Goldblatt, and Jonathan Perraton (1999) *Global Transformations: Politics, Economics, and Culture*, Stanford, CA: Stanford University Press.

Hopkins, A. G. (ed.) (2002) *Globalization in World History*, London: Random House.

Hutchings, Kevin, and Julia M. Wright (eds.) (2011) *Transatlantic Literary Exchanges, 1790–1870*, Farnham: Ashgate.

Johnson, David (2012) *Imagining the Cape Colony*, Edinburgh: Edinburgh University Press.

Kane, Paul (1996) *Australian Poetry: Romanticism and Negativity*, Cambridge: Cambridge University Press.

Keane, Patrick J. (1994) *Coleridge's Submerged Politics: The Ancient Mariner and Robinson Crusoe*, Columbia, MI: University of Missouri Press.

Kelsall, Malcolm (1998) "'Once did she hold the gorgeous east in fee . . .': Byron's Venice and Oriental Empire", in Tim Fulford and Peter Kitson (eds.) *Romanticism and Colonialism: Writing and Empire, 1780–1830*, Cambridge: Cambridge University Press, 243–60.

Kitson, Peter (2014) *Forging Romantic China: Sino-British Cultural Exchange, 1760–1840*, Cambridge: Cambridge University Press.

—. (2010) "John Thelwall in Saint Domingue: Race, Slavery, and Revolution in *The Daughter of Adoption: A Tale of Modern Times* (1801)", *Romanticism* 16.2: 120–38.

Landsdown, Richard (2009) "Romantic Aftermaths", in Peter Pierce (ed.) *The Cambridge History of Australian Literature*, Cambridge: Cambridge University Press, 243–60.

Leask, Nigel (2009) "Romanticism and the Wider World: Poetry, Travel Literature and Empire", in James Chandler (ed.) *The Cambridge History of English Romantic Literature*, Cambridge: Cambridge University Press, 271–92.

—. (2002) *Curiosity and the Aesthetics of Travel Writing, 1770–1840: 'From an Antique Land'*, Oxford: Oxford University Press.

—. (1992) *British Romantic Writers and the East: Anxieties of Empire*, Cambridge: Cambridge University Press.

Lee, Debbie (2004) *Slavery and the Romantic Imagination*, Philadelphia, PA: University of Pennsylvania Press.

Lester, Alan and David Lambert (2006) "Introduction: Imperial Spaces, Imperial Subjects", in Alan Lester and David Lambert (eds.) *Colonial Lives Across the British Empire: Imperial Careering in the Long Nineteenth Century*, Cambridge: Cambridge University Press, 1–31.

Lukács, Georg (1937/1963) *The Historical Novel*, trans. Hannah and Stanley Mitchel, Boston: Beacon Press.

Majeed, Javed (1992) *Ungoverned Imaginings: James Mill's "History of British India" and Orientalism*, Oxford: Clarendon Press.

Makdisi, Saree (1998) *Romantic Imperialism: Universal Empire and the Culture of Modernity*, Cambridge: Cambridge University Press.

McKusick, James C. (1993) "'That Silent Sea': Coleridge, Lee Boo, and the Exploration of the South Pacific", *Wordsworth Circle* 24.2: 102–106.

Manning, Susan (2002) *Fragments of Union: Making Connections in Scottish and American Writing*, New York: Palgrave.

Maxwell, Richard (2000) "Inundations of Time: A Definition of Scott's Originality", *English Literary History* 68.2: 419–68.

Melman, Billie (1992) *Women's Orients: English Women and the Middle East, 1718–1918: Sexuality, Religion and Work*, Ann Arbor, MI: University of Michigan Press.

Mills, Sara (2005) *Gender and Colonial Space*, Manchester: Manchester University Press.

Moore, Jane (2011) "'Transatlantic Tom': Thomas Moore in North America", in Jim Kelly (ed.), *Ireland and Romanticism: Publics, Nations and Scenes of Cultural Production*, Basingstoke: Palgrave Macmillan.

Moore, Thomas (1806) *Epistles, Odes, and Other Poems*, Philadelphia: John Watts.

Moretti, Franco (2000) "Conjectures on World Literature", *New Left Review* 1: 54–68.

Mukherjee, S. N. (1968) *Sir William Jones: A Study in Eighteenth-Century British Attitudes Towards India*, Cambridge: Cambridge University Press.

O'Brien, Karen (2007) "Uneasy Settlement: Wordsworth and Emigration", in Claire Lamont and Michael Rossington (eds.) *Romanticism's Debatable Lands*, Basingstoke: Palgrave Macmillan, 121–35.

Otto, Peter (2005) "Romantic Medievalism and Gothic Horror: Wordsworth, Tennyson, Kendall, and the Dilemmas of Antipodean Gothic", in Stephanie Trigg (ed.), *Medievalism and the Gothic in Australian Culture*, Turnhout: Brepols.

Pitts, Jennifer (2005) *A Turn to Empire: The Rise of Imperial Liberalism in Britain and France*, Princeton: Princeton University Press.

Pratt, Mary Louise (1992) *Imperial Eyes: Travel Writing and Transculturation*, New York and London: Routledge.

Regan, John (2014) "'No 'nonsense upon stilts': James Mill's *History of British India* and the Poetics of Benthamite Historiography", in Porscha Fermanis and John Regan (eds.) *Rethinking British Romantic History, 1770–1840*, Oxford: Oxford University Press, 72–93.

Richardson, Alan (1998) "Darkness Visible? Race and Representation in Bristol Abolitionist Poetry, 1770–1810", in Tim Fulford and Peter Kitson (eds.) *Romanticism and Colonialism: Writing and Empire, 1780–1830*, Cambridge: Cambridge University Press, 129–47.

—. and Debbie Lee (eds.) (2004) *Early Black British Writing*, Boston: Houghton Mifflin.

Roberts, Daniel Sanjiv (2012) "'Dark Interpretations': Romanticism's Ambiguous Legacy in India", in Carmen Casaliggi and Paul March-Russell (eds.) *Legacies of Romanticism: Literature, Culture, Aesthetics*, London and New York: Routledge.

Robertson, Fiona (2014) "Historical Fiction and the Fractured Atlantic", in Porscha Fermanis and John Regan (eds.) *Rethinking British Romantic History, 1770–1845*, Oxford: Oxford University Press, 246–70.

Robertson, Roland (1992) *Globalization: Social Theory and Global Culture*, London: Sage.

Said, Edward (1977) *Orientalism*, London: Penguin.

Sánchez, Juan (2007) "Helen Maria Williams's *Peru* and the Spanish Legacy of the British Empire", in Claire Lamont and Michael Rossington (eds.) *Romanticism's Debatable Lands*, Basingstoke: Palgrave Macmillan, 172–85.

Sharpe, Jenny (1993) *Allegories of Empire: The Figure of Woman in the Colonial Text*, Minneapolis, MN: University of Minnesota Press.

Smith, Charlotte (1796) *Marchmont: A Novel*, 4 vols, London: Sampson Low.

—. (1793) *The Emigrants*, 2 vols, London: Sampson Low.

Thelwall, John (2013) *The Daughter of Adoption: A Tale of Modern Times*, ed. Michael Scrivener, Yasmin Solomonescu and Judith Thompson, Petersborough: Broadview Press.

Thompson, Carl (2007) *The Suffering Traveller and the Romantic Imagination*, Oxford: Oxford University Press.

Trumpener, Katie (2007) *Bardic Nationalism: The Romantic Novel and the British Empire*, Princeton, NJ: Princeton University Press.

Turcotte, Gerry (1998) "Australian Gothic", in M. Mulvey-Roberts (ed.) *The Handbook to Gothic Literature*, Basingstoke: Palgrave Macmillan, 10–19.

Waters, Malcolm (1995) *Globalization*, London and New York: Routledge.

Wellek, René (1949) "'The Concept of 'Romanticism' in Literary History (The Unity of European Romanticism)", *Comparative Literature* 1: 147–72.

White, Dan (2013) *From Little London to Little Bengal: Religion, Print, and Modernity in Early British India, 1793–1835*, Baltimore, MD: Johns Hopkins University Press.

Williamson, Karinna (ed.) (2008) *Contrary Voices: Representations of Indian Slavery, 1657–1834*, Kingston: University of the West Indies Press.

Winch, Donald (1965) *Classical Political Economy and Colonies*, Cambridge, MA: Harvard University Press.

Wolfson, Susan (2000) "Charlotte Smith's "Emigrants": Forging Connections at the Borders of a Female Tradition", *Huntington Library Quarterly* 63.4: 509–46.

Wood, Marcus (2002) *Slavery, Empathy and Pornography*, Oxford: Oxford University Press.

Young, Robert (1995) *Colonial Desire: Hybridity in Theory, Culture and Race*, London and New York: Routledge.

Conclusion: Legacies of Romanticism

Alsen, Eberhard (ed.) (2000) *The New Romanticism: A Collection of Critical Essays*, New York and London: Garland Publishing.

Beer, John (2003a) *Romantic Consciousness: Blake to Mary Shelley*, Basingstoke: Palgrave Macmillan.

—. (2003b) *Post-Romantic Consciousness: Dickens to Plath*, Basingstoke: Palgrave Macmillan.

Bennett, Andrew (1999) *Romantic Poets and the Culture of Posterity*, Cambridge: Cambridge University Press.

Borges, Jorge Luis (2000) *Selected Non-Fictions*, ed. Eliot Weinberger, New York: Penguin.

Bornstein, George (2006) "Yeats and Romanticism", in Marjorie Howes and John Kelly (eds.) *The Cambridge Companion to W. B. Yeats*, Cambridge: Cambridge University Press, 19–35.

Bradley, Matthew (2012) "Pole to Pole: Romantic Apocalypse at the Victorian *Fin de Siècle*", in Carmen Casaliggi and Paul March-Russell (eds.) *Legacies of Romanticism: Literature, Culture, Aesthetics*, New York and London: Routledge, 130–48.

Casaliggi, Carmen and Paul March-Russell (eds.) (2012) *Legacies of Romanticism: Literature, Culture, Aesthetics*, New York and London: Routledge.

Cronin, Richard (2002) *Romantic Victorians: English Literature, 1824–1840*, Basingstoke and New York: Palgrave Macmillan.

Di Tommaso, Lorenzo (2014) "Apocalypticism and Popular Culture", in John J. Collins (ed.) *The Oxford Handbook of Apocalyptic Literature*, Oxford and New York: Oxford University Press, 473–510.

De Sola Pinto (1967) *Crisis in English Poetry, 1880–1940*, London: Hutchinson.

Douglas-Fairhurst, Robert (2002) *Victorian Afterlives: The Shaping of Influence in Nineteenth-Century Literature*, Oxford: Oxford University Press.

Eisenhauer, Robert G. (2008) *After Romanticism*, New York and Oxford: Peter Lang.

Faflak, Joel and Julia M. Wright (eds.) (2004) *Nervous Reactions: Victorian Recollections of Romanticism*, Albany: State University of New York Press.

Harris, Alexandra (2010) *Romantic Moderns: English Writers, Artists and the Imagination: from Virginia Woolf to John Piper*, London: Thames and Hudson.

Hay, Daisy (2010) *Young Romantics: The Shelleys, Byron and Other Tangled Lives*, London: Bloomsbury.

Hockenhull, Stella (2012) "Neo-Romantic Visionaries: Picturing Britain in the Second World War", in Carmen Casaliggi and Paul March-Russell (eds.) *Legacies of Romanticism: Literature, Culture, Aesthetics*, New York and London: Routledge, 179–97.

Hogle, Jerrold E. (2005) "Film", in Nicholas Roe (ed.) *Romanticism: An Oxford Guide*. Oxford: Oxford University Press, 631–41.

Joyce, James (1993) *Ulysses*, ed. Jeri Johnson, Oxford and New York: Oxford University Press.

—. (1992) *Poems and Exiles*, ed. J. C. C. Mays, London: Penguin.

Larrissy, Edward (2012) "Seamus Heaney and Romanticism", in Mark Sandy (ed.) *Romantic Presences in the Twentieth Century*, Farnham: Ashgate, 105–16

—. (2006) *Blake and Modern Literature*, Basingstoke: Palgrave Macmillan.

—. (ed.) (1999) *Romanticism and Postmodernism*, Cambridge: Cambridge University Press.

McIntire, Gabrielle (2008) *Modernism, Memory, and Desire: T. S. Eliot and Virginia Woolf*, Cambridge: Cambridge University Press.

Makdisi, Saree (1998) *Romantic Imperialism: Universal Empire and the Culture of Modernity*, Cambridge: Cambridge University Press.

Mole, Tom (ed.) (2009) *Romanticism and Celebrity Culture 1750–1850*, Cambridge: Cambridge University Press.

—. (2007) *Byron's Romantic Celebrity: Industrial Culture and the Hermeneutic of Intimacy*, Basingstoke: Palgrave Macmillan.

Morton, Timothy (2005) "Environmentalism", in Nicholas Roe (ed.) *Romanticism: An Oxford Guide*, Oxford: Oxford University Press, 696–707.

O'Neill, Michael (2007) *The All-Sustaining Air: Romantic Legacies and Renewals in British, American, and Irish Poetry since 1900*, Oxford: Oxford University Press.

Østermark-Johansen, Lene (2003) *Romantic Generations: Text, Authority and Posterity in British Romanticism*, Copenhagen: Museum Tusculanum Press.

Raby, Peter (1988) *Oscar Wilde*, Cambridge: Cambridge University Press.

Radford, Andrew and Mark Sandy (eds.) (2008) *Romantic Echoes in the Victorian Era*, Aldershot: Ashgate.

Rommel, Gabriele (2004) "Romanticism and Natural Science", in Dennis F. Mahoney (ed.) *The Literature of German Romanticism*, Vol. 8, Rochester, NY: Boydell & Brewer, 209–28.

Rosen, Charles (1995) *The Romantic Generation*, Cambridge, MA: Harvard University Press.

Sandy, Mark (ed.) (2012) *Romantic Presences in the Twentieth Century*, Aldershot: Ashgate.

Shelley, Percy Bysshe (2000) *The Poems of Shelley: Vol. II 1817–19*, ed. Kelvin Everest and Jeffrey Matthews, London and New York: Routledge.

Sim, Lorraine (2010) *Virginia Woolf: The Patterns of Ordinary Experience*, Farnham: Ashgate.

Strathman, Christopher A. (2006) *Romantic Poetry and the Fragmentary Imperative: Schlegel, Byron, Joyce, Blanchot*, Albany, NY: State University of New York Press.

Tabbi, Joseph (2012) "Present Prophesy: the Transformation of Romantic Rhetoric in and by New Media", in Carmen Casaliggi and Paul March-Russell (eds.) *Legacies of Romanticism: Literature, Culture, Aesthetics*, New York and London: Routledge, 260–74.

—. (1995) *Postmodern Sublime: Technology and American Writing from Mailer to Cyberpunk*, Ithaca, NY and London: Cornell University Press.

Vaughan, William (1994) *Romanticism and Art*, London: Thames and Hudson.

Walford Davies, Damian and Richard Marggraf Turley (eds.) (2006) *The Monstrous Debt: Modalities of Romantic Influences in Twentieth-Century Literature*, Detroit, MI: Wayne State University Press.

Wallace, Diana and Andrew Smith (2009) *The Female Gothic: New Directions*, Basingstoke: Palgrave Macmillan.

Wheeler, Kathleen (ed.) (1984) *German Aesthetics and Literary Criticism: The Romantic Ironists and Goethe*, Cambridge: Cambridge University Press.

Worthen, John (2001) *The Gang: Coleridge, the Hutchinsons and the Wordsworths in 1802*, New Haven, CT: Yale University Press.

Yeats, William Butler (2008) *The Major Works: Including Poems, Plays, and Critical Prose*, ed. Edward Larrissy, Oxford: Oxford University Press.

Index